DAVID O. MCKAY LIBRARY

3 1404 00715 3478

D0742628

MAR 1 2 2000

PROPERT O .
DAVID O. McKAY LIBRARY
BYU-IDAHO
REXBURG ID 83460-0405

WITHDRAWN

SEP 1 2 2022

DAVID O. McKAY LIBRARY
BYU-IDAHO

CIVIC JUSTICE

CIVIC JUSTICE

FROM GREEK ANTIQUITY

TO THE MODERN WORLD

PETER MURPHY

Humanity Books

an imprint of Prometheus Books
59 John Glenn Drive, Amherst, New York 14228-2197

Published 2001 by Humanity Books, an imprint of Prometheus Books

Civic Justice: From Greek Antiquity to the Modern World. Copyright © 2001 by Peter Murphy. All rights reserved. No part of this publication may be reproduced, stored in a retrieval system, or transmitted in any form or by any means, digital, electronic, mechanical, photocopying, recording, or otherwise or conveyed via the Internet or a Web site without prior written permission of the publisher, except in the case of brief quotations embodied in critical articles and reviews.

Inquiries should be addressed to
Humanity Books
59 John Glenn Drive
Amherst, New York 14228-2197
VOICE: 716-691-0133, ext. 207
FAX: 716-564-2711
WWW.PROMETHEUSBOOKS.COM

05 04 03 02 01   5 4 3 2 1

Library of Congress Cataloging-in-Publication Data

Murphy, Peter, 1956–
    Civic justice : from Greek antiquity to the modern world / Peter Murphy.
        p. cm.
    Includes bibliographical references and index.
    ISBN 1-57392-951-4 (cloth : alk. paper)
    1. Justice—History. I. Title.

JC578 .M84 2001
320'.01'1 — dc21   2001024674

Printed in the United States of America on acid-free paper

CONTENTS

Acknowledgments   7

Introduction   9

1. Kallipolis — The Beautiful City   15

2. Metron — The Common Measure   39

3. Kosmopolis   65

4. The Birth of Humanism   93

5. The Commune   123

6. Kosmopoiêsis   139

7. The Scales of Justice   163

8. The First Modernity   193

9. Commonwealth and Contingency   221

10. The Republican Empire   255

11. The City Beautiful   281

Conclusion   315

Bibliography   317

Glossary of Greek and Latin Terms   327

ACKNOWLEDGMENTS

*C*ivic Justice was begun in late 1991 and substantially drafted by January 1996; revisions to the text were done in mid-1997 and November–December 2000. I want to thank the Modern Greek Program at Ohio State University for hosting me on a number of occasions during this time. I am grateful to Dimitris Dimiroulis and his colleagues at Panteion University for their hospitality during my stay in Athens over the months November 1995 to January 1996. In San Francisco, John Ely has always made me feel "at home" on my many visits. In Texas, Dwight Allman made a year-long stay in unfamiliar surroundings at Baylor University memorable.

To my colleagues at *Thesis Eleven* (Sage Publications), I owe a debt of gratitude for providing enduring intellectual companionship and stimulus, and for their unflagging worldly curiosity.

The voices and thoughts of many people invariably shape the writing of a book. Over the years I have had many fruitful and interesting conversations with Dwight Allman, Wendy Allman, Johann Arnason, Anna Ayala, Georgios Anagnostu, Richard Bernstein, David Blaazer, David Boucher, Peter Beilharz, John Carroll, Cornelius Castoriadis, Marios Constantinou, Sarah Crisp, Michael Crozier, Dimitris Dimiroulis, John Ely, Ferenc Feher, Gerald Fitzgerald, Julie Fletcher, Claudio Fogu, Eduardo de la Fuente, Ron Gallagher, Andrew Giles-Peters, Lydia Goehr, Agnes Heller, Trevor Hogan, Paul Harrison, Michael James, Gregory Jusdanis, Gerasimus Katsan, Peter Kirkpatrick, Artemis Leontis, Michael Lykoudis, Simon Marginson, Blaine McBurney, Ted Murphy, Sigrid Mueller, Christopher Race, Ambrose Ransley, Michael Riley, David Roberts, Gillian Robinson, John Rundell, Bernie Schedvin, Lewis Sieglebaum, David Spratt, Franz Timmerman, Louis Ruprecht, Candice Ward, and John Winkelman.

During the writing of *Civic Justice*, a sharpening and deepening of my ideas came from long discussions with Vassilis Lambropoulos.

This book is dedicated to Christine Mintrom in love, and Vassilis Lambropoulos in friendship.

T he author and publishers would like to thank the following for their permission to reproduce photographs: the Archivi Alinari-Firenze (photograph of the church of S. Giorgio Maggiore, Venice, page 186); John Varriano (the interior dome, Chapel of the Holy Shroud, page 200); Ron Gallagher (the Piazza di San Pietro, Vatican, Rome, page 202); Dell Upton (Thomas Jefferson's villa, Monticello II, page 285); and the Museum of New York (the Chrysler Building, page 300).

The photograph of the Parthenon, Athens (page 68), from *An Outline of European Architecture* by Nikolaus Pevsner (Penguin Books 1943, Seventh edition 1963), copyright © Nikolaus Pevsner, 1943, is reproduced by permission of the publisher.

The photograph of Savanna, Georgia (page 262), is reproduced courtesy of Historic Urban Plans, Inc., Ithaca, New York.

Text (page 160) from Ovid's *Metamorphoses* (1987), translation copyright © 1986 by A. D. Melville, is reprinted by permission of Oxford University Press.

Text (pages 143, 146) from *The Divine Comedy* by Dante Alighieri, translated by John Ciardi, copyright © 1954, 1957, 1959, 1960, 1961, 1967, and 1970 by the Ciardi Family Publishing Trust, is used by permission of W. W. Norton & Company, Inc.

Every attempt has been made to trace accurate ownership of copyrighted material in this book. Errors and omissions will be corrected in subsequent editions, provided that notification is sent to the publisher.

INTRODUCTION

This book traces the passage of the civic idea of justice from the Classical World to the New World. Its starting point is the emergence of the *polis* in ancient Greece (in the centuries prior to the Persian Wars) and the revolution in thinking wrought by the pre-Socratic Ionian enlightenment. From the pre-Socratics came the vocabulary of ancient philosophy and its constitutive ideas of moderation, limit, harmony, the union of opposites, equilibrium, reason, form, and constancy. *Civic Justice* explores the parallels between this bundle of philosophical ideas and the political practices of citizenship, the development of agonistic public culture, the patterns of journeying and colonization, and the ethos of friendship and hospitality that characterized the Hellenic world. The Greek city embodied a particular (civic) conception of justice: justice as an equilibrium (an isonomy) of contending powers and forces. Citizenship and justice were symbolized and objectified in the built environment of the city — in the public places and buildings that the Greeks created.

This work of *kosmopoiêsis* — the making of the "rational order" of the city — was not without its self-destructive aspect. For along with its brilliance came the tragic legacy of fifth-century B.C.E. Athens — the rise of Athens to preeminence in the Greek world, its assimilation, then disavowal and destruction of the Ionian images of isonomy, *kosmos* (order) and *kallipolis* (the beautiful city), its imperialism and its defeat in war, and eventual incorporation into the patrimonial Hellenistic empire. Against this background, I discuss how the pre-Socratic conception of justice was employed in Plato's philosophical criticism of Athens's imperial democracy, how the agonistic and isonomic ethos of the Hellenes declines in the Hellenistic age, and at the same time how this decline is compensated for by the rise of the *kosmopolis* (the world city) and the stoical ethos of natural law, federalism, and sympathy.

Hellenistic cosmopolitanism, in its turn, was subsumed and incorporated by the Romans in their world conquest. Rome both transformed the Greek world and was transformed by that world. The Romans synthesized many different Greek philosophical ideas and schools. The result was the Roman *humanitas*, or humanism, which influenced European culture and politics time and again over the centuries, and which was the crucible of Roman notions of republicanism, citizenship, civic virtue, public space and place, natural law, and justice. Rome, like Greece, had its self-destructive aspect. The parallels between the cosmopolitanism of the humanist idea and the expansion of Rome, an expansion that eventually destroyed republican Rome and ushered in the empire, are unmistakable. The imperial reconfiguration of humanism, through the transition from republic to empire, and its continuing influence on Augustan Rome, is an episode rich in tensions and ambiguities. The idea of the city lived on, and for a time even flourished, but it could not sustain the weight of an increasingly patrimonial social system encouraged by the emperors and an Augustinian Christianity that looked askance at the earthly city.

After the fall of Rome, the city form withers and almost disappears. The Latin West becomes an agrarian and patrimonial, feudal and hierarchical world. Public things (*res publicae*) — public buildings and spaces, virtues and institutions — are devalued. Trade across the Mediterranean, the lifeblood of the ancient city, is halted by the rise of Islam. This condition continues until the geopolitics of the Mediterranean basin finally permits the revival of the cities, along with the renaissance (in the twelfth century) of civic culture and humanistic learning, and the reemergence of city governments in Tuscany, the Veneto, and elsewhere. Dante's allegory of *kosmopoiêsis* (world making) in the *Divine Comedy* is illustrative of the difficulties of refounding the city. The strongly Neoplatonic character of Dante's humanism lends it an ambiguous nature: partway between a Christian and an imperial Roman worldview. This kosmopoietical ambiguity mirrors the instabilities of the emergent Italian city republics, and their inability to properly solidify as a political and social form or to find a constitutional "ordering" fully their own. This ambiguity is never completely resolved but at least is mastered sufficiently to permit the renaissance of the Italian cities.

The civic idea finds expression not only in the political arrangements of these cities, and their modes of citizenship and justice, but also in their art and architecture. The work of the humanist architects — Filipo Brunelleschi, Leon Battista Alberti, Andrea Palladio — embodied the political and social aspirations of the Renaissance city, and this work remained, long after the demise of the Italian city-republics, an enduring legacy and symbol of the classical humanist project. As much can be learned about the nature of civic justice from the architects of the Renaissance city as can be learned from the political theorists and philosophers. Indeed, a fully rounded *philosophical* conception of the city develops only *after* the city-republic is in decline. It appears in Machiavelli's *Discourses* where the author reworks classical ideas of the just equilibrium of forces and civic virtue, taking ancient republican Rome as his model. The Neoplatonism of humanist intellectuals like Ficino and Pico points to the inability of Renaissance philosophy to arrive at a consistent classicism, choosing instead to synthesize the corpus of classical learning (from Pythagoreans to Stoics, Epicureans to Skeptics) with the learning of other Mediterranean cultures (Judaic, Christian, and Egyptian).

After the glories of the High Renaissance, the city idea again becomes superannuated. It is not a renewed patrimonialism but the "first wave" of modernity in the European seventeenth century that causes its decline. The dynamism of the absolutist state (the forerunner of the modern nation-state) emerges as the central signification of modern society. Classical humanist imagery — "conflict that yields harmony" and "diversity that yields beauty" — gives way to images of tension, disorder, crisis, and an attraction to the exotic and the twisted. The classical sense of order (*kosmos*) is replaced by a fascination with change, movement, and transformation. Civic art and architecture turns in the direction of the baroque. Grandeur and excess prevail over moderation and limits in urban design and conception. The images of the capital city and the grand avenue, expressive of a centralized, increasingly bureaucratic power, replace the ethos of the republican city and its balance of powers. Hobbes's Leviathan overshadows Machiavelli's Florence. Modern reason (doubt) displaces classical reason (constancy). Sovereign power dislodges the constitutional equilibrium of powers of the classical city. The concept of a dynamic justice eclipses the idea of the just proportion and symmetrical reciprocity of contrary forces.

This eclipse was neither complete nor permanent. There was a partial (which is also to say equivocal) revival of the classical humanist ideal in England in the late seventeenth and early eighteenth centuries. The claims of absolutism in seventeenth-century England led to civil war; the cultural and spiritual atmosphere of those times was conducive to religio-political extremism and antinomian currents. Exhausted by all of this, and seeking to avoid a repeat of it, the English turned first to gothic and commonwealth models of constitutional monarchy, and then to classical and humanist models: to Renaissance Venice, to imperial and republican Rome, and to Hellenism. Shaftesbury in particular brilliantly reworks classical humanist ideas of moral beauty, political virtue, and just proportion. But the influence of this ethos cannot withstand the rise of the concepts of the sublime and of aesthetics. The Hellenism of Shaftesbury, and all it represents, was no match for the expansionary significations of emerging modern capitalism, bureaucracy, and mercantile imperialism.

A new nonclassical idea of the citizen as consumer is anticipated in the aestheticized reaction against Shaftesbury's Pythagorean-Platonic idea of art. At the same time as the rise of the aesthetic, the model of imperial Rome is appropriated by the English Crown as a legitimating basis for the construction of a transoceanic empire. The irony of this Augustan imperial model is that it becomes the unintended vehicle of, and stimulus for, the translation of images of the classical *civitas* into the New World. Americans turn to republican Rome as a model for resistance to England's Augustan and imperial Rome. Drawing on the experience of English commonwealth radicalism, the Dutch Republic, Renaissance city republics, the Roman republic, Greek city leagues, Hellenistic and Roman stoicism, the Americans construct a constitutional order in answer to English sovereign power.

Jefferson epitomizes this. His political thought is underpinned by a humanist scholarship of great breadth, and his architecture draws deeply from the well of Palladian and Roman models. Jeffersonian America creates a full-fledged republican constitution based on the quasi-classical ethos of "checks and balances" of contestatory forces. Yet, the agrarianism of Jefferson meant that the American Constitution was detached from the city. The Ciceronian-style country villa (Jefferson's Monticello) was an inferior substitute for "the city beautiful," and its entanglement with the plantation economy left a tragic and debilitating legacy. Other Americans imagined a republic made up of small farmers — in the hope of recreating either the gothic yeomanry of the English commonwealth or else the citizen-farmer-soldier of Cato's Rome or Sparta. In the absence of a strong city foundation, the American Republic became a continental empire, republicanism evolved into liberalism, and the constitutional order turned into a legal-institutional structure.

What was lost in this American transfiguration was the constructive ethos of the engaged city dweller who prefers the beautiful ordering of the city to the laws and commands of the state, the productivist ethic of republican citizenship to the distributivist ethic of the modern consumer, and who refuses to allow the architectonic justice materialized in the city to be overwhelmed by the demands of the abstract liberty of modern life. As we can see all around us today, in the greatest of the modern republics, there is a failure of *kosmopoiêsis*. The symptoms of this are legion: urban deterioration (epitomized by the decline of the inner cities in the

United States); amorphous suburbia; electoral cynicism and distrust of government; the proliferation of unskilled jobs in the service-consumer economy; the inability of modern welfarism or familial privatism to effectively motivate or provide constructive affiliations and loyalties; the shoddiness of public spaces; the loss of appetite for civic greatness; the formlessness generated by boundless growth and the worldlessness of those preoccupied with psychological (self) exploration.

It is doubtful whether calls for greater civic virtue or democratic participation offer much of a corrective to this. Rather, it is a much more fundamental human attribute that has been allowed to atrophy: viz., the creative/constructive power of ordering, pattern making, modeling, i.e., the power to give shape to human action and objects. To revitalize that power requires the stimulation of more than moral self-sacrifice ("giving") or collegiate political forms (committees, associations). It requires reacquaintance — through education and example, work and deed — with the architectonic arts and the human power of creative artifice.

Peter Murphy
pwmurphy@ozemail.com.au
June 2001

1

KALLIPOLIS —
THE BEAUTIFUL CITY

THE HOUSEHOLD SOCIETY

Greek-speaking peoples who settled in the Mediterranean beginning around the 1100s B.C.E. brought with them a patriarchal and
clannish social structure. These nomadic invaders, capping nearly a millennium of similar waves of migration from the north, supplanted the
centralized monarchy of the Myceneans, a civilization that had passed its
prime.* The first consequence of this invasion was a kind of cultural
regression, so that a less sophisticated social organization replaced the
palace culture of the proto-Greek-speaking Myceneans. The Aegean
world was cast into a dark age, and the literacy and artistic refinement of
the Myceneans was lost. What is remarkable about the invaders is that in
time, long past their inauspicious appearance, they were to create a city
culture that departed in unprecedented fashion from the patrimonial and
patriarchal organizing principles that hitherto all forms of society had
been based on.

At the start, the society of the archaic Greek invaders was structured
around the patriarchal clan—the *genos*.[1] The members of each clan were
descendants—some by adoption—of a common ancestor, and they wor-
shiped this ancestral figure as a god. All of them gathered around a
common hearth, and lived (figuratively) under a common roof. Such great
households incorporated hundreds of kin.[2] All relations in this household
(*oikos*) society were thought of in familial terms. The only consciousness of
duty that existed was duty to one's kin. Property, livestock, slaves, land,
pasture, vines, or chards, gardens, and forests belonged to the whole

---

*As well as can be determined from the limited available evidence, the Myceneans
entered the Aegean region around 2000 B.C.E. The Trojan War, dated 1250–1200 B.C.E., seems
to have destabilized Mycenean power, which was successfully attacked by Greek-speaking
tribes in 1200–1150. The Mycenean world would subsequently disperse into flows of
refugees, invaders, and migrants.

group, as did responsibility for the actions of members of the group. The group's activities were organized according to a familial hierarchy. The chief of the *genos* was the clan member who, by male succession, traced his origin most directly to the divine ancestor. Significantly, though, the chief of the *genos* — contrary to the case of many Middle and Far Eastern kingships — was regarded not as a deity, but as a priest of the divine ancestor. While exercising enormous authority over all household members, the chief at the same time interpreted and executed the *themistes*, the infallible decrees (a kind of superhuman wisdom), of the ancestor god. Such decrees were revealed to chiefs through the medium of dreams and oracles, and were handed down from father to son. The *themistes* formed a sacred and mysterious code of family justice (*themis*).[3] A clan member who violated the code acted against the clan, and was exposed to divinely inspired wrath — to punishments meted out by the chief, or to ordeals set by him, that would expiate the transgressions of the offender.

The clans had a life largely independent of each other, and treated neighboring clans as enemies. Blood feuds, vengeance, vendettas, and raids against neighbors were the norm. Yet for some purposes, especially for warring, clans would combine to form larger groupings, in the first instance brotherhoods or phratries (*phratriai*). When larger warring expeditions required more than warrior bands (the *phratores* or *phrateres*) provided by a brotherhood, the phratries would combine into a small number of tribes (*phulai*). Each tribe had its own god, its own war cry, and its own "king," the *phulobasileus*. For certain, again limited, purposes contiguous tribes would combine, recognizing in their turn a supreme "king," the *basileus* in chief. This "king of kings" acquired over time the role of attenuating blood feuds between families. In the office of *basileus* in chief was concentrated an authority of a circumscribed kind that stood above the clans.

Another way of developing bonds cutting across clans was for family leaders to host feasts and entertainments for male companions (*hetairoi*). Feasts were held in the great hall (*megaron*) of a chief's house. Through acts of generosity and hospitality, strangers (*xenoi*) were transformed into guests (*xenoi*) and hosts (*xenoi*). Ties of guest-friendship united strangers, and the feast became a way for chiefs to form bonds with enemy clans. Reciprocal hosting replaced the bloody reciprocity of vengeance and feuds. Crucially, because these were not ties of marriage or kinship, this prepared the way for the emergence of a new social form that was not structured on household lines. In tandem with this, the supreme chiefs encouraged the process of *sunoikismos*, the concentrating of dwelling houses (of rival families) in the *asty* (lower town) around a common citadel.[4] This citadel was the original *polis* — the *akro-polis*, or high-town.

It was the site of the residence of the "king" (the *basileus* in chief) and of the temple of the god whose worship united local families. The high-town was fortified. It was built on a hilltop so it could be defended, and was usually located in the midst of a plain.

While united in phratries and tribes, clans did not abandon their vendettas. However, under pressure of town life, they were compelled to subordinate these feuds to common rules that came to constitute a law that was higher than *themis*, viz. *dikê*. Via the rule of *dikê*, the spiral of vengeance for the bloody mischief of a clan member could be suspended. The *basileus* in chief could arrange for the exile of a murderer or for the payment of blood money by the responsible group to atone for crimes committed. Supreme chiefs also encouraged the broadening of feelings of duty by arranging for kinsmen of different feuding clans to intermarry or be adopted into rival clans. Treaties of friendship or alliance (*philia*)[5] between enemy families followed such arrangements, and thus gradually through *dikê* an interfamily, though not yet public, law was built up.

Whereas *themis* was conveyed through the medium of dreams (it was a type of truth that came from the revelations of oracles), *dikê* was the product of the demonstrative gesture. The word *dikê* is derived from the linguistic stem meaning "to show" or "to point out."[6] Accordingly, the chief who was *dikaios* (just) in-*dic*-ated ways of conduct that were "straight" (*orthos*). The dispenser of *dikê* was protected against "crooked" judgments by the taking of an oath (*horkos*).[7] *Dikê* provided clear rulings in disputes between parties. It pointed to ways of reinstating a customary-familial order of things that had been violated (e.g., by murder). It showed, in the manner of the pointed index finger, what was just. An in*dic*ation, though, is not a command, no matter how authoritative it might be. It is something closer to arbitration: a "law" that made allies or friends of warring clans, replacing the bloody reciprocity of vengeance with a peaceful reciprocity (*philotês*). Where the arbitration of the *dikaioi* (the just ones) was accepted by the disputing parties, there could be a coalescence of clan groups who were originally unconnected. In this, *dikê* prefigures politics. Politics combines and connects the distinct. Still, *dikê* is not yet politics, for it does not refer to the common thing (*to koinon*) defined by the public objects and public spaces around which parties assemble, and about which they discuss, contend, and dispute.

The archaic assembly functioned as a mute sanctioning force for *dikê*. *Dikê* was enforced primarily by pressure from the *dêmos* (the whole mass of clans assembled together). The *dêmos* exerted — in the guise of *nemesis* (the personification of retributive justice, the righteous anger that distributes "what is due")[8] — an influence that no single clan alone could ignore. Significantly, the *basileus* in chief did not develop an enforcement staff, and was not a monopolistic landowner. While certain communal lands were reserved for the *use* of these chiefs, such lands were not part of their *patrimony* (i.e., their household). Consequently, no Eastern-style centralized monarchy developed among the Greek-speaking peoples.[9] Rather the *basileus* in chief was a *religious* officiator acting in the name of the tribes at whose apex he stood; he held communion with the gods and appeased their wrath. His hearth was the common hearth around which the leading men of the tribes and clans gathered to make their offerings to the gods and to decide about matters of common concern. To support the palace of the *basileus* in chief, and the modest household staff needed to carry out the religious and juridical responsibilities, he levied customs duties and other dues. The "king of kings" was a mediator between human beings and the gods, a representative of gods among men, a leader in war, and a maker of peace treaties. In these functions the *basileus* in chief was not fundamentally different from the other chiefs, and was in many respects no more than a *primus inter pares* (first among equals). All chiefs possessed a scepter by which they received knowledge of the *themistes*, the supernatural principles of the familial society. Although subject to *themis*, none of the chiefs were subjects of the "king of kings." Rather they were counselors to the supreme king; collectively they formed a council (*boulê*). This council met on the initiative of the "king of kings," but he could not act effectively in matters of great moment without the council. The counselors were the "table companions" of the monarch. Banquets attended by the great men, also known as the elders (*gerontes*), typically preceded official business.

As well as the supreme king and the council, there was the assembly (*agora*) of all of the people—originally the assembly of warriors, free men capable of bearing arms. The *agora* was the place—perhaps originally a field—of the plenary assembly of all the *agathoi* (the valiant) of all of the tribes, who assembled on the initiative of the "king of kings." Before it came everything that concerned the people (e.g., repatriation of immigrants, questions of pestilence, war and peace). The people, while assembled together, were silent. Normally, after the king opened the session, only the elders spoke. Silence, of course, is relative—no doubt the feelings of the people had ways of being expressed via body language, mood, atmosphere, murmurings, and so forth. All the intangible, prerational expressiveness that gives a body of people "presence" in an assembly cannot be eliminated. But such feelings could never acquire rational form. The people could not articulate a program, an idea, or an opinion. Only the elders could speak, and then only within the terms of the semi-mystical *themis* or sacred family justice.

Because the counselors, like their monarch, were possessors of the secrets of the *themistes* (the decrees of the ancestor god), and executors of the law in their own clan, unsurprisingly, as the demands of *dikê* on the supreme king increased, so the elders gradually assumed responsibilities for administering the interfamilial law of *dikê*—in effect arbitrating private vendettas when disputing parties consented to, or were pressured into, arbitration. Gradually they supplanted the role of the monarch, to the point where, in the last centuries of the dark ages of archaic Greece, the power of the office of the *basileus* in chief all but disappeared, subsumed by the collective membership of the council. Kingship became nothing more than a magistrate's office with little power. It ceased to be a hereditary and life office, evolving instead into an annual office open to candidates from all of the powerful families.

The tribal societies of the Greek-speaking peoples, in other words, became subject to the collective rule of the council of nobles, and the councils of the chiefs of the powerful families became the masters of the towns that were created by *sunoikismos*. These families were wealthy, and their position brought them land and revenue; but it was not their wealth that legitimated their position as rulers, but rather their *status* as families that traced their respective origin to an ancestor god.

THE CITY AS A SOCIAL FORM

In the eighth century B.C.E. a rupture begins that radically reshapes the Greek-speaking societies. At that point these societies had already passed through a number of changes, but all those changes had been played out within the frame of the patriarchal or familial-hierarchical principle of social organization. (This age-old principle had provided the form of all but the most elementary of human societies.) A shift, tantamount to a break in time, begins in the eighth century and lasts—to the extent that such a thing can be understood in temporal or narrative terms—through the sixth century. What causes this upheaval is the rise of a new organizing/shaping principle of society, a new type of social form (*eidos*) that integrates the elements of society around a new core. The patrimonial culture that was displaced was an "organic" culture. Each tribal community was *rooted* to a particular place. The new social form that emerged in the eighth, seventh, and sixth centuries was, in contrast, *moveable*—transportable across the seas, easily displaced and reborn in another place.

In taking on board this new shaping principle of society, the Greek-speaking agricultural peoples of the Aegean, in a practical sense, had to learn the ways of seafaring and, in a metaphysical sense, had to develop a *universal ethos* ("way," ethic, form of life) that was readily relocatable, or, more precisely, carried its own location within itself—this, from peoples who had no name for the sea when they first settled in the Aegean region.[10] The universal ethos that emerged was the ethos of the city (*polis*). One way of describing what a city ethos is is to say that its principal defining force is not the family but the *city center*—the public spaces of the city. The locus of identification of the city dweller proper is not the household—be it a clannish, tribal, monarchical, or imperial household—but the life of the streets, the places of assembly, the public theaters, and so on. Life in the city is shaped not by customary patterns and folkways, generations, networks of family affiliation, local gods, concrete obligations, or reciprocities of the clan—none of which can relocate well or easily—but by abstract norms (virtues) that govern public life and competition, by *logos* (the speech of reason), and by the love of public activity and civic beauty.

For such an ethos to emerge, the Hellenes had to create (in the sense of give form to) places of *logos*—places of intersection where one social part could be orientated to another, and one thing related to another thing. *Logos* (speech, reason; the speech of reason) was a connective, assembling, orientating medium. *Logos* "gathered" persons and things,[11] and laid them next to each other in the public world. It was a connective principle that joined things together *beautifully*. The "reason" for something was the connection (cause, assembling factor, orientating precept) that could be publicly spoken about. To "give a reason" was to give an account of what lies *between* people, what relates and binds them in a public way. Such connections can be spoken of publicly because such speech arises *from the same place* (the *en meson*, the "in the middle," the center of things) in which public assemblages, joins, and connections are made. As *logos* was asserted, simultaneously a public life emerged in the spaces beneath the citadels of the cities of *sunoikismos*, towns that had no precedent in the hitherto existing urban form—the palace-cities of patrimonial monarchs. Gradually conversations of friends in the marketplace, religious processions, assemblies of citizens, and festivals—a great assortment of public activities—became central to the life of city dwellers (*politai*).[12] Even "knights," warrior-nobles, gathered together in nonfamilial companionate associations—in *hetairiai* characterized by homoerotic rather than familial or clannish bonds.[13]

During the time of change the natural (familial) economy of the household was rivaled, though never replaced, by the public market of the *agora*, which doubled as a meeting place of tribes located below the *akropolis*. The closed household economy no longer produced everything people needed. More specialized artisan production grew up, its products sold in the *agora*. Such goods were produced by *demiourgoi*,[14] i.e., smiths, potters, metal-workers. These were the "men who worked for the people" in the market-place, rather than consuming the products of their own labor or living as fringe dwellers, *perioikoi*, on the periphery of great houses, serving the nobility's needs for handmade goods. Others—often landless and trade-less, many of them affected adversely by the growth of markets, or else lacking a clan and therefore falling outside of the traditional social structure—hired themselves out for wages. The place where products were sold or exchanged, or labor hired out, the *agora*, became a meeting place in a more general sense—a place to spend leisure time, a place for walking and talking with others. The countrysider acquired the reputation of being a rustic country dweller in contrast to the *asteios*, the sharp wit, of the city dweller. Even the nobility lived in town. This represents the beginning of an *active* life, a life spent outdoors away from the household, a life spent in leisurely intercourse with others who were not necessarily kin or brothers.

Where there was assembly, there was contest. *Agôn*, signifying both assembly and contest, was the sign of a society in which the strife of battle was being civilized into the competitive game, and in which the prowess of the warrior was being sublimated into the skill of the performer (the singer-poet, the athlete) whose *aretê* (excellence) in contest was displayed and honored in public.[15] This was a society animated by contest, in-trigued by the skill of the contestant, yet at the same time detached from the contest in the sense of being devoted to watching the contest without taking sides, or being absorbed in listening to accounts (*logoi*) of great contests and great performances. As spectators in the audience looking on or as performers in the middle of things, the city dwellers partook of the creation of their society. Each public performance, with its actors and audiences, contestants and spectators, was a recreation of the *kosmos* (order) of the city dwellers (*politai*). The aim of the contestant or performer was to stand out (*ekprepês*), to shine brilliantly—to evince the wonder (*thauma*) of the audience. The actor gave pleasure or delight (*terpsis*) to spectators through the exercise of consummate skill—excellence, forth-rightness, risk-taking, courage, self-restraint in action—in competition and performance.[16] Even those who fought actual battles (in wars between cities and families) wanted not just victory but to be remembered, to be represented in the story-songs and odes and dances of the public. They wanted to endure in memory—remembered for their prowess/excellence that had withstood the test of the contest. The public space was a theater in which rivalry had become a gamelike *agôn*. Such gamelike rivalries were played out not only between actors in the city, but also between cities. In the time of great change in the 700s and 600s B.C.E., the period that saw the emergence of the *polis* and its accompanying public ethos, cities fought each other as families and clans had done (and still did). But cities also met *en meson*, at the great intercity festivals. The Ionian *politai* met at Delos and at the feast of the twelve cities at the cape between Ephesus and Miletus.[17] The contestants at these assemblies were aware of the need to give audiences pleasure,[18] to satisfy their rational-emotions: their wonder at and delight in the way in which everything came together in the beautiful performance of the great athlete or singer.

The athletic and poetic publics were the first publics. They preceded (and if we think ahead to the Hellenistic age, outlasted) the administrative public that took shape only by the overcoming of great obstacles. Through their use of councils to govern, the nobility contributed decisively to the emergence of public forms of administration. Originating among the archaic chiefs, this nobility was initially small in numbers. In the 600s, however, the size of councils expanded to accommodate the claims of medium-sized landholders. As military tactics changed decisively in mainland Greece, away from cavalry warfare to hoplite warfare, the stratum of medium landowners — who could afford the armor and shields of the hoplite soldier — found it possible to claim worth like that of the great families, and thus a share in citizenship. Still even with this enlarged constituency, the councils of the cities (*poleis*) remained relatively exclusive. Or more to the point: a much broader, and more interesting, public ethos developed outside of the city council.

This was the ethos of the *kallipolis*, the city beautiful, objectified in the public places and built forms of religious ritual, sporting competition, and dance and song. The ones who created these places (the sculptors, builders, and painters) and many of those who performed in them (like the singer-poets or teachers) were not citizens but *residents*, that is, citizens and free men and women, *demiourgoi*, and servant "out dwellers" from *other* cities. These *metoikoi* (middle dwellers between the great houses on the hill and the out dwellings of the near-servant artisans; a group that was "in-between" houses, not really part of the household society) constituted a *public class*. Metics were not as privileged as citizens. They could not deliberate in councils and were not consulted in assemblies, and could not own land[19] (the prize of the ruling class). At the same time, they were liable for military service and taxes just like citizens. Despite this, the status of the *metoikos* was not unattractive.[20] The readiness of many Hellenes to forgo citizenship for residency — denizenship — abroad is explained by the fact that *another public*, with its own privileges and freedoms, emerged in the Hellenic world alongside the council-public. All of the *metoikoi*, men and women, enjoyed a dispensation from the more archaic sense of duty of the ruling class, and were free of certain of its ties to homeland (*patria*) and hearth. "Residents" (denizens) might settle but they were always between houses. If, eventually, they might return home or else be granted citizenship in their adopted city, and embrace its civic hearth, in-between times they were relatively free to wander the periphery (*peras*) of the Mediterranean that was being opened up by colonization in the eighth, seventh, and sixth centuries.

Colonization was initiated by the council nobility of home cities. One practical reason advanced for this is that the nobility of the period wrestled with the fact that there was not enough land to pass on to their children. (Pressure on land was conditioned by the fact that Greek inheritance required equal division between sons.) Yet, even if early colonization was triggered by the need to ensure an adequate patrimony to descendants, the colonizing movement acquired its own raison d'être, and in doing so also further undermined the patrimonial conception of things already starting to disappear from the Greek world. (The existence of a council nobility was itself a sign of this transformation.) Under Ionian auspices especially, the Greek-speakers shifted from being a rooted, agricultural people to being a colonizing settler people capable of uprooting and settling elsewhere.* This shift of outlook perhaps owed something to the origins of the Greek-speakers as a *nomas* people, wandering herders. In any case, the Greeks (in a planned fashion) began to found cities—*apoikia* (away-homes, emigrant colonies, settler societies)—around the Mediterranean.[21] These cities were not in the main trading outposts of a mother city, as had been the case with the Greeks' great rivals in the Mediterranean, the Phoenicians.[22] Indeed the Greeks, despite their geographical spread, were not really international traders of a monopolistic kind as the Phoenicians were, but instead were comparatively free-dealing coastal traders.[23] In turn, this meant that the cities that they created tended to be based on a mix of farming, mining, and artisan production rather than on long-distance trade. The self-representation of Greek cities as self-sufficient (*autarkês*) both reflected and defined this

---

*Most particularly, due to the influence of Ionian cities on the islands of Chios and Samos, and on the central mainland of Asia Minor. The Ionians of Asia Minor had migrated from mainland Greece (especially Athens) around 1050–950 B.C.E., part of the population shifts that destroyed the Mycenean Greek world. These population shifts were reflected in the distribution of Greek dialects. Doric Greek speakers came to dominate the Peloponnese (once the center of Mycenean Greece) and spread to Crete, Rhodes, and southern Asia Minor. In the Arcadian mountains and Cyprus, a kind of Mycenean Greek survived. In Northern Asia Minor, the Aeolic dialect was spoken with strong connections to the language patterns of central and northern mainland Greece (Boeotia, Aetolia, and Thessaly).

reality. Self-sufficiency extended to political independence from the mother city. The existence of settler cities—"away homes"—signified a new practical-ethical phenomenon: the development of the first-ever *universal ethos*. Such an ethos allowed for the founding of independent communities with distinctive economic and social structures, customs, gods, and so on, yet which shared certain universal values that gave them a common (Pan-Hellenic) character, that made travel and cultural exchange between them possible, and which allowed the development of large communities of foreign residents—the *metoikoi* or "co-dwellers"—in the majority of Greek cities: all of this no matter their self-sufficiency, and no matter what rivalries, disputes, or wars might break out between the cities from time to time.

Here we see emerge a new kind of human commonness. Previously what had given form (shape) to a human society, which is also to say what bonded human beings and the different parts or elements of societies together, was the household in its different incarnations, whether it be the clan, band, tribe, monarchy, or patrimonial empire. In contrast, the Greeks who spread themselves around the watery margins of the Mediterranean did not belong to a great household or homeland. Despite this, they did enjoy a common character born of the city.

It took time, of course, for this form—this new shaping-formative power of society—itself to take form, to reach self-consciousness.

This was a consciousness that one's ethos is not connected to one's homeland and does not die out if it is uprooted, if one leaves a home-land for other places which are not even primarily landed, but are city-sites to be found at many different possible locations. This is a conciousness of looking outward to the sea, looking out to other possible locations of other cities still to be founded, looking out toward the sea to other cities that can, and will, someday be visited, out toward a sea that invites and welcomes travel and voyages and journeys, a sea across which it is possible to carry one's ethos to distant places—places some of which are surrounded by other (landed) peoples with whom the city-dweller learns to coexist without extinguishing them, as the Greeks learned living close to the Scythians in southern Russia, the Thracians along the northern Aegean, the Sicels or Sicans in Sicily.[24]

This emergent consciousness is summed up at a much later time by the words of the Athenian general Nikias to his troops: "Consider that you constitute a *polis* the moment you settle down wherever you are."[25]

THE TRAVELER AND THE ETHOS OF GUEST-FRIENDSHIP

Homer's *Odyssey* prefigures this extraordinary capacity to constitute a polis, wherever that may be.* It represents the first moment of this emigrant consciousness just as it is the culminating moment of the archaic-heroic culture of chiefs and knights and warriors. The Homeric hero Odysseus is a "king of kings," yet in his travels he hardly behaves as we would expect a patriarch to behave—leaving his household-palace behind him for so long. (In fact, he is not at all an orthodox figure—his inheritance [*klêros*] from his father is pitiful, and he makes his way in society instead by his sea-raiding prowess.) Even the writing down of this voyaging epic points toward the beginnings of a transportable ethos, one no longer rooted in the land and passed on by oral means and memory alone; one that is no longer defined by a specific customary context or homeland but rather by an ethos, including a protoliterature that can be read and can form readers in different places and social contexts. This ethos finds its summation in an art that is enacted by traveling companies that perform wherever they can find an audience.

Homer represents the beginning of the consciousness of belonging to an ethos that is not rooted in (or of) a single society or country or landscape. Homer's *Odyssey* is the story of a daring voyager who throughout his journey encounters tests, and who has to rely not on his kin but on his own *aretê* (excellence) to survive. Visible here is a new human type, who is guided by abstract (that is to say, relatively context free) calculations and norms of virtue rather than by the patriarchal rule of *themis* or of *dikê*. What propels the wandering Homeric hero is not a sense of duty to others (to the clan, to the home) but rather a duty to himself in the sense of a duty to his great journey and what that epic journey requires of him. He is an *actor*—he strives after excellence and the public recognition of that excellence, and in this we can see the basis of the universal ethos of the Greek cities. The Homeric hero, of course, is a warrior, not a citizen, but the ethos of excellence made possible the citizen. The Homeric hero is a transitional figure, caught between two human types; on the one hand, the *basileus*; on the other hand, the traveler who has *empeiria* (experience) of the world.

What makes possible the emergence of the traveler is the ethos of *xenos* (stranger-guest-host-friend). As this ethos—first seen as a way of

---

*The Homeric epic reaches its mature form around 750–700 B.C.E., most likely. Homer is associated with Ionian Chios and Smyrna. The Homerids, the professional guild of Homeric performers, were located on the island of Chios, possibly for a number of centuries before Plato.

bridging between rival clans—became generalized in the Ionian-Homeric world, the possibilities of journeying were greatly expanded. "[The] *basileus* could expect to be welcomed on his travels by men of the same class as himself: with them he would establish, or find already established by his ancestors, that relationship between guest and host . . . which was especially sacrosanct. . . . The stranger traveled empty-handed, but he was given not only board and lodging: everywhere he received also gifts (*xeinia*). . . ."[26] This hospitality (the feasting of strangers and the giving of gifts) created a new social bond. The traveler provided news, stories, and companionship, and at some future time would be expected to accommodate his host. This was a reciprocal giving (*antapodosis*). As this guest-friendship network expanded across, and beyond, the Ionian world, contacts, movement, and travel grew. As city life developed, spurred by the guest-friendship ethos, the guest-friendship relationship in turn was broadened beyond its original aristocratic parameters. Doctors, artisans, and teachers became regular travelers between cities, as did the singer-poets, sculptors, and painters. Cities themselves used a "public guest-friend" (*proxenos*)—usually a scion of a prominent local family—to represent themselves for purposes of trade and diplomacy in other cities. Many cities developed forms of hospitable residency (*metoikos*) for strangers who came to stay, such as statutes making assistance for *metoikoi* under attack a legally enforceable duty.[27]

Not all cities, though, were this accommodating. The principal exception was Sparta. The Spartans were *xeno*phobic. Theirs was a closed society. They kept few written records and were very secretive. They were wary of travelers and foreigners, or any commercial activity that might bring them into close contact with other societies—particularly from the seventh century onward—and they refused to allow other cities to appoint *proxenoi* to represent them at Sparta. The Spartans ensured sufficient land to themselves by the exceptional tactic of conquering their neighbors, the Messenians, in the late eighth century, and only ever established one colony overseas, Tarentum in southern Italy, and then only to accommodate the sons of Spartan nobility who were excluded from the distribution of Messenian land (either because they were the offspring of non-Spartan women or because they did not fight in the Messenian war).[28] The Spartans looked away from the sea. They were not in spirit coastal dwellers ready to accommodate travelers along the perimeter of the sea. There were no "strangers in the city" in Sparta, no *metoikoi*, no public class of residents. This is not to say that a public culture did not develop in Sparta. On the contrary, the Spartans went to extremes to deny the household's place as the central signifying institution of their society.

The Spartans instead took as the model of their society the companionate associations, the *hetairai*, of the old warrior-nobility — associations distinguished by homoerotic instead of familial or clannish bonds. As in other Greek cities, the Spartan definition of the warrior changed — in effect, expanded — as military tactics changed, and the ranks of hoplite soldiers superseded mounted noblemen in the seventh century. The hoplite soldiers assembled were the citizens, the ultimate rulers, of Sparta. Marks of earlier times persisted, though. The Spartans retained two kings, but powerful overseers (*ephoroi*) monitored the kings. A council of elders, (*gerousia*), dominated by leading families, prepared business for the citizen body, but such residual signifiers of the household society (family lineage or age as a determinant of power) were quite secondary. The signifying (meaning-generating) core of Spartan society, which shaped or formed the Spartan citizen, was composed of a set of institutions derived from the aristocratic-warrior companionate associations (*hetairai*) but modified to take account of the hoplite development. Central to these was the *sussitia*, the dining club or mess, of the male Spartan community.

The Spartans were not unique in embracing the institution of the public meal. In a number of Greek cities, men were expected to take the main meal of the day together in one or other public mess, and to contribute from their estate to its support.[29] The Spartans, however, pushed this practice to an extreme. The messes doubled as basic units of the Spartan military, and were typically composed of about fifteen adult members. Belonging to one of these messes was a criterion of Spartan citizenship. The citizen was one who dined publicly. To be able to do this required land and a household of sufficient size in order to support the long periods the male citizen spent in the mess, in combat and competition, and to provide the equipment needed for this. Given the conditions that land rarely changed family hands, that the Spartans held commerce in low regard, and that non-Spartans were barred from citizenship, citizenship became effectively the hereditary preserve of Spartan men whose households farmed the land. These men, though, spent the better part of their lives in a public world entirely removed from their households. To be eligible for election to a mess, a man had to have passed through the *agôgê*, the Spartan "upbringing." This upbringing instilled in the citizen-to-be an ascetical public ethos: one of discipline, frugality, austerity, courage, and inurance to pain and hardship. Taciturnity was encouraged rather than public wit. *Logos* played little part in Spartan public life; its role was replaced by an asceticism that prepared the initiate for a life of combativeness. At the age of seven, male children were removed from the household and put into "packs." Henceforth, they returned to the household only as visitors, and were publicly educated in music, war, and gymnastics. A parallel system of public education existed for women, who were instructed in music and athletics. Combat, music, and sport were each a different kind of public *agôn*. Competitions of choruses, for example, could be occasions, as much as war, for great feats of endurance. For citizens at least, this competition was offset by the society of companions of the messes, in which intimate bonds were formed with non-household members. The norm of pederastic relations between men and teenaged boys set the scene for this. A man joined a mess when he was twenty, and until he was forty-five he spent his nights in the public house of the mess-hall (or else on active military service), while women, in their parallel world, were responsible for household management.[30]

Whereas most Greek cities opened themselves up to forms of *xenia*, the Spartans wanted to eliminate the element of the stranger from the signifying core of their society. They idealized a kind of relationship that was not familial, and yet was transparent, a quasi-public relationship from which any trace of the stranger was absent. The deepest aspiration of Spartan society was revealed in the wedding night ritual, when the bride dressed as a man and cut her hair like a man. Marriage partners — whose relationship, perhaps more than any other human relationship, engenders familiarity — were thus transformed symbolically into nonfamilial companions (*hetairai*). Spartan xenophobia, though, was not at all typical of the Hellenes. Even where *xenoi* were discriminated against in law, strangers in the city were commonplace through most of the Greek world. Strangers brought with them unfamiliar customs, dialects, artistic techniques, but at the same time belonged to an overarching common ethos, and shared a common nature (*phusis*). At the center of this ethical nature was an Odyssean love of exploring but not transgressing the limits (*peras*) of the world. It was this love that animated Greek colonization, and at the same time allowed the citizen-founders of one city to see something of themselves in the strangers who had come from another city.

ARISTOCRATS, METICS, AND MOBILE WEALTH

During the age of colonization, Greek civilization spread across a vast area from the Black Sea littoral to the east coast of Spain. The Greeks built cities on the coastal margins of Asia Minor, on the Aegean islands, in southern Italy, and in eastern Sicily. Greek cities appeared on the Thracian and Libyan coasts. Greeks founded the trading post (*emporion*) of Naucratis in the Nile Delta in Egypt, and established the original Marseilles, Monaco,

Naples, and Syracuse.[31] The chief colonizing cities were the Euboean towns of Chalcis and Eretria, Corinth and Megara, and the Ionian cities of Miletus and Phocaea.[32] The most adventurous of the city founders were the Ionians. The scope of their colonization was very much in the spirit of the Ionian epic song of Homer. Tiny Phocaea brilliantly illustrates this. It established a colony at distant Massalia (Marseilles) around 600 B.C.E. Subsequently the Massalians leap frogged trading settlements along the trade route between Spain and Italy — at Monoecus (Monaco), Nicaea (Nice), Antipolis (Antibes), Agathe (Agde), and Emporion (Ampurias). As well as founding these littoral colonies, the Massalians exploited the internal river routes of France, allowing them to trade throughout Gaul. Indeed, such was the mettle and skill of these navigating people that a Massalian, Euthymenes, passed through the Pillars of Hercules (the Straits of Gibraltar) and traveled southward along the African coast, it would seem as far down as the Senegal River.[33]

The great city-founding endeavor was a phenomenon of the Mediterranean (and Black Sea) littoral. Greek civilization was a *civilization of the sea*, of the coastal periphery, *not of the land*. Greek cities were rarely ever sited more than twenty or twenty-five miles inland from the coast. Plato's Socrates called it living about the sea like ants or frogs around a pond. Being on the periphery of the sea shaped the character of the Greek city. The *polis* was not rooted in the land — it was not inland, so to speak, which also meant that Hellas had no territorial borders. This did not mean that the *polis* was undefined or indefinite. Rather it was defined by the routes of the sea and the Greek travelers on the sea, and by the fact that, while they were capable of making extremely long voyages, journeys were mostly coastal in nature. In this way Greek navigators avoided the formless expanse or boundlessness (*apeiron*) of seas far from landfall.[34] The coasting voyage (*periploos*) was the limit (*peras*) of *to Hellenikon*. "The Greek thing" was defined by the boundary (*peirar*) that was the shoreline rather than by a border that was laid-down as if it were an ordinance of a *hêgemôn* or sovereign power. The idea of Hellas was, thus, borderless but not boundlessness. The Hellenes did not covet vast territories. On the contrary, colonization occurred because there was a sense of definite limit to the size of the *polis*. While pragmatic calculation, such as the ratio of population to arable land, played its part in this, more important was the role of ratio in another sense, viz., the Greek idea of reason that understood reason in terms of limits. The Greeks, with a deep respect for limits, thought that the good city life, which was also the good life, depended on the city not growing too large, and where it threatened to do so, the citizens would resolve, as a collective act, to create a new city. Plato, much later in *The*

Republic [*Politea*], set the ideal size of the city at five thousand citizens (which, including foreign residents, slaves, household members, and so on, amounted to a total population of around fifty thousand). Hippodamus, the town planner who laid out Piraeus, the port of Athens, said the ideal number of citizens was ten thousand. In practice only three Greek cities reached population levels of over twenty thousand—Syracuse, Acragas in Sicily, and Athens. At the outbreak of the Peloponnesian War, the population of Athens is estimated at three hundred and fifty thousand, of which one-third (a century later one-half) lived in urban districts.[35]

Colonization—together with the phenomenon of the *demiourgoi* (traders and artisans working for the public), many of whom were travelers, moving from city to city and welcomed as *xenoi*—created a new mobile wealth in opposition to the landed wealth (mines, farms) of the noble families. The *demiourgoi* accumulated wealth to the point where wealth became a source of a claim to power (*kratos*). This in turn touched upon the central significations of Greek society. One of the things most prized in that society was freedom. Freedom meant not being in the servile state typical of the subjects of monarchies and empires. Where patrimonies existed and kings had a claim on all of the property of society, everyone was in a condition of unfreedom. The Greeks arranged things so that individual households owned the land. Whether the household was great or small, the proprietor was still free. The worst fate that could occur to a Greek was to fall into servitude, and those who did, and who accepted their fate, became objects of scorn, regarded as cowards who had put life before independence.[36]

There were many kinds of servitude.[37] To be forced to work as a wage laborer was tantamount to slavery. In the Homeric imagination "the life of a laborer [was] scarcely different from that of a beggar, for both are free men who have lost their position in society as completely as they can. . . . [Free] men would not willingly put themselves in the power of another by hiring themselves out on a regular basis."[38] The poor might be forced, of necessity, to work for someone else. But in so doing they lost their self-sufficiency (*autarkeia*). Another kind of servitude was that of the household servant. Such servants—often Greek women and children captured in interpolis wars, while men were put to death—were menial members of the household, *oiketikoi*, obliged to carry out daily tasks under direction but not chattel slaves to be bought and sold at market. Then there were the *perioikoi*, out dwellers who lived on the peripheries of large households and who catered to the productive needs of these households. The Spartans further distinguished between *perioikoi*—originally outlying villagers who were excluded from the citizen elite but who performed productive services for the citizens — and helots (conquered Achaean and Dorian peoples) who were reduced to a kind of serfdom with limited family and property rights, who tilled the fields or served as prison guards, mess attendants, and household servants.[39] Additionally, the Greeks had chattel slaves. Of the lowest status, the chattel slave, the *andrapodon* ("man footed thing"), was generally — and to the Greek mind preferably — of non-Greek speaking "barbarian" origin.* As far as the Greeks were concerned, servitude was part of the nature (*phusis*) of non-Greek speaking societies. In other words, there was a kind of "slavery by nature." The Greeks observed the patrimonial condition of non-Greek speaking societies, and concluded that there was a fundamental difference in nature between themselves and others. It was only the later, Hellenistic Greeks who (for the first time in *any* society) posited the idea of a *universal* nature (so that the argument against slavery per se became possible).

Mobile wealth played havoc with the distinction between freedom (*eleutheria*) and servitude. Traders performed services for others. Yet such services were governed by contracts. Was fulfilling a contractual obligation the same as working for another? Take the even knottier conundrum of the artisan. Did artisans work for themselves or for others? In the older household society, artisans were marginalized "dwellers around" who worked in a servile manner for a handful of powerful families. But in the new *polis* society of intercity mobility and the *agora*, the artisan took on a new appearance: of working independently. Even more perplexingly, a slave-owner could provide the capital to establish a slave in a business in the *agora* (and take a share of the profits),[40] while a smallholder, who could not afford chattel slaves and who toiled in the fields, possessed a notional freedom, but his hard labor seemed like that of a slave. The smallholder had no time for leisure, (*scholê*), no time for free activity (*praxis*) not compelled by necessity, no time to contemplate and enjoy things of beauty: the goods of the skilled artisans or the performances of the epic singers.

Beauty presaged freedom, not landed freedom (the traditional freedom of archaic Greek society) but the freedom of the city.[41] In the eyes of the city dweller, to live without beauty was to live without freedom. Beauty was a sign of freedom, of not being subject to the tyranny (*despoteia*) of anyone or anything. This freedom was not license. Beauty signified order, not chaos. It signified the freedom of order (*kosmos*) without obsequiousness or spiritlessness. The beautiful thing was a wonder to behold. Even aristocratic city dwellers were entranced by the beautiful, in spite of the fact that the noble class habitually demeaned those who made beautiful objects. As Plutarch

---

*The "barbarians" were the non-Greek-speaking *barbarophônoi*, or *bar-bar* speakers.

much later remarked of this persistent attitude: "Oftentimes we take pleasure in the work, but despise the workman [*demiourgos*]."[42] The most socially transforming of these tradesmen were the *metoikoi*: freed slaves or freeborn men and women or citizens of other cities who had been allowed to dwell in the city as residents.

The metics were "in-between houses," a middle group who provided the material forms of an agonistic society. They were the ones who measured its shape. The work of the *metoikoi* created the stage for and reenacted (in epic song and so on) the contestations of Greek society. Yet the *metoikoi* were not *actors* in these great conflicts. They made things, sang about deeds, but were not the *doers* of outstanding deeds. They had their own *agôn*: singers and sculptors were no less competitive than the nobility. But there was still a profound difference. The deed of the councilor or the cavalryman was frail — it left no trace behind, except in fallible memory.[43] The *metoikoi*, on the other hand, objectivated themselves in melodies and meters, buildings and sculptures. The nobleman who acted did so out of a spirit of independence. Great deeds were imaginable because the aristocrat was nobody's servant. The aristocrat possessed a freedom that came from the possession of land. He did not bend to the dictates of a patrimonial monarch or theocracy, although he did, as a city ruler or household master, issue dictates to others. The *metoikoi* also possessed a freedom: a freedom of movement. But even more significantly than this, the *metoikoi* possessed the power to create a beautiful world, the *kallipolis*, which — like the aristocrat's independence — intimated a freedom from despotism. The beauty created by the metic denizen and the *demiourgos* — the melodies of the epic singers, the ideal proportions of the temple, the harmonic ratios of public buildings — heralded an order free from the dictates of masters and kings, tyrants and despots, and even from noble judges and magistrates. Yet this beauty these same aristocrats admired and financed. Councils and citizens desired a great city in order to perpetuate the memory of their deeds, and the mark of the great city was the beauty created by the *demiourgoi* whom they disdained, by the *metoikoi* whom they held at arm's length.

How to escape these contradictions? The Spartans did it by shutting themselves off from intercity contact. They enforced the exclusion or expulsion of foreigners. But this was atypical among Greek cities, and as a consequence of it, Spartan culture stagnated. Cities like Corinth and Athens encouraged foreign traders and artisans, freedmen or citizens of other cities, to settle as residents, which was a way of avoiding the question of whether they were fit for citizenship. While such cities benefited from the taxes on wealth that the residents generated, the landed families still distrusted the accompanying commerce, partly because it threatened their office-monopoly and partly because of the view that the cultivated field was the "father of life." The marketplace — the commercial public — threatened the agrarian-based household society by raising the specter of the alienation of household property through sale. In the household society, property was passed down through the generations and retained in the clan. (Inheritance laws and customs were carefully regulated by the archaic *polis*.) Alongside but separate from the household, the agrarian householders collectively created a realm of citizenship centered on the institution of the council (*boulê*). At the same time they insisted that the merchant or artisan lacked the time to devote to governance or to warfare. This was a world, we must remember, without a bureaucratic or professional class to carry out the business of ruling, and in which there was no professionalized or bureaucratized army of a modern kind.[44] The management (*oikonomia*) of the landed household economy could be done by wives or by stewards/slave-managers (*epitropos*), giving the male head time to devote to city politics. But the merchant-traveler (*emporos*) of necessity journeyed extensively while the artisan's energies were taken up by the making of things. Their economy of time was unlike that of the great houses. Yet, once a person with a commercial background made enough money and retired from business, these considerations had much less force, and the wealthy individual might lay claim to parity with the well born. Even so, to be rich was not in itself a qualification for the soldiering or office holding of the citizen. To be a citizen required the possession (or at least the attribution) of an agonistic virtue. The art of moneymaking would not suffice. It had no moral merit.

Metics were welcomed in the city as social actors ready to venture in the fortuitous sphere of mobile wealth that the citizen abjured. But this world was potentially limitless. In contrast, land on the Mediterranean margins was scarce, and real estate for sale was practically nonexistent.[45] Land changed hands through inheritance, not markets, and did not easily pass out of the hands of the household or the clan. Commercial wealth was unbounded, while the Hellenic ethos embraced limits. By coasting the boundaries of the Mediterranean, and staying as a guest of host cities, the merchant-traveler acquired wealth. But this wealth had no obvious end or limit, nothing to signify sufficiency. It was not clear where acquisition ended, and acquisitiveness and greed began. Virtue, in contrast, was premised on a sense of limit, and one that had real effects: Greece was a world almost entirely without palaces or private mansions.[46] (Indeed many cities passed sumptuary laws prohibiting extravagant display by the wealthy.) The wellborn landowner/householder (the farmer citizen) claimed to be virtuous because he acted with an end in sight: the city. Correspondingly, war was rarely for the sake of conquest or dominion—Sparta's conquest of Messenia in the eighth century was a rare exception—rather it was a testing of the customs, rites, and laws of one city against another. The preclassical Greeks fought for the law embodied in the civic hearth. Cities with similar laws rarely went to war against each other.[47] The (noble) armed farmer citizen acted courageously in war for the sake of the *polis*, and over the course of the seventh and sixth centuries, the same increasingly applied to the medium or modest landowner, as war became dominated by the hoplite phalanx in place of cavalry. The hoplite was the armored soldier who stood in ranks and fought in close formation.[48] The virtue of the hoplite soldier farmers was that they supplied their own helmets and shields on behalf of the city, and they possessed the courage to stand firm in battle and not break ranks.[49]

Measured against this, moneymaking, even if it was energetic, had no inherent virtuous character. But the wealthy did have the capacity to *endow* the city, to express a public spiritedness by employing their wealth not in endless acquisition but in financing public works, in helping to build the middle in which the *agôn* of society was dramatized, providing interest-free "friendly" loans (*eranoi*) to the city for civic purposes. Through such activity, the wealthy could demonstrate a virtue (generosity), and make good their claim to share in the offices of the city. Undoubtedly the fact that the *gerontes* (the nobility of blood and line) were an *urban* nobility—they did not live in the countryside, in a feudal manner, on country estates—smoothed the way for the ascension of the wealthy into the ranks of the rulers in the eighth and seventh centuries, when rule came increasingly to be shared between the "best men"—those of the illustrious ancient noble families—and the rich men. Such rule could no longer be described as that of an aristocracy but rather as that of the few (*oligoi*). In different cities, oligarchic rule varied in specific character, according to whether it was more or less dynastic in character, more or less open to wealthy newcomers, more or less open to those who had once practiced a trade, and according to how high or low the property qualifications were set for the admittance of the wealthy to the council of nobles.[50] Whatever the variations, the numbers of rulers, the wielders of power (*kratos*), remained small.

Oligarchy was an inherently unstable form of rule. It always had to face the uncertain question of what *level* of wealth was sufficient to gain admittance to the council of rulers. What is more, the wealthy who *did* gain admittance typically then sought the luster of being an "old family," and would ape the dynastic and patrimonial characteristics of archaic families, which had the effect of underscoring the power of prestigious families over the city. Yet insofar as they conducted governance through a council system and not through a household-style hierarchy of an imperial or patrimonial kind, even this way of ruling prefigured public or civic power. This was not a popular system of governance, but insofar as it operated through the medium of assembly (where conciliar oratory was a valued practice), it was an intimation of a new social and political form. The best ideal of this age—the ideal of *kalokagathia*—aimed at a unity of nobility, wealth, and public agonal excellence. But it was a precarious unity, expressive of a set of overlapping but contradictory meanings.

NOTES

1. There are many general accounts of the clan society and the rise of the polis out of it. Among the best of these accounts is G. Glotz, *The Greek City and Its Institutions* (New York: Alfred Knopf, 1930). See also H. D. F. Kitto, *The Greeks* (Harmondsworth: Penguin, 1951), chaps. 1–5; M. I. Finley, *The Ancient Greeks* (Harmondsworth: Penguin, 1966 [1963]); Victor Ehrenberg, *The Greek State*, 2d ed. (Oxford: Basil Blackwell, 1969), pt. 1, chap. 1; Philip Brook Manville, *The Origins of Citizenship in Ancient Athens* (Princeton, N.J.: Princeton University Press, 1990), chaps. 2, 3.

2. Oswyn Murray in his *Early Greece*, 2d ed. (London: Fontana, 1993) argues against the idea that the *genos* was an extended group, incorporating related families (pp. 38–39). In Homer and Hesiod, he suggests, the *genos* appears to have little significance beyond immediate kin, and obligations do not seem to be owed to a wider group. Yet if we assume the absence of the extended, clannish *genos*, we can make no sense of later aristocratic factional politics. It is not possible to explain the factional power of (e.g.) the Alcmeonid family in Athens or the Bacchiadaein in Corinth if we think of them as nucleated families. The aristocratic family-party requires extensive family networks, even reaching (by intermarriage) between cities. Indeed, as Murray himself (p. 214) reminds us: "Marriage was for the upper classes an occasion for creating political and social ties between different families and so enhancing the status of the *genos* within the individual city-state, or among the wider circle of international aristocracy."

3. On the concept of *themis*, see John L. Myres, *The Political Ideas of the Greeks* (New York: Abingdon Press, 1927), Lecture III. The word *themis* was derived from the stem *the*, signifying firmness, steadfastness, and, upward from that root, from the verb *tithêmi*, meaning to lay down, to establish.

4. William Reginald Halliday, *The Growth of the City State* (Liverpool: University Press of Liverpool, 1923), Lecture IV; Kitto, *The Greeks*, p. 68.

5. On the development of this concept, see Vassilis Lambropoulos, "The Rule of Justice," *Thesis Eleven* 40 (Cambridge, Mass.: MIT Press, 1995).

6. It is related thus to words like *deiknumi*, which means to show, point out, bring to light, to display, exhibit, make known, etc.

7. A cognate of *herkos* or "fence."

8. As in the goddess of retribution who personifies retributive justice and righteous indignation.

9. For a description of the Eastern centralized monarchy, see, e.g., Karl Polanyi, *The Great Transformation* (Boston: Beacon Press, 1957), pp. 51–52.

10. Ehrenberg, *The Greek State*, p. 4.

11. This image of "gathering" is emphasized by Martin Heidegger. See, for example, his *The Principle of Reason* (Bloomington: Indiana University Press, 1991), p. 107.

12. Ehrenberg, *The Greek State*, p. 6.

13. Ibid., pp. 11, 19.

14. On the character of the *demiourgoi*, see Indra Kagis McEwen, *Socrates' Ancestor* (Cambridge, Mass.: MIT Press, 1993), pp. 72–76.

15. M. I. Finley, *The World of Odysseus* (London: Chatto and Windus, 1977 [1956]), pp. 119–20.

16. Charles Segal, "Spectator and Listener" in *The Greeks*, ed. Jean-Pierre Vernant (Chicago: University of Chicago, 1995).

17. Jack Lindsay, *The Ancient World: Manners and Morals* (New York: Putnam, 1968), pp. 41–42; Segal, "Spectator and Listener," pp. 195–96.

18. The contestants were—in the words of the Homeric *Hymn to Delian Apollo* addressed to the festival audience—"mindful they give you pleasure with boxing and dancing and song, as often as they hold their contest."

19. They could farm land as tenants, though.

20. The most famous example is Aristotle: a citizen by birth in his native Stageira in Khalkidike, he lived his adult years in Athens as a *metoikos*.

21. Finley, *The Ancient Greeks*, p. 22; Kitto, *The Greeks*, p. 81.

22. The Greeks did establish the trading *emporion* in some cases, primarily in the border areas of civilization: the Levantine coast, Etruria, Egypt. The *emporion* was made up of permanent communities of resident Greeks from different cities. See Murray, *Early Greece*, pp. 73, 107, 228–31.

23. J. Holland Rose, *The Mediterranean in the Ancient World* (New York: Greenwood Press, 1969 [1934]), p. 49.

24. Finley, *The Ancient Greeks*, pp. 37–38.

25. Jacob Burckhardt, *History of Greek Culture* (New York: Ungar, 1963), p. 95.

26. Murray, *Early Greece*, p. 48; Finley, *The World of Odysseus*, pp. 61–62, 64–66.

27. Paul A. Rahe, *Republics Ancient and Modern*, vol. 1 (Chapel Hill: University of North Carolina Press, 1994), p. 55.

28. Murray, *Early Greece*, p. 164.

29. Rahe, *Republics Ancient and Modern*, p. 57.

30. And because, under Spartan law, women could inherit in their own right, women owned much, perhaps eventually as much as two thirds, of Spartan property.

31. Finley, *The Ancient Greeks*, p. 3; Ehrenberg, *The Greek State*, p. 5; Meyer Reinhold, "Greek and Roman Civilization" in *Hellas and Rome*, ed. Robert Douglas Mead (New York: New American Library, 1972), p. 32.

32. Michael Grant, *The Ancient Mediterranean* (New York: Penguin, 1969), pp. 166–84; *The Founders of the Western World* (New York: Charles Scribner, 1991), chap. 2.

33. Euthymenes believed himself to have rounded Southern Africa and to

have located the source of the Nile in a huge freshwater sea. (James S. Romm, *The Edges of the Earth in Ancient Thought: Geography, Exploration and Fiction* [Princeton, N.J.: Princeton University Press, 1992], pp. 210–11.) This Massalian exploratory culture was persistent. Somewhere around 300 B.C.E., Pytheas of Massalia became the first recorded Greek to sail to the North Atlantic reaching the British Isles and possibly Scandinavia. (See Romm, p. 22.)

34. Ernle Bradford, *Mediterranean: Portait of a Sea* (London: Hodder and Stoughton, 1971), p. 94; Romm, *The Edges of the Earth in Ancient Thought*, chap. 1.

35. Kitto, *The Greeks*, p. 66; Finley, *The Ancient Greeks*, p. 52; Reinhold, "Greek and Roman Civilization," p. 2.

36. Rahe, *Republics Ancient and Modern*, p. 19. In the matter of slavery, Yvon Garlan dates this attitude to the era of the Persian Wars, citing the move of Aeschylus in 472 in *The Persians* to represent the battle of Salamis as a confrontation between the principle of liberty and slavery. (Garlan, *Slavery In Ancient Greece*, trans. Janet Lloyd, revised and expanded edition [Ithaca: Cornell, 1998], p. 120.) It makes sense that closer contact with Asiatic patrimonial societies, especially under conditions of war, would dramatize the slave/free distinction in the Greek mind. In the archaic era in contrast slavery could be considered a hazard of war between households without invoking broader geopolitical meanings or principles. Symptomatic of the growing importance of geopolitics is the fact that in the classical age, a slave is more likely to be a non-Greek than was the case in the archaic era. (N. R. E. Fisher, *Slavery in Classical Greece* [Bristol: Bristol Classical Press, 1993], p. 23.) But we must keep in mind that contact between Greeks and Eastern patrimonies occurs with increasing frequency in the centuries leading up to the Persian Wars, so there is also no reason to think that the liberty/slavery distinction was unheard of before Aeschylus and his generation.

37. On the subtle distinction of types of servitude, see Paul Cartledge, *The Greeks* (Oxford: Oxford University Press, 1993), chap. 6; Hannah Arendt, *The Human Condition* (Chicago: University of Chicago Press, 1958), p. 81.

38. Murray, *Early Greece*, p. 42.

39. Ibid., pp. 163–64; Cartledge, *The Greeks*, pp. 140–41.

40. Slave artisans, who "dwelled apart" (*choris oikountes*) from the household, might be allowed to set aside part of what they earned towards the purchase of their manumission.

41. Exemplifying this, women who were of free status but not of the citizen class had more liberty of movement than those who were from the households of the ruling class. The protective ethos characteristic of a landed, armed nobility [cf. Oswyn Murray, "Life and Society in Classical Greece" in *The Oxford History of Greece and the Hellenistic World* (Oxford: Oxford University Press, 1986), pp. 249–56.] — not to mention the legacy of aristocratic feuding — restricted the latter almost entirely to the household.

42. Indeed, an Athenian citizen could sue for defamation if described in public as a "tradesman." Cf. Mogens Herman Hansen, *The Athenian Democracy in the Age of Demosthenes* (Oxford: Blackwell, 1991), p. 120.

43. As Hannah Arendt stressed in *The Human Condition*.

44. Rahe, *Republics Ancient and Modern*, chap. 1.

45. Leasing of farms and houses, on the other hand, was a common practice.

46. Finley, *The Ancient Greeks*, p. 151.

47. Rahe, *Republics Ancient and Modern*, p. 95.

48. Murray, *Early Greece*, chap. 8.

49. This contrasted with the virtue of the nobleman, a virtue that was much more "heroic," in the sense that aristocratic combat was much more "individualized."

50. On the awarding of citizenship to noncitizens and the growing arbitrariness surrounding the question of "who is a citizen?" — see Ehrenberg, *The Greek State*, pp. 39–40.

2

METRON –
THE COMMON MEASURE

SOLON

The growth of the money economy in the Greek world during the seventh century stimulated the increasing social and economic weight of the *demiourgoi*, "those who worked for the public." The corollary of this was the decline of small landholders. For the small and unprestigous families of the archaic order, the expansion of a commercial economy was often crippling. Used to the ways of the "natural" patriarchal economy, they could not compete on commercial markets, and had difficulty paying for the goods produced by artisans that were quickly becoming necessities of life. To keep up, some contracted loans, fell into debt, and were reduced, along with their families, to a nonchattel slavish condition to clear the debts. To large, mercenary landowners, this was a boon. It offered a solution to the perennial problem of land shortage. There was no market in land to speak of. But if smaller neighbors could be ensnared in debts that they could not repay, they would forfeit their land and their freedom. Compounding the sense of injustice experienced in the face of such conditions was the secretive nature of the "justice" handed down by the judges of city councils – "justice" in the tradition of *themis*, which treated law as a kind of divine revelation (*alêtheia*). When tallied with the sectional interests of landowners and *oligoi*, this made law an arbitrary and "crooked" thing. Laws were divined and interpreted outside of public view.

The first significant attempt to redress this corrupted order was to bring in law givers, most notably in Athens. Athens becomes a leader in the attempt at reform, not because it was the most advanced of the Greek cities of the time, but because of its relative *backwardness*. It was backward in the sense that seventh-century Athens was not a colonizing city (Athenians' identification with their soil was too strong to permit it); nor was

Athens a big exporter of artisan products. This meant that Athens did not have the safety valve of overseas settlement to release the pressure of land shortage; nor did it have nonservile city employments available to it for those forced off the land due to the monetization of the economy.

This combination of factors put into question the central significations of Attic society. If there was an archaic Greek concept of freedom, it was *the identification of freedom with land*. The Greek landholder was free—compared with the one who held land at the pleasure of a patrimonial emperor, or compared with the hired laborer or slave. This landed freedom was always equivocal. For the freedom of landed householders meant at the same time submission to the house—to its head, to its divine ancestor, and so on. Still, it was central to archaic Greek identity; it distinguished Greek from non–Greek-speaking peoples who lacked landed independence. To lose land was thus a devastating thing, made even more devastating if the ruling council of the city—dominated, as Athens was, by noble landowners—acquiesced or abetted in the manipulation of debts by largeholders intent on dispossessing smallholders. The council might rest its judgments on the divine character of its ancestry, but as the other chief significations of society fell into crisis, this legitimation of authority seemed hollow.

Drako's publication of Athenian laws in 621 B.C.E.—the writing down of the *themistes*—was an attempt to demystify them. This was a step toward the law becoming a public property rather than the possession of a few persons who had inherited it from the gods.* Once published, the law was stripped of some of its mystery. Under Solon's guidance—he was made *archôn*, chief magistrate in Athens in 594–93 B.C.E.—a *corrective justice* was attempted.[1] Solon cancelled the punitive debts of the *hektemoroi*, the poorest class of farmers. His law recognized the sanctity of their person and guaranteed their freedom. They could no longer be forced into servitude. Under Solon material wealth (or more precisely, income from landed property) was formalized as the basis for holding office, and categories of wealth were more precisely defined in correspondence with matching political rights.[2] The bottom income order, the *thêtes*, was confirmed in its right to participate in the Athenian Assembly, while the old ruling council, the *Areopagus*,[3] lost significant power.

Traditionally, the *Areopagus* was made up of former chief magistrates. On finishing office, an *archôn* would join the council to sit alongside his predecessors. An *archôn* always came from an ancestral noble family. He was proposed for office by the *Areopagus*, conditional on acceptance by the Assembly of Athens. Solon altered this arrangement. The *archôn* was

---

*The Greek idea of law in effect evolved from revelation to arbitration (*dikê*) to legislation of public rules (*nomoi*)

henceforth selected from among the ranks of highest landed income order – an innovation that in principle, although probably not in practice, broke the connection between office-holding and ancestry. The chief magistrates still retired to the *Areopagus*, but after Solon's reforms they first had to give an account of their term in office to the Assembly, and this account had to be accepted by the Assembly before they could take up a place in the *Areopagus*. Further, the *Areopagus* lost its power to propose – that is, to initiate the business of the Assembly, to set its agenda (including nomination of candidates for office.) Under Solon, the Assembly acquired its own executive Council of Four Hundred[4] to prepare its business. Statutes were publicly displayed in the center of Athens, and a right was created for anyone, not just the injured party or his family, to bring a lawsuit on behalf of someone personally wronged. The effect of this was to open up the access of the less wealthy to the courts. (There was no public prosecutor in Athens: the old "self-help" genos-based tradition of justice prevailed at least in this respect.) The Athenians, guided by Solon, turned the care of orphans into a public responsibility. A civic center was formally established, and residences were banned from the center. A law of *stasis* was enacted requiring citizens to take sides in public controversies (punishment was loss of citizenship).[5] Grants of citizenship were permitted to permanent exiles and those who had come to Attica from other cities with their entire household to practice a trade.[6] The *agora* was cleared and marked out as a place for speeches (*logoi*). And, beginning what was perhaps a more ambivalent trend, for the first time certain sacrifices, public feasts, and religious rituals were authorized for the shared benefit of all Athenians. (The Athenians even instituted a common festival of the dead to complement family rituals. Rites such as these previously had been the preserve of the families and the tribes.)

For all of this, the *polis* order was not yet established. Solon's contribution to its establishment was ambiguous, if not contradictory. He opened up rule to those whose qualification for ruling was property, i.e., not ancestry but wealth. But because the only wealth he recognized was *landed* wealth, he lapsed back into reliance on the old system of social meaning. Another part of what he did was to help give form to the emergent public world of the *polis*. He defined public responsibilities, he made a gesture to the metics, the immigrants; he wanted the law publicly displayed (and thus publicly talked about, even argued about). He wished in effect that the *polis* were organized around controversy, taking sides, political opposition. At the same time his reforms suggested that there was a kind of public hospitality that made all citizens of the city – whatever their differences – friends.

Solon's reforms failed in the sense that within thirty years Athens succumbed to the rule of tyranny. Much of the attraction of tyranny to Athenians can be explained by the fact that Solon left much unaccounted for by his reforms. This was not a personal failing, but rather an indication of the difficulties of reform in circumstances where the very signifying core of a society is exhausted, and the reformer must work in between old and new systems of meaning. In this setting it is unclear to the reformer whether he is making institutions for the old world or the new world. As a result, Solon's reforms left much unresolved. Even if he outlawed opportunistic debt slavery, he could not prevent successive generations of small farmers cultivating more and more marginal plots, and eventually being forced by circumstances off the land — to do what? To be hired hands (which in Greek eyes was just a kind of slavery by default). *Solon did not envisage an alternative to the patriarchal landed economy.*[7] Likewise, making wealth the criterion for holding office did not answer the question of legitimate rule. In truth, wealth by itself did not possess moral legitimacy in Greek eyes. We see Solon struggling to take account of the illegitimacy of wealth when he makes income the qualification for holding office but in the same breath he recognizes only income from land — knowing that there remained powerful tacit connections between landowning and noble ancestry, and that few of the mercantile wealthy would be able in practice to buy the land that bequeathed political rights. Yet this equivocation was played out in a social context where the aura, the mystery, the divinity of ancestry was losing its meaning, while those with mobile wealth were becoming a social force.

Solon did not answer the question of how this new *social* force could acquire a legitimate place and authority in the order of things. Solon does not see the possibility that wealth can legitimate itself by generosity — by donations to the city, by the giving of interest-free loans for public works. Later on this was to become a significant practice in the Greek world but Solon was blind to it. His reforms did not give form to the power of wealth; nor did they define a place for the artisans and merchants in Attica's social order, who thus remained outside the scheme of things. Solon gestures toward the inclusion of them when he raises the prospect of metics getting citizenship. But even this was never realized in practice — most probably Athenian patriotism precluded it (with the further consequence that metics became major supporters of tyranny).

TYRANNY

The inability of the emergent *polis* order to properly define itself, or stabilize itself, is indicated by the turn of the *poleis* to the rule of tyrants, commonplace in Greek cities in the century after 650 B.C.E.[8] These tyrants were not Eastern-style despots—they did not rule society as masters over slaves. Rather the tyrants were a curious transitional phenomenon in the Greek cities—one more staging post in the shift from the patriarchal city to the city of citizens. They symbolized a rejection of the council rule of noble families, and for periods of time often enjoyed considerable popular support. Tyrants ruled by strength and ability rather than under the constitution (*politeia*) of the city. They came to power as a retribution for the *hubris* of the wealthy. The *hubris* (the insolent overstepping of the mark) of the oligarchs was unavoidable. Wealth, the chief good of the oligarchs, knew no bounds. The object of the wealthy was to acquire greater wealth, if necessary, from small or vulnerable property holders. Wealth was an object without form, and for that reason it encouraged the exceeding of limits. The lawlessness and disorder of the *oligoi* followed in its wake.

In the place of oligarchy, the tyrants instituted a kind of pseudocivic regime, one that aimed to correct oligarchic injustice but not through a constitutional ordering of things. Strikingly, the tyrannies could not consolidate themselves; the tyrannies of Thrasybulus of Miletus and of Cypselus of Corinth, as examples, lasted two generations. The *anomia* of the tyrant also ended in injustice—its own kind of *hubris*—and in the demand of the populace for the restoration of good order (*eunomia*).

Peisistratos's regime in Athens (after 564 B.C.E.) exemplifies this.[9] The regime maintained the framework of civic institutions—the Assembly and the Council of Four Hundred that Solon had instituted—and generally respected legalities. It redressed certain oligarchic biases, introducing a program of agricultural loans to help smallholders and a system of traveling judges to go into outlying rural districts. The regime settled some of the landless ex-smallholders on estates that it confiscated from the nobility, and otherwise provided jobs for those leaving the land by encouraging the expansion of crafts and trades in the city as well as an export trade in wines and pottery.[10] The Peisistratid regime initiated a major program of civic enhancement.[11] It undertook an extensive scheme of public building (including a fountain and pipe system for the city— important in a country that suffered water shortages); it demolished the old city walls, improved roads, and sponsored a city festival (in which tragic drama had its origins). It encouraged a civic religion. Shrines to city gods were built as an alternative to the household-based cults. In particular, increased attention was paid to Athena, the goddess of Athens. The regime erected the first temple of Athena Polias. (It also began constructing one for Zeus Polias, but it was on such a scale that it was only eventually completed six hundred years later by the Roman emperor Hadrian.[12]) Theseas was sponsored as a national hero in opposition to the Dorian Heracles.[13] In the interstices of this civic devotion emerged a cult of Athens that foreshadows some of the ailments of fifth century Athens. While the Peisistratid regime took the city further away from the old clannish patriarchy, it did so in the direction of a civic *patria*tism. Under these conditions, the city, instead of the household, became a kind of *patria*—a place of roots, to which its citizens could be tied in feeling and deed. This stands in contradistinction to the "*apoikia* ethos" that wherever one settles, one recreates the ethos of the *polis*. This in turn encouraged Athenians to become not primarily *polis* dwellers but, first and foremost, Athenians; to become not travelers or settlers but imperialists. It is under the Peisistratid regime that Athens begins to accumulate power in the Aegean—laying the groundwork of what was to become the Athenian Empire of the fifth century—by conquering the Megaran port of Nisaia, gaining hegemony over the island of Naxos, and establishing links with the kingdoms of Thrace and Macedon.[14]

Tyranny was a simulation of a public culture. It displayed some but not all of the significations of a public culture. The tyrant developed the material infrastructure of the public, but not its all-important limits or sense of possessing a boundary (*peras*). Tyranny was *matter without form* and an expression of the lack of certainty of the Hellenes about the shape of the new sociopolitical formation (the *polis*) that was struggling to emerge. Tyranny adopted some of the superficial trapping of this new social and governmental form but it was at odds with its spirit. The problem was that this spirit was far from self-conscious. In particular, until the spirit of the *peras* was sedimented in thought, the *polis* would lack a definition of itself—a sense of itself (its shape) continuing over time—and therefore would be susceptible to corruption. It was to three figures in particular that fell the task of "thinking the *polis*," conceiving its form in thought. One was a young man when Solon's reforms were instituted, Anaximander of Miletus (ca. 610–548 B.C.E.); another, from Ephesus, was Heraclitus (ca. 521–487 B.C.E.); the third, Pythagoras of Samos (ca. 580–500 B.C.E.), left Samos for southern Italy in 538 B.C.E., not long after the time of Anaximander's death.

THE IONIANS – PUBLIC POWER AND *ISONOMIA*

The form of the *polis* gradually emerged as traders, travelers, and colonists crisscrossed the Mediterranean and Black Seas. This littoral world proved to be the cradle of an urban life quite unlike that of earlier patrimonial or imperial societies. The life of the seaboard Greek city was not dominated by *one* social power: be it divine kings, priests, bureaucrats, aristocrats, or merchants. There was not a single, *uncontested,* force in this city life. *In nuce,* we see the outline of a new formative power; a formative power that *drew together a variety of social forces and held them in a kind of equilibrium.* The king's palace, the emperors' forbidden city, the priests' temple – none of these dominate the center of the *polis.* The *polis* center was (symbolically at least) a place through which different social forces could pass. The life of the city was composed of disparate activities linked, or drawn together, in what Pythagoras called a "union of opposites." The effect of this "union of opposites" was to allow different parties to exercise mutual restraint: no one overwhelmed the other, as long as each balanced the other. No one social force – religious, bureaucratic, commercial, and so on – could subsume and dominate the others. Rather there was an equipoise established between different – often ebullient and maneuvering – forces in the city. This equipoise, however fragile, was the essence of the *polis.* The heart of the city was the public space where different social forces could interact: where they could experience the virtues and vices of each other; where each was visible to the other; where each *contested* the other.

The proliferation of cities in the Mediterranean from the eighth century B.C.E. on marks the beginning of Western civilization. The building of cities, and with them the formation of city-states, took place with the most extraordinary vitality. This vitality indicates that the city was a meaningful entity for its inhabitants, one which connected their activities, their individual parts in the social drama with their fellows. In most societies before this time the sense of social wholeness had come from a belief in hierarchy. A chief, a god-king, or an emperor surmounted a hierarchical arrangement in which everyone had a place that defined their social role and power. We should not underestimate the capacity of hierarchy to give meaning, even to the most humble of people's lives. To even begin to imagine replacing a hierarchically arranged society, it is necessary first to be able to offer an alternative principle for tying together the disparate parts of society. If hierarchy is not to be the cement of society, then what is to be the binding factor? In the Mediterranean of the period from the eighth century B.C.E. to the third century C.E., two other ways of cementing society appear. The second, and later of these, was the *principle of expansion* – the principle of expansive change—that proved so disastrously seductive in the case of the Attic Empire, and that reappeared in the Hellenistic and Roman Empires, both of which, at least for a time, derived their meaning from their very movement, before collapsing back into the patterns of patrimony. The first, and earlier, of these new ways of thinking about the way in which society meaningfully coheres was *the principle of balance*. This principle found its most articulate expression in the sixth-century Ionian enlightenment, which had a profound influence on later antique thinking, not least of all on both Plato's and Aristotle's conceptions of the just city.

The Ionians were the first to think through a new conception of form. This thinking through—in the guise of a theory of order: a *kosmos logos* or cosmology—came about to meet the demands of the developing Ionian cities, of which Miletus was the most important. What evidence we have of this thinking through is fragmentary, but the fragments that are extant of Milesian thought suggest a marvelous depth of reflection. The most important thought fragment that has come down to us is that of Anaximander of Miletus. Anaximander seeks to explain the *kosmos* of things. In doing so, he rejects the preexisting mythological account, in which a single element or part of the world, a *monarchia*, dominates all other parts. In the Anaximandian theory there is no *monarchia* to establish and maintain order. There is no place for the *monarchia* of one element over all of the rest. Indeed the rule of one element over all of the others is identified as being destructive. But what ties the parts together, if not some kind of hierarchical arrangement? The Milesian answer was to postulate an *isonomia*, or balance, of parts, and more specifically, a balance of *opposing* parts. This cosmology addressed the needs of the emergent city for the representation of itself as a social and political arrangement radically different from the patrimonial arrangements of the past.

The city was a social and political form in which parts were arranged in opposition rather than in hierarchy. Hierarchies still persisted in the familial and household arrangements that coexisted with the city proper. But the city, no matter how compromised by these older forms, was a radical departure from them as well, not least of all because the emergent city involved a revaluation and reconstruction of the idea of opposing or contending forces in society. The idea of opposition lost the connotation of enemy or deadly rival in the sense of an enemy locked in mortal combat in a tribal setting. Enemies were the enemies of one's household or clan. War (*polemos*) in the precivic setting meant the overcoming of an adversary—asserting one's superiority over the other, conquering the other, dominating the other, forcing the other to submit. This was often associated, in the case of the archaic warrior, with exaltation or frenzy, the *lussa,* into which he was thrown — as though beside himself — by *menos*, the ardor inspired by a god.[15] Domination and submission was a form of order. The old mythological conception of the universe, which predated the rise of the Greek city, exalted the power of a god (Zeus) who ruled the entire universe and who had vanquished all of his rivals (such as the Titans). In the mythological, as opposed to the cosmological, conception, rivalry was the harbinger of chaos and disorder, of formlessness. Rivalry, struggles, and battles led society to the edge of the dark abyss — the bottomless hole. Rivalries threatened to allow the darkness of the underworld to erupt into daylight, and were that to happen, the stability of society would be subsumed by chaos. Only the victory of a single dominating force could ensure stability and form. Order was dependent on the ordering agency of the monarch.

Anaximander, in contrast to this, postulated that order was achieved not by the assertion of hierarchy, that is by the dominance of a king or chief, but rather by the achievement of an equilibrium or balance between opposing elements or forces in society. Anaximander said that the infinite, the unbounded, the formless was the principle from which all things came into being, and that things came into being by the separation of opposites from the infinite. For Anaximander, the separation and then combination of four opposing physical qualities — hot/cold, dry/moist — could account for the origin of the universe. In the cosmological conception, in the creation of the universe, no element is privileged, and no element is infinite. If one element were infinite, other elements could be destroyed by that element. Instead the infinite was something other than the elements, something from which they arose. So the *kosmos* was composed of finite or limited elements, which were opposed to each other but which could not eliminate each other. As opposites, though, these elements constantly encroached on each other. Their encroachments represented a denial of their finitude, an overstepping of limits, and an invading of other elements, causing "destruction" or "offense." And yet, for all of this, rivalry and strife were not the harbinger of formlessness and chaos. They were not inherently evil. Rather what was problematic was the transgression of limits: when determinate things behaved as if they were indeterminate. What kind of arrangement was it where such things did not occur? It was an arrangement where there was a balance or equilibrium between opposites — where neither was strong enough to dominate the other, to encroach on the other, at least without having to make amends for the encroachment. Where such an arrangement existed there was a state of justice; where it did not exist there was a state of injustice. Where injustices occurred — as Anaximander believed they would —

each part would, under the ordinance of time, make amends, give reparations to each other for their offense, and in that way equilibrium would be restored.

Like the old myths, the Ionian cosmology had a political and social meaning. It alluded to a political order—the city—that was not arranged in the shape of a patrimonial hierarchy. In the city, conflict or strife between the parts of society was not wrong. What was wrong was the excessive strength of any one part of the city. Anaximander's *adikia* denoted the victory of one opposing power over another. But if a monarch did not order society, who or what did? Order in the city was achieved by the keeping of equilibrium, an *isonomia*, between competing social forces. *Isonomia*, though, was not a kind of *dikê*. To put this in terms of a rational reconstruction of events: *Nomos* (law or rules or conventions that were written down) superseded *dikê* (the indicative arbitration of chiefs) in the ordering of the city. Thus there could be no *isodikê*. *Isonomia* was achieved in the Ionian world by creating a center of equilibrium—a city center—in which different forces, elements, sections, and classes in the city could come together and forge a balance or equilibrium of forces—the balance (*iso*) of different laws/rules (*nomoi*). In the space of the city was gathered together those with allegiances to different households, clans, brotherhoods, and tribes. Gradually, as different civic spaces—markets, theaters, academies, assemblies, and so on—formed, a variety of sometimes conflicting *nomoi* emerged. There had to be an overarching just equation that could hold together these competing laws and norms.

Such an equation was provided by *isonomia*. *Isonomia* was a kind of equality. But it was not an arithmetical equality. Arithmetical equality [A=B] can be expressed as a ratio of equal numbers, $1/1$.[16] From the Ionians onwards, the Greeks thought not of the equality of two elements, but of an equality of more than two elements.[17] This *isometria* involved a *geometrical* equality* among three or more elements. In giving an account of the physical *kosmos*, the Milesian would not equate heat with dryness, but equate the ratio of hot to cold with the ratio of dry to wet. Translated into quantitative terms, these were ratios not of equal but of unequal numbers. Geometrical equality yielded a world that was well proportioned, and the sense of what might be dubbed isonomic proportions was a key to spirit of the city.

Nowhere was the stamp of geometrical equality more visible than in the plan of the city and its buildings. Unsurprisingly, the first reputed town planner was an Ionian: Hippodamos of Miletus.[18] In the Milesian

---

*An *isotês geômetria*, an equality of ratios.

order the laying out of a center for the city was crucial. This was not a center in the sense of domination — that is, the rule of the center over the periphery. Rather it was a center in the sense of an ontological condition of "being centered," or of not being unbalanced. This center, what the Greeks called the *agora*, was an assembly space. It was not filled with a temple, or a palace, or a chief's house, or any one dominant social signifier. It was instead an open space surrounded by all kinds of social signifiers — temples, craft workshops, temporary stalls, political and legal offices. Bordering the city center was typically a council chamber, a town hall (executive), and the stoas or colonnades used as stores, places of philosophical debate, picture galleries, and law courts. The architectural form of these buildings was correspondingly crucial. For it was during the sixth century B.C.E., the age of the Ionian enlightenment, that the essential character of architecture — what was to become "the classical" architecture of the West — emerges.[19] In its infancy this architecture — distinguishable from both the vernacular building of everyday life and the monumental building of patrimonies and empires — was distinguished by Doric and Ionic orders. *This architecture was a visual analogue of the isonomic politics of ordering.* In architectural terms, this ordering meant the arrangement of space and mass in a way that was well proportioned, regular, and symmetrical, and that as a result formed, in the person who viewed the architects' massing or who walked through the spaces of a building, a sense of clarity, beauty, and completion. From all of this flowed an authority, the authority of the ordering. Its completeness, its clarity, above all its beauty — its *kallos* — justified the ordering. The ordering was beautiful. It was beautiful because it was well — which is also to say justly — proportioned. Beauty, justice, and goodness were ultimately one and the same. Like all core systems of social meaning, the meaning of the *kallipolis* was internal to itself and circular.

The symmetry of the individual Greek classical building intimated a balancing of forces around a central point or axis. Such a centering was replicated in the structure of the city. All of its many, different, often cluttered activities and buildings were grouped in a loose "U" shape around the central space of the city. The *agora* was the place where people gathered together to exchange goods, to assemble for political discussion (if they were citizens), to meet friends. The center was a place of conversation, encounters, and meetings. It represented the beginning of *public* space — the possession of no one, and no one authority, in particular. Like the earth at the center of Anaximander's universe — equidistant from all points on the celestial circumference, and therefore motionless, with no more reason to sink than to rise, to move to one side rather than the other—the *agora* was metaphorically equidistant from all households in the city. While the household was still a hierarchically structured space, the city privileged no one household, no one clan, over another. The house was a place of domination: slavery, patriarchy, hierarchy were its essence. By contrast, those who entered the city center, even slaves, were not ruled by anyone in that domain. The power of *kratos* (mastery) was absent from the public domain. Power in the public domain was the power of judgment (*gnôsis*)—the power of judging the performance of rivals and opponents in the civic domain. Not everyone could enter into the game-like rivalries that were played out in the city center. But, whatever the social constraints operating on the ambit of this new kind of power, the fact of its existence was momentous.

What the existence of this kind of power, and what the Ionians and later Greek civilization generally assumed, was that conflict/strife did not necessarily imply chaos. The center was a place where rivalries could be played out in friendly contests, where those in opposition or dispute could meet without being driven by the need to vanquish one another. Rivals could appear in the public arena without destroying each other. Rivalries took on the form of an *agôn*,[20] a friendly yet competitive contest, and thereby bloodlust was transformed into games governed by rules. These were public events, public spectacles—watched by citizens and noncitizens—where the contestants had to demonstrate their prowess. The sanction of the public was dependent on the excellence of the contestant. Rivalries were transformed from the old private vendettas between (or within) households/families into public things for public display and judgment. Rivalries were no longer carried out in a vengeful spirit or in a spirit of frenzy. They came instead to be pursued by such things as lawsuits in the public space of the courts, dependent on the skill of representation of the advocate. In the public court the aim was not to seek revenge or to kill those who may have caused harm, or to seek as a supplicant the beneficial redress or ruling of a king or some powerful patrimonial figure, but to gain justice via the judgment of the court. The court in the city involved a public contest—an adversarial engagement—with plaintiff and defendant arguing, and others sitting in judgment on the excellence of the cases of the contending parties.

Even the war (*polemos*) between cities, as opposed to the discord (*stasis*) within cities, was transformed by the nature of the city. In post-Homeric times cities waging war against each other sought not so much in the time-honored fashion to annihilate their adversary or destroy its army but rather to force the other side to acknowledge their fighting skill demonstrated in a test that was as rule-bound as a tournament.[21] War had a time limit (normally summer); it was fought on a chosen ground; to win often required only to break the lines of an opponents' heavy infantry. Armies did not pursue their opponents to vanquish them. There was no fighting to death in order to extinguish the enemy as a social or religious entity; there was no conquest in order to absorb the opponent totally.[22] War in classical Greece was an *agôn*, a game (albeit a deadly one), and indeed so much so that military operations would be suspended, or passage of athletes and spectators guaranteed, for the Great Pan-Hellenic Games where rivalries were conducted in a framework of rules not so different from the contest of war.

CONFLICT IS JUSTICE: THE UNION OF OPPOSITES

Heraclitus, a native of Ephesus on the coast of Asia Minor just north of Miletus, portrayed the sense of agonistic rivalry well. For Heraclitus, the nature of things was constructed according to conflict (*eris*): "One must realize that war (*polemos*) is shared and conflict is justice, and that all things come to pass in accordance with conflict." *Polemos* is common in the sense of being universal, all-pervading, *and* unifying. In Heraclitus's conception, *what is shared is division.* Conflict is justice because conflict does not involve the triumph of one force over another. Rather, conflict unites: the counterthrust brings together, oppositions concur; the fairest connection comes from things that differ; from discordant tones comes the finest attunement (*harmonia*).[23] This is what the *kosmos* is: something that, in differing, agrees with itself.[24] Conflict is justice because discordance attunes; it harmonizes.

   This harmony or union is not the unity of the patrimonial and hierarchical order, but the harmony/union of hostile powers; the convergent divergence, the consonant dissonance of opponents bonded together by what they share: conflict, *polemos*, and by the desire to maintain that conflict so that it is not cancelled by the strength of one party. There is a common measure (*metron*), whose preservation throughout each round of thrust and counterthrust ensures the justice of conflict. Heraclitus's fragmentary cosmology identifies this common measure as "fire." This is normally taken to mean that Heraclitus rejected Anaximander's notion of *archê*, of an undifferentiated boundlessness from which opposing constitutive elements of the cosmos emerge; and that he held instead the notion that fire was the preeminent element in the universe, and that all things that compose the world are a differentiation of just one of them.[25] However, there is no need to understand the common measure as the *source* of all things. When Heraclitus says that "all things are an exchange for fire, and fire for all things,"[26] he is indicating how things not the same, and likely to be subsumed by their opposites, are equilibrated. Cold things grow hot, heat cools, the wet dries, and that which is parched moistens.[27] The elements of the physical universe (fire, earth, water) can be equilibrated, but not by saying that the physical components of the universe are equal (in mass and so on) to each other, or are reducible to one element, but that they can be brought to the point of equilibrium where the relationship (of volume, weight, and so on) of water to *fire* in the cosmos is equal to that of *fire* to earth. Fire "governs" or "steers" all things because it is the *metron* or common measure that allows for the positing of a geometrical proportion. In the spirit of Ionian commerce, Heraclitus draws the analogy: all things are an exchange for fire and fire for all things, as goods are for gold and gold for goods.

The balanced measure (*isometria*) of the cosmos implies that it is not any particular social or physical force that is the unifying factor but rather ratio. Ratio provides union in the midst of conflict and struggle. In the Heraclitean world, combativeness no longer assumes the death or extinction of the other party. *Polemos* is carried on in a civic manner instead. This requires or implies a new system of power: *public power*. Public power does not dominate parties in society. Public power is what maintains spaces, and sets the rules, for contestatory engagements. The contest is governed by rules and norms. Those who confront each other in public are not the same. The *nomoi* of their family, household, class, or function in society *sets them apart*. They aim for different, and conflicting, things. In the city there is no "father of the people" to assign them a place. There is no hierarchical order, or order of strength even, to make each part of society the servant of some other (higher) part, as in the case of even chiefs and kings who serve mythological divinities. Without such ties, parties in society will encroach on one another, and will seek to redress such encroachment. Justice is deciding where the limits are, and is not attained without struggle. Such struggle helps to define the limits of the respective parties, but without one party triumphing over its opponent.

In a public struggle, to do well in the struggle requires human excellence. It requires qualities of courage, self-discipline, prudence, and so forth. The contestant wins not by frenzy and aggression but by the possession of *aretê* (virtue). In the *agora* of public power there are rules, but no rulers. *Instead of rulers there are judges, juries, assemblies, spectators.* They exercise judgment. The backing of public power for one's cause is not necessarily easy to attain, nor does it flow to the most deserving without this desert being tested. The adversary, the contestant, the performer in public can win the backing of public sanctions but not without effort, work (*ergon*) and activity (*energeia*). To gain the support of the civic courts, for example, one must engage in an adversarial contest, or at least confront an opponent, and in doing so, exhibit *aretê* and the practical knowledge that allows one to avoid *hubris* and to act in a "measured" way. It is the same in the law-making assembly: political opponents confront each other. They confront each other to redress social injustice, to draw the limits that establish the determinacy of social parties.

All things, not only justice, *come to pass in accordance with conflict*. Conflict is to be found on the sports field, among philosophers in the academy, or artisans in the marketplace. Conflict is a stimulus to excellence. The best, the most skilled, the ones who excel, can receive the sanction of their respective publics. These contests are played out in the city center. In the *agora* there were contests of potters, horse breeders, singers, military companies, composers, and dramatists.[28] The city center was the place for exhibition, exposition, competition; the assembly (*ekklêsia*) a place for the contest of statesmen-citizens. The gymnasium, the enclosed sports ground, set in a grove of trees, was the place for athletic competition. The Pan-Hellenic Games (Olympian, Pythian, Isthmian, Nemean) raised this to a higher level. The post-Homeric Greek world was a world where *conflict was a source of meaning rather than the harbinger of chaos*. Yet that was so only as long as conflict yielded equilibrium – the balance of contending forces; as long as public space functioned as a fulcrum for competing forces; as long as it yielded *a union of opposites*.

This paradoxical but brilliant image of the union of opposites was elaborated most fully by the Pythagoreans. The idea of order that had been developed in Miletus and other Ionian cities in the first half of the sixth century was carried westward by settlers like Pythagoras of Samos, who left the Ionian cities for Magna Graecia (today's coastal southern Italy) in the second half of the sixth century. Just like other Ionian traditions, the Pythagoreans sought the meaning-generating power of society neither in the Being of the old hierarchical world nor in the Becoming of a dynamic empire, but in Balance (in the union of opposites). The Pythagorean answer to the problem of meaning was the doctrine of the mean. The Pythagoreans conceived of the parts of society as opposites – opposites that had a tendency to encroach upon each other. Like Anaximander, Pythagoras regarded such encroachment as a state of injustice. Justice, in contrast, was a condition where each opposite kept to itself. But how was this conceivable without a place – a station – for each part in a hierarchy? By, Pythagoras argued, the maintaining of a *balance* between opposites. In this schema, *the image of hierarchy is replaced by the image of scales*. The scales of justice establish a balance in society. The condition of reconciliation or civil peace, sought after by the Pythagoreans, was "an attunement of opposites, a unification of the many, a reconciliation of dissentients." Opposites were neither hierarchically subordinated nor things to be radically transformed into something else. Rather they were what stood in equilibrium around a mean or middle point.

Pythagoras observed that the weights of different hammers striking an anvil sometimes produced concordant musical tones. The pounding of light and heavy weights might have been expected to produce nothing more than noise — chaotic or incongruous sounds, cacophony. And yet, sometimes the pounding hammers harmonized — because of the ratio between the weights of the hammers. A five-kilogram hammer and a ten-kilogram hammer, standing in a ratio of 1:2, produced the concord of the octave. This union of the light and the heavy was illustrative of a more profound conception: that things of radical difference, when they were combined together in certain ideal ratios — most particularly the ratios of the intervals of the musical scale — could generate a surprising synthesis. This was so because a well-scaled or well-proportioned part of a whole meant that it did not overwhelm or obscure other parts. No part was excessive. This encapsulated the Greek idea of *logos*, which meant on the one hand "the intelligible, determinate, mensurable as opposed to the fantastic, vague, and shapeless" and on the other hand "the proportions of things both in their internal structure and in their relations with one another."[29] The proportionality implied in the Greek idea of reason was related closely to ideas of limit, moderation, and order. The parts of what was well proportioned were limited, and they were thereby well ordered in their relationship to each other. This concern with limits and order was, of all the ancient Greek theories, most beautifully conceived by the Pythagoreans, who believed that the world was living, divine, good, and efficient because it was limited and because it displayed an order in the relations of its component parts. The limited and the unlimited were contrasting principles. The Pythagoreans believed that evil belonged to the unlimited and good to the limited. The world is good because it is limited, and where limits are observed, each part that makes up a whole has its own existence; others do not encroach upon it. It was this condition that made a *union of opposites* possible. It was this condition that was just.

CLEISTHENES'S REFORMS AND THE MIXED POLITICAL ORDER

Ionian thought prefigured the emergence of the *polis* as a fully formed social and political order. One might say that what the first philosophers thought through, the Athenians, under the guiding hand of Cleisthenes, were the first to realize. But this role probably would not have fallen to Athens had it not been for the Persians.[30] In 559 B.C.E., when Cyrus came to the throne, Persia was a vassal kingdom of the Medians. Twenty years later, Persia's overlords, along with the kingdom of Lydia, Babylon, and the Greek cities of Asia Minor, had fallen to Persia in the 540s B.C.E.[31] The Persians installed tyrants in the Greek cities that they conquered. The effect of coming under Persian hegemony was to cut off Ionian political evolution. The promise, for example, of the moderate government that had emerged in Miletus (after decades of factional and oligarchic strife) could not be realized. Simultaneously the Persian presence triggered the westward migration of Ionian thinkers. Heraclitus stayed in Ephesus, but in 538 B.C.E., the older Pythagoras left Samos, which had come under the control of Polycrates, a home-grown tyrant who cultivated good relations with the oriental palace monarchies.[32] With Asia Minor under Persian hegemony, the transition from tyranny to an isonomic regime was only conceivable somewhere to the West. As it happened, this shift was eventually undertaken by Athens. In the interregnum, though, the destabilizing presence of the Persians was a trigger for the installation of a tyranny in Athens.

The tyrant Peisistratos ruled Athens from 546 to 528 B.C.E., and was succeeded by his sons, until one of them, Hippias, was expelled by Athenians in 510 B.C.E., and Attica set about, with Cleisthenes at the helm, establishing an isonomic constitutional order. The Peisistratos regime was not an oriental despotism; but it was not unambiguously opposed to the Persians either—for these Greek tyrants had an orientalizing side. (There are some parallels between the palace building of the East and the monumentalizing public works of tyrants.) When, after 520 B.C.E., the Persian king Darius had set his sights on European conquest, attacking Thrace and Scythia, the Peisistradids could not be relied upon to stand firm against the Persians, and their expulsion was inevitable. For the Athenians—like all the Greeks—the thought of the loss of independence was intolerable.[33]

With Hippias exiled, Cleisthenes introduced to Attica the practice of ostracism as a defensive measure against the Peisistratids (or other powerful families like the Alcmeonids) because of mistrust of their connections with Persia.[34] But with the Peisistratids out of power, the Athenians faced a much more difficult question: What political regime could they institute? If the regime was to be neither tyrannical nor based on the kind of tribal-clannish principle that had produced aristocratic factionalism or had degenerated into oligarchy, then who was to rule Athens, and what was to be the ethos of that rule?

Before the time of Cleisthenes, qualification for citizenship was membership in a phratry.[35] The citizen body was still notionally a tribal community, composed of old Attic clans. Solon had passed a law stipulating that membership of the clans be open to nonclansmen, but the oligarchs obstructed the implementation of this measure. Unsurprisingly many of the immigrants who continued to be excluded from the phratries — because they lacked a "pure" tribal descent — later became supporters of the Peisistratids. One of the reasons for Solon's failure in these matters was the legal form of his reforms. Solon's laws had been *thesmoi*. (*Thesmos* meant more or less the same as *themis*; that is, a law laid down by sacred tradition and repeated through usage. The word for *thesmoi* appears only once in Homer, but is frequent in the Attic authors. Draco also legislated via the *thesmoi*.) Solon used the legal forms of the nobility to reconfigure the social regime — a strategy that could achieve only so much. Cleisthenes's laws by contrast were *nomoi*[36] — public laws passed through the Athenian assembly, while Solon's laws had simply been an uncovering (*alêtheia*) by Solon of something otherwise inaccessibly sacred. For Solon's generation, justice remained intertwined with a divine truth that only someone with revelatory authority could pronounce. Cleisthenes on the other hand offered a no longer divine but mathematical and geometrical (rational) image of justice — a system of justice based not on oracular pronouncements but on numbers, on social metrics.

Under Cleisthenes's initiatives, civic participation was no longer organized through the clan, but the neighborhood (*dêmos*). The clans, tribes, and priesthoods of the old order continued on, but were stripped of significance. This in turn made possible the enfranchisement of many people of "impure" birth — those whose tribal descent was questionable. Many non-Athenians and freed slaves were enfranchised in the new neighborhoods.[37] Ten new artificial "tribes" replaced the four traditional Ionian tribes (*phulai*) of Attica. To reinforce the transformation of identity or affiliation that this involved, from 508 B.C.E. citizens were officially known by their deme rather than by their father's name — by the demotic rather than the patronymic.* The neighborhood units were grouped into thirty *trittues*, and those *trittues* were classified as city, coast, or inland.

---

*This measure was ever only partially realized, and led in practice to a varied and often arbitrary use of names.

The *trittues* were then assigned by lot to the ten artificial tribes. The result was that each artificial "tribe" had a mix of city, inland and coastal dwellers, and each neighborhood was a mix of different clans or families. The mixing of the Pediaei, Paralii and Diacrii—the inhabitants of the plain, the coast, and the hills—was central to Cleisthenes's design. These were the basic geopolitical forces (parties) in Athenian politics. The plain was dominated by the still clannish large landed estates and the agrarian power of the nobility; the coastal region was mercantile in its ethos: this was the trading world of the Athenian middle class and resident aliens; while the hills region was the locale of the poor: the dispossessed peasants and immigrant aliens who worked the plutocrat's quarries and mines, and the herdsmen who had acquired freedom under Solon's reforms but no land.[38]

The significance of the Cleisthenian reforms (508–500 B.C.E.) lay in the instituting of a mixed political order instead of the old household-based, segmented structure of rule (*kratos*). Of course, the old patriarchal system did not die in toto. But then the fact that it did not is indicative of the depth of the shift that was being initiated. The Greeks were embarking on a reconstruction of the core signifiers of their society. It is unwise to think that such an enterprise could be completed overnight or even—considering that we are talking about a transportable source of meaning—over the lifespan of a *particular* society.

To take one example: For the Attic Greeks, admission to citizenship, with its civic right to enter and speak in the public assembly, to speak in court, and to hold property was the possession of males. But even where a man (husband, father) was the *kurios* ("sovereign"/guardian) of a woman in public matters—or else where, as in many cities, residents (*metoikoi*) had to have a guardian (*prostatês*) to bring a lawsuit[39]—this did not make men the *despotês* (arbitrary task master) over women in the household, or even kings in the house. Rather the relationship of husband and wife—as Aristotle, who had no interest in giving a liberal interpretation of these matters, describes it—was much more subtle: a husband and a father ruled over his wife and children,[40] both of whom were free, but the rule differed in each case; rule over children was royal, whereas rule over wives was *constitutional*. Under this schema, the male was by nature fitter for command than the female, yet, Aristotle acknowledged, in constitutional states citizens *rule and are ruled in turn*.[41] This presupposed the considerable authority of women in the *household* domain. Such authority extended in many Greek cities to the point where women could inherit and could own property in their own right, and indeed, in some cities, could act on their own in court, that is to say, in the *public*

domain.[42] The Pythagoreans, though the exception, encouraged participation by women in their associations and clubs, and in these circles
women were a significant intellectual presence. In general it is true to say
that women in the Hellenic world were not public beings, and that predominately their sphere was the household. But there were interesting
exceptions to this. Women of high status held civic offices as priestesses[43]
(e.g., the chief religious official of the Athenian polis was the priestess of
Athena Polias); free women of lower status worked outdoors and sold
vegetables and perfumes in the marketplace; metic women made shoes
and costumes; and in Sparta women, like men, participated in musical
and gymnastic competitions.[44]

It was to take more than two thousand years of the unfolding of the
universal ethos that underlay the Attic deme before housebound women
or household dependents (such as servants) gained a full public standing.
Today, to accuse the Hellene deme order — the ordering of society through
public assemblies based on neighborhoods — of complicity in the rule of
patriarchy[45] is to miss the enormity of the step that the Greeks took in their
partial refusal of the patriarchal principle. Anyone who has a little more
patient perspective will observe that development of the Greek cities in
the Hellenistic age (from the age of Alexander to the age of Augustus) is
marked by a noticeable "feminization" of the *polis* — as women participated in more and more public activities, art, and culture. It is important
to understand the city tradition as *the epic unfolding of a form over centuries*.
To reconstruct the core meaning of society is fraught with difficulty. Contemporaries today, infatuated with the promise of reform constantly made
in bureaucratic societies, mislead themselves if they suppose that the frequent rule changes of the bureaucratic society amount to something substantial, or believe that the reconstruction of the core meaning of a society
("the spirit of its laws") can happen with the flick of a pen, when all that
such Faustian endeavors do is strip away meaning from social life.

Civilizational change — the tectonic shift from one meaning-generating principle to another — is enormously complicated, and is constrained by the fact that even the least socially advantaged may still draw
deep meaning from the established organizing principle of their society,
and may remain deeply loyal to that principle precisely because it
imparts a meaning to their lives. We should not underestimate the pull of
old signifiers on human actions and emotions. We see this, for example,
in the way that, over time, in the post-Cleisthenian era, the deme gradually reacquired a familial character. The original members of the deme —
those who were recognized in the Cleisthenian ordering as citizens —
were adult males resident in one of the designated neighborhoods at the

time that the Cleisthenian constitution was adopted. In subsequent generations, however, membership of demes was determined by descent. The Athenian assembly could grant citizenship, but this procedure was used sparingly. In practice, overwhelmingly, a citizen *inherited* citizenship from his father, and this citizenship was fixed to a particular deme. No matter where he might reside a son belonged to the same deme as his father, as his father had belonged to his father's deme. Thus the deme tended over time to grow into a corporate body of kinsmen with its own chief and customary life.

In short, there was no way that the household was going to be erased overnight as a locus of identification and source of meaning in matters of governance. But, equally, we should not underestimate the importance of the breach (with the old regime of meaning) represented by the Cleisthenian ordering. What Cleisthenes did, after the spirit of the "first philosophers" (the Ionian philosophers), was to conceive of another way of arranging the parts of society so that those parts combined to form a meaningful whole, recognizable as a whole by the members of society. As Aristotle observed of Cleisthenes, he wished to mix up men from different parts of the city, so they could share in citizenship.[46] Such mixing meant taking those with different religious, tribal, and household affiliations, and those with different functional—agrarian, artisanal, commercial—orientations, and mixing them together. A *union* was created out of such a *mixture* by the practice of *isonomia*, the balancing of norms. (The popular twentieth century translation of the term *isonomia* as "equality of rights" or "equality before the law" tells us more about the philosophico-political preoccupations of the twentieth century than it does about the antique practice of *isonomia*.) Each of the parts of the *polis* had its own *nomos*. The *isonomia* was the constitutional ordering of all of the *nomoi*. This ordering—the good order (*eunomia*) of the *nomoi*—was achieved by the *iso*, balancing, of *nomoi*. This constitutional ordering was a kind of *sunkrasis* (compound) and *sunopsis* (general view) of the parts of society.[47] Through the image of the constitutional order the members of the society were able to see themselves as part of a whole, a whole that was ordered through the balancing or equilibration of those parts.

The bearers of different *nomoi* achieved this balance, in the first place, by entering public space. In the *ekklêsia*, the assembly of the people, each citizen had freedom of speech, *isêgoria*, to address the assembly. The days when only nobles could speak publicly were officially over. The assembly, at Cleisthenes' initiative, was confirmed in its responsibility for voting war and peace, passing death sentences, and choosing military officers. The meetings of the assembly took place in the city center, where the bearers of the different *nomoi* gathered together. They entered the public space, each representing a claim to excellence (*aretê*, virtue) — the courage of the soldier, the self-control of the artisan, the prudence of the judge, and so on — and each displaying a readiness to demonstrate that *aretê* in speech or deed. *Nomos* competed against *nomos* — in the public *agôn* of politics. In turn, this competition was dramatized in the theater of the city, in the performances of tragedy, in the work of the tragedians. The bearers of different *nomoi* had the right to speak, to argue, to plead their causes — the causes of making war and peace, of commerce, of city-building, and so forth — and of contesting each other's cause. Yet, underlying such contestation was an awareness of limits, moderation, and measure.

The Greeks developed a strong dislike of *hubris*, of overstepping the mark, e.g., because of improper ambition. (The Attic procedure of ostracism was employed as a response to *hubris* — a citizen could be exiled from Athens for ten years if a majority of the quorum of six thousand citizens voted against him.)[48] Because the *polis* was constituted as a *civic* order, no one of the *nomoi* could expect to conquer or to master (*kratein*) the other. Cleisthenes's *polis*, the mature *polis*, was not a democracy (*dêmokratia*), any more than it was an oligarchy or an aristocracy. It was not a *dêmo-kratia* in the sense that it moved away from the practice of "ruling in the mode of *kratos*" (in fact it appears that the term *dêmokratia* was not coined until around the 460s B.C.E., and perhaps later.)[49] The Cleisthenian ordering was, in principle, *a-kratein*; yet it was not dispossessed of the authority that leads, that provides political initiative. Rather it bracketed the desire for *kratos*, for mastery. To give up the desire for mastery is at the same time to learn that one's scope for action (*praxis*) is *limited*; that — irrespective of which of the *nomoi* one identifies with or sides with in the political conflicts (*stasis, polemos*) of the *polis* — one's speech or deed must ultimately be "measured." It must be "moderated." It must accord with "the mean," with a measure of all of the *nomoi*. This signifies that even the toughest conflict of forces gravitates toward equilibrium, a balancing of opposites; in other words, toward a just way of living together.

NOTES

1. On Solon's reforms, see Philip Brook Manville, *The Origins of Citizenship in Ancient Athens* (Princeton, N.J.: Princeton University Press, 1990), chap. 6; Oswyn Murray, *Early Greece*, 2d ed. (London: Fontana, 1993), pp. 189–200.

2. Solon created four property classes: the *pentakosiomedimnoi*, the *hippeis*, the *zeugitai*, and the *thêtes*. Membership of these classes depended on returns from landholding. However, the first three classes, as Oswyn Murray (*Early Greece*, p.

194) points out, were roughly equatable with the older aristocratic stratification. The first class were more or less "men of good birth" (those of the most important families); the second class were knights, those who could afford their own horses for military service as cavalrymen ("mounted warriors"); the third class were those who could afford the armour of the hoplite soldier; the fourth were below the military census. The positions of *archôn* and state treasurers were reserved for the highest class. The *thêtes* had no share in offices. (All income classes, though, could vote for magistrates.) As Athens developed a blue water fleet, the *thêtes* served in the navy as marines or rowers. But, by that time, the formal exclusion from higher office was dropped.

3. The "hill of Ares" where it assembled.

4. A hundred for each tribe of Attica.

5. Aristotle, *Athenian Constitution*, trans. P. J. Rhodes (Harmondsworth: Penguin, 1984), 8.5.

6. Murray, *Early Greece*, p. 198.

7. Even if he advised fathers to teach their sons a trade – good advice, perhaps, but it had no institutional resonance.

8. Victor Ehrenberg, *The Greek State*, 2d ed. (Oxford: Basil Blackwell, 1966 [1963]), pp. 44–45; James F. McGlew, *Tyranny and Political Culture in Ancient Greece* (Ithaca, N.Y.: Cornell University Press, 1993), especially chap. 2; A. Andrewes, *The Greek Tyrants* (London: Hutchinson, 1956).

9. Manville, *The Origins of Citizenship in Ancient Athens*, pp. 168–69; George Thomson, *Studies in Ancient Greek Society: The First Philosophers* (London: Lawrence and Wishart, 1955), p. 221; A. Andrewes, *The Greek Tyrants*, chap. 9.

10. According to Andrewes, *The Greek Tyrants*, pp. 111–12, the pottery industry of Athens reached its zenith at this time, while the circulation of coin improved markedly under the tyranny.

11. On Periander's comparable public works program at Corinth, see Andrewes, p. 51. Andrewes remarks that such public works "were a feature of every tyranny," as indeed they were. The sixth-century tyrant Thrasybulus built a new acropolis and harbor in Miletus. Polycrates (ca. 533–522 B.C.E.) of Samos was preoccupied with engineering, and built a harbor mole and water tunnel far in advance of its time. Periander laid a roadway across the Isthmus at Corinth, so ships could be hauled between the Gulf of Corinth and the Saronic Gulf. The Doric temple form, of central importance in Greek architecture, emerged in Corinth during the period of tryanny. On the latter, see Murray, *Early Greece*, p. 152.

12. Thomson, *Studies in Ancient Greek Society*, p. 221.

13. Andrewes, *The Greek Tyrants*, p. 114.

14. Periander of Corinth likewise established close relations with the kings of Lydia.

15. Jean-Pierre Vernant, *The Origins of Greek Thought* (Ithaca, N.Y.: Cornell University Press, 1982), pp. 63–64.

16. This view is at odds with that of Gregory Vlastos, in "Isonomia," *American Journal of Philology*, 74:4, and in "Equality and Justice in Early Greek Cosmologies" in David J. Furley and R. E. Allen, *Studies in Presocratic Philosophy* (London: Routledge, 1970), vol. 1.

17. See, e.g., Charles Kahn, *Anaximander and the Origins of Greek Cosmology* (New York: Columbia University Press, 1960), pp. 187–88.

18. Hippodamos worked in the period after the Persian Wars. He adapted the orthogonal grid, already used in Greek colonial cities, to the ideal proportions of Pythagorean theory.

19. On the origin and nature of architecture, see Peter Murphy, "Architectonics," in J. Arnason and P. Murphy (eds.), *Agon, Logos, Polis* (Stuttgart: Franz Steiner, 2001), pp. 207–32.

20. The Homeric word for public assembly or assembly place as well as contest.

21. Jean-Pierre Vernant, *Myth and Society in Ancient Greece* (London: Methuen, 1982), p. 27.

22. Ibid., p. 31.

23. Jonathan Barnes, *Early Greek Philosophy* (Harmondsworth: Penguin, 1987), p. 115; Charles H. Kahn, *The Art and Thought of Heraclitus* (Cambridge: Cambridge University Press, 1979), p. 193.

24. Barnes, *Early Greek Philosophy*, p. 102; Kahn, *The Art and Thought of Heraclitus*, p. 195.

25. See, e.g., G. Vlastos, "On Heraclitus" in Furley and Allen, *Studies in Presocratic Philosophy*.

26. Kahn, *The Art and Thought of Heraclitus*, p. 47; Barnes, *Early Greek Philosophy*, p. 123.

27. Barnes, *Early Greek Philosophy*, p. 115.

28. Lewis Mumford, *The City in History* (Harmondsworth: Penguin, 1966 [1961]), p. 137.

29. W. K. C. Guthrie, *A History of Greek Philosophy* (Cambridge University Press, Cambridge, 1962), vol. 1.

30. Though, as I discuss in chapter 3 (*Kosmopolis*), the fact that Athens was to pick up the mantle of the Ionian enlightenment was not necessarily propitious, for Athens was far from perfectly fitted for such a role.

31. Cyrus' son Cambyses conquered Egypt in 525.

32. Polycrates cultivated both Persia and Egypt in order to play them off each other; he was eventually killed (ca. 522 B.C.E.) by the Persians for his efforts.

33. The Athenians wagered all on their war against the Persians. The Athenians, along with all of the Greeks, knew what independence (*autarkeia*) was. What they most disliked was the loss of this independence. To be Hellene meant not to hold life dearer than liberty (*eleutheria*). This is what was at stake in the confrontation with Persia. Contemporary liberal opinion (cf. Paul A. Rahe, *Republics Ancient and Modern* [Chapel Hill: University of North Carolina Press, 1994], vol. 1, pp. 19–20) finds the Greek attitude that one should fear slavery more than death puzzling and disconcerting. This modern view is premised on the Hobbesian assumption that the greatest evil is death. If you assume this, the Greeks are incomprehensible, and it is impossible to make any sense of the Greek attitude toward the "barbarians." It looks like just another ethnocentrism (as Cartledge, *The Greeks* [Oxford University Press, Oxford, 1993], chap. 3, believes it is) when the Greeks say that they are "naturally" free and the *barbarophonoi* are servile by nature. But Persia, Egypt, Thrace, and so on were societies whose central signifying core was patri-

monial, and who made subjection and obedience the central tie of society. In the eyes of the modern liberal, oriental despotism does not exist—it is a stereotype (cf. Paul Cartledge, *The Greeks*, p. 62). The modern liberal cannot understand a society whose *phusis* determined that people feared the loss of independence more than death. For the Hellenes, the worst thing, say, about being poor was not the discomfort, or hunger, but the lack of control over oneself—being compelled to do slavish things, falling into helpless dependence, not being able to speak frankly. Only a person who was independent could do or say something of note, could be the best, could act distinctively, excel, shine, be remembered in others' stories, be noticed by the *polis*, and thereby become immortal.

34. Murray, *Early Greece*, p. 286.

35. On Cleisthenes, see Manville, *The Origins of Citizenship in Ancient Athens*, chap. 7, and Thomson, *Studies in Ancient Greek Society*, pp. 223–27. See also the astute comments of Cornelius Castoriadis, "The Greek Polis and the Creation of Democracy," in *Philosophy, Politics, Autonomy*, ed. David Ames Curtis (Oxford: Oxford University Press, 1991), especially p. 111.

36. M. Ostwald, *From Popular Sovereignty to Sovereignty of Law* (Berkeley: University of California Press, 1986), p. 87.

37. Mogens Herman Hansen, *The Athenian Democracy in the Age of Demosthenes* (Oxford: Blackwell, 1991), p. 34.

38. Thomson, *Studies in Ancient Greek Society*, pp. 216–19; Andrewes, *The Greek Tyrants*, pp. 102–104; Ehrenberg, *The Greek State*, p. 29. By contrast, the notion (of Ellen Meiksins Wood in *Peasant-Citizen and Slave* [London: Verso, 1988]) that the Athenian *polis* was dominated by a peasant-smallholder culture misses its mixed character.

39. Hansen, *The Athenian Democracy in the Age of Demosthenes*, pp. 117–18.

40. There is a habit of contemporary commentators to follow Aristotle no further than this in his chain of reasoning, as instanced by Cartledge, *The Greeks*, pp. 69–70.

41. *Politics*, 1259b1.

42. Ehrenberg, *The Greek State*, p. 42.

43. Priestesses and priests were officials of the city, whose function it was to carry out rituals.

44. Jack Lindsay, *The Ancient World: Manners and Morals* (New York: Putnam, 1968), p. 94; James Redfield, "Homo Domesticus," in *The Greeks*, ed. Jean-Pierre Vernant (Chicago: University of Chicago Press, 1995).

45. Cartledge, *The Greeks*, chap. 4.

46. Aristotle, *The Athenian Constitution*, 21.2; *Politics*, trans. Ernest Baker (Oxford: Clarendon Press, 1946), 1319a19.

47. Cf. the nomoscopic analysis of Greek politics pursued by Vassilis Lambropoulos in "The Rule of Justice," *Thesis Eleven* 40 (Cambridge, Mass.: MIT Press, 1995).

48. Manville, *The Origins of Citizenship in Ancient Athens*, p. 196.

49. Rahe, *Republics Ancient and Modern*, vol. 1, p. 94.

3

KOSMOPOLIS

POWER

With Cleisthenes's isonomic reforms, Athens inherited the mantle of the Ionian Enlightenment. But the soul of Attica, notwithstanding the brilliance of its philosophical minds, was not equipped for the bearing of this legacy. Through much of the sixth century Athens had been a relative backwater, much more of an agricultural "stay-at-home" society than the Ionian cities. Tellingly, in this "home society," artisans and traders were stigmatized. When sixth-century Athens did experience broader horizons, it was at the behest of the Peisistratids, whose promotion of artisanship and trade was inextricably connected with a program of monumentalizing public works and the imperial control of trade routes via the domination of the Aegean. Isonomic Athens was heir to this ethos, and its influence on Attica was pernicious.

Athens had participated little in the colonizing diaspora of the archaic Hellenic world. Athenians thus had little collective sense of the "away home." Attica, by Greek standards, possessed a sizeable territory, and could in the eighth and seventh centuries accommodate an expanding population at home. In this there is a parallel with Sparta up to a certain point: the Spartans, by conquering the southwest Peloponnese, managed to avoid overseas settlement. The Athenians, however, were not motivated by a distrust of contact with the world as the Spartans were. Athenians traveled, and citizens of other cities settled in Athens. Yet they were not a thalassocentric people.[1] Having no experience of the "away home," they believed themselves to be aboriginal settlers on their territory who had a special relationship to the soil of Attica,[2] and thus special reason not to settle abroad.[3] When population pressures and inadequate farm land threatened grain shortages at the end of the seventh century, the first thought of Athenians was to seize Sigeum at the entry to the Hellespont (Dardanelles) in an effort to control the Black Sea grain trade. It was this same pressure on land that caused a swelling of numbers of landless poor, and that forced, in the midst of aristocratic faction fighting, Solon's reforms of 594–93 B.C.E. These reforms, though, were inseparable from the view of Athenians that their city could trace its origins back to the Bronze Age without break. Thus, along with his legal reforms, Solon initiated specifically Athenian rites, and urged his fellow citizens to annex the island of Salamis. The Peisisratid regime subsequently expanded the city cult and the annexation strategy. Pericles, finally, immortalized both.

The fifth century is thought of as the period of "classical" Greece, and Athens its shining emblem. But the fifth century was also a time of enormous self-destructiveness. It is true that fifth-century Athens hosted many of the greatest minds of the ancient world. But what preoccupied so much of their thought were the disasters that Athenians had brought upon themselves. Athens, alongside Sparta, defiantly and brilliantly stood up to the Persian invasion, and, against all of the odds, was decisive in the defeat of the Persians. But subsequently she turned the alliances she had made with other Aegean cities against the Persians into a none-too-glorious imperial hegemony. The isonomic regime lived more in words than in reality in classical Athens. Of course, that it persisted in words was important for posterity.

The idea of an isometric regime entered (what we retrospectively know as) European culture directly from Pythagorean sources and indirectly via Plato and Aristotle. It articulated another, and highly influential, way of understanding the relation between the elements of society — one that was not patrimonial. The isometrical image of a *centered* society — one that had the quality of *sôphrosunê* — was inextricably linked to the social form (*eidos*) that we know as the city. The city proper has played a significant, if contested, role in the history of the West. Challenges to the social form of the city have come from two principal sources: from the image of society as a patrimony and from the image of society as expansionary. We see these forces aligned against the classic city in the Greek world of the fifth century B.C.E. Athens was reconstructed under Cleisthenes's leadership at the tail end of the sixth century, and encapsulated a political equilibrium of old and new social forces. Yet by the time of Pericles's (mid-fifth-century) leadership, Athens had come to see itself less as a balanced city and more as an expansionary force ready to dominate and coerce its neighbors. In a pattern already established by the Peisistratids, Pericles promoted a naval empire for Athens and legitimated this by turning Athens into a *patria* for its citizens: into an object of divination. This was not a Spartan fear of strangers, but a cult that emphasized the purity of citizen descent. Where the Spartans feared the outside world, the Periclean regime relished the irony that the Spartans themselves were outsiders — Dorians—ruling over an "indigenous" population. In response—and in no small part motivated by political ends—the Pericleans stressed the autochthonous nature of Athens,[4] and in this spirit Pericles introduced a law[5] requiring a citizen to have both an Athenian mother and an Athenian father that increased the difficulty of metics gaining admission to citizenship. Irony of ironies, Pericles then asked for an exemption for Aspasia, his learned and beautiful companion who was, alas, a Miletian.[6]

The government of Periclean Athens (460-429 B.C.E.) spent large amounts of money on civic art, festivals, and buildings, but in a way that corroded the civic spirit and made the citizen one who was devoted to a patron deity. This is epitomized in Pericles's rebuilding of the *Acropolis*. Athenians were encouraged to worship their origins. On the hill-site of the earliest settlement,[7] they built a monumental entrance (the Propylaia)[8] to the sacred enclosure of the Acropolis. Rising above this was the Parthenon, the temple to Athena.[9] Nearby, the Erechtheion commemorated the dispute between the sea-god Poseidon and Athena for possession of Attica, and celebrated Athena as the guardian of Athens. The cult of Athens is inseparable from the city's imperial tendencies — viz. its growing hegemony over the Delian League (of more than 150 cities) that had begun as a defensive measure against the Persians.[10] Athens had acquitted herself well, even brilliantly, in standing up to the threat of Persian despotism earlier in the century, and had organized an effective alliance (*philia*) of cities against Persian ambitions to control the Aegean. Now Athens turned this civic collaboration into an arrangement of dominance and subordination. Contemporaries were right to call Athens a "tyrant city." Member states of the Delian League were forced to contribute money to support a massive fleet of ships that were provided, manned, and controlled by Athens. Again in the Peisistratid pattern, the Periclean administration strengthened diplomatic ties with Thrace and southern Russia. The imperial policy was a disaster for Athens. Sparta, formerly the great ally of Athens against the Persian Empire, was understandably threatened by the build-up of Athenian naval power and by its imperial proclivities. Smaller cities, fearing their loss of independence, allied with Sparta against Athens. The Peloponnesian War (431-404 B.C.E.) ended in total defeat for Athens. She was stripped of her fleet; her empire was dissolved.

Athens never completely recovered from the defeat. The loss of life and wealth, and of confidence and morale, had been enormous. Stripped of military power, Athens—ever dynamic, even in defeat—reconstructed

Athens, the Parthenon, 447–438 B.C.E.

herself as the cultural center of the Greek-speaking world. The founding of the Platonic and Aristotelian schools in Athens set the model that would bring a succession of the best minds of the Eastern Mediterranean to Athens over the next two centuries to create or lead philosophical schools. In a manner of speaking, these schools were founded on the disaster of the Peloponnesian War. The mature discipline of philosophy emerged through a painful reflection on that war and the responsibility of the Athenian neighborhood (*dêmos*) constitution (*politeia*) for the war. The key figure in this painful reflection is Socrates, or more precisely Plato's Socrates. The figure of Socrates, as he appears in Plato's dialogues, sets the tone for subsequent Hellene philosophy, with the partial exception of Aristotle and his school. Socrates personifies philosophy's abandonment of politics. This is often understood as a rejection of democracy. If it is meant by this that Socrates held the Athenian *dêmos* responsible for the aggressive and blighted policies of an imperial democracy, this is correct enough. Who else could one hold responsible for Athenian myopia? Yet the particulars of blame are important. What, exactly, was at fault? Was it the deme order in toto, or the deme order that resigned its orderliness in favor of the designs of *kratos*? What is to be called to account: the deme order or the deme kratos?; the *isonomia* of Cleisthenes with its synoptic breadth or the *dêmokratia* in which the deme fancy themselves looking down from the Acropolis, masters of all they see — masters of all the seas, masters of all they can imagine they can see? The eyesight of *dêmokratia* is myopic, and not only because of the desire for mastery. Something else is at work here. A new kind of power emerges out of the Athenian well-spring. This power is not public power either. It is something different again. Let us call this power *plastic-promethean power*. It is the power of *dunamis* as opposed to the public power of *energeia*.[11] It thrives on constant change, transformation, and with this, expansion. At the same time, it is a destructive form of power. *To create, it must destroy.*

Thucydides observed that Athenians of the Periclean age were "addicted to innovation."[12] They became "adventurous beyond their power, and daring beyond their judgment." In consequence, they were "swift to follow up success, and slow to recoil from a reverse." This addiction to innovation meant on the one hand "a scheme unexecuted is with them a positive loss;" while on the other hand for Athenians to conjecture something was practically to enact it, "for they alone are enabled to call a thing hoped for a thing got, by the speed with which they act out their resolutions." Here indeed is a new kind of power. The personification of this power of innovation — this *dunamis* — in Athenian politics was Alcibiades (ca. 450–404 B.C.E.), the brilliant, destructive ward of Pericles. Alcibiades was a significant player in many of the irrational acts perpetrated by Athens during the Peloponnesian War, culminating in the Sicilian adventure. He was a prime mover of, and had command of, the military forces Athenians sent in their unfathomable attempt (in 415 B.C.E.) to conquer Syracuse at a time when Athens's Eastern-style behavior as a *hêgemôn* (one who commands) was being sorely tested by the Spartans and their allies. This adventure ended in disaster, and the episode epitomizes the departure of *logos* from the public arena during the time of the Peloponnesian War. It also epitomizes what replaced *logos*. Thucydides's phrase "addiction to innovation" is as sharp a way as any of describing the replacement for reason. What Alcibiades offered the Athenian Assembly (*ekklêsia*) in place of the speech of reason was the rhetoric of adventurousness and daring. This rhetoric was brilliant, seductive and calamitous at the same time. Wherein lay its seduction? Herodotus — through the figure of Megabyzus — spoke of the temptation of democracy to "[rush] headlong into undertakings and [press] forward in them without reflection, like a winter torrent."[13] Yet this, again, was less a question of democracy per se, than an incisive description of the heady, inciting power of *dunamis*. This is a power that the early Roman Caesars—Julius and Octavius—personified; it is a power that the Princes whom Machiavelli describes (in his late Renaissance treatise) also personified.

That an imperial democracy might get caught up in the bracing rush of the winter torrent was less a matter of who ruled and more a matter of the nature of power and its attractions. The exercise of power requires effort and sacrifice, and it must offer as requital for this some source of attraction. Alcibiades exemplifies the attractiveness of the power that flows like a winter torrent. There is no question that he was attractive, or that he was a brilliant speaker on behalf of a protean power. The source of his attractiveness lay in the fact that his soul was plastic. He was the first great chameleon politician. Cornelius Nepos describes him thus: "Though he was rich, when circumstances demanded it, he could be hardworking and tough. He was generous, lived elegantly, was affable, courteous and yet a shrewd opponent. As soon as he had relaxed, and there was no need for mental exertion, he proved to be luxury-loving, dissolute in behavior, lustful, and intemperate. As a result, everyone was amazed that there could be such great opposites and so varied a nature in one man."[14] More disturbingly, these variations or opposites were not contained by their mutual conflict—there was no *harmonia* in Alcibiades's soul. Rather the variations and oppositions expressed themselves by the unceasing drive of the personality to change from one thing to another. To be one moment hard-working, dissolute the next. Such a protean personality is persuasive—both in a positive and negative way. The changeable persona is fascinating, and therefore attractive; at the same time this persona is not committed to anything and therefore can tell its audience what it wants to hear, or can say different things to different people according to circumstance. Such a soul has spirit and drive and daring but no character to see its designs through to the end. It is thus brilliant but also destructive. When the Athenians realized this—and the disastrous mistake of the Sicilian adventure (too late of course)—and sought to impeach Alcibiades, he, ever the chameleon, simply fled to Sparta (the opposite side) and became as Spartan as the Spartans: "People who saw him wearing his hair close cut, bathing in cold water, eating coarse meal, and dining on black broth, doubted, or rather could not believe, that he ever had a cook in house, or had seen a perfumer, or had worn a mantle of Milesian purple."[15]

Let us be clear: the Peloponnesian War was popular in democratic

Athens. For one thing it provided jobs—in a world that dealt (often effectively) with unemployment not by the provision of welfare but by public works. The prosecutors of the Athenian empire, in this respect, simply reiterated the pattern established by the earlier tyrannies. But Alcibiades represented still something more: a politics of daring beyond judgment that entirely confounds reason; that makes reason look and sound timid and conservative and nay-saying. So what did the *philoi sophias*, the friends of wisdom, make of this? Their commitment, from the time of the first philosophers, was to the good—temperate—order of the city and to reason. If the deme oversaw a time of disorderliness—if it was subject to a winter torrent—an understandable conclusion was that the deme had to be rejected. Philosophy, in its Socratic mode, becomes wary of the deme. And yet its wariness is much more than this. It goes much deeper; its implications are much more radical. The philosopher becomes wary of politics per se.

Interestingly, part of what is at stake here is the question of love. The destruction of Athens was caused by the excessive love of Athenians for Athens—a love that blinded them to the independent existence of other cities, a love that made them myopic. The philosophers did not share this love. Neither Socrates nor Plato was a phil-Athenian. In fact, both were attracted to Sparta, Athens's enemy. They admired the Doric constraint of the Spartans—their conservatism as opposed to the innovativeness of the Athenians, a conservatism that evinced a discipline that Athens lacked, or had lost. The philosophers put *sophia* before Athena, and this allowed them to sympathize with Periclean Athens's mortal enemy. But this was not a "political sympathy" in any straightforward sense, primarily because philosophy had become animated by disgust with politics. Socrates's life as a philosopher is roughly simultaneous with the debacle of the Peloponnesian War. Socrates disdained what the politicians had done to Athens—not out of a love of Athens, but out of his respect for *eunomia*. And thus he withdraws almost completely from the political life into the discursive life of the friend of wisdom.[16] Socrates turned his life into a gesture. What this gesture betrayed was the flight of *logos*, reason, from the *agora* into the philosophical circle. There was, after all, nothing reasonable about the conduct of the Athenian assembly fueled by dreams of empire. Public speech became overbearing, inhospitable, hectoring: demagogic. War was turned from contest into bullying. Consequently *logos*, the speech that gathers together, sought refuge in the conversations, the *dia-logos*, of the philosopher with his interlocutors. These conversations turned away from concrete matters of everyday politics—the matters of war and peace, diplomacy and strategy, public works and new markets. What the friends of wisdom talked about was the nature of justice, of piety, of what is it that gives *form* to the *polis*. The philosophers turned to the ultimate questions—the nature of beauty, goodness, creation, and finally late in the day to the *theo-logos*—to reflections on the nature of the soul (its eternity compared with the mortality of the body).

SOUL

Because Athens had been fatally fractured by its imperial adventure, Socratic-Platonic philosophy posed *the question of meaning*—the question of the constitution of meaningful order out of the chaos of dark times. But philosophy declined to see the constitution of meaningful order as a political constitution, as one pertaining to the public speech and deeds of *citizens*, to the life of "speaking in the assembly and practicing rhetoric and playing the politician."[17] The *agora* had become a place of wild opinion instead of reasoned speech (*logos*).

In the philosophy of the fifth century, politics no longer appears as the condition of the just city. *Philosophy retreats from politics.* The just city becomes conceivable without politics. Plato's city drew freely on pre-Socratic images. Like Pythagoras, Plato imagined that the external constitution of the city was an analogue of the internal constitution of the soul. As Plato extrapolated from the Pythagorean view of the *psuchê*, the condition of human happiness was for the three parts of the soul—reason, passion, and desire—to be brought into *harmonia* (fitting together; attunement).[18] A fourth element of the soul responsible for attaining this accord was the element of justice. Justice was the maintaining of reciprocity (*philotês*) between reason, passion, and desire. *Sôphrosunê* (temperance) was the virtue of the soul as a whole. Temperance was exhibited in the smooth working together of all of parts of the psyche: ensuring that no one element swamped or extinguished another. Doubtless there were individual differences in the way the balance was struck: some persons were more spirited than others; some more acquisitive; others more calculating or reflective, and so on. But without the presence of opposite qualities to counterbalance the temperamentally leading trait, the consequence would be unchecked behavior, and thus unhappiness.

The unlimited rule of any single quality or power was necessarily destructive, and not only for the individual *psuchê*. The same, Plato insisted, applied to the city as a whole, where three contrary qualities—*courage* (of those in conflict or in battle, who have to confront and control the passions of fear and fright), *wisdom* (of those who must calculate not just about their own good but the good of the state as a whole), and *self-*

discipline (of those who have to master the passions of appetite and acquisitiveness) — must somehow be brought into accord if the city is to flourish. A city completely dominated either by soldiers, or by administrators, or by wealthy artisans or merchants would be primed for ruin. It would be a city *devoid of justice*. It would lack *proportion*. The sense of justice or proportion so crucial to the city did not mean the rule of equality. It did not mean a city where everyone was a soldier, or where everyone had a public office, or where everyone was wealthy. What made the city good was not the fact that the parts of it were identical, but rather that the different parts balanced one another. However, in Socratic-Platonic philosophy, it is not the *agônisma* of politics — the meeting of forces from an opposite direction — that achieves this balance. Justice is not the result of the warring of elements, the counterthrust that brings together. No longer can it be said that all things come to pass in accordance with conflict. *No longer can it be said that conflict is justice.*

The retreat from politics meant scrutinizing again the principles of order (the *archê-kosmos*) and of the city. The ordered city, the *kosmos-polis*, would become — when the philosophers had finished reviewing it — apolitical. The philosophers' answer to the fact that politics in fifth-century Athens had become a battlefield of speeches (productive of only inflated imperial ambitions and a crippling internal *stasis*) was the reconstitution of the *kosmos* of the *polis*. This reordering, the philosophers believed, could be achieved by the initiative (*archê*) of a founder, and once it was constituted it could be maintained by the initiative of expert administrators (knowledgeable captains who could steer the ship of state) rather than by the speech and deeds of citizens.

The problem with any beginning, even a beginning-again, though, is: What is the basis for the beginning? Who or what begins the beginning, who or what sets in train the *eunomia*? What makes that beginning a source of meaning, and not simply an arbitrary act? The exercise of initiative normally occurs within a frame of meaning. As far as governance is concerned, such a frame of meaning might be the household or the *polis*. However, if we speak of the beginning of the household or of the *polis*, we enter a conceptually very difficult terrain, and risk setting upon a course of infinite regression. Socratic-Platonic philosophy set itself this task: to give a rational account of *archê*.[19] The Greeks, not distant from the time of Socrates, had been witness to two remarkable instances of *archê*: Solon and Cleisthenes. These instances of *archê* had been productive of the deme order. But that order, in the time of Periclean imperial democracy, had become disordered. The great intuition of philosophy was to return to the moment of *archê* and to see if it was possible to give an account of *archê*, or rather of the right *archê*: one that was productive of a coherent social order in the sense of *eunomia*.

The Socratic-Platonic argument was that the *archôn* would have to be, in the first place, something like an expert. *Archê* would rest on knowledge. As this proposition unfolds, we see that this knowledge is both an art and the knowledge of virtue.

As Socrates explains it in the dialogue *Gorgias*, ruling is an art (*technê*). Legislation is akin to the art of gymnastics, while the administration of justice is akin to medicine.[20] By contrast, oratory, the speech of the *agora*, is simply an impersonation of governance, a pretense to knowledge that produces no principle out of itself. It can give no rational account of itself, and therefore is not rational. Oratory is speech, but not the speech of reason. It is sophistry, and sophistry is to legislation what cosmetic beautification is to gymnastics, or cooking is to medicine.[21] All aim at producing some kind of pleasure but the cook and the orator do this without knowing anything of good and evil. The ruler and the doctor, by contrast, can give a *logos* — a rational account — of the nature of pleasure and its cause. The rhetoric of the *dêmos* is to justice what cookery is to medicine. While rhetoricians, like tyrants, may possess great power in Greek cities, Socrates's view was that it was power without intelligence.

The *archôn*, the ruler who initiates or leads the way, on the other hand, is a figure comparable to a farmer who is an expert with good sound knowledge about the soil. The knowledge of the *archôn*, though, is not about soil, but about virtue.[22] And via this knowledge, the *archôn* is able to *govern himself*. He is temperate and in control of his appetites.[23] The artistry of the *archôn*, unlike the oratory of the public speaker, is unpretentious and orderly. It does not put on airs or make believe that its accomplishments are astonishing. The pilot who possesses such an art, and who achieves the good results of the art, goes ashore and walks alongside his ship with modest bearing.[24] Comparably, the *archôn* exemplifies an order of life that is satisfied with what at any time it possesses.[25] The ruler has an ordered and disciplined soul, and such orderliness means temperance and justice.[26] In ruling, the *archôn* thinks only of how justice and temperance may be implanted in, and indiscipline banished from, the soul of citizens.[27] All the endeavors of the city, like all of the endeavors of the good man, should be devoted to the single purpose of ensuring that justice and temperance dwell in each person.[28]

Socrates noted that the followers of Pythagoras had said that the heavens and the earth, gods and men, are bound together by fellowship and friendship, order, temperance, and justice, and for this reason the Pythagoreans called the sum of things the "ordered" universe (*kosmos*) —

not the world of disorder and riot.[29] Socrates's personal experience of the *polis*, during the time of imperial democracy, had been one of disorder and turbulence and intemperance, a disorder productive of great unhappiness. Socrates reiterated the need for a geometrical (proportionate) equality among gods and men alike. But Athenian politics, rather than producing the balance of landed, middle class, and poor of Cleisthenes's design, had found itself torn by a fierce *anta*gonism of those forces. After Alcibiades' Sicilian adventure, the middle class and the old families pushed out the poor and created a short-lived oligarchy (411 B.C.E.); then, after the Spartan coalition finally defeated Athens, the *oligoi*—this time even conspiring against the middle class—attempted a similarly short-lived, and thuggish, tyranny (404 B.C.E.). The pungent irony of this tyranny was that the instigators of it were close associates of the philosopher. The anger of the victims of the oligarchs turned itself on Socrates. Socrates was brought to trial in 399 B.C.E. The charge against him—corrupting youth—carried a death sentence, but such a sentence was rarely carried through to finality in ancient politics. Socrates, however, chose not to make the routine plea for the commuting of his sentence to ten years' exile. Athenian politics had descended into the under-belly of the city, into the sewer of factionalism and chaos. Socrates's anguish and bitterness in the face of all of this is palpably evident in his choice to die, as was his deep foreboding about the future of the *polis*.

THE CITY OF PHILOSOPHERS

Plato drew from Socrates's sobering example the conclusion that the denizens of the *polis* required an art to save them from death—something like a pilot's art that can save the lives and the goods of the passengers traveling on the ship of state from the gravest dangers. Where would such a pilot come from? Plato proposed that such a pilot would come from the cradle of philosophy. The *archôn* would be a philosopher-*archôn*, and in that role, like the captain of a ship, would be a *mon*-archon. Why a philosopher? First, because the philosopher has knowledge of the forms, the organizing patterns of things that underlie the world of appearances. Just as the idea of the vase precedes any particular instance of the vase, so the idea of justice precedes any particular instance of justice. When we look at an artisan's well-wrought vase, we see the surface of the vessel, its ornamentation, color, and so on, but we also recognize that it belongs to a type. We may not know much more than that it is a type of vase. Employing more sophisticated typologies, we may be able to identify the vase by the school of artist who made it, or by the region in which it was produced—that is, according to genre type. We are able to do this—identify an object by type—because we can classify the object by common recurring shapes, lines, and plastic features. Such identifications are what make the world an orderly place—when we view a vase, we do not ask ouselves each time, "What is this?" Likewise, when we view a just deed, a graceful action, or a beautiful countenance, we recognize the thing in question by bringing to mind the form (the idea) of justice, grace, or beauty.

The forms are what give shape, which is to say, meaning, to existence. Ordinary existence is mutable. Yet *eunomia* requires that there is something that persists through all those changes; something that gives shape to human existence. The something that persists is form—the forms of justice, goodness, truth, beauty—and their opposites. These forms are eternal and unchanging; they constitute a reality that endures. The philosopher is the person who thinks about, who has *knowledge* of, these forms. But the philosopher, as well as possessing knowledge, has a certain character or temperament, a philosophic temperament. The philosopher, the friend of wisdom, has a constant desire for any knowledge that will reveal something of the ultimate reality of the forms.[30] This is the pleasure of the philosopher, and it is the pleasure of the soul. For the philosopher all other pleasures (of the body, of money, and so on) are feeble by comparison. The philosophic nature cares about truth (wisdom), not about lavish spending, connections, or strength. The proposition of Plato is that one *begins the city* with the philosopher, with the founder whose mind has dwelt upon the organizing patterns of *eunomia*, patterns that provide the city with a basis of good order, a just stability, and a temperate existence. This *archôn* will not only be knowledgeable, but will also be a good man. The temperament of the friend of truth, Plato proposes, will be fair-minded, gentle, and sociable, unpretentious, courageous, and generous. But why is this so? What rationally accounts for the connection between friendship of truth and good character? The answer—in the Socratic-Platonic account, which is also at its root the Pythagorean account—is that truth is goodness. How so? Because goodness is proportion, and there is a close affinity between proportion and truth. How so? Goodness is beautiful proportion because the good person is a balanced person—and from the knowing sense of balance (of the good person) arises the ethical qualities of justice, moderation (temperateness), the capacity to give as well as receive, and to hold steady in the face of danger and threat. The stamp of a balanced person is that all the elements of this person's makeup are brought together in a well-proportioned way. They bear the mark of composure. Thus knowledge, truth, goodness, justice, and the virtues are ultimately one and the same. This conclusion should not surprise us. For Plato is concerned with the order of things, with the ordering of the *polis* that gives life in the *polis* (whatever its contingencies and mutations) *meaning*. And meaning concerns the whole. The meaning of particular human deeds and speech, human feelings and imaginings arise from their embeddedness in a whole.

There is a wonderful elegance about Plato's account, but also an inherent flaw. For even if we accept that truth is goodness, and goodness is justice, temperance, courage, and generosity, Plato has not shown how or why the friend of truth is of necessity a good person. Indeed friendship of truth requires devotion to the search for truth (not the archaic truth of revelation but the knowledge of good proportions). This search may outweigh other considerations — of justice, temperance, and the rest. Friendship implies partiality for the befriended (in this case knowledge-wisdom-metrics), not the impartiality of justice, nor even the impersonal generosity of the city benefactor. Friendship exists *beyond justice*.[31] The friend of truth cannot act out of friendship and out of justice simultaneously — even if the friend of truth can tell us much about the metrics of justice and generosity and so on. This does not imply that the philosopher-*archôn* will be a tyrant, let alone a despot, even if he is a mon-*archôn*, a single ruler.[32] But it does suggest that the philosopher-*archôn* will lack the all-roundedness, the human wholeness, the sense of being "in the middle" required of the founder of the city, the initiator of the *eunomia* of the city.

The friend of truth is a *part* of the city, not its *architektonikos* (builder-maker-founder). The founder must be part philosopher, but *more than* a philosopher.

The problems of Plato's account do not finish there. For what happens when the work of the *archôn*, the initiator, is finished, when the city is established; when the *archôn* has, like Solon, resumed his travels or retired to his private life? The city that the *archôn* has begun rests on the equilibrium of its parts. It must be a centered city, as those who dwell in the city are centered beings. Plato provides us with a sketch of a possible *eunomia*. In this sketch, the city is divided along functional lines. Each of the functional parts has its own excellence, and each is balanced by the others so as to produce a good order. Plato imagines that one of those parts — the administrators — will be, through their possession of the virtue of prudence, instrumental in achieving the *eunomia* of the city. But how can *one part* play the role of the mediator of *all* the parts of the city? Or to put it another way: The virtue of prudence (an intellectual virtue) is a necessary accompaniment of *all* the ethical virtues, and to the extent that all are prudent, all parts of the city can play a role in the centering of the city. But this, of course, returns us to the very thing that Plato wanted to escape: *politics*. It returns us to the public space at the center of the city, where assertion defies assertion, where deed counters deed, where conflict produces a just ordering, where *logos*, the speech of reason, lays the parts of the city side by side. When Plato, in the *Laws*, expresses the view that only the beginning is entitled to rule (*archein*), he—momentarily at least—returns to the Anaximandrian notion that there is an impersonal principle, rather than a personal principal, from which order arises. Though Plato has no inclination to do this, one might conjecture that, in politics, the public space is the impersonal principle from which all opposing forces come into being. Politics is the conflict, the rivalry, the encroachments, and the equilibration of opposites born of the public space at the center. Plato's city in the clouds, in contrast, lacks a center, and because it lacks a center where all the forces of the city concentrate, and contest one another, then one part of the city must inevitably be accountable for the whole, whether this one part is the administrators or the philosophers. The city in the clouds must be centerless because Plato, like Socrates, is disillusioned with politics. Public speech, in the age of Attic imperial democracy, had become inflated and excessive. Rather than doing the work of reason, of laying the parts of the city side by side, speech had been partitioned, separated, and factionalized. It had become exaggerated and reckless. So, no politics.

This did not mean no public talk and no public life. Socrates rejected the life of the citizen, but what he recommended in its place—the discursive life of the philosopher spent contemplating the forms—retained certain parallels with the life of the citizen inasmuch as the philosophers engaged animatedly in certain kinds of public talking, although this was no longer in the public assembly but amongst the followers and friends, interlocutors and rivals of the philosopher. Philosophers founded their own small publics. Anyone who was a citizen could join in the political discourse. Anyone who was a friend of wisdom could join the philosophical discourse. Philosophy envisaged the little public of philosophers and their auditors as the refuge of reason when it was felt—not without justification—that the great public of the demos had betrayed reason.[33]

GEOMETRIC PROPORTIONALITY

Aristotle—younger than Plato, and not marked in the same way as either Socrates or his disciple Plato by the debacle of the Peloponnesian War, and also not a native of Athens—did not exhibit quite the same radical disillusionment with politics as the Socratic-Platonic philosophers. Aristotle could still envisage a political life as a form of the good life, and he still believed (echoing Cleisthenes) that a mixed constitution — which balanced the claims of birth, virtue, and number — was possible and desirable.[34] Yet in Aristotle there is a toning down of the political spirit. Struggle and conflict — the agonistic aspect — do not resonate in Aristotelian politics, even if there remains in his work an abiding regard for the isometric condition of politics.

Aristotle maintained that justice rested upon proportional reciprocation,[35] and such that reciprocation was the thing that held the city together. Proportional reciprocity meant the mutual adjustment of one part to another, but not their equation. Proportionality required a union of opposites, not the making of identical parts (by eliminating their opposition). The ancient city was a social state; i.e., it was composed of social classes. Landholders, artisans, and merchants made up the social base of the state. There was no specialized apparatus (military, administrative, party) that was separate from ancient classes and households. Thus landholders, artisans, and merchants contributed arms, taxes and technologies, public utilities and monuments to the city. Had the ancient philosopher supposed simple (arithmetical) equality in the state, then the artisan would have been expected to die for the city and the soldier would have been expected to accumulate wealth for public purposes. But this appeared to ancient eyes to be absurd — warrior-merchants, technologist-farmers did not seem to make much sense then, and if we are honest about it, they make no more sense today. To put this proposition another way: the different parts of society have different qualities to contribute to the city. They have *different natures*.

If we accept this, then, is there any way these natures can be compared? Is there any "common measure" of these different natures? Not directly. We cannot compare the producer, the administrator, and the soldier according to the standard of bravery. We cannot make them equals before the standard of bravery because, while the conquest of fear is central to the life of the soldier, it is only from time to time demanded of the administrator, and hardly ever at all of the manufacturer. Yet we can compare them *indirectly*. We cannot say that one part of society cannot be larger (e.g., in bravery or in the honors that attend bravery) than another, or that each part must be equal in magnitude (e.g., in honor or wealth or office) to any other part of the social whole. What we can talk about instead is the congruity, or the good proportioning, of parts: the *equality of ratios* between two pairs of quantities. It is not necessary that A=B or that B=C (where A is the bravery quotient of the producer, B is the bravery quotient of the administrator, and C is the same of the warrior), only that the ratio of A:B is equal to the ratio of B:C. This avoids the artifice of making every part in a whole the same as every other part, whether in magnitude or in nature, just as 2 does not equal 4 and 4 does not equal 8 but 2:4 does equal 4:8. Another way of conceiving of this is to think of contributions to society. The soldier who is properly brave (who is not foolhardy, who does not kill in terror or panic), the office holder who is properly conscientious (who does aggrandize power in the delusion that this is a public service), the producer who steadily builds up a business but who is not greedy—each acts, contributes, and is rewarded according to his specific capacities and talents. There can be a proportional equality between them. The soldier stands in relation to the administrator as the administrator stands in relation to the producer. The different qualities and different natures that they bring to the city as a whole are contrary, and are not directly commensurable. We cannot expect all the variegated parts of society to be equal in courage, in feeling, in wealth, in reason. But it is possible to imagine each contributing to, and taking from, society in a well-proportioned fashion.

This was the fundamental political lesson of the Ionian enlightenment. From the vivid cosmological speculations of Heraclitus, the image of a geometrically proportional universe took shape. Pythagoras provided a serious mathematical base for these speculations. Cleisthenes translated mathematical cosmology into a social metric and a constitutional order,[36] while Hippodamos translated the mathematized cosmos into the outline of an elegant urban order. Plato then took the idea of geometrical proportionality and used it to imagine the internal state of a just individual, while Aristotle employed the idea of geometrical proportion to explain the nature of distributive justice and just exchanges in the marketplace. But then, suddenly, this extraordinary train of speculation was interrupted. The tradition of isonomic politics, stretching between Heraclitus and Aristotle, is abruptly arrested by the conquest of the Greek world by Macedonia.

That Macedonian suzerainty of the Greek *poleis* decisively changed the acceptability of "political geometry" is unquestionable. In the Hellenistic Empire created by the Alexander the Great and his successors any social metrics was marginalized. Yet, the transportable nature of Greek thought meant that speculations about metrical justice survived the upheavals wrought by the Macedonians. The survival of isometric speculations was further ensured by the institutionalization of knowledge in the Hellenistic library—which was able to store ideas even if they were not applied in practice. Even if it opened up a gap between theory and practice, through the means of the library the imaginary of Greek isometrics was able to be passed down through the centuries, always available as a potential source of inspiration, a frozen resource waiting to be shaken into life.

LIBRARIES AND PUBLICS

The conquest of the Greek cities by Philip II of Macedonia and Alexander the Great (357–323 B.C.E.) in the second half of the fourth century created a patrimonial empire—the Hellenistic empire—that spread from the Black Sea to the Indus, almost as a mirror image of the westward movement of Greek colonization in the eighth, seventh, and sixth centuries. Alexander's was an unusual patrimony partly for the reason that it was divided among three successors of his—the Macedonian, Ptolemaic, and Seleucid kingdoms—and partly because the Greek cities managed to retain a certain degree of independence within the body of the post-Alexandrian monarchies that composed the empire. All the same, empire meant the disappearance of the idea of the city as a political constitution, as an impersonal order or public stage where political contestations and dramas could unfold, where opposites could meet, engage each other, and eventually find some kind of reconciliation (or else tragic denouement). The power of monarchy was asserted over cities. While *poleis* in the Hellenistic world, especially those under the Macedonian kings, typically retained some municipal independence, it was of a limited kind, and citizenship lost its luster.[37] This is not to say that public life disappeared, or that life retreated to the confines of the household. Rather the pattern was for micropublics to substitute themselves for the greater public of the *polis*. Perhaps this happened in a spirit of consolation, but it was not without significance.

Logos, the speech of reason that draws people together outside of their households, found forums other than the *agora* in a certain kind of associational life. (This was a kind of public life that, among other things, was more open to women than the public life of the classical *polis* had been.)[38] This new associational life included the spread of philosophical circles and schools throughout the Hellenistic world. Epicurus's garden is one example of the way in which, in this age, men and women gathered together to talk about things that mattered. They did not do so (figuratively) as brothers or sisters; rather they did so as friends, *philoi*, who assembled to hear each other speak, and who gained pleasure and enjoyment from that talk, and whose imaginations were stimulated by that talk.[39] As well as philosophical circles, all kinds of nonpolitical associations and clubs flourished in the Hellenistic age—associations of traders and foreign nationals, and the *eranoi* and the *thiasoi*—the guilds that served the combined functions of friendly society, dining club, and burial club.[40]

Another example of the "new publics" of the Hellenistic age was the public schools. Classical Greece was a literate society, but higher forms of education remained private and largely aristocratic. Public (gymnasium) education, by contrast, was widespread in the Hellenistic cities and supported by the contributions of the wealthy. Again, symptomatic of the expanded conception of the public, women as well as men participated in this higher education, as they participated in the new reading publics, in the creation of new popular literatures and in the growth of professional (liberal, nonstate, and nonhousehold) employments such as medicine and magistracies that accompanied the spread of higher learning.[41] The gymnasium classroom, readers' and writers' circles, and professional work of a nonhousehold kind — each constituted a public realm. But something crucial was missing from these publics: the spirit of the *agôn*, the contest. The inheritors of Alexander's mantle extinguished the contestatory spirit. It bore too many political connotations for them. One cost of this was a loss of striving for *aretê* (excellence) in creation. Hellenistic literature rarely approached the aesthetic unity and concentration of language achieved by the classical tragic dramatists or by the Homeric epic.

The Hellenistic peoples were great travelers, a sign of their urbanity, of the fact that they were not rooted in the soil of a *patria*. They traveled for purposes of trade, the professions, theatre, diplomacy, and scholarship. They produced a wealth of travel guides and travelers' tales, and one marvelous but ultimately failed attempt at epic literature, the *Argonautica* by Appollonius (b. 295 B.C.E.). The quest of the Argonauts lacked the consistent ethos of *aretê* and *empeiria* of the *Odyssey*. It substituted a protoromantic ethos for Homeric calculation. At the most decisive moment, Jason's quest is fulfilled because of the magical art of Medea, not because of Homeric-style resourcefulness. While the topography of the epic is extensive — encompassing the Euxine (Black) Sea, Asia Minor, the Danube, the Adriatic, and so on — the extrovert character of the Homeric hero and heroine is replaced by a romantic psychologizing of Jason's relationship with (and abandonment of) Medea.[42]

The *Argonautica*'s author lacked the ability of Homer to integrate a diversity of episodes, folktales, parallel events, and so on, into a whole. Perhaps it was something more than accidental that Appollonius was chief librarian at the Library of Alexandria. This library was a storehouse (akin to the granaries of patrimonial empires) of great cultural wealth, and one that benefited from the patronage of the Hellenized Ptolemaic dynasty. State libraries appeared in the three court-cities of the Hellenistic kingdoms: at Alexandria, Antioch, and Pergamum. (The Library and Museum at Alexandria, founded by Ptolemy I, was the grandest.) Writers and literary publics gravitated to these court-cities. But despite lavish patronage in the imperial cities, real intellectual thought, and even the education of the most talented servants of the monarchs, occurred in the older cities.

Culturally, Alexandria gave the world the ambivalent benefit of textual criticism. Its librarians were the first philologists. One of its chief librarians, Zenodotus of Ephesus, invented the art of textual criticism by comparing manuscripts. The Alexandrian culture busied itself producing compilations, editing books of poetry and prose, and publishing guides to authors, commentaries, and criticisms. Much of value, not least of all the philosophies of metrical justice, were preserved and passed on in this fashion. Yet for all the great accumulation of cultural *wealth* that this represented, the librarian-philologists evinced a disproportionately smaller cultural *power*. The best of the Alexandrian works were items like Eratosthenes's (of Cyrene, 275–194 B.C.E.) *On Geography*. Producing a richly detailed and comprehensive geography of the known world, Erathosthenes, librarian at Alexandria under Ptolemy III, fixed in words something of the real exploratory and traveling spirit of the Hellenistic age — a spirit that reached its peak with the astonishing voyage of Pytheas, a sea captain from Massalia (modern Marseilles) who (around 320 B.C.E.) navigated the coast of Spain, Gaul, and Britain, traveling via the Shetlands perhaps as far north as Jutland, and who recorded his voyage in a book appropriately called *On The Ocean*. Yet Alexandrian geography, for all its interest, lacked the meaning-generating power of the fully realized epic. The librarians of Alexandria managed to gather details from all over the known world but did not intellectually unify this material. Their enterprise lacked a signifying power of the first order. One of the reasons for this was that the library was a place of learning without *agôn* — unless we mistake the backbiting and rivalries of the librarians for an *agôn*. There was none of the competitiveness — the theatrical contests — that produced the great tragic dramas of Athens, and there were no competitions because there could be no ebullient or forceful civic life under the Hellenistic monarchs. There was governance, of course; there were little publics; even astute maneuvering by the cities to keep a measure of independence. But no full-blown *politics*.

The Hellenistic kings demanded, like all patrimonial rulers, acquiescence, patience, and discipline — the waiting virtues. The Hellenistic city was well ordered, well sewered, prosperous, but lacking in a civic *agôn*.[43] Tribute monies and the booties of war were pumped back into lavish and monumental public works which, in part, functioned to keep the subjects of the city in awe of the centralized monarchs who dominated their lives. Public places correspondingly lost some of their drawing power. Being in the streets was less compelling in the Hellenistic period than in the classical age. Where the private houses of classical Greece had been quite rudimentary, and their arrangement and architecture neglected,[44] the private houses of the Hellenistic period were considerably more commodious and lavish.[45] Correspondingly, with features such as the roofed courtyard (*atrium*) — borrowed from the Etruscans — there was also a move to develop a public space *within* the household.

The public life of the times acquired patrimonial features in more than one way. For example, the Hellenistic monarchs claimed a divinity of sorts (usually after their death). Official cults worshipping the dynastic line were sponsored in the cities, and divine pedigrees were invented for these dynasties. Dynastic figures were worshipped as saviors and benefactors. The cherished function of kingship was held to be *philanthropia* — helpfulness to subjects. Beneficence and magnificence were the watchwords of an ascendant and powerful patrimony. Beneficence kept subjects in comfortable subjection; they did not feel themselves oppressed and tyrannized, merely docile. Docility implied respectfulness toward authority while magnificence implied awe of authority. Such magnificence was no better represented than in the aesthetic arrangement of long unbroken vistas devised for the Hellenistic cities as a visual metaphor of power. Long avenues marked by continuous open arcades formed of stoas — roofed colonnades that protected city dwellers from the elements — provided the signature of Hellenistic grandeur.

THE STOICS

It was in the shade of the stoa that Zeno of Citium (333–262 B.C.E.) and other Stoic thinkers (named after those very colonnades) formulated a new sense of the city.[46] If the municipal city was denied to them, a world city, the *kosmo-polis*, was not. The Stoics might not be able to conceive of the city drawing together *agonistic* social and political forces, but they could see it at least as a place of intersection of disparate cultures from the Mediterranean littoral, from Asia Minor, and further afield. The imperialism of the Hellenistic monarchies produced significant population movements — migrations of prisoners, slaves, refugees, displaced persons,[47] — and the Hellenistic city proved in practice more open to these "foreigners" than Greek cities of the Classical period that had remained protective of their nationality. In the older *polis*, *ethico-political* virtues were the key aspect of a good (meaningful) life—courage in defending the city or in civic conflicts, generosity in endowing public places, self-control or ordinary justice in business dealings, wisdom or prudence in administration—all related to aspects of *public* conduct (even the market-place was a semipublic domain). These did not die out entirely in the Hellenistic age. For example, the public liberality of the wealthy persisted. Expectations of the wealthy included: bailing cities (that generally lacked effective budgets) out of financial difficulties; going on embassies for their city without remuneration; paying for bridges, gymnasiums, temples, schools, festivals, citizen's banquets, and other public projects.[48] But the agonistic spirit that had once attended these things was missing. Festivals, processions, and on so became occasions to celebrate kings' birthdays or visits—and less and less contests for the display of hard-sought excellence. The Greek love of distinction (*philotimia*) remained, but distinction was earned through the medium of largess and contribution that was no longer marked by a real competitive effort. There was civic virtue but without the spirit of strenuous civic contest.

When the Hellenistic empire swallowed up the Greek city, the ethos of the city did not die but instead was radically transformed. The massive migration of people within the Hellenistic world stimulated and guaranteed social heterogeneity in the city which, while no longer having a truly active citizen body, saw the development of a new kind of extracommunal authority—the authority of the *kosmo-polis*, the idea of a "world city" in which different cultures, peoples, and religions might intermingle. The cosmopolitan ideal was most clearly formulated by the Stoics, for whom the *kosmopolis* combined together the idea of city (*polis*) with the idea of universal order (*kosmos*). The Hellenistic city was a place where people of heterogeneous backgrounds and cultures were brought together. The rules of no one *ethnos* could fully apply in the *kosmopolis*. As a consequence people, groups—if they were to get along together—had to relate via the medium of abstract *nomoi* (ethical virtues) rather than concrete *nomoi*; that is, they had to relate via the universal norms of nature: steadfastness, courage, and so on. Moreover, and more importantly still, they had to learn to modulate *nomoi*—concrete or abstract—to move between them, and blend them as circumstances required.

Rather than the rules of clan or tribe or city hearth holding sway—rules that define and protect what is "one's own"—virtue (*aretê*) created *common human possessions* (the spectacle of the actor, the temple built at the expense of the rich benefactor). *Aretê*, as in the case of courage, sometimes required standing up to one's particularistic feelings (especially those of fear) occasioned by threats to what was "one's own." In the kosmopolis, fear is especially the fear of unknown others — the fear of the displaced, migrants, travelers, pilgrims, those of other faiths, and those with other habits, languages, customs, or appearances. The inhabitant of the kosmopolis must learn to hold fear at bay, to create things and deeds that are a common human possession, and act justly towards others. Yet there is no strict rule (code, social custom) that tells the inhabitant what to do, how to behave in the cosmopolitan city. The in*habit*ant, ironically, is bereft of a socially effective *habit*. *Aretê* is not a set of rules. Moreover, there are various kinds of *aretê*. Accommodation of these different excellences requires justice. Thus also in the *kosmopolis*, justice is not strict. Justice lays each of the virtues (the varying powers and qualities that create the common human possession) side by side, taking each into account. Justice arises out of a process of give and take, adjustment, or "blending" of the many forces and qualities that make up the *nomoi* of the *kosmopolis*.

The vehicle of such adjustment was what the Stoics called reason (*logos*). The binding force of the Hellenistic *kosmos* was not agonistic conflict but synthetic reason. The Stoics argued that the governing principle (*hêgemônikon*) of the *kosmos* is the *logos* that makes the world an orderly structure (*kosmos*). This *logos* is universal. It is common to all things, directs all things; it is the cause of all happenings. It directs all events ultimately to purposes that are good. Reason is also nature, God, Zeus, an all-pervading intelligent material, breathing (*pneuma*) entity. Reason is the connective that holds the world together. Although it was not the pre-Socratic equilibrium of powers arising out of chaotic strife, reason nonetheless remained an alternative to hierarchy (patrimony) as a connective principle of the world. And, as such, Stoic reason gave coherence to all other things, binding the parts or elements of the world, including the social world, into a meaningful whole.

This holding of things together, though, was not without stresses and strains. The Stoics spoke of the tension that exists between individual parts of the whole, as when muscles press upon muscles, or ligaments upon the bone. A healthy state of things — to carry forward the biological metaphor — involves tension and countertension that yields an equilibrium. A sickly state of things involves *atonia*, the absence of tension and flaccidity that yields imbalance. An overwrought state of tension can likewise lead to friction and ruin. In general, a lack of proper tension between the parts of the whole can lead to disorder, turbulence, confusion, chaos, convulsions, and debilitation. The right tension is struck, the Stoics argued, via the power of *sumpatheia* (sympathy), which can be described as the medium of cohesion in a tense world. Sympathy yields a kinship of things united in feeling, in aspiration, and in extension. *Sumpatheia* means, on the one hand, connection, integration, bonding, kinship. At the same time it refers to the operation of different, distinct parts of the whole on each other.

The Stoics were interested in the question of what is a good "kinship" of things. In answer to this, they assumed that one and the same unit of space could be occupied by more than one object, that all sorts of pairs of (seeming) opposites and irreconcilables, e.g. life and death, can be *coextensive*. Opposites can mix in the same space as "one." But how exactly does this happen? Certainly, elements can be mechanically combined as when grains of barley and wheat are mixed together. But this is a juxtaposition of elements rather than what the Stoics regarded as significant—viz. a blending (*mixis* or *krasis*) of elements. Certain mixtures, e.g. of water and wine, occur when bodies are completely extended throughout the substance and properties of one another while maintaining their original substance and properties in this mixture. This *mixis* or *krasis* falls short of a complete fusion where the original properties of each part are destroyed to form a new body, yet, unlike the case of mere juxtaposition, the component parts are coextensive. They extend throughout one another: "body passes through body," *soma dia somatos chorei*. There is an integration of identities but each of them is preserved as a specific identity.

Socially speaking, this ordering of the universal and the particular is rather difficult to achieve. The Stoics were the first to admit that were such bondedness to fail, or misfire, there would be confusion rather than a confluence of identities. Each part would affect the other but not so as to produce *kosmos* but instead disorder, and thus havoc, disturbance, turbulence, and suffering. Yet the image of a *mixis* or *krasis* was a powerful answer to the question of what constitutes an organizing principle of society (a formative or shaping principle) if hierarchy (or patrimony) is rejected. The Stoic sympathy of parts paralleled—yet had a different metaphorical basis (more medical-biological than mathematical) in comparison to—the older Greek *isonomia*.

CITY LEAGUES

One interesting application of the principle of sympathy was the idea of the federative league (*to koinon*) between cities. Cities retained some municipal independence under the Hellenistic monarchs. Their combination into leagues gave them greater bargaining power with the monarchies, as well as a way dealing with the traditional destructive discord between cities. These leagues were understood to be either *sympolities* or *isopolities.*[49] The idea of *sumpoliteia* — in effect Greek federalism — took hold principally in areas of Greece that had been less developed in the Classical age. The two most important examples of *sympolity* were in Aetolia and Achaea. When a new city joined sympolitically a league (let us say the Aetolian League), its people became Aetolians and attended the Aetolian assembly. Each city in the league kept its identity — its own constitution, law courts, system of citizenship, magistracies, and so on — but other functions, such as foreign policy, army, weights, and measures, became federal responsibilities. Decision making about federal responsibilities was conducted by the act of the citizens of the federated cities assembling together, although the Aetolians also developed the practice of an executive council composed of city representatives elected in proportion to city size (a rare example of the representative idea at work in ancient politics). In the case of the *isopolitic* relationship, a city became an *ally* of the league, and its citizens became citizens of the league only *potentially*. Their citizenship became actualized if they settled in and became citizens (as they had a right to do) of the *sumpoliteia*. The principles of *sympoliteia*, or even of *isopoliteia*, could ever be only partially realized in the Hellenistic world. Such civic principles were always effectively constrained by the presence of monarchy and all of the rest of the institutions of the ancient patrimonial world, from slavery to the patriarchal structure of households.

Perhaps with time the principle of *sympolity* would have spread more widely, and might have eventually provided an alternative to the *kosmos-oikos*, the universal household of the monarchs, that the cities had to live under. But such time was not available. The First Illyrian War in 229 B.C.E. announced the coming of the Romans. Soon after the Hellenistic world would be Roman. But despite that, Rome did not spell the end of the city ethos, any more than Macedonia had — for the city ethos was universal. Rather than die, it traveled to Rome, where educated Romans eagerly absorbed it. With the inevitable modifications, it was to deeply inform the Roman *civitas*, the successor of the *polis*.

This westward journey of the city ethos is a potent sign of its character: it travels well. In this, if nothing else, it retained something of the wandering (*nomas*) spirit of the first Greek-speakers. The city ethos is never tyrannized by distance. The bearers of the city ethos are not fearful of journeying. Yet they are not masters of space like Alexander, with his "world imagination" — the creator of an unbounded empire, geopolitical space without limits. Rather, it is the case that wherever they settle, city-dwellers will recreate a city. They do this simply by standing in the middle of things and marking out a central space to be bounded by close-set buildings, giving it a three-dimensional depth. In this bounded central space all the diverse forces of the world can gather. It sets these forces going—for it is this depth-space that is the *archê* of them all—in opposition to each other, but at the same time this depth-space is productive of a reason that unites them all and holds them together, side by side. And it is precisely because this space belongs to no one in particular—because it is a *public* space, belonging to no one *ethnos*, set of customs, faith, property-owner, or even (as the translation of Greek ideas into Latin was to show) language, the civic ethos travels well. A possession of no one in particular, it is potentially the possession of everyone.

NOTES

1. The foundation myth of Athens illustrates this. Cecrops, a Phoenician, came to Attica where he founded a city of the rock near the sea. The gods of Olympia proclaimed that the city should be named after the deity who could produce the most valuable legacy for mortals. Athena (the goddess of wisdom) and Poseidon (the god of the sea) contended for these naming rights. Poseidon struck his trident and caused a spring to flow from the Acropolis; Athena made an olive tree grow—a sign of fertility. As the latter was deemed more valuable, Athena was adopted as the chief deity of Athens, while Poseidon was one of the most popular deities of the sea-going cities of Greece. The Erechtheion monument on the Acropolis (built 421–395 B.C.E.) stands on the spot where Athena and Poseidon were supposed to have contested for Athens. The dedication of the temple to *both* Athena and Poseidon represents a reconciliation of the two deities after their contest.

2. In many cities, free noncitizens were barred from owning land. While once again not unique, citizenship and landholding were strongly intertwined in the self-image of the Athenians. At the end of the fifth century, three-quarters of citizen families still owned some landed property, even if much of their income came from trading or manufacturing sources (M. I. Finley, *The Ancient Greeks* [Harmondsworth: Penguin, 1963], pp. 71–72).

3. Though it must be noted that Athenians were prepared to resettle the *polis* elsewhere rather than submit to the Persians.

4. On the attractions of this autochthonous self-representation for modern romantic philhellenes, especially for the German romanticism that culminates in Heidegger, see my "Romantic Modernism and the Greek Polis," *Thesis Eleven* 34 (Cambridge, Mass.: MIT Press, 1993).

5. In 451 B.C.E.

6. G. Glotz, *The Greek City and Its Institutions* (New York: Alfred Knopf, 1930), pp. 128, 296.

7. There are signs of Neolithlic and early Helladic ("Pelasgian") settlement on the Acropolis going back to 5000 B.C.E. A Mycenaean royal palace existed on the Acropolis ca. 1500–1200 B.C.E.

8. Built by Mnesicles in 437–432 B.C.E.

9. Designed by Ictinos and Callicrates under the supervision of Pheidias. Begun in 447 B.C.E., it was completed in 438 B.C.E.

10. Indeed, the Parthenon, the largest Doric temple ever completed in Greece and the greatest architectural glory of ancient Greece, had the purpose, in addition to housing the great statue of Athena, of housing the treasury for tribute money that was moved from Delos as Athens's grip over the Delian league tightened.

11. On the emergence of *dunamis* in the Athenian context, see Murphy, "Romantic Modernism and the Greek Polis."

12. Thucydides, *History of the Peloponnesian War*, trans. Rex Warner (Harmondsworth: Penguin, 1972), I.70–71.

13. Herodotus, *The Histories*, trans. Aubrey de Selincourt (Penguin: Harmondsworth, 1954), III.81.

14. Cited by Meyer Reinhold, "Greek and Roman Civilisation," in *Hellas and Rome*, ed. Robert Douglas Mead (New York: New American Library, 1972), p. 195.

15. Plutarch, *Alcibiades* in *Plutarch's Lives* trans. Dryden, revised by Arthur Clough, vol. 1 (New York: P. F. Collier, ca. 1909), p. 397.

16. In the entirety of his life, he held only one official post. "I am no politician, Polus, and last year when I became a member of the Council and my tribe was presiding and it was my duty to put the question to vote, I raised a laugh because I did not know how to." Plato, *Gorgias*, in *Socratic Dialogues*, ed. and trans. W. D. Woodhead (Edinburgh: Nelson, 1953) 473E–474A.

17. Plato, *Gorgias*, 473E–474A.

18. Plato, *Republic*, V.

19. Such a polysemic word! *Archê* means office, rule, magistracy, source, beginning, fundamental cause, the supreme principle that governs, and so forth.

20. Plato, *Gorgias*, 464B–C.

21. Ibid., 465C; 500B; 501A–B.

22. Ibid., 490E.

23. Ibid., 491D–E.

24. Ibid., 511D–E.

25. Ibid., 493E.

26. Ibid., 504D.

27. Ibid., 504D–E; 507D.

28. Ibid., 507D.

29. Ibid., 507E–508A.

30. Plato, *Republic*, 484A–484A.

31. Agnes Heller, *Beyond Justice* (Oxford: Basil Blackwell, 1987).

32. A "king," yes, but not in an archaic sense of that word. In the *Laws*, Plato makes clear (677B–683B) that *dunasteia*-style patriarchal chieftains or lordship, the *basileia*-style kingship, even the Dorian-type *ethnos* are earlier and superseded forms of governance.

33. It is unsurprising, also, that at the time when philosophers were creating these "small publics," other citizens of the *polis* were also creating clubs and associations, the *hetairiai* with memberships of 20–50, for purposes of conversation, drinking, sociability, symposiac sex, musical enjoyment, and mutual aid. These constituted places where "sacrilegious" comments could be made about the cult

of Athens. Some of these clubs had an aristocratic coloration; others were just places for the ironically or skeptically minded—the ones not swept along by Athens' winter torrent. The *hetairiai* were also one of the places of public meeting or association in Athens where women were welcomed. Martha Nussbaum in *The Therapy of Desire* (Princeton, N.J.: Princeton University Press, 1994) recognizes the freedom, literacy, and intellectual sophistication of the companionate class. To say, as is usually done, that the *hetairiai* women were "courtesans" is overdetermined by centuries of Christian scholarship. The *hetairiai* certainly had an erotic role. But this goes back at least to their archaic origins where the bonds of association were male homoerotic. It is possible to sense a very Christian assumption—buried in the deep, archaeological layers of scholarship—that if one was not a housebound woman then, perforce, one was a prostitute.

34. See my "Is The Philosophy of Rights Enough?" *Thesis Eleven* 32 (Cambridge, Mass.: MIT Press, 1992).

35. Aristotle, *Ethics*, V.

36. On this see Peter Murphy, "The Triadic Moment: The Anti-Genealogy of Hellenist Marxism," *Thesis Eleven* 53 (London: Sage Publications, 1998), pp. 102–13.

37. Tarn and Griffith made the point: "Considered from without, the constitution of the self-governing Greek city, in the third century, looked much the same as it had always done; it had its assembly, Council, and magistrates . . . . But in reality . . . the actual political life of the city, considered as a thing in which all shared, was losing its former importance and interest." Willian Tarn and G. T. Griffith, *Hellenistic Civilization*, 3d ed. (London: Methuen, 1952), chap. 2.

38. Michael Grant, *From Alexander to Cleopatra* (London: Weidenfeld and Nicolson, 1982), pp. 194–213.

39. The other side of this coin, certainly so far as relations between men and women were concerned, was that men and women were no longer assumed to be married for life. Divorce in the Hellenistic Age became easier, and marriages less and less arranged between the males of households. Intimate and emotional life in other words became less subject to the patterns and the dictates of the household.

40. Tran and Griffith, *Hellenistic Civilization*, pp. 93, 260; F. W. Walbank, *The Hellenistic World* (Trenton, N.J.: Humanities Press, 1981), pp. 64–65.

41. Grant, *From Alexander to Cleopatra*, pp. 200–203.

42. Unsurprisingly, the Jason story was strongly promoted by nineteenth-century romantic philhellenes. The story of the *Argo*'s voyage was retold by Grillparzer in the *Golden Fleece* (1820), Nathanael Hawthorne in *Tanglewood Tales* (1851), and Charles Kingsley in *Heroes* (1855). The English romantic socialist William Morris did a medievalizing version of the Argonaut story, and in so doing created the longest modern epic poem (7,500 lines), *The Life and Death of Jason*.

43. For a general discussion of the Greek city in the Hellenistic age, see Tarn and Griffith, *Hellenistic Civilization*, chap. 3; Lewis Mumford, *The City in History* (Harmondsworth: Penguin, 1966 [1961]), chap. 7.

44. Glotz, *The Greek City and its Institutions*, p. 302, describes them as rustic in appearance, small, badly built, and scattered in haphazard fashion along narrow and tortuous little streets.

45. Grant, *From Alexander to Cleopatra*, pp. 145–46.

46. On the Stoics, see Brad Inwood, *Ethics and Human Action in Early Stoicism* (Oxford: Oxford University Press, 1985); R. D. Hicks, *Stoic and Epicurean* (New York: Russell and Russell, 1910); A. A. Long, *Hellenistic Philosophy* (London: Duckworth, 1974). According to A. A. Long (p. 109), on the authority of Diogenes Laertius, about 301/300 B.C.E. Zeno began to pace up and down in the Painted Colonnade (*stoa poikilê*) at Athens and engaged in philosophical discourse there: "The Stoa bordered one side of the great piazza of ancient Athens, and from it, as one can see today, those who promenaded there looked directly at the main public buildings, with the Acropolis and its temples towering in the background. Unlike Epicurus, Zeno began his teaching in a central public space, which came to stand as the name of his followers and their philosophical system." Zeno came to Athens roughly ten years after the death of Aristotle and Alexander, and shortly before Epicurus established his garden.

47. Mumford, *The City In History*, p. 198.

48. Tarn and Griffith, *Hellenistic Civilization*, pp. 108–109.

49. Tarn and Griffith, *Hellenistic Civilization*, pp. 71–73; Walbank, *The Hellenistic World*, chap. 8; Grant, *From Alexander to Cleopatra*, chap. 2.

4

THE BIRTH OF HUMANISM

LIBERTY AND POWER

Rome's beginning was an act of conjunction. This was as true for Romans themselves as for later admirers and interpreters. The Romans saw their city-state as the outcome of a union of various foreign tribes from neighboring hills (by tradition sometime in the eighth century B.C.E.). Rome was founded on a treaty-law between different and hostile peoples.[1] For the Romans, this law (*lex*) gave effect to justice (*ius*). The root idea of *ius*, of *iustus* and *iustitia*, is a joining or fitting together — a *iungere*, a union — of contraries, of conflicting, warring, disputing parties. Symbolic of such union, at the heart of the Roman city (*urbs*), was *the forum*, the approximate equivalent of the Greek agora[2] — a place of assembly, contests, and exchange; a place for shrines and temples, council buildings, the basilica or public hall used for meetings and law courts, rows of shops, offices, and open spaces framed by colonnades where orators could speak as well as the place where the *civitas* (the union of citizens) gathered together, and where games and shows were held.

This space was *multidimensional*, and to be perpetuated, such multi-dimensionality required on the part of Romans a sense of justice. Justice was the leading quality of the city. Without justice, the city proper could not be sustained. If diverse social forces (classes, tribes, ethnicities) were to find a *union* in the city, then ways had to be found of *adjusting* one force to another. The word adjustment comes from a .constellation of Latin terms with its source in the root *iu-*, meaning *to bind*. This constellation includes terms like *iungere* (joining, union) and *subiungere* (to join under a yoke). In Latin, adjustment (*adiuxtare*, from *ad*, to [toward] and *iuxta*, a union of things in close proximity) had connotations of a settling, a placing justly, a putting side by side, an arranging of different things near to one another. To adjust requires a sense of *impartiality* — a capacity to

93

detach oneself from the claims and emotions of the primary parties, to distance oneself from one's own *patria*. Impartiality was a key condition of the city.[3] The city drew together people whose backgrounds were different, who did not come from the same tribe, and whose life stories were tangential. These people, because they did not share the same narrative of life, the same rituals, the same conventions, the same traditions, had to find some way to adjust conflicting forms of life.

Rome was to develop far beyond its city limits—first as an expansive republic, then as an empire—but, despite this, for centuries it retained something of its original city spirit. In the simplest terms, this can be described as a flair for adjusting and blending customs and characters, ambitions and philosophies of a remarkable variety, and giving them a common form, a distinguishable Roman stamp. In symbolic terms, this quality was summed up in the popular image of being Janus-faced (two-faced)—looking both ways. This was not the Homeric capacity for deceit and cunning—the Romans were never so poetic about these matters, and they took very seriously the virtue of honesty. But, at the same time, the Romans could live with antitheses. They were never apostles of truth.

The ability to live with antitheses, like most things Roman, had a political origin. At a certain point in their history, the Romans concluded that a city, filled as it was with tangential life stories (and thus drawing to itself those whose speech was ambivalent and whose deeds were enigmatic), was no place for kings. Kings were rulers who looked in one direction, while the Romans, through the experience of emergent city life, found themselves symbolically looking in more than one direction at the same time. This shift in mentality occurred sometime in the period between the eighth and sixth centuries—in the same period when the city form emerged in Greece—and it paved the way for an ultimate break with the institution of kingship. The Romans were always at ease with power, but were attracted to a regime of multiple, countervailing, and antithetical powers.

Inferences from the archeological record aside, most of what we know about this shift in mentality comes from the interpretation of Roman myths, or rather interpretations of the recounting of Roman myths of origin by the Roman historian Livy (59 B.C.E.–17 C.E.). The Roman myth of foundation provides pointers to the rational reconstruction of the emergence of Rome as a civic institution. In Roman myth the twins Romulus and Remus created a tribal twin town—traditionally ca. 750 B.C.E.—an allegory for the amalgamation of Latin communities living on the Palatine and Esquiline hills. Romulus—after whom the town was named—killed his brother in a struggle for power. Under Romulus's tutelage, the hill town was plagued by a shortage of women, and to redress this shortage, Romulus took advantage of an annual Latin festival to abduct the town's guests—women from the neighboring Sabine tribe (also hilltop dwellers)—with the intention of forcing them into marriage. The result was war between the two communities. In the myth, just as the two armies are poised to meet in combat, the Sabine women intercede and appeal for peace. The fighting is halted, and the leaders of the communities agree to a merger of the states. A co-monarchy is created with Romulus sharing power with the king of the Sabines.

The myth has political saliency. In story form, it describes the condition of possibility of the classical city—i.e., not the urban settlement, hill town or palace-city, but "the city" that is founded on antitheses, "twins in opposition," the union of two or more elements, the paradoxical "capture that is concord." Roman myth strongly suggests that the "state of antitheses" is possible only where monarchy is transfigured. The co-monarchy of the Latins and the Sabines was the earliest representation that the city life of Rome—as a union of antitheses—could not flourish under the rule of kings of an archaic kind. In the mythical account, the dual monarchy of Romulus and his Sabine counterpart ended with the death of the Sabine king, at which time Romulus became a sole ruler again. The power of monarchy continues with the rule of the Etruscans over the Romans (traditionally 616–509 B.C.E.). But, as the mythopoesis of the Romans intuited, such kingship could not satisfactorily steer the processes of civic amalgamation and interrelation that produced increasing levels of social compounding and the enigmatic natures of city dwellers (who were Latin *and* Sabine by virtue of intermarriage). The image of dual power persisted as the subterranean prefiguration of another kind of power, in latent opposition to kingship.

Archaic kingship was the culmination of the familial, clannish, tribal principle of social organization. Household heads, clan bosses, tribal chiefs, and kings were all "the fathers of their people," and the pivot of a precivic society in which identification with lineage, blood ties, and family signifiers was preeminent. In the city, by contrast, such things are less significant. Law, reason, character, friendship, and public life are the ties that bind the denizens of the city—adjusting one to the other. Consequently, kingship cannot symbolize the city, nor can it provide effective rule over it. Unsurprisingly, then, the condition of Rome's flourishing as a city was the expulsion of its kings. In their place, Rome developed an impersonal *constitutional order* that contained aristocratic, popular, and executive forces: the Senate, the assembly of the People, and the Consuls, and it organized them into a constitutional balance. This constitutional order was republican. It was premised on the Roman idea of *libertas*, of life without kings.[4] *Libertas* signified a state that was not subject to the arbitrary will of a single person. In contrast, the subjects of an absolute monarch were slaves. The slave was one who owned no property and over whom the master had the power of life and death. The expulsion of kings and the coming of republicanism symbolized the end of political servitude, even if the Romans continued with forms of social and economic servitude. Freedom, for the Romans, consisted not in having a just master but in having no master at all.[5]

Roman liberty was achieved by overturning the archaic monarchy in the sixth century B.C.E. In the time when various tribes had formed the proto-city of Rome, kings held executive power (*imperium*) in the city, and dispensed justice, appointed officials, and commanded armies. A senate — a council of the heads of the leading families — advised these kings. This senate had authority, but not power. For instance, it could propose a new king, but could not make the appointment unless the people approved. Even this archaic arrangement supposed something of the later Roman republic viz. that a variety of social forces shared in the state. A republican constitution, though, only came into being after the episode of the autocratic rule of Rome by the Etruscans (traditionally the later seventh and early sixth centuries B.C.E.). Romans henceforth displayed a loathing of kings, and of arbitrary rule, that was to endure for most of Rome's history. When self-government returned to Rome, the power (*imperium*) of the king was divided among two magistrates (consuls) who had the power to veto each other's proposals in the case of disagreement, in effect an institutionalization of the idea of a balance between opposing forces (something present in the mythological account of the origin of Rome in the story of Romulus and Remus). The consuls held office for one year. The whole people in assembly, from whom they received their *imperium*, appointed them. This choice had to be ratified by the Senate.

The people and the senators, between themselves, constituted the body of citizens. Not all Romans, not even a majority, were citizens. The status of citizen meant freedom. It meant freedom in a political sense. (Citizens, and the part they played in a complex constitutional balance, reduced the arbitrary and despotic aspects of the state.) The status of citizen also meant freedom in a civil sense — freedom to move without the consent of a master or household head. Most of the Romans who were not citizens were unfree in a civil, and not only in a political, sense. They were dependents, or slaves, of the Roman household (*familia*), subject to the head of the household (*paterfamilias*). The slave, of course, was the worst off in this arrangement: the slave could be bought, sold, given away, flogged, put to death, and bequeathed at the discretion of the master.

Unlike modern constitutional arrangements, the Roman constitutional balance was a balance not only of offices but of social classes as well. It was a union of the *populus* (the Roman people, plebeians) and the senatorial class—who together shared in the "public thing," the *res publica*. These social classes had their roots in the patrimonial-patriarchal household. Senators and *populus* were all citizens. Each citizen, each member of the *civitas*, the union of citizens, entered the public domain as a (male) head of a household that was the place of slaves, servants, women, and children. The nonpatrimonial world of the public was based on the patrimonial domain of the social. The Roman Senate had originated as a council of the heads of leading families. It never completely lost this character. As long as familial rather than functional principles dominated economic and social organization in Rome, this was inevitable. But, it should be stressed, the Roman Senate, and the senatorial class, was never a closed oligarchy. Membership was open, and the senatorial class recruited those of talent to its ranks.

By the first century B.C.E., the *nobilitas*—the aristocracy—included any family of which one member at least (past or present) had attained a consulship.[6] Consulships were elected posts, elected by the *comitia centuriata*, one of the "assemblies of the whole people." It must be said, of course, that the *comitia centuriata* was not a particularly democratic assembly. While it contained both patrician and plebeian citizens, its voting procedures had a strongly oligarchic bias. The *comitia centuriata* was divided into property classes, and those classes in turn were divided into voting units known as centuries. A mix of age and wealth determined membership of centuries. This arrangement was itself conditioned by the fact that Roman citizenship, at least at its beginning, was closely connected with the capacity for soldiering. The Roman citizen in the beginning had been a citizen-soldier, and citizenship originally implied military obligations and a capacity (conditioned by age and wealth) to fulfill those obligations. The consequence of this was that the *comitia centuriata* was structured in an oligarchic fashion with precedence given to those with the greatest wealth (which originally meant those with the greatest ability to provide certain kinds of fighting equipment). The wealthier one was, the greater one's say. For example, it required only the unanimous vote of the first class of the *comitia centuriata*, joined together with the larger part of the second class, to produce a winning majority on any question.[7] Unsurprisingly, it was rare for the last classes (the fourth and the fifth) to be called to actually vote for consuls or for any of the other high magistracies (the praetors and censors) chosen by the *comitia centuriata*.

Consulships—the key point of entry to the Roman nobility—were not hereditary posts. They were achieved. At the same time, however, nobility itself was an inherited status. Rome thus equivocated between a civic and a patrimonial arrangement. Before being passed onto family descendants, *nobilitas* had to be achieved. Achievement was defined not—as in the case of the modern social arrangement—bureaucratically or procedurally, but ethically. In republican Rome, the holding of public office ideally required the demonstration of what the Romans called *virtus* in public service[8]—which broadly meant the carrying out of the public duties (*officia*) of the magistrate or military commander in a manner that was both great (or at least expedient) and morally right at the same time. The office holder was expected to be effective in office, and was encouraged to seek fame (*gloria*) through public office, yet to do so in ways that were moral and just, in particular that demonstrated preparedness to redress wrongdoing, to curb personal ambition, to fulfill promises made and to be courageous in public life. Of course, many office holders did not behave justly or morally; many came to office through patronage rather than because of demonstrated moral capacities or greatness, and feathered their own (family) nests and those of their backers.

Rome was perpetually caught between collegiate civic idealism and a corrupting patrimonialism. This was not without constitutional consequences. To protect themselves against consular injustice, the plebeians demanded and got a council in which they dominated and magistrates of their own. A counterweight to consular power emerged in the guise of the *comitia tributa* (or the *concilium plebis* that was for all intents and purposes the same as the *comitia* excepting that the *concilium* could only be convened and presided over by a magistrate of the plebs, an aedile or tribune, whereas any magistrate, including one elected by the *comitia centuriata*, could convene a *comitia tributa* meeting). The *comitia tributa* elected junior magistrates—quaestors, aediles, military tribunes, extraordinary magistrates (such as agrarian triumvirs or decemvirs), and most crucially the magistrates of the plebs, the *tribuni plebis*. These plebeian magistrates, or tribunes, were denied *imperium*, but were given a special limited power (*potestas*) to aid plebeians against individual unjust acts—such as arbitrary floggings and executions—by patrician magistrates.[9] This power was designed to give effect to the liberty of the ordinary citizen,[10] a popular liberty that paralleled the liberty of senators and magistrates to speak their minds freely.[11] Tribunes were protected by the mightiest of things Roman, the oath; their persons were declared sacred and they had the right to intercede their person between any plebeian and a consul's *lictor* (attendant) attempting an arrest—helping to ensure, thereby, an ultimate appeal to the *populus Romanus*, the Roman people. This tribunate power was later expanded into a power of veto that covered the whole field of government. The plebeian magistrate acted as a check against the misuse of the *imperium* by consuls, and here we see, once again, the development of a fundamental aspect of the *res publica, viz.* the idea of one kind of power checking another kind of power, power balancing power in the state.

This balancing was evident in legislative as well as executive matters. The Senate was the place where policies and laws were initiated and discussed. But true to its origins as a consultative body, the Senate did not make binding decisions. It had authority, not power.[12] It advised. Senators consulted with the magistrates. Such *consul*tation had immense weight. It was backed by the *auctoritas* (authority) of the senators — so much so that not only was it sought, it normally prevailed. The authority of senators rested on experience, age, ability, and service to the state. This authority, however, was not the command of the master. It was not based on threats or coercion. It did not demand submission or groveling. When a legislative power did evolve under the Roman constitution, it was not the Senate but the countervailing plebeian dominated council or *comitia* that exercised law-making power.

The *comitia tributa* was a more democratic body than the *comitia centuriata*. It was an "assembly of the whole people" divided into "tribes" (notionally territorial groupings of voters) rather than into classes and centuries. The tribes, like the centuries, were collective voting units. Voting in Rome was always indirect and collegiate in nature — i.e., mediated through collective units. For a law to pass the *comitia tributa*, it required the initiator of the law — i.e., whatever magistrate proposed the law — to garner a majority of tribes in support of it. After 287 B.C.E. it was established that the resolutions (*plebiscita*) of the plebeian dominated assemblies were binding on the whole state. From that time onwards the legislative activity of the *comitia centuriata* declined sharply. It became simply a gatekeeper regulating access to the highest offices in the Roman republic. But just as assemblies in this fashion were stakeholders in the election of executive officers in the state, so those magistrates in their turn were stakeholders in the exercise of legislative power by the Roman *comitia*. This was a "check and balance" arrangement. *Comitia* could be called together only by a magistrate. The Roman *comitia* (the assembled people) did not initiate or debate laws. That was the province of magistrates. Magistrates made proposals, usually ones previously discussed by the Senate. The *comitia* listened to the speeches of various magistrates for and against proposals, and either ratified or rejected the proposals.[13] The role of the people was not to debate, but to vote. Such voting, though, could occur only in assembly, and such assemblies could take place only within the city of Rome. The people would be summoned to Rome at least twenty times a year for law-making purposes (a total commitment of some forty to sixty days in Rome), and at least seven times a year to elect magistrates (a commitment of fifteen days or more in Rome). For citizens who did not live in Rome, this meant extensive travel. There was no obligation on a citizen to attend an assembly, and assemblies would thus be more or less frequently attended. It was up to sponsors and opponents of bills and candidates to ensure a good turnout for their side. In 225 B.C.E. probably about three hundred thousand adult men had Roman citizenship; in 28 B.C.E. the figure was around the 1.7 million mark. A good voting turnout at an assembly would have been one hundredth of the total citizen body. Citizens who were also Roman residents were advantaged by this arrangement; rural residents were disadvantaged—although the more serious the matter, the more reason there was to travel to Rome.[14]

The Roman constitutional order existed (figuratively) as a result of an agreement (*pactio*) made by the various elements in the state. It established a modus vivendi between different classes and offices in the state. This agreement was a reiteration of an original pact that founded the city of Rome, as in Sallust's description of the beginnings of Rome: "In a short time a scattered and wandering multitude became a *civitas* through *concordia*."[15] Sometimes this constitutional order is called "Polybian" after the Greek-Roman historian Polybius, who gave an influential description of it in his *Histories* in the second century B.C.E.; the other principal, systematic, account of the Roman constitution is Cicero's *De re publica*, written in the first century B.C.E. when republican Rome was on its last legs. The virtue of the Roman constitution, in the eyes of the philosopher-statesman Cicero, lay in its mixed (*mixta*) nature. This was not, though, just any kind of mixture but one that was "balanced and moderate" (*aequatum et temperatum*).[16] It combined together elements of *regnum* (kingship), *optimates* (aristocracy), and *civitas popularis*, in a manner that was well regulated. The essence of this good regulation was to create a balance of different powers in the state. Cicero was clear that a constitutional order could not be seen in terms of arithmetical equality, because the powers of the executive, Senate and the populace were incommensurable. Nothing could directly equate the different powers of the one, the few, and the many, precisely because they were different kinds of powers exercised for different purposes. In essence, the people voted, the Senate influenced, and the magistrates ruled. What the ideal of the Roman constitution embodied was, according to Cicero, "a fair (*aequabilis*) balance of rights, duties and functions, so that magistrates had enough power (*potestatis*), the counsels of the eminent citizens (*in principum consilio*) enough influence (*auctoritatis*), and the people (*populo*) enough liberty (*libertatis*)."[17] What was *aequitas*, or fair, was not what could be counted but what could be weighed; the balance of the constitution was like the balance of a pair of scales, the scales of justice.[18]

EXPANSION AND REFORM

Even as the city of Rome became imperial in ambition and scope, it maintained, for a long time, the sense of justice as an adjustment. This needs some explanation, as empires, in the normal course of things, are vehicles of obliteration or assimilation, not conciliations of antitheses. How could the city ethos resonate in an empire? To answer this, we must understand the fatal flaw of the ancient city-states: their relationship with other cities. Or to put it another way: their size. Cities are most likeable, and most just, when they are not gigantic.[19] Yet, militarily and commercially, there are definite advantages in mass. So then, how can a city remain limited in size, yet gain the advantages of largeness? One answer is to build federations (confederations, alliances, leagues) of cities. The Greeks experimented with these in the fifth century B.C.E., but seldom very successfully, partly because the civic character of the Greek *poleis* was undermined by the tendency to forge federations on a shared ethnic basis. The Delian League that Athens led was (initially) Ionian; the Peloponnesian League, largely Dorian; the Achaean League claimed a (mythical) Mycenaean basis.[20] In these leagues, civility was often lacking, as one city would dominate others (extracting tribute, coercing decisions, and so on). It was only when, in the fourth century B.C.E., *poleis* entered into nontribalistic or nonethnic associations (*sumpoliteia*) — like the Achaean Confederation or the reformed Boeotian Confederacy — that a fully political union was possible. Essentially the ties of *patria* (home/land) or *ethnos* (nationality/ethnicity) had to be replaced by *impersonal* ties of political assembly (*ekklêsia*) in which the citizens of confederated cities could participate and make decisions jointly in a noncoercive atmosphere. The alternative way for a city to expand was to *colonize* other cities, either by founding subject cities or conquering other cities. When the aristocracy of Rome, in the name of *gloria*, pursued this imperial strategy, it had grave consequences for the constitution of Rome.

To understand the very peculiar nature of Rome, and Roman imperialism, we need to understand that it did not, in significant measure, reiterate the patterns of the patrimonial empires.[21] What even late Roman jurisprudence retained — and precisely because it was a juris-*prudence* — was the sense, derived from the foundations of Rome as a city, that it could enter into a treaty-partnership, some kind of "fitting together," with those it conquered, while at the same time retaining the sense that there was an impersonal order that bound all Romans whatever their specific background, class, or ethnicity. Roman peace, as Hannah Arendt pointed out, was determined not by victory and defeat, but by the alliance of erstwhile warring parties who became partners, *socii* or allies, by virtue of the new relationship established in the war itself and confirmed through the instrument of *lex* or Roman law.[22] Like Virgil's Aeneas, the *aim* in principle was not personal domination (the plundering of provinces) in the name of *gloria* but *reconciliation* and *unification* of the Roman world based on law. This ethos was established in the second century B.C.E., and continued for hundreds of years. Cities (or monarchies or tribes) conquered by Rome were offered not subject status, but "alliance" with Rome — on a variety of terms, some as "friends" of Rome, some as "free" cities, some as "stipendiary" cities.[23] Tribute was extracted from these allies, but the burden of tribute was not crushing. Crucially, cities absorbed by Rome were able to maintain the better part of their constitutions and laws under their agreements with Rome. In other words, local autonomy was preserved. The Roman habit was to leave things as they found them. They allowed the laws and structures of conquered cities to remain in force, and superimposed over the top of such structures the *imperium* of provincial magistrates responsible for tax collection and military garrisons. This *imperium*, or absolute power of the provincial governors, was never properly reconciled with the Roman respect for *lex*.

The expansion of Rome in the second century B.C.E. was astonishing. In 211 Rome was still fighting for her life against a foreign enemy (Carthage) at her gates. Sixty years later, Rome dominated the Mediterranean.[24] The Roman *provincia* (designating a sphere of official duty rather than territorial domain; the city was not a territorial state) rapidly expanded to include Sicily, Corsica, the Spains, Africa, Macedonia, Asia, Crete, Syria, and Egypt. This expansion, however, destroyed the republican constitution of the city — and its tradition of citizenship — and led to the rule of the emperors. Rome simply grew too large to be governed as a city-republic. The flood of tributary corn and money — from those provinces (especially Asia) that were remunerative — transformed Rome from a city that had the rough and ready look of a country town into a city beautiful. The borrowing from Greek culture was instrumental in this transformation.[25] Romans imitated the temples, basilicas, colonnades, and atrium houses they saw in Greek cities. Yet, despite this cultural growth, the city of Rome, during the second and first centuries B.C.E., experienced a social decline. During the wars of the second century, especially against Carthage, four hundred Italian townships were destroyed. The Italian countryside was depopulated. The numbers of free farmers and smallholders declined significantly. Much land either passed out of agriculture or into the hands of plantation owners who organized *lati-*

fundia (large landed estates) using slaves.[26] The cheap corn that came as tribute from Sicily and Africa plugged the hole that this caused in the supply of foodstuffs to Rome. But what could not be redressed was the social impact of the thousands who gravitated to Rome to live in ill-built and ill-drained quarters of the city. This uneducated and underemployed proletariat was conducive to the client politics that helped destroy the virtue of the Roman senatorial aristocracy. The purchase of gangs of supporters and of clients took politics out of the bright light of the public arena into the dark recesses of the patrician antechambers. This decline was compounded by the fact that the Republic drew its soldiers, crucial to its expansionary ambitions, from its citizen or free farmers. The republican army was not a professional but a citizen armed force. The tribute-paying citizenry bore arms as part of their citizen duties. During long periods of campaigning, their farms might be stolen, encumbered by debt, neglected, or ruined.[27] The senatorial class created no arrangements of compensation or redress for this. Indeed amongst their number were land grabbers. The consequence of this was to make soldiers susceptible to the promises of generals to settle them on the land, and thus loyal to the generals rather than the Republic. The generals set about creating colonial towns, many of them in Italy, which had the further destabilizing consequence of displacing existing landholders.[28]

All of this underlines the fact that bonds of *concordia* (union, concord) were never the only bonds binding Roman to Roman. Those of "clientship," *clientela*, also played a key role. The lower ranks of citizen society were often bound to great houses and noble families in a relationship of mutual "benefit." Patrons "protected" their clients; clients "supported" their patrons in various ways (including votes).[29] Such clients were by no means automatically compliant tools of their patrons.[30] The outright purchase of votes was illegal. Clients were often patronized by competing great households, diluting the political significance of the client-patron relationship and causing divided loyalties. Still, the client system represented the latent persistence of the patrimonial model of a "beneficiary" state that constantly threatened to erode the civic order and replace a condition based on an impersonal *concordia* with a hierarchical model of personal dependence.

Rome in the second and first centuries B.C.E. could not reform itself. There were attempts, for example by the Gracchi,* but they were

---

*Tiberius Gracchus, in his capacity as tribune (133), initiated a process of land reform (133–121) involving the reclaiming of pubic lands and their redistribution to landless citizens. Tiberius was killed for his efforts, but his reformism was carried on by his brother Gaius and others.

thwarted by upper-class Romans, the senatorial class, and the equestrian (capitalist) class, many of whom had lost their moral faith, the faith that sustained the constitution of the city-republic. There was real pressure to correct social distortions created by the wars of the second century — pressure to redistribute land, reduce indebtedness, and set up land commissions to deal with land grabbers who had stolen much of the arable land in Italy after the devastations of war, and who had turned it into *latifundia* based on slave labor. There was also pressure to extend Roman citizenship to conquered cities. The latter at least was gradually achieved. In 90–89 B.C.E., Italian townships pushed for enfranchisement,[31] and then took up arms successfully against an attempt to rig the voting system and make the votes they were granted worthless. The social question, however, remained insoluble, and even Gracchi-style reform proposals often had a patrimonial flavor (as in the case of the recurrent proposal to control corn prices or distribute free grain) and betrayed the ambivalences of attempts to reform the Republic. Cicero had a point in his consistent opposition to land redistribution and the cancellation of debts. This might be easily read as an apology for the cliques of great and rich families that increasingly dominated the political and economic landscape of the late Republic.[32] But it can also be read as an antipatrimonial, that is to say, republican, stance. What the Republic pioneered was an unconditional conception of private property.[33] The significance of this can be measured against what preceded it historically — viz. conditional property ownership, conditional on the command of a king or emperor. Arguably, Cicero feared that land redistribution would again make ownership conditional on political loyalty, just as he feared that debt cancellation (or moratoriums on the repayment of loans or reductions of the capital to be repaid) represented an erosion of the Roman moral ideal of *fides* (to trust, put confidence in), a key social bond of the Republic. What, however, is also clear is that Cicero did not offer a workable solution of his own. The republicans could not imagine a nonhousehold form of *production* to parallel the nonhousehold form of *res publica*; even if, in matters of property and exchange, Rome moved hesitatingly toward a *political* economy, the despotic (slave) household dominated production in the countryside, as imported skilled artisans did in the city. Rome failed to develop a balanced city economy, and thus had no way of properly employing its proletariat. It imported luxury goods, normally associated with a rich city life, from all over the Mediterranean, but exported only its administrative, political, legal, and military skills, not the products of its skilled hands. Indicative of this, the artisans who rebuilt Rome, turning it into an architectural masterpiece, were predominately Greek.

Only the "liberal arts," those concerned with virtue, were appropriate for the free man. While medicine and architecture were partial exceptions to this—in part because "questions of character" were raised by these arts—the world of the workshop, the trader, and the financier, although tolerated, lacked the *dignitas* (worth, merit) of the political or public office or of the occupation of the farmer.[34]

HUMANISM

Just as the city of Rome imported things of beauty, so did it import much of its intellectual culture. From the start of the second century B.C.E. (after the Second Punic War of 218–202), Rome experienced a cultural flourishing. This was the time when Rome became a player in the affairs of the Hellenistic kingdoms and cities. Foreign ideas—especially Greek and Hellenistic ideas—entered Rome. The circle around Scipio Aemilianus (184–129 B.C.E.), a close friend of Polybius (ca. 203–120 B.C.E.), was key in this cosmopolitan development from which emerged the Roman ideal of *humanitas* (humanity), an ideal that encouraged the sympathetic reception of ideas from other civic cultures. The good will toward other ideas and intellectual currents was an antidote to the provinciality of older Romans, and proved to be both an enduring force throughout Western history and a keystone of the tradition of humanistic inquiry that has been a distinguishing feature of Western civilization. Rome, though, was not simply a passive receptor of these (foreign) ideas. Rather, humanism operated as a bridge between Roman and Greek ideas, causing a transformation of the Greek ones as much as the Roman ones.

The case of the Stoic Panaetius of Rhodes (ca. 185–109 B.C.E.), an intimate of Scipio Aemilianus and his circle, exemplifies this. Panaetius modified Stoic teachings to make them acceptable to a Roman elite that placed a high value on political action and the holding of public office. Stoic virtues of fortitude and courage had been, in the Hellenistic setting, antipolitical virtues—ways of coping with the arbitrary impositions of Hellenistic monarchs. Now they became models of behavior for republican political actors coping with the ups and downs of military and political fortune. Rome, in the second and first centuries B.C.E., was the inheritor of the philosophies of the Peripatetics and Academics *and* the "art of living" of the Stoics, both developed in the Eastern Mediterranean. The former appealed to Romans because of the centrality of ethico-political argument in the philosophies of Aristotle and Plato. Rome was a *civitas*. Romans identified with the *res publica*. Public service, public duty, and public endowment were central to

Roman character. The chief business of the upper class (the *nobiles*) in republican Rome was politics. The claim to power of this class was asserted on the basis of moral worth: political right was the right of *virtus*, exemplified by great deeds done in the service of Rome through public office. Courage in fighting for one's country and the use of wealth for public ends were idealized. But alongside belief in the public realm, the Roman politician was expected to act on the basis of staunchness and faith. Courage in the face of natural evils and good faith towards one's allies or clients, devotion to office rather than private interest or ambition, were simultaneously idealized. Republican Romans were drawn to a tripartite arrangement of the ethico-political good, Stoical endurance and Roman faith. Each of these represented a basic moral truth for the Roman citizen.* Each of these moral truths represented a form of union for Roman citizens whatever their disagreements, rivalries, backgrounds, or customs. As Roman intellectual life grew, it reflected this mixing of moral truths. What emerged from this peculiarly Roman "enlightenment" was the enduring ideal of *humanitas*—an attitude of receptiveness to a variety of civic mores and to the variety of positional "truths" that they embodied. *Humanitas* provided a bridge between the different "moral truths" that entered into and circulated through the Roman world.

Unquestionably, enlightened Romans were eclectic in their reception of world views. Cicero is a prime example of this. At various times he defends Stoic views that pain and other evils can be endured, and that such endurance is virtuous, yet he does not accept that a happy or good life is simply one of stoical virtue. To be able to deal well with the blows of fate, and not get agitated or distressed by those blows, is part of what makes a good life, but only a part. A good life also must have available to it the goods of the body, the external things of mine-and-thine, and public things. Dealing well with the loss of such goods is not and cannot be the whole of virtue. In asserting this, Cicero is saying that Stoicism can be modified to take account of other philosophical positions. In the Roman world of Cicero's time, the Academics, Peripatetics, and Stoics all made compromises; all retreated from dogmatic certainty. Early in the third century, the systems of the Academy, the Peripatetics, and the Stoics had been distinct. After that time they underwent a process of fusing and blending.[35]

Cicero's attitude was decisively shaped by the New Academy and by two of his teachers, Philo of Larissa (ca. 160–80 B.C.E.) and Antiochus of Ascalon (ca. 130–68 B.C.E.). Cicero was deeply influenced by Antiochus's attempt to modify Stoic ethics and psychology, and to reconcile it with Pla-

---

*This was truth in the sense of practical knowledge, not revelation.

tonic and Aristotelian strands of classical thought. For Antiochus, the leader of the New Academy after Philo, the Peripatetics, Stoics, and Academics were part of a common tradition. Distinctions that once had been decisive were blurred to the point where Stoic doctrine was presented as a development of the Academic tradition. The humanist spirit of the age is played out in a paradoxical way. For example, where Antiochus embraced the Stoic doctrine of the validity of perception, Philo before him rejected it, preferring the doctrine of probability. Yet Philo's rejection of absolute certainty contributed to an atmosphere conducive to a breakdown in rigid doctrinal differences. Plato was accepted by the New Academy as the progenitor of skepticism[36]—i.e., of an intellectual style where no positive assertion is made, though *many arguments are advanced on both sides*; where inquiry into all things is made but no definite (certain) conclusion is drawn. For the ancient skeptic, action was based on probability, on deciding the most probable thing to do in the face of competing truths. The skeptic did not frontally reject the idea of truth, but rather the notion that human beings could act with absolute certainty. The skeptic realized that there were difficulties knowing what to do amidst a multiplicity of moral systems and definitions of the good. The other side of this was the attempt to create compounds out of rival moral systems. Antiochus, for example, compounded the Stoic view that moral worth and human good required detachment from concerns about material or bodily advantages or public life with the Platonic-Aristotelian view that material or bodily advantages and public things were crucial to human good and moral action. In a humanistic and skeptical context, this by no means amounted to a contradiction in terms. Admitting the ethical significance of natural or material advantages or public life did not preclude adopting a stoical attitude to the loss of such advantages. For Antiochus this amounted to no more than eliminating inconsistencies in the Stoic tradition and remedying weaknesses apparent in *both* Platonic and Aristotelian traditions.

Of course, a kind of flexibility was inherent, and deep-set, in any regime based, as Rome was, on the cultivation of political associations and alliances (*amicitia*). In a world of alliances, the one-dimensional grip of truth must inevitably be loosened. When Romans of Cicero's day opened themselves up to different (rival) conceptions of truth—to Greek, Hellenistic, and Roman axioms, to Greek ideas of public happiness, to Hellenistic ideas of endurance, and to their own native sense of *fides*—the intellectual corollary of this was a kind of humanistic skepticism. Such a skeptical standpoint is neither the modern critical standpoint (that seeks to critique and to devalidate particular axioms in their entirety), nor is it the standpoint that accepts only the authority of a single *ultimus finis*, or ultimate end. The skeptical attitude, rather, sees something in a variety of different truths or ends. As Cicero put it, if the Stoics were right in their definition of the ultimate good, then the question was settled. It would inevitably follow that the Stoic wise man was always happy. But the humanistic procedure was to inquire also into the view of the other schools and to see how the splendid pronouncements of the Stoics could be *harmonized with* the attitudes and systems of every school.[37] The skeptical attitude does not identify with one or other completely; it does not reject one or other completely either. Such eclecticism, of course, can become devoid of meaning. It can become Alexandrine, a byword for a museum culture that collects bits and pieces from here and there and puts them on display without any connective thread of meaning, producing nothing more than a heap or shapeless mass. Skepticism can be a meaningful worldview, but only where there is an arbitral process that *adjusts* heterogeneous truths (and their implicit ethical norms) to one another by reference to the spirit of the city. That is to say, skepticism can be a meaningful worldview only *where skepticism takes the form of (civic) humanism.*

PATRIMONY

In the late Republic, the connective thread of meaning was indeed in danger of breaking. The problem, though, was not the presence of a skeptical humanism. If anything, the birth of humanism was a sign of the vitality of Rome. Rather, the crisis of meaning that Rome faced was due to its inability to reconcile civic and patrimonial sources of meaning. In other words — in its practices and at the level of ideas — Romans were never able to institute a consistently civic orientation. The tension between patrimony and *civitas* is evident in the late Republican conception of justice. Justice, the fitting together or union of the *civitas*, was in Roman eyes achieved by the *constantia* (steadiness, firmness, constancy) and *fides* of the citizen (*civis*) in the public spaces of the *civitas*. Constancy in facing the vicissitudes of mortal life, good faith in the marketplace, and a capacity to finance, build, use, and appreciate public spaces and places were the building blocks of the union of citizens. But, in contradiction to this, the Romans could never shake off more archaic images either of the protected life of the *domus* (house), the violent and faithless relationships of the *latifundia*, or of the cruel spectacles and pseudo-"public" grotesquery of patrimonial power.

Romans understood justice or right to mean, firstly, the delivering to citizens the interest that each has in the safeguarding of their body. (Soldiers and sailors contributed to the safety and security of the *civitas*. So did the criminal law and so forth.) But how—*by what method*—was this to be delivered to *all* citizens? The Romans were disinclined to rely on a patrimonial model of provision. If benefits were to be provided by a king in return for obedience or loyalty, citizenship would be killed off. The Romans stressed instead the virtuous action of the citizen as the guarantee of the safety of the state. Romans made much of the courage of the citizen in the face of threat, invasion, want, poverty, floods, plagues, natural disasters, hazards, and accidents—indeed any of the evils that imperil elementary human security and that trigger human fear. The citizen was expected to control such fears, and to act courageously in the face of death and pain and physical agony, enslavement and exile and poverty.[38] The citizen was expected to rise above the outward circumstances of life and death, displaying staunchness and detachment. The Roman response to the natural evils of death and want was intuitively stoical. Courage, character, endurance, and fortitude were the stock answers to human pain and physical sufferings.[39] They were not the only answers. It was recognized that it was a duty of the state to supply the necessities of life.[40] But the Romans sought to do so in a manner that made the best of the moral quality of self-control, and they did so to avoid patrimonial monarchy and to sustain republican citizenship.

The Romans never quite discovered how to combine the material supply of necessities by the state with the moral character of the citizen; they never quite found out how to achieve the right balance—to avoid the patrimonial model but also avoid callousness, cruelty, and indifference to suffering. Of course, as most in Roman society were still household dependents, paternalism was a widespread response to suffering, as was (in the case of slaves) despotic indifference. Standing outside the patrimony of the household, the citizen was assumed to have certain resources (arms, money). The Romans never worked out how to help the impoverished or poorer citizen except by invoking the image of stoical endurance on the one hand, or the patrimonial dole or else the neopatrimonialism of public banquets sponsored by powerful politicians on the other hand. Cicero talked of a moral duty of liberality, of offering services or money to fellow citizens who are poor but deserving,[41] but this fell short of a systematic arrangement. However, it must be emphasized that courage and character provided important bonds of union between Roman citizens; the common admiration of these qualities linked Roman citizens together. They could expect their fellow citizens, whatever their way of life, to be unflinching, unwavering, staunch, and steadfast in the face of calamity, and to act steadily, without panic or alarm, and without falling into a mad frenzy or paralytic terror and hysteria.

The removal of the prospect of panic, frenzy, and alarm from the lives of citizens was both a condition and an effect of the just union of the city. Likewise, this just union was both a condition and a symptom of a climate of confidence and trust in others, an atmosphere of *fides* in which relations of hiring, selling, buying, partnerships and commissions, friendships and treaties could flourish.[42] *Fides* was the basis for relationships between equals, and for the friendship (*amicitia*) that tied together the members of the senatorial or the equestrian class; likewise it was the basis for the relationships of unequals (patrons and clients). The parties entering all these relationships promised something to one another, raising expectations that in time something was due to each one of them. *Fides* was the faith, the trust that this something would be delivered. Correspondingly, one of the worst acts that a Roman could commit was a breach of faith — to break a promise, an oath, an undertaking. For this was precisely to break the bond of society.[43] Morality was *honestum*. To act honestly, to deal with integrity, and to live an honorable life was something desirable, and not just for the sake of interest but for its own sake. *Honestum* brought people together. Violations of *honestum* undermined common life. All parties had an interest in honest and honorable action. Reciprocally, justice demanded of all who entered into voluntary arrangements that they act honestly and with integrity. Legal justice went further. The courts enforced good faith. The Romans developed, much further than any society before, what today we would call civil law or contract law. Ensuring that anyone who had the legal capacity to make a contract would, to the greatest practical extent, fulfill "promises made" was central to the working of justice in the city. But, at the same time that contractual relationships emerged as central to commercial and social relationships, the Romans maintained the despotic relationship of master and slave, a relationship that was in effect the antithesis of the relationship of *fides*. Again, late republican Romans cast themselves in a quandary. They elaborated a moral ideal of *honestum* which was to prove of enduring significance for Western mercantile and group relationships; yet, in the same breath, they desecrated productive relationships with the arbitrariness and faithlessness that marks slavery. Such a contradiction could not be sustained without undermining the sense of meaningful order in the late Republic. Wars, land grabbing, and the rest contributed their part, but the loss of spirit of the Romans — the loss of effective belief in their own world of meaning — sealed the fate of the Republic.

A civic order of meaning combines many different and opposing elements. Yet, some things cannot be combined in such an order. Some things are absolutely — and lethally — antithetical to the *civitas*. Patrimonial practices, institutions, and beliefs are prime among these. The bonds of the *civitas* and the bonds of a patrimonial order cannot be reconciled. The most important civic bond or union is the *public* union, the bringing together of people in public spaces. An essential part of Roman justice was the creation of spaces where all citizens could mingle. This was achieved by the creation of *res publicae*, public things or common property—the buildings, temples, theaters, and so forth that articulated such three-dimensional spaces. Good faith, trust, and confidence contributed to such public union, of course, as did a basic sense of security. But beyond this, it was the liveliness, drama, and theater of public life in public spaces, indeed often the very fact of civil dissension or disagreement, which drew people together in the public forum. Romans even disagreed on how money should be spent on the *res publica*. Were public games a gigantic, endless, and wasteful expenditure, as Cicero contended?[44] Were the sums devoted to walls, dockyards, harbors, and aqueducts more or less important than expenditure on theaters, porticoes, or new temples? Was it better for citizens to spend their money on such public infrastructure or public display or for those citizens to expend their energies in appearing in public in the assemblies and courts of the city, to speak, to argue, to orate, to deliver a speech in public debate, or to defend someone in court, someone honest and worthy but poor, against oppression and persecution by the powerful and corrupt? Roman citizens were divided over these issues. The paradox of the city was that disunity united. The union of citizens involved rivalries, conflict, argument, divergence, struggles, and disagreements, yet these confirmed an underlying union or *concordia*, viz. a belief in the *res publica*. But, on a deeper level, some divisions were symptomatic of the unbridgeable *differend* that afflicted Roman life.

The public theater, so much part of any *civitas*, was also a site of patrimonial largess. Republican (and later imperial) politicians were drawn into fêting the urban proletariat of Rome with spectacles of cruelty in order to guarantee their political acquiescence. The theater of cruelty of patrimonial society became the prop for, and then a cause of, the debasement of the politics of Rome.[45] Even the most astute figures, like Cicero, who saw the corrosive contradictoriness of this could do nothing to obviate it, and were often, as a condition of their political survival, required to sponsor bloody or sadistic contests that parodied, mocked and dragged into the gutter the dramatic contestations of a *civitas*. The stoic coldness of the intelligent republican politician forbade any sentimental objection to the blood sports. The *caritas* (love, affection) of the Christian was not yet a force in Roman society, and would be a long time

The Colosseum. Amphitheater, Rome. Built 69–79 B.C.E.

coming, and in its own way as lethal to the *civitas* as the theater of cruelty. Sentiment aside, the republican could not find an effective rebuttal to the violent pleasures of patrimonial life, and each small acquiescence to theatrical bloodiness was a further nail in the coffin of the Republic.

THE EMPERORS

The death of the Republic saw a reassertion of a hierarchical ordering of society. This was due both to the patrimony of the emperors and the influence of Christianity. At first this was muted. Roman law counterbalanced imperial caprice, and Latin civilization flourished. The two centuries of the Principate were a great period of architecture and city building. Indeed Gibbon called this "the period in the history of the world during which the condition of the human race was most prosperous and happy."[46] Rome during the time of the Principate remained a peculiar mixture of patrimonial and civic elements. The Caesars were drawn to the patrimonial model of Ptolemaic Egypt. Julius Caesar presented himself as a "savior" who offered a pathway out of the confusion to which the late Republic had succumbed. His great-nephew and adopted son Octavian built a state around the notion of the *princeps* (the foremost one) who maintains order. Yet the republican ideal of *libertas*, of public life without a king (*rex*),[47] was deeply entrenched in Roman civilization. The Caesars could not claim for themselves the title of *rex*. When Octavian, the emperor Augustus, imposed order on Rome, he did so in the name of his "father's deified benefactions" to the state and as the "savior" of his countrymen. Yet he exercised power as the wearer of the ambivalent "civic crown" of oak leaves, and as the *princeps*, which was not the title of an office but an expression of dignity.[48] The authority of the *princeps* was real and effective, but it had to respect a notional framework of republican institutions. The Senate and its magistracies continued in existence. Yet there was no real equilibrium between the *princeps* and the Senate. Augustus ensured this through his control of all the soldiers in Italy, his unprecedented garrisoning of soldiers in Rome itself, and his personal control of the provinces of Egypt, Spain, and Gaul.[49] The latter guaranteed him enormous patronage. Occasionally over the next two centuries, the Senate asserted itself, but rarely. On the other hand, its quiescence required the *princeps* to respect senatorial traditions and formalities, and above all to avoid the use of the term *dominus* (master, possessor, ruler, lord).

This begs the question, though: was the *princeps*, in reality, a *dominus*? In part, it is clear that the Caesars ruled patrimonially. For one thing, they assumed the patrimonial mantle of feeding the people. The condition of this was that the *princeps* took the place of the people in the Roman constitution. Augustus's successor, Tiberius, effectively suppressed the *comitia* and thereby abrogated the *populus Romanus*. Military conscription was ended, and the citizen soldier, crucial to the republican arrangement, ceased to be.[50] The juridical function of the populace was extinguished, as was the system of popular elections that had been the principal route into the Senate and its magistracies. Instead the *princeps* became "the father to his country," a patron who sponsored cheap corn and public shows. Yet, for all this, the Caesars organized a system of administration that was in many respects *less* patrimonial in character than the one that the Senators in the late Republic presided over. The origins of professional bureaucracy can be traced to this time. The Caesars put in place what was in fact a professional body of public servants, the "new men," recruited from the ranks of the Roman knights and freedmen.[51] Governors were now paid regular salaries, and a uniform tax system was created.[52] A corollary of this was the beginning of the rule of a territorial state, as opposed to the ethos of a city-republic. City magistracies ceased to have importance.[53] Imperial officers (curators, accountants, and so on), who traveled from province to province all over the Roman Empire, replaced them. The Roman military likewise became professionalized. Permanent armies and standing fleets were created. Such proclivity for professional administration, however, did not stop the Caesars from sponsoring, in typical patrimonial style, the introduction of a state religion. Yet even this reflected the profound ambivalences of the Principate. The temples that spread throughout the Empire were dedicated to Rome and Augustus,[54] in other words, to the city *and* the *princeps*, not just to the *princeps* alone. And in the established Roman fashion of leaving things as they were, this state religion coexisted with all manner of religious observances throughout the Empire. The Romans — as one would expect of an "importing" society — were tolerant of other religions.[55] The state religion required no inward faith but only outward signs of *loyalty* to the *princeps* (the patrimonial condition) *and* the sign of *patriotic allegiance* to the city of Rome, the worship of the city and her glorious destiny.

The Caesars played their part in the worship of the *civitas*, even if they often employed patrimonial means to do so. Augustus, once again, established the pattern of things. With the tribute of his personal provinces at his disposal, Augustus was the city benefactor *par excellence*. There were few towns in the Empire that did not have a splendid building that bore witness to this benefaction.[56] In imitation of the Caesar, each municipality would have its *patrons* who furnished the town with baths, temples, basilicas, fora, bathhouses, circuses, amphitheaters, libraries, statues, and colonnades. During the Principate, Rome entered a great period of city building,[57] the influence of which was to be deeply felt in the Renaissance and beyond. From the Theater of Marcellus (13 B.C.E.), which provided the model for Michelangelo's design of the inner court of the Farnese Palace at Rome, to the Roman temple at Nîmes known as the Maison Carrée, which inspired Jefferson's design for the Virginia Capitol building, the architecture of the Principate and its symbolic associations (including the latently republican ones) was to affect very deeply the civic architecture and politics of all subsequent ages that have regarded "the public thing" as the central signification of society. During the Principate, Rome itself was transformed from a city of brick to a city of marble.[58] Artists from Greece and Asia Minor carried out this rebuilding. Romans, though, modified Greek architectural forms. They dispensed with the *peristyle* or surrounding colonnades of the temple, introduced a wider span in roofing (by means of vaulting), and exhibited a preference for the Corinthian order of column rather than the Doric or Ionic. The Romans excelled at public works — at engineering, building, water supply, and drainage[59]—and they built for permanence. Material civilization reached a point under their guiding hand that was probably not generally reached again until the late nineteenth century in Europe. A real civic ardor remained during the Principate, in some ways almost as a compensation for the loss of republican citizenship. A powerful sense of patriotism, of city worship, impelled the rich to devote a large part of their fortunes to the embellishment of their native towns.[60] The rich also contributed to the foundation of schools, a practice that was, understandably, most highly developed in the historically Greek parts of the Empire because of like-minded Hellenistic precedents. Such schools undertook the maintenance of poor children, educating girls as well as boys.[61] Such efforts ensured that education was more widespread and more accessible to the poor in 200 C.E. than in 1850 C.E. in Europe.[62]

This system worked on the scale that it did only because the Romans respected the relative autonomy of cities throughout the Empire. As Rome outgrew its own city boundaries, it incorporated a multitude of regions, languages, and cultures with their own customs, habits, and traditions. Rome could have attempted to digest these, incorporating them like a traditional patrimonial empire. But such a structure would not have lasted long. Like Alexander's empire, it would have fragmented very quickly. The Romans did not have the resources to administer a patrimonial empire on such a scale. Instead, they permitted a large amount of self-government at the municipal level.[63] The Romans distinguished between *ius civile* (applying specifically to Roman citizens), *ius gentium* (a mix of Roman and foreign law applicable to foreigners), and *ius naturale* (applying to the Roman world as a whole). The articulation of the sense of Rome as a universal city was facilitated by the categories of Stoicism, categories that allowed for heterogeneity (of custom and social prescription) on the municipal level and, on the cosmopolitan level, the homogeneity (universal Nature) that is a prerequisite of meaning. The Roman administrator, the Roman jurist—the "new men" who rose to positions of power under the Empire—had to recognize, without fear or favor, the claims of different traditions and customs, yet at the same time to fit them together in a meaningful whole. What made such a synthesis possible was the Roman idea of humanism—in particular, the sense it conveyed of bringing rival types of ethos into concordance within the bounds of the city. And to do this required on the part of each administrator, each jurist, the impartiality that came from a universal justice that was meant to give what is due to each particular part of the world city (or *kosmopolis*) of Rome. Stoic natural law contributed a great deal to making this possible. But it was a distinctively Roman stoicism. For unlike the original Greek stoic, the imperial Roman jurist or administrator was a *public* officer. Not, of course, a politician of old, but nonetheless someone whose sense of duty came out of a *civic* tradition, someone for whom the ethico-political good was still of importance. Rome under the Empire (in particular the Principate) did not disown the idea of the *res publica*, but reinterpreted it.

CHRISTIANITY AND THE ESTATE SOCIETY

The rule of emperors did not destroy the tradition of the *civitas* straight away. One should rather speak of a gradual process of "patrimonializa-tion" — or erosion of the civic order — over three centuries. What remained in imperial Rome, for a long time, was the Roman sense of justice, of legal and administrative impartiality, of *virtus* as the unremitting and impartial administration of affairs of state by public office holders — the image of which passed through the centuries, long after the Empire was gone, leaving its stamp on the Western world. A part of this was a cosmopolitan sense of law that disposed the Romans, within the framework of the Empire, to allow disparate systems of law to exist alongside a system of *universal law* that was binding on all Romans.

But the spread in the third century of Christianity paralleled a deep shift as the Principate gradually gave way to the Dominate. Emperors from Aurelian (270–275) onward required the Eastern (despotic) ceremonial of full-length abasement before the Emperor, and beginning with Diocletian (284–305), "dominus" became the official title for the emperor. The spiritualization of domination by Christianity was also anticipated in this period by the neo-Platonic philosopher Plotinus (205–270). The Principate had been an urban civilization. It had sponsored a remarkable process of city building, but it did not manage to create a sustainable urban economy. The city was an agency of Roman expansion. It was the locus of political, legal, and military know-how. This was not without economic significance, however. Expansion generated tax revenues, loot, and slaves captured in war, but when the dynamics of expansion slowed to a halt, the weakness of Rome became apparent. Its fiscal basis began to dry up. The city of Rome did not have any other way of generating finance. In fact, the population of Rome was largely parasitic. In the mid-fourth century, three hundred thousand Romans held bread tickets that entitled them to draw free rations from the government. A century later, with a much smaller population, there were still about one hundred and twenty thousand receiving this largess.[64] In the fourth century, Rome found itself no longer fighting wars of expansion, but fighting wars of defense on its northern frontiers. To defend itself against invasion, it needed to support a military and civil administration that could no longer recover its own costs via expansion. The end of the imperial *dunamis* had a shattering effect: Rome could no longer afford a fully professional army. From the beginning of the fourth century, it reintroduced conscription.[65] As it had been in the past, country, not city, dwellers — small farmers — were affected by the draft. In the Republic, soldiering had been seen as the honorable duty of the citizen-farmer. But this sense of citizenship was long past. The free farmer no longer saw soldiering as an obligation but as mere servitude.[66] Military service now was something to be evaded. The state fought draft dodging with tough laws. But to the extent that these laws were successful, they garnered reluctant soldiers and caused the neglect or abandonment of cultivated soils. When conscription failed to give the army sufficient personnel, the army turned to Germans it captured to fill its depleted ranks. This also had a paradoxical effect. Previously, war captives had been the main source of slave labor for the Italian *latifundia*. Now this source of agricultural labor dried up because of military demands. Further compounding the pressures on the countryside were the punitive taxes that the state levied on smallholders. Taxes escalated in the fourth century to alleviate the loss of revenue from conquest. Rome now drew ninety percent of its tax revenue from taxes levied on land — regressive taxes that hit the poor harder than the rich. In one estimate, by 350 C.E. the sums extracted from this source had multiplied three-fold in living memory.[67] What is more, methods of tax collection had become increasingly abusive. What followed from this was an escalation in social destitution, poverty, and distress.[68]

This mix of factors congealed in the direction of a localized or decentralized patrimonialism. Small landholders in the countryside sought protection from tax collectors and conscription. Large landowners, the senatorial aristocracy, were in a position to deliver this protection — to resist the demands of imperial tax officers, to negotiate exemptions to military service for their labor force, and so on. Small landowners fled their properties and sought refuge behind the walls of the great estates. In exchange for this protection, the landed magnates demanded submission to their will. The kind of submission demanded, though, was not the same as that extracted from the slave. The landowner was assumed to exercise the right over these new tenants with the care of the parent as well as the power of a master.[69] This represented a more benign kind of servitude than that endured by the slave, even if in certain ways it resembled the condition of enslavement, as when Valentinian I, in the mid-fourth century, denied tenants the right to move from the landlord's estate without the consent of the landlord. Theodosius I, late in the fourth century, declared that, though such tenants appeared to be free-born by condition, they should nevertheless be considered as slaves to the land to which they were born. In other words, they were tied to the soil. The magnate landowners were in effect creating a new social-political form out of the ruins of the Empire, though, interestingly, this was as much a consequence of their retreat from active politics as anything else. The Senate, under the emperors, had lost its capacity to steer the direction of the state. As individuals, the aristocrats had continued to accumulate wealth, and even in the fourth and fifth centuries bureaucratic offices, but increasingly they stood aloof from the responsibilities of holding high office in the state and were excluded from service on city councils. They turned their attention instead to leisure and estate management. Politics had become a dirty word for them.[70] Yet on their estates emerged a new social and juridical form, or, rather, a recasting of the patrimonial form. The Empire responded (unsuccessfully) by trying to outlaw such arrangements. The estates of the landed magnates were reorganized around tenant instead of slave labor. The estates had their own prisons and armed force. The landlords could eject tax collectors, harbor deserters, and so on with impunity. They presented themselves as defenders of the poor. They exempted themselves from any municipal responsibilities and taxes. They created their own world, even with its own scholarly infrastructure. The scribes and the libraries of these landowners were crucial to the transmission of learning through the days of the disintegration of the Empire.[71]

In the fourth and fifth centuries, the foundations were laid for a renovated hierarchical conception of government. Christianity played the key role of giving this new arrangement moral validation.[72] Landlords found legitimation for their actions in the fourth-century Christian emphasis on the protection of the poor. Likewise the paternal submission required by the landlords was mirrored in Christian attitudes: God had erected in the heavens different ranks, and accordingly these found their replica on earth.[73] When Christians emphasized humility and self-abnegation, it was presupposed that the formative power over society and state was the principle of hierarchy. Society and state were formed by the hierarchical bonds between lords and servants. Christianity spiritualized these arrangements.

The Roman state officially recognized the power of the church when Emperor Constantine (312–337 C.E.) sought to convert Rome from paganism to Christianity. This recognition was expressed in a very Roman manner, with state funds flowing to Christian churches and church building, unleashing a vigorous process of turning Roman *basilicae* into

Christian edifices. Constantine's other monumental decision was his choice of the Greek city of Byzantium as a new capital (Constantinople) and effectively a "new Rome" (replete with its own Senate, Forum, and dole). While the choice was dictated by military needs—Byzantium was in striking distance of the major war zones of the Danube and the Euphrates—from the moment that there were de facto two "Romes," the basis was laid for the eventual schism of the Empire into two parts (Western and Eastern), two languages (Latin and Greek), and two Christianities (Catholic and Orthodox). As Rome's Western Empire collapsed, the impersonal order of the Romans was ousted by the image of society as a family with God-the-father, our Lord, and bishops and priests as fathers, ruling over their children. Secular princes and lords similarly assumed parental responsibilities for their feudal dependents. The significations of the city were marginalized. The Roman *civitas* vanished, a memory only. In the East, while the city (Constantinople) retained greater symbolic and emotional power, theocratic, imperial patrimony and provincial agrarian life dominated the world of Byzantium. Here also, Rome was memory.

NOTES

1. Hannah Arendt, *On Revolution* (Harmondsworth: Penguin, 1973).
2. E. J. Owens, *The City in the Greek and Roman World* (London: Routledge, 1991), p. 154.
3. Richard Sennett, *The Conscience of the Eye* (New York: Norton, 1992), p. 136.
4. "*Libertas* in the Republic," in P. A. Brunt, *The Fall of the Roman Republic and Related Essays* (Oxford: Clarendon Press, 1988).
5. Cicero, *Republic*, II.
6. In the previous century it had been the attainment of any curule magistracy (consulship, praetorship, curule aedileship). Donald Earl, *The Moral and Political Tradition of Rome* (London: Thames and Hudson, 1967), p. 12.
7. C. Nicolet, *The World of the Citizen in Republican Rome* (London: Batsford, 1980), chap. 7; Brunt, *The Fall of the Roman Republic and Related Essays*, p. 343.
8. Earl, *The Moral and Political Tradition of Rome*, pp. 20–21.
9. R. H. Barrow, *The Romans* (Harmondsworth: Penguin, 1949), p. 48; Brunt, *The Fall of the Roman Republic and Related Essays*, pp. 331–34.
10. Brunt, *The Fall of the Roman Republic and Related Essays*, p. 331.
11. Ibid., p. 328.
12. Hannah Arendt, "What Is Authority?" in *Between Past and Future* (Harmondsworth: Penguin, 1977); Brunt, *The Fall of the Roman Republic and Related Essays*, pp. 322, 325.
13. Cicero, *Republic*, I; Brunt, *The Fall of the Roman Republic and Related Essays*, p. 315.

14. Nicolet, *The World of the Citizen in Republican Rome*, chap. 7; J. C. Stobart, *The Grandeur That Was Rome*, 4th ed. (London: New English Library, 1965), p. 38; Barrow, *The Romans*, p. 49.

15. Earl, *The Moral and Political Tradition of Rome*, p. 123.

16. Cicero, *Republic*, I, II.

17. Cicero, *Republic*, II.

18. Cicero, *Republic*, VI; *On Duties*, II.

19. What counts as gigantic varies with time and socio-economic conditions.

20. Murray Bookchin, *The Rise of Urbanism and the Decline of Citizenship* (San Francisco: Sierra Club Books, 1987).

21. On the nature of the patrimonial empires, see S. N. Eisensdadt, *The Political Systems of Empires* (New York: Free Press, 1969).

22. Arendt, *On Revolution*, p. 210.

23. Stobart, *The Grandeur That Was Rome*, pp. 61–62.

24. Ibid., chap. 2.

25. Ibid., pp. 66, 73.

26. Perry Anderson, *Passages from Antiquity to Feudalism* (London: Verso, 1974), pp. 56, 60.

27. Barrow, *The Romans*, p. 54; Anderson, *Passages from Antiquity to Feudalism*, pp. 61–68.

28. Owens, *The City in the Greek and Roman World*, pp. 113–15.

29. Earl, *The Moral and Political Tradition of Rome*, pp. 15, 28.

30. As Brunt stresses in "*Clientela*" in *The Fall of the Roman Republic and Related Essays*.

31. Although the voting system for some time was rigged to make these votes worthless.

32. This is the view of Anderson and of Wood. See Neal Wood, *Cicero's Social and Political Thought* (Berkeley: University of California Press, 1988).

33. Anderson, *Passages from Antiquity to Feudalism*, p. 66.

34. Barrow, *The Romans*, p. 139.

35. H. A. K. Hunt, *The Humanism of Cicero* (Parkville: Melbourne University Press, 1954), pp. 2, 5, 7.

36. Ibid., p. 21.

37. Cicero, *Discussions at Tusculum*, V.

38. See, e.g., Cicero, *On Duties*, II.

39. Cicero, *Discussions at Tusculum*, V.

40. Cicero, *On Duties*, II.

41. Ibid.

42. Ibid., III.

43. Machiavelli's comment that Roman citizens "were more afraid of breaking an oath than of breaking the law" is apposite. Machiavelli, *The Discourses*. Edited with an introduction by Bernard Crick, trans. Leslie J. Walker, revised by Brian Richardson (Harmondsworth: Penguin, 1970), Book 1, Discourse 11, 139.

44. Cicero, *On Duties*, II.

45. Lewis Mumford, *The City in History* (Harmondsworth: Penguin, 1961), pp. 264–73.

46. Edward Gibbon, *The Decline and Fall of the Roman Empire*, ed. D. A. Saunders (Harmondsworth: Penguin, 1981[1776–1788]), p. 107.

47. On this see Jose Ortega y Gasset, "Concord and Liberty," in *Concord and Liberty* (New York: Norton, 1946).

48. Stobart, *The Grandeur That Was Rome*, chap. 4; Michael Grant, *The Founders of the Western World* (New York: Scribners, 1991), p. 179.

49. Ibid.

50. Anderson, *Passages from Antiquity to Feudalism*, p. 71.

51. Stobart, *The Grandeur That Was Rome*, pp. 234, 238; Michael Grant, *The Climax of Rome* (London: Phoenix, 1997 [1968]), p. 75.

52. Anderson, *Passages from Antiquity to Feudalism*, p. 72.

53. Stobart, *The Grandeur That Was Rome*, p. 240.

54. Andrew Lintott, *Imperium Romanum: Politics and Administration* (London: Routledge, 1973), chap. 12; Stobart, *The Grandeur That Was Rome*, p. 177.

55. Ibid., p. 258.

56. Ibid., p. 167.

57. Ibid., pp. 251–55; Owens, *The City in the Greek and Roman World*, chap. 7.

58. David Shotter, *Augustus Caesar* (London: Routledge, 1991), chap. 8.

59. Owens, *The City in the Greek and Roman World*, pp. 118, 158–63; Barrow, *The Romans*, p. 132.

60. Owens, *The City in the Greek and Roman World*, p. 122; Stobart, *The City in the Greek and Roman World*, p. 244.

61. Ibid., p. 246.

62. Ibid., p. 242.

63. Lintott, *Imperium Romanum*, chap. 8.

64. Michael Grant, *The Fall of the Roman Empire* (New York: Macmillan, 1990), p. 60.

65. Ibid., p. 37.

66. Ibid., p. 39.

67. Ibid., p. 57.

68. Ibid., chap. 3.

69. Ibid., p. 62.

70. Ibid., p. 74.

71. Barrow, *The Romans*, p. 193; Grant, *The Fall of the Roman Empire*, p. 75.

72. Peter Brown, *Power and Persuasion in Late Antiquity: Towards a Christian Empire* (Madison: University of Wisconsin Press, 1992).

73. Walter Ullmann, *Medieval Political Thought* (Harmondsworth: Penguin, 1975).

5

THE COMMUNE

THE RETREAT OF THE CITY

Neither feudalism nor the conquest of the Western Roman Empire by the Germanic tribes—decisive by the beginning of the fifth century—completely erased city life. The aim of the invaders, the historian Henri Pirenne reasoned, was not to destroy Rome but to occupy and enjoy it.[1] Perhaps we cannot, with Pirenne, really know what the aim of the invaders was, but consequences are more easily determined. As Pirenne describes it, "by and large, what [the invaders] preserved far exceeded what they destroyed or what they brought that was new." Roman provinces were transformed into Germanic kingdoms.[2] The Vandals were installed in Africa, the Visigoths in Aquitaine and in Spain, the Burgundians in the Valley of the Rhône, the Ostrogoths in Italy. Pirenne argued that while decline accompanied the invasions, there was preserved a physiognomy—or, I think more properly speaking, a *topography*—that was still distinctively Roman.[3] Look at the *scope* of the conquests, he suggests. "It includes only Mediterranean countries, and little more is needed to show that the objectives of the conquerors, free at last to settle down where they pleased, was the sea—the sea which for so long a time the Romans had called, with as much affection as pride, *mare nostrum*. Toward the sea, as of one accord, they all turned their steps, impatient to settle along its shores and enjoy its beauty."[4] The sea, this sea, was the space that linked cities, drawing them into a common destiny, at least as powerfully as the roads of an imperial administration.

Historically, the linkages of the sea—of the *Medi*-terranean, the middle of the earth—were: (i) those of navigation, commerce, exchange, itinerant scholarship, and travel; (ii) colonization by metropolitan cities, translating the city form around the shores, the watery margins, of the big lake, so that "home" became the being-away-from-home of the *apoikiai*; (iii) the beauty of the sea, its capacity to draw all human kinds to its shores, to look upon its

123

azure as a common pleasure; and (iv) the spirit of honesty, amicability, and alliance that made traffic between port cities possible. Pirenne argues that the importance of the Mediterranean did not diminish after the period of the invasions. "The sea remained for the Germanic tribes what it had been before their arrival—the very center of Europe, the *mare nostrum*."[5] As long as the sea remained open to traffic (to the exchange of commercial goods and ideas) especially between the bifurcated parts of the Roman Empire— the Byzantine East and the West—there was yet no end to "that common-wealth of civilization created by the Empire from the Pillars of Hercules to the Aegean Sea, from the coasts of Egypt and Africa to the shores of Gaul, Italy and Spain."[6] The linkage to Byzantium was crucial to this continuing Mediterranean civilization.[7] Byzantium was a key conduit of a Hellenized classical culture after the fall of Rome. Constantinople was founded as a New Rome by the Roman Emperor Constantine in 330 C.E. in his attempt to strengthen the empire, and the vision of that city as an heir to Rome was maintained through the centuries. Even later emperors of Greek origin called themselves Roman, and continued to refer to their capital as the New Rome. Through much of its history, Byzantium acted as a bulwark against incursions of Persians, Turks, Arabs, Slavs, and Russians into the old Roman world. Byzantium preserved and transmitted important aspects of classical culture, though mainly of Greek rather than Latin origins. Politically, Byzan-tium looked to the West. Justinian I's (527–565) attempted reconquest of the West, although short-lived, was symbolic of this, as was his recodification of Roman law. Even the way Byzantine civilization acted as a filter for Persian, Arabic, Syrian, and Armenian influences to enter into the West[8] resembled the old "Roman capacity for fusing the most varied characteristics."[9]

The fact that Byzantium was both urbanized and more commercial-ized than the West at this time was crucial to the staying alive of cities in the West. The continuance of maritime commercial activity after the dis-integration of the Western Empire meant the survival of towns and thus the survival of something of the civic form. "By means of shipping which was carried on from the coasts of Spain and Gaul to those of Syria and Asia Minor, the basin of the Mediterranean did not cease, despite the political subdivisions which it had seen take place, to consolidate the eco-nomic unity which it had shaped for centuries under the imperial com-monwealth."[10] The maritime economy sustained city life from the fifth to the eighth century, as if a ghostly trace of the Roman world.[11] As in the days of the Roman Empire, all the largest cities of Merovingian Gaul were still to be found south of the Loire, and like the commercial face of Gaul itself, they were oriented to the Mediterranean. Marseille, the great port of Gaul in the eighth century, was a lively economic center whose shipping bound it to Syria, Africa, Egypt, Spain, and Italy. Here something of the old *kosmopolis* remained, evident in the residence of foreign merchants — Jews and Syrians mainly — in the city. Something also of the old culture remained. As Erwin Panofsky notes, right through to the time of the Carolingian Empire, "oases [of classical culture were] left in regions such as Italy, North Africa, Spain, and South Gaul, where we can observe the survival of what has been nicely termed a 'subantique' style. . . . "[12] But to speak of "survival" is to indicate the weakness of these cities. They lacked the political superstructure of either the Roman *res publica* or Augustan Caesarism. Lodged in the southernmost bowels of the barbarian kingdoms, they existed precariously. They enjoyed none of the benefits of an ascendant civilization or of a supervening political artifice whose anchor was the city. The transplanted Germanic kingdoms were patrimonial in structure and agrarian in orientation. Their culture, politics, and economics were that of the household. Whatever the attractions of the sea, at the base their élan was Germanic, not Mediterranean. It was the spirit of the landlocked *domus*, not the maritime *emporion*. The best, trade-wise, society-wise, such kingdoms could offer was the *domus negociantum*, the local market tied to the household and the manor.

The ineffectiveness of the political superstructure of the Germanic kingdoms for the purposes of the city is demonstrated by the emergence of Islam in the Arabic world. From the time of the prophet Muhammad (571–632), the power of Islam spread rapidly, incorporating Syria (634–636), Egypt (640–642), Africa (698), and then on into the heart of the old Roman world, colonizing part of Spain (711).[13] Politically the Germanic kingdoms were ineffectual in the face of the Islamic advance. As Pirenne puts it, "its sudden thrust . . . destroyed ancient Europe. It . . . put an end to the Mediterranean commonwealth in which it had gathered its strength. The familiar and almost 'family' sea which had once united all parts of this commonwealth was to become a barrier between them."[14] The basis of the Mediterranean economy — trade between the West and the East — shriveled up.[15] By the ninth century the port of Marseille was silent, and Provence, once the wealthiest part of Gaul, had become the poorest. The Muslims consolidated their grip on the Mediterranean with the capture of the Balearic Isles, Corsica, Sardinia, and Sicily. The conquest of Sicily in the ninth century brought a typical change of focus: until that time the chief city of Sicily had always been Syracuse, which looked eastward across the Mediterranean to the Greek world. The arrival of the Muslims forced a reorientation toward Tunisia, and the consequent rise of Palermo.[16] All over, the Muslims founded new ports: Tunis, Cairo, and Palermo (their base in the Tyrrhenian Sea), while their raiders pillaged the coasts of Provence and Italy.[17]

Byzantium maintained a presence in Southern Italy (centered on Bari).[18] This kept open a limited space for West-East transactions of a classical type, and significantly it is in this tenuous space that the city of Venice developed.[19] In 811, when sailors and traders from nearby Malamocco settled in force on the lagoon islands — in order to defend themselves against Frankish attack — the history of the watery city began.[20] Venice developed a "neoclassical" pattern of trade and economy. Byzantium, with its Hellenic accent on refinement, adornment, and iconography, was the perfect partner in this. The Venetians took to heart the classical love of public appearances and its stress on the pleasure of the eye. Everything to them became a surface to be adorned, a stage to be set, a facade to be observed by the passerby.[21] The Venetians imported rich materials (golds, silks, and gems) from Byzantium and exported the work of local artists — embroidery, lace, gold work, jewelry, and crystal of extraordinary design.[22] Yet this economic space, created by the Byzantine presence, with its echoes of the classical world, was exceptional rather than normal. Whatever dreams the Byzantines had of founding Rome anew, Byzantium in time became more and more preoccupied with the Slavic world, and less and less interested in challenging the power of Islam.

The Germanic kingdoms of continental Europe were equally ineffectual. The consolidation of these kingdoms under the auspices of Charlemagne and the Carolingian Empire in the eighth century had made little difference to Europe's rim cities. The Carolingians could not effectively defend their sea borders against Islamic or Norse raiders. The spirit of the Germanic kingdoms lay inland, not on the beaches. The North Sea, the Channel, the Gulf of Gascony, and the Mediterranean in this period were not beachheads of power but permeable boundaries into which raiders made easy forays, even down into the river systems of the Rhine, the Meuse, the Scheidt, the Seine, the Loire, the Garonne, and the Rhône.[23] The economy and society of ex-Roman territories became, for a time, almost completely patrimonialized — composed of agrarian household units, ecclesiastical and lay demesnes dominated by hereditary landed proprietors (*seigneurs*) to whom a peasantry (bound to the soil) owed service. This arrangement secured production mainly for local or subsistence needs. The medium and long-distance commerce in luxury goods, central to the old economy of the city, virtually disappeared. The supervening political structure — that of a universal monarchy — mirrored the social arrangement, with the *seigneurs* organized into a loose hierarchy of feudatory obligations. Reflective of the agrarian character of the state, the palaces of the Carolingian princes were no longer located in the towns.[24] By the eighth century the civic economy had largely disappeared, and

Mediterranean cities survived principally as episcopal cities where bishops resided. Symbolically Rome—the imperial city—had become the pontifical city.[25] Both spiritually and politically, cities had become *defensive* entities, no longer outward looking. The church had come to dominate the heart of the city, offering refuge from the tumult of the disintegrating *civitas*. The urban center for Christians was neither a crossroad nor a public space, but an ecclesiastical shelter—a sanctuary. In the period from the sixth to the tenth century, secular space, in what remained of the old urban areas, became more and more jumbled and intestinal in structure. Meanwhile church space retained a ghostly trace of Roman clarity, but making a different point: the church (representing the transcendent) was the only thing visible and clear in contrast with the mess and confusion of the world. In less symbolic terms, the church at the heart of the diminished *urbs* (walled town) offered immunity from a dangerous world. In defense against the systemic violence of the agrarian-feudal world, the city became surrounded by a walled enclosure. It became the *castellum* (fortress, stronghold), the *burgus* (castle, fortress), fortified against raiders. The city-as-fortification represented the extension of the seigneurial mentality into the very fabric of the city. Seigneurs offered their dependents protection in exchange for service and loyalty. Fortress populations now came under their protection. Typically each local prince had a house (*domus*)—which doubled as a storehouse for the produce of neighboring demesnes—in each *burgus* of his territory, where he and his retinue stayed on occasions when military or administrative duties required it.[26] The *burgus* was not a city in the true sense of that word. It had a castellated rather than civic character, and earned its keep as fortification for the landed powerful. The labor and produce of the demesnes kept towns going. They were in effect colonies of the seigneurial world.

THE REVIVAL OF CITIES

The reversal of this situation, and the revitalization of cities, began with the loosening of Islamic power over the Mediterranean. Christianity played its role in this, and in no small measure because of its own revitalization in the tenth century, due to the Cluniac reforms.* Toledo and Valencia in Spain fell to the Christians (1072–1109).[27] Norman knights pushed the Muslims out of southern Italy (as they did Byzantium). By the

---

*Modeled after the example of the Burgundian Abbey of Cluny, a reform monastery in the Benedictine tradition. Cluny was founded in 910 by William of Aquitaine, and its practices were widely imitated in Western Europe.

end of the tenth century the Venetians were able to negotiate a trading agreement with the Muslims. The pressure on Islamic power was stepped up when the Franks launched the first of the Crusades against Islam in 1096, with the consequence that the Mediterranean was opened up yet further to Western shipping. The commercial cities, notably Venice, happily provisioned the Crusaders for a price. (In the Venetian case, this was the one and a half quarters of Constantinople after the sack of that city in 1204 as well as control of numerous coastal cities on the Adriatic Gulf and the Albanian shore.)[28] Under these conditions, the city could breathe again. In the eleventh and twelfth centuries, what occurred was an economic diaspora, as Italian merchants and seamen journeyed once more to the Levant, the Black Sea, and the North African coast.[29] Traders from Pisa, Genoa, Venice, Milan, and, a little belatedly, Florence created a commercial revolution. What followed, in parts of central and northern Italy, and in the Toulouse region, was a renaissance of the city.

The expansion of city life also took place on the shores of the Baltic (Lubeck and Hamburg), along the Rhine river (Worms, Mainz), and in the Netherlands (on the shore of the sea and along the banks of the Meuse and the Scheldt).[30] But it is in Italy that commerce was revived with a *public-aesthetic* character that, to a large extent, eluded the northern cities. As Murray Bookchin observes, the cities involved in the revitalized Mediterranean trade made their fortunes largely from luxury goods such as silk, spices, gems, well-wrought armor, gold and silver ornaments, and the like, while German cities tended to deal in the making and sale of coarser cloths, tools, simple armor, food staples, and raw materials.[31] Where Genoa and Venice acquired wealth mainly from exotic goods, Hamburg grew rich from brewing, and Lübeck from herrings and the furs of eastern European forests. These northern cities had a much closer relationship to the staple producers, and thus to the communal *mores* of the agrarian world. The Germanic cities therefore had a somewhat stodgy, "stay at home" character, while the Italian cities developed a *theatrical* quality, and a much closer relationship to the *mores* of the public world of the actor. The *vita activa* (active life) was a much stronger part of the fabric of the Latin city than of the cities of the north.

Florence epitomizes this southern theatricality. Even its staple good, woolen cloth, evinces this character. The Florentine woolen goods industry was premised on aesthetic refinement. Indeed, here, there was no clear differentiation between art and industry. They were on a continuum. And it was this art-industry that elevated Florence from a small provincial town — still at the end of the twelfth century overshadowed in size by her neighbor Pisa — to one of the most populous cities in Europe by the middle of the thirteenth century.[32] This art-industry also was the basis for a far-flung network of Florentine traders. Agents of Florentine firms lived and worked in Rome, Venice, Paris, London, Constantinople, and Damascus.[33] Something of the old Greek sense of *apoikiai* — in this case a remarkable capacity to live and work abroad — is evident in the Florentine mercantile elite. What accompanied this was an evident facility of mind — fluency in more than one foreign language; knowledge of many different systems of coinage, tariffs, weights, and measures; and a capacity to translate between different systems with ease. The transactions of the large trading firms encompassed hundreds of cities, from Edinburgh and Stockholm to Beirut and Alexandria. Contact with foreign people and world traveling were valued by the Florentines, and the occupation of international trade was a prestigious one. Building on the wealth from textiles and the networks established by their traders, Florentines established a flourishing banking industry, although one that for a long time existed in a twilight of semilegality because of Christian prohibitions against usury.

The basis of Florence's economy lay in the Florentine feel for beauty and excellence. It was not their trading sense but the *quality* of their textiles that eclipsed their rivals (e.g. in the Flemish cloth industry). And this was quality in the sense of *artistic* quality. Florentines did not draw a strong distinction between art and craft. To be an artisan — or the master of a craft: a mason or carpenter, embroiderer, sculptor, painter, or goldsmith — was to be an artist, and vice-versa. *Production was the production of beautiful things*, things for aesthetic display: captivating to the eye, fine to touch, and so on. As Gene Brucker observed, the appreciation of quality, and the corresponding disdain for the shoddy and the inferior, became a characteristic feature of the Florentine mentality. Here we see a renaissance of the classical idea of excellence (*aretê*). The artisans and merchants of Florence were engaged in a competitive struggle, not simply for self-aggrandizement, but to produce work of quality that would enhance the beauty and reputation of the city, and that would thereby enter into public memory, bringing fame to themselves and their city at the same time. The Florentine guild system played an interesting part in this. The guilds carefully regulated the competitive struggle but not in an insular way. The role of the guild was to enforce standards of quality — to ensure that competition did not undercut quality. Such quality earned Florentine merchants, capitalists, and artisans impressive returns. But here again we need to be aware of the distinctive ethos that governed such moneymaking. Wealth was not simply for private benefit or even just for business expansion. A substantial part was directed to public ends — to the support of poets, scholars, and civic art, the endowing of public buildings and schools — all of which was meant to enhance the greater glory of the city.

Florence's art-industries attracted a flood of immigrants (skilled and unskilled alike), which in its turn stimulated the expansion of the city. Parallel phenomena occurred in many North Italian cities, where a city revival was signaled by the growth of the merchant class along with a middle class of professional notaries (lawyers), skilled artisans, and literate professionals. The appearance of these independent classes, which stood outside of the household economy, shook the patrimonial-episcopal domination of the city. In the revitalized cities, functional titles began to replace noble titles, and feudal patterns of behavior were discouraged. Patrimonial power was gradually displaced, although by no means eradicated, by the rise of the *commune* — originally a private association of city dwellers that over time encouraged the transfer of responsibilities for defense, protection, endowment, and so on from private-familial or ecclesiastical-pastoral to lay-public hands.

THE RISE OF COMMERCE

The political and commercial revolution of the eleventh, twelfth, and thirteenth centuries that followed the retreat of Islamic power in the Mediterranean basin was intimately connected with the revival of the city. And yet the rebirth of the city happened with great difficulty and uncertainty. The reborn city lacked the promise of permanence, surrounded as it was by an aura of disturbance and instability.

The reemergent Italian cities, their citizens and their denizens, were torn in their allegiances. The commercial revolution was premised on the revival of what might be called Roman values. The long-distance trading of the cities depended on high levels of trust, honesty, and reliability — on the Roman *fides* — as well as upon a Hellenistic-Roman sense of cosmopolitanism: on education of a broad scope, amicability toward foreign people, a readiness to learn about foreign customs and conventions, and so forth. The good management of urban workshops, on the other hand, required values that were part Christian, part Stoic: prudential caution, restraint, ascetical thrift. At the same time, the encompassing end of production was public display, a value underpinned by the Hellenic-Byzantine love of beauty. Parallel to this, yet at the same time distinct from it, was a Greco-Roman admiration for public-political life and for friendship. Had the cities been simply the recipients of a Greco-Roman-Byzantine classicism, the mix would have been quite manageable. But instead the classical was placed side by side with the familial and the Christian: the medieval inheritance. It was not easy to reconcile the axioms of the classical and the medieval, because the very medium of reconciliation in each case was different: one through public discourse, the other through paternal care. Take for example the classical value of friendship—friendships crossed familial lines, and were capable of forging human bonds as powerful and as enduring as familial ones. Friendships flourished in the city atmosphere. Yet the family remained a key source of identity in the revitalized cities. City dwellers were thus often torn between family and city.

Allegiance to family over city meant factiousness, lawlessness, uncivil rivalry, nepotism—as powerful households fought each other for preeminence and greater power, or as they attempted to buy influence, office, even release from punishment for their wayward affiliates. Even if idealized medieval notions of chivalry were foregone—as households became more and more commercialized—patrician families were still liable to defend family codes of honor with aggression and vengeful pride. While the church provided asylums from this violence, its preaching of peace was largely ignored. In this respect at least, familial "self-help" predominated over Christian faith in redemption. The key test for the civic regime was whether it could do any better. In the twelfth century, feudal fighting was still common among leading families in the resurgent cities of northern Italy. A powerful family would tend to dominate a neighborhood; the symbol of this domination was the defensive tower. Relatives, dependents, retainers, and clients of the family banded together in the neighborhood for protection and defense against rival houses.[34] The urban community thus broke down into family nuclei. The family ethos was one of solidarity, acting as group for survival. It was to the family that the individual owed primary obligation. Street fighting, vendettas, blood feuds, and hatreds mutilated interfamilial relations. Still, the formation of family *consortia* (protective alliances with other families) indicates the different dynamics of the *urbs* in contrast to the landed world. The *consortia* were based on *promises* of mutual aid, not *oaths* of feudal loyalty. They were unconscious testaments to the centrality of the contract in city life, and symptomatic of the subtle pressures on noble families to urbanize and shed their feudal ways. Spiritually these families might have lived in the world of chivalric myths, service obligations, honor, and warring, yet practically they lived in increasingly citified contexts that denied the relevance of the landed hierarchical form of life. In the city contractual reliability, rather than loyal service, was in demand.

The nobility was thus under pressure—both internal and external—to transform itself into a citizen nobility. To facilitate this, Tuscan, Veneto, and Lombard cities, in the twelfth century, turned to the institution of the *podestà*, a kind of chief executive cum juridical officer. (In the thirteenth century, the *podestà* lost administrative power but retained juridical power, becoming something like a chief justice with police authority.) The creation of the office of *podestà* had the effect of placing the principal executive/judicial power of the city in the hands of someone who came from *outside* the city, who was appointed for a limited term, and who therefore had no close association with particular families. The *podestà* was a neutral figure not caught up in the web of discords, intrigues, revenges, and conspiracies of the powerful families.

The office of *podestà* was one of several interrelated institutions that helped define the twelfth century Veneto-Lombard-Tuscan cities as distinctive entities independent of seigneurial power. A new type of power displaced patrimonial power. This was *civic power*, derived from the collective agreements of the citizens of the *commune*. The citizen became the determining force in city life. The citizen usually was someone who owned household property of a certain substantial value, who had not been exiled and had not been a murderer, who was resident within the city limits for at least nine months of the year, and who had been born in or lived in the city for a certain time. Citizenship required participation in civic affairs. It involved duties. Citizens were required to obey the laws and officers of the city, to attend meetings and give counsel, to make their houses and fortified towers available to the city for military purposes, and to perform some (part-time, unpaid) administrative duty in the city or participate in making laws in the city's council. In the earliest days of the communes citizens made decisions in assemblies of all of the citizens. But as cities grew and citizenship became more inclusive, this was difficult to sustain. Increasingly councils replaced the deliberations of assemblies. In some larger cities "great councils" had over one thousand members, but these spawned smaller "inner" councils. Membership of councils was determined variously (indirectly, by lot, by outgoing councilors), and was normally for a short tenure only. Councils functioned procedurally with debating rules, with both secret ballots and public votes, with two-third majorities for key decisions and so on—procedures varied according to the specific commune. The *podestà* was an officer of the council, an executive administrator and head of the city's judiciary.

Other measures, aside from the institution of the *podestà*, were directed against the magnate families. For example, to curb the power of the families, Florence promulgated the Ordinance of Justice (1293).[35] The ordinance provided harsh penalties for clan-motivated violence and effective judicial means of enforcing this. Under the Ordinance of Justice powerful magnate families were excluded from the commune's highest offices (though this by no means ended the influence of great families). Magnate families were even required to post bond guaranteeing their good behavior. Such tough measures had an effect. By the late fourteenth century violent factiousness had decreased significantly. The passage of measures like the Florentine Ordinance of Justice symbolized a shift in the power structure of the city. In the course of the thirteenth century, citizenship in cities like Florence had come to be dominated by the *popolo*, affluent artisans and arriviste-burgher capitalists bound by a common guild identity. Measures such as preventing a family member taking office as a magistrate conducting the public business of the city if another family member was already serving in that capacity helped the *popolo* constrain the power of the families.[36] Nobles continued to play prominent roles as ambassadors and military advisers, and more often behind the scenes of the public stage. But in effect, in many northern Italian cities, magnates were allowed only what amounted to a fixed degree of participation in city councils and offices. This ceiling on the power and influence of the feudal nobility was mirrored in the increasing use of city regulation to strip this class of its explicitly feudal character. The city councils gradually outlawed seigneurial justice, private prisons, vassalage, and retinues; they imposed laws to regulate the height of the domestic fortified towers and prevent nobles from feuding. This did not change patterns of behavior overnight — even in the late fourteenth century, in Florence, patron-client relationships instigated by powerful families were still a significant force, especially during times of political unrest.[37] But over time it had an impact.

The driving force behind the regulation of the nobility was the *popolo*, the urban class of traders, lawyers, scribes, craftsmen, and financiers. The city became a kind of *balance of power* between the noble citizenry and the *popolo*. There was an explicit sharing of offices in the city between classes. The number of offices that nobles could hold was restricted; at the same time, there was the understanding that there were certain qualities that the nobles could contribute to the city. In military and diplomatic fields the formative training of the patrician had explicit value. *La potenza degli Oltimati* (the influence of the big ones) could not be denied, but it was counterbalanced by the influence of *il governo popolare* (popular government). As a counter to patrician power in the second half of the thirteenth century, the *popolo* became more organized. It often had its own councils, militia, and officials. Even more significantly, the thirteenth century saw the rise of the office of the *Capitano del Popolo* as a counterweight to the office of *podestà* that was usually staffed by a patrician. The office of *podestà* lost its administrative power and was transformed into a largely judicial office, while the *Captain of the People* was transformed into a leading executive office. (And, it has to be said, in so doing, both offices lost something of their class character and acquired something more of a functional character.)

IMPERIALISM IN ITALY

The civic institutions which were worked out in the twelfth and thirteenth centuries did not last. The Italian cities were unable to stabilize them. Through the fourteenth century the cities increasingly came under the governance of the *signoria*, the Modern Princes. Even where city life and business remained ebullient, the political superstructure of the city passed into the hands of powerful ruling families cum political factions albeit ones of a substantially urbanized character.

One central reason for this was the lack on the part of city protagonists of a strong conception of the city as belonging to a *kosmos* (an ordered arrangement of things). The cities lacked, in their dealing with each other, a genuinely *cosmopolitan* feeling, which was ultimately to poison their internal politics as well. Thus despite the *mercantile* cosmopolitanism of the twelfth and thirteenth centuries—exemplified both in the capacity of Florentines, Milanese, and Venetians to work together abroad and in the imaginings of the mercantile diaspora of a common Italia that existed in no one else's minds—and despite the interchange of *podestà* between cities, despite even the provincial alliances of city factions,[38] fierce antagonisms, fired by particularistic and patriotic sentiments, often broke out between north Italian cities. While "the greater glory of the city" supposed a shift of allegiance from the family or the church, it lacked a properly cosmopolitan dimension, and it proved to be a narrow and often destructive allegiance. It lacked even the pretensions to universal scope of the church, or even the nostalgia for the scope of empire exhibited by the (Germanic) Holy Roman emperors. Because of this, divisions between cities could be quite rancorous, while alliances, when forged, were shifting and uncertain. Bereft of a sense of the city as part of the ordered arrangement of the *kosmos*, the city mentality could be quite petty and ugly.

When internecine and nasty bickering or struggles festered between cities, the practical question was raised: How could things be otherwise arranged? Four practical alternatives to narrow city patriotism were raised:

(1) *A league or confederation of cities.* This represented a revival of the Hellenic idea of federalism. But without the underlying ethos of the *kosmopolis,* it could not progress very far, except under certain conditions of threat, as for example when the Lombard communes came together in the twelfth century to resist the claims of the Germanic emperors to control them.

(2) *The incorporation of the city into a sovereign form of government (a kingship) based on a common language.* As it happened, none of the Italian monarchies, including Milan and Naples, were powerful enough to lay effective claim to the peninsula, while the French monarchy tried but unsuccessfully. In the medieval period, until Dante, there was no common vernacular literary/cultural language. In other words, the condition of a "national history" did not exist. Linguistic differences between regions stood in the way of the ethno-linguistic unity of a dynastic national state. There was no Italian monarchy capable or prepared to do what the French-speaking monarchy had done in conquering south of the Loire: eliminating the *langue d'oc* and the civilization of city-states that lived through this language.

(3) *The incorporation of cities into the Vatican State.* The church had ambitions to rule Italy, and it intervened aggressively in the power politics of the peninsula. From the time of Gregory VII (1073–1085), the papacy appealed to all Italians against the pretensions of the German emperors.[39]

(4) *Subsumption under the (Holy) Roman Emperor.* The Holy Roman Empire was a semifictional legacy of Charlemagne's effort to revive the scope of the Roman Empire on a *continental* basis. What was actually a medieval Germanic empire was seen somewhat bizarrely as the heir of the Roman Empire.[40] The Albrechts and the Heinrichs were thus supposedly successors of Augustus, and a unified Italy sat neatly with this myth of descent.

The last serious effort of the Holy Roman Empire to unify Italy was pursued by Frederick II in the thirteenth century, and this doomed attempt exemplifies all the ambivalences of Italian politics that paralyzed the emergent cities and destabilized them. Frederick began his Augustus-imitating quest by imposing his will over the Sicilian kingdom he inherited from his Norman mother; in the course of this he crushed a defiant nobility, defeated a Muslim brigand state that maintained a foothold on Sicily, intervened in episcopal elections on behalf of his candidates, and founded the University at Naples to train bureaucrats for his imperial administration-to-be.[41] But all these actions turned to impotence. The League of Lombardy reorganized itself against this fake Roman Empire in the making. The papacy under Gregory IX forcefully resisted Frederick's imperial ambition (seeking, naturally, a restoration of "ecclesiastical liberties" in Sicily). The church offered alliances to the towns against the imperial force. It excommunicated Frederick and organized a crusade against him, effectively blocking his ambitions in central Italy, in much the same way that the Lombard League blocked his claim on northern Italy.

Actually, had it ever come to pass, Frederick's mock "Augustan" imperialism would have been, in practice, as much Muslim as Roman. Like the "baptized sultans" — the Norman kings of Sicily who had preceded him — Frederick moved easily in the Islamic world. He had a working knowledge of Arabic; he negotiated armistices with Muslims in the Crusades (rather than fighting them); he patronized translations of Arabic works in the natural sciences. Frederick's kingdom was in fact a medieval patrimony. It was based almost entirely on landed wealth, with few traders or skilled artisans in evidence. The wealth of the state was extracted, in patrimonial fashion, by royal warehouses and royal monopolies. Frederick liked to present himself as a "father and lord in dispensing justice," and set to work on a legal code whose main effect was to consolidate the king's power by prohibiting private warfare and the bearing of arms, and by outlawing cities that appointed their own officials.[42] Under this code, it was intended that local systems of law be preserved, yet without any *ius naturale* to bring them together in a rational manner. Privileges of the nobility were entrenched (trials were reserved to their peers), and oaths of fealty of vassal and lord were strengthened.

The effect of Frederick's imperialism on the cities of northern Italy was to lay yet another level of factiousness over that of normal patrician rivalries. It caused the solidification of city factions committed variously to empire or to church. Finding themselves exposed and vulnerable because of their size, yet unable to form lasting alliances or federations because of a lack of trust of each other and a lack of a sense of how cities might enter into an orderly arrangement of contending forces (a *kosmos*), the northern cities looked to the protection of the church against the empire, or alternatively to the empire against the ambitions of the church. Two parties (factions) emerged in the northern cities — the party of the church (the Guelfs) and the party of the empire (the Ghibellines). City dwellers would side with these powers for a variety of reasons. Sometimes for no more than gaining support in familial battles for control of a town; other times because of a belief that either empire or church could institute a peace over the factiousness of the cities; other times in order to play off one power against another and gain breathing space for the city.

One notable casualty of this extremely internecine politics was Dante Alighieri, Florence's great philosophical poet.

It happened that the *Parte Guelfa* was the dominant party in Florence (indeed until 1280 it was part of the city's constitution). But, signifying the decline of the imperial threat to Florence and the way in which familial struggles and ambitions often overdetermined church or imperial allegiances, in the period 1295–1300 the Florentine Guelfs split into Blacks and Whites. Naturally enough, the leaders of these factions within a faction were personal-familial enemies. But the split reflected a deeper shift in the topographical interests of the Guelf "new men" who were increasingly doing business with Ghibelline cities and territories. The conflict of the factions came to a head during the pontificate of Boniface VIII, who supported the Blacks "by all the considerable means at his disposal,"[43] and who even entered into an alliance with the French monarchy to pacify the city. With church and French support, the (pro-church) Blacks exiled the compromise-minded Whites from the city in 1302. Amongst their number was Dante, a White who was in practice an ardent admirer of the imperialist idea, but by default a moderate (a White) in a Guelf city. After being expatriated, Dante never returned to Florence, and lived out his life in peripatetic exile, composing his great epic of the poet-wanderer, the *Divine Comedy*, and exorcising his disgust with the factious city.

NOTES

1. Henri Pirenne, *Medieval Cities: Their Origins and the Revival of Trade* (Princeton, N.J.: Princeton University Press, 1952), p. 8.
2. Ibid., p. 7.
3. Ibid., p. 9.
4. Ibid., p. 7.
5. Ibid., p. 9.
6. Ibid., p. 10.
7. Jack Lindsay, *Byzantium Into Europe: The Story of Byzantium as the First Europe (326–1204 AD) and Its Further Contribution till 1453 AD* (London: Bodley Head, 1952).
8. Edward Burman, *Emperor to Emperor: Italy before the Renaissance* (London: Constable, 1991), p. 110.
9. Jack Lindsay, *Thunder Underground: A Story of Nero's Rome* (London: Frederick Muller, 1965), p. 49.
10. Pirenne, *Medieval Cities*, p. 16.
11. Ibid., pp. 17–19.
12. Erwin Panofsky, *Renaissance and Renascences* (New York: Harper and Row, 1969).
13. Pirenne, *Medieval Cities*, p. 24.

14. Ibid.

15. Ibid., p. 30.

16. Burman, *Emperor to Emperor*, chap. 3.

17. Pirenne, *Medieval Cities*, p. 30.

18. Burman, *Emperor to Emperor*, chap. 4.

19. This was formalized in the Treaty of Aquisgrana of 802, which assigned North Italy and Istria to the Franks, and Venice, Sicily, Calabria, and Naples to the Byzantines.

20. Vincent Cronin, *The Flowering of the Renaissance* (London: Pimlico, 1992), p. 176.

21. Mary McCarthy, *The Stones of Florence; and Venice Observed* (Harmondsworth: Penguin, 1972), pp. 244–45.

22. Cronin, *The Flowering of the Renaissance*, p. 177.

23. Pirenne, *Medieval Cities*, p. 31.

24. Ibid., p. 62.

25. Ibid., pp. 60, 64.

26. Ibid., p. 73.

27. Ibid., p. 80.

28. McCarthy, *Venice Observed*, chap. 2.

29. Gene Brucker, *Renaissance Florence* (New York: Wiley, 1969), p. 52.

30. Murray Bookchin, *The Rise of Urbanization and the Decline of Citizenship* (San Franscico: Sierra Club, 1987), pp. 154–57; Pirenne, *Medieval Cities*, pp. 93–105.

31. Bookchin, *The Rise of Urbanization and the Decline of Citizenship*, p. 154.

32. Brucker, *Renaissance Florence*, p. 52. Only Paris, Venice, Milan, and Naples were larger.

33. Ibid., p. 69.

34. Ibid., pp. 23, 90.

35. Ibid., p. 116.

36. Leonardo Bruni, "On the Florentine Constitution," in *The Humanism of Leonardo Bruni: Selected Texts*, ed. G. Griffiths, J. Hankins, and D. Thompson (Binghampton, N.Y.: SUNY Press, 1987).

37. Brucker, *Renaissance Florence*, p. 97.

38. Robert E. Lerner, *The Age of Adversity* (Ithaca, N.Y.: Cornell University Press, 1968), p. 2.

39. Ibid.

40. Ibid., p. 3.

41. Ibid., p. 19.

42. Ibid., p. 28. "Any official, '*podestà*, rector, or consul elected by the men of a town' shall suffer death; the town where such an election has been made shall be given over to 'perpetual desolation' and 'all men of the same town shall be held as serfs in perpetuity.' "

43. J. K. Hyde, *Society and Politics in Medieval Italy: The Evolution of Civil Life 1000–1300* (London: Macmillan, 1973), p. 137. On the role of the imperial and church factions more generally, see Hyde, pp. 132–41.

6

KOSMOPOIÊSIS

THE MAKING OF WORLDS

Dante's cantos are a work of *kosmopoiêsis*. They are a thinking through, poetically, of how a good order might arise in an Italy that existed only in the mind of exiles. And yet, like the checkerboard politics of his time, his *kosmos* is a hybrid—part-Christian but antichurch, part-Roman but imbued with a Christian desire for a mystical "oneness" that was quite un-Roman.

The first of the great Italian humanists, Dante Alighieri (1265–1321), exhibits the deep ambivalences of a humanism that is at the same time Christian, and of a learning that has Pythagorean-Platonic roots and Virgilian-epic ambitions, yet takes its cue from a Neoplatonic and Christian disgust with the city. The classical sense of forging accord out of the *agôn* of contending parties was difficult to square with Christian disdain for the discord of the city—its sense that discord equated mayhem, murder, or parricide. Christianity offered a vision of a unified society, hierarchically organized and anchored in the transcendental. The protagonist of the *urbs* saw the form of society arising *out of its very division*, and anchored in public places.[1] Where contending forces could be equilibrated, the city took shape. Early Italian humanism expressed the transition from an episcopal to a citified form of society, from Christian pastoral love to the friendship-amity of the city dweller. In the twelfth and thirteenth centuries, humanism represented the intersection of Christianity with classical law and learning. It sought to make a *unity* out of the *diversity* of transcendental and urban forms. Arguably, this was an attempt to reconcile the irreconcilable—humanism was bound eventually and necessarily to give way to a consistent classicism, or tear itself apart.

Dante's *Divine Comedy* is reminiscent of the Neoplatonic revival of pagan thought in the fourth century C.E.—the last stand of the pagans against Christianity in the Roman west, although one which, because of the conditions of the times, was a halfway house between Christianity and a strand of pagan thought to which Christian theology was open. Of course by Dante's time another key strand of the thought of antiquity, viz. Aristotelianism, had been assimilated into Christianity via the scholarship of the Arabs. The infusion of Aristotle into the Christian canon by the Spanish Moor Averroës (1126–1198) produced Thomism, whose crucible was the northern French kingdom and its Parisian university culture. Where the French appropriated their pagan classics from the Spanish Muslims, the northern Italian cities appropriated the classical from Byzantine sources. As has been noted before, the Byzantine Empire for a long time maintained a presence in southern Italy. When the northern Italian city blossomed, Byzantium became a trading partner and a powerful cultural influence and conduit to antiquity. Like the Christian west, Byzantium had its significant Christian writers whose works displayed a Neoplatonic undertow — Gregory of Nyssa (d. 394 C.E.) and the convert Dionysius the Areopagite (ca. 500 C.E.), for instance. From the ninth century onward, Plato was copied and studied in Byzantium. But most interestingly, what occurred in the eleventh century, in the context of an important Byzantine renaissance,[2] was the development of an explicit synthesis of Neoplatonic philosophy and Christian theology begun by Michael Psellos.[3]

The exiled Dante adapted a loosely Neoplatonic schema as the philosophical frame of the *Divine Comedy*. But while Neoplatonism was the categorical frame, the structure of the *Comedy* was epic. And this is not at all contingent. For epic is a key, perhaps *the* key, way of thinking through *kosmopoiêsis*. It is the symbolic form in which the meaning of the whole — the whole of a society in formation and its underlying *kosmos* (order, arrangement) can be grasped. More particularly, what can be grasped through the epic is the *making* of this order, that is, the *kosmopoiêsis*. The epic (poem) is the telling of the story of the making of this order. The giving of an account of the birth of a form — the most difficult of all accounts (*logoi*) — is a very rare thing. It has sometimes been achieved by philosophy (Heraclitus, Plato), and sometimes by poets (Homer, Virgil). Epic epitomizes in a panoramic way an entire form of life. In the epic all the multitudinous elements that make up a society in formation are brought together and rationally connected, most commonly by the journey (which is also the *logos*) of the wanderer. The journey makes connection between "points" on a *topos*. The epic is a *topo-graphy* that is at the same time, to coin a phrase, a *choros-logos*. Different kinds of journey are possible. But all true epic journeys will share something of the spirit of the first visionary journeys of the Greek sailors who sailed by coasting around the earth, with the boundaries of their world (the coast) close at hand. The epic journey takes place in a timeless region—it is outside time, outside the normal (chronicled, historiographical) sequences of cause and effect, and so forth. Meaning *takes place* rather than originates *in time*. The epic journey reveals the core signifiers of a society. Historical action (and description) *occurs* within the limits of these core signifiers. Meaning, on the other hand, is uncovered in the *topo-graphy* of the wanderer: in the story of the long and winding and difficult journey of the wanderer in a time-free place, a *parousia*. This is a place where actors and events do not go forward, nor are they recalled sequentially, but are rather *simultaneously present as part of a self-contained totality of meaning*. Dante encounters republican Romans and imperial poets, Constantine and Charlemagne, and so forth, in his journey. The epic *topos* is *the place of meaning-for-itself*. By the end of the journey we grasp the self-contained totality of meaning of a social world—its *kosmos*—that is struggling to come into being, and struggling to become conscious of itself.

Dante's epic is one of disenchantment with the city—a journey away from the city. The destiny of Aeneas to found the city is missing. Yet, for all Dante's profound disillusionment with his city of Florence—a disillusionment of which his epic is born—the *Divine Comedy* is shaped by an ethos that is as much Roman and Virgilian as it is Christian and Augustinian. The journey begins in the *inferno*, which is a realm of particularity (of human beings isolated from each other). At first glance, Dante's hell is full of sinners in the Christian sense, those who—because of their unchristian greed, lust, violence, and selfishness—have broken the bonds of humanity. But underneath this conventional Christian surface is a set of preoccupations that are quite Roman in nature. Those who are assigned to hell lack faith, not just in a Christian sense, but in the more fundamental Roman sense of *fides*. Their faithlessness is their lack of character, which in turn is their lack of morality. The Romans understood that to behave morally was to have a character, and a character, first of all, was that which persisted over time in the human persona, and which thereby enabled personalities to stand up to the vicissitudes of human existence, to stand firm in the face of terror and bribes, threat and seduction alike. A person who had a character was reliable, steadfast and courageous in the face of hostilities, and temperate or moderate in disposition, which is another way of saying: not prepared to give way to the extremes of human appetites. At the heart of Roman character was *fides*—faithfulness to friends, office, *civitas*. Such *fides* recapitulated the earlier Greek admiration for reason and permanence above flux. Both the Romans and the

Greeks held in high esteem that which endured (as opposed not only to flux but also to that which was eternal, and which never had to mark out a place for itself in the midst of flux).

As we turn back the veil of Dante's Christic language, we find, as we follow the poet-wanderer through the hellish city of Dis—in part modeled, in Dante's imagination, on Florence, a city populated by those without a moral character in the *Roman* sense. The further significance of this is that the moral defects of those in the inferno are defects not just of the individual soul in the sense of the good neighbor, the good member of the Christian family, etc., but also of the city dweller. These souls are not only unfit as Christians—lacking appropriate self-sacrifice or self-denial in the name of family, community, and God—but they are also unfit as city denizens. Because of their lack of character they are unfit to engage in the friendships, markets, associations, and offices of the city. We find assigned to Hell not only the glutton[4] (whose feeding of his body is a sign that he pays attention only to himself), or the self-aggrandizing churchmen (who avariciously accumulate property rather than giving to others through charity and teaching),[5] or the misers (who hoard what others could have), or even the Christian-familiaphilic targets of the sodomite[6] and the suicide,[7] but also statesmen, kings, officeholders, and leaders who are treacherous, factious, and fraudulent.

Treachery, factiousness, theft, and fraud all erode the trust—the *fides*—on which a city is built. Trust—knowing that one can rely without question on the *fides* of another—is not equally important in all forms of society. In a hierarchical society, obedience is more important than trustworthiness. In a bourgeois (modern-dynamic-bureaucratic) society, enterprise is more important than reliability. But in a pure city society, where individuals are not tied together hierarchically or institutionally, familially or bureaucratically, trustworthiness (fidelity) is of utmost importance—as it was for the Florentine merchants who traveled the Mediterranean and the North Seas. The word (*logos*) is the bond both of the city dweller and of the traveler who recreates the city wherever that person settles. To break one's word (promise, commitment, *fides*) is to break apart *logos*, the horizontal connection of the city dweller-traveler.

How is trustworthiness/fidelity undermined? In Dante's inferno, we are presented with a number of ways:

(1) *Hypocrisy.* The saying of one principled thing (an *archê-logos*), the doing of another thing instead. When, in politics, hypocrisy flourishes, what follows are cynicism and the loss of faith by the citizen in government.

(2) *Fraud.*[8] The perpetrator of a fraud preys on people's trust. Fraud

is committed by false promises, false declarations, false testimony. It is the antithesis of *honestum* (morality, virtue).

(3) *Theft.*[9] Theft is a kind of dishonest robbery—it occurs secretly, rather than with the open violence of the bandit. Theft is committed by trusted employees, by responsible officeholders, and so on. Dante compares theft with the metamorphosis of the soul, that is, the loss of identity of the soul. The thief, in the act of stealing, loses possession of his or her character.

(4) *Betrayal.*[10] All of the denizens of the city are capable of betrayal: friends betray friends' confidences; business partners betray business partners' secrets; soldiers betray their comrades-in-arms; teachers and doctors betray their vocations; party supporters betray their cause; leaders betray their followers; cities betray their allies, their laws—even their own citizens.

Reflecting on his own bitter experience of the metamorphoses of his native Florence, Dante complained of her:

> How often within living recollection
> have you changed coinage, custom, law, and office,
> and hacked your own limbs off and sewed them on?
>
> But if your wits and memory are not dead
> you yet will see yourself as that sick woman
> who cannot rest, though on a feather bed,
>
> but flails as if she fenced with pain and grief.
> Ah, Florence, may your cure or course be brief.[11]

Dante's lesson is this: without trustworthiness, there can be no reliability; without reliability, there can be no consistency; without consistency, there can be no justice. Civic justice is a kind of extension of trustworthiness.

To act in the spirit of *fides* is to act consistently; likewise to act justly is to act consistently. The unjust person is one who is inconsistent. That person cannot treat like cases alike. The unjust *ruler* is also one who is inconsistent. The worst type of unjust ruler, the despot, is one whose rule is arbitrary. The despot is one who enjoys an *arbitrarium* (freedom) from any *archê-logos*; there is no law, no principle (*archê*) that governs the ruler's actions from day to day or from case to case.

It is not only untrustworthiness that corrupts a city. Dante also emphasizes the infernal role of factiousness and graft. Factiousness is the way in which the patrimonial-familial regime corrodes city politics. Factious personalities treat the space of the city as a battleground between families or family parties.[12] Graft[13] and simony[14] are traffic in civic and ecclesiastical office which wealthy families resort to in their struggle for precedence. This struggle, moreover, is often a violent one, driven by short tempers and explosive passions—by archaic feelings of vengeance, hatred, and frenzy that often end in sudden killings or other violent harm,[15] and that confound the continuities of a city society.

In Dante's view, factiousness is fed by pride, by the hope of succeeding by the suppression of rivals or rising by another's fall. Factiousness is also fed by envy, by the fear of losing power because of another faction's success. Pride and envy often result in a touchy overreaction to an offense caused by a rival, and this turns to wrath,[16] to the desire to hurt and to destroy so as to avenge an injury. What destroyed the ancient city of Troy was pride, and it was centuries before the city could arise again in Rome. Dante warns, in effect, that Florence is on the road to becoming another Troy. Pride and envy are traits not just of city dwellers, but of cities themselves. Florence and Siena are neighboring cities. They could be allies, Dante observes, but instead they engage in rancorous conflict.

For Dante the Italian city-republic—meaning Florence in particular—had become the captive of factious struggles of a diabolical kind. On the losing side of an internecine struggle between Black and White Guelfs in Florence, Dante was forced into wandering exile by the victorious faction. Parallel to this, the journey of the poet-wanderer in the *Divine Comedy*, as he leaves the Inferno and begins the ascent of Mount Purgatory, is a journey to discover how the deceit, betrayal, and factiousness of the Florence of his trials may be overcome. Part of the answer to how this might be achieved lies in Purgatory, a realm governed by a kind of Pythagorean principle: the balance of opposites. For each cause of moral corruption—in either a Christian or a civic sense—there is a countervailing force for good. Thus in Purgatory members of opposing political factions are portrayed as being on friendly and cooperative terms. Instead of perpetrating the destructive violence of feuds, they attenuate the violence by the forgiveness of others[17]—by a refusal of revenge and vindictiveness. In Purgatory words are exchanged, hymns are sung: language is no longer used as a weapon. The bitter antisocial atmosphere of Hell—with each person standing apart from the other—starts to be undone in Purgatory. Gestures of Christian humility play their part in the overcoming of the destructive force of factiousness, pride,[18] rage,[19] and familial arrogance, while Christian charity counterbalances familial envy.[20] The root of charity and humility is the selfless love of the Christian.[21] But this is not the Christianity of the church, which Dante regards as a greedy wealth- and power-acquiring institution.[22] Rather it is a Christianity of self-denial,[23] based on poverty and giving,[24] and which counters ascetical temperance to gluttony[25] and chastity to lust.[26] The structural principle of Purgatory is a pseudo-Pythagorean counterbalancing of Christian love to the earthly perversions of love (pride, envy, and anger) or to the excessive loves for temporal goods (avarice, lust, and gluttony).

Those who go through Purgatory and enter Paradise find it to be a place of harmony rather than factious discord. Paradise is a place of unity. But this heavenly unity is not, at least in the first instance, a simple homogeneity of outlook and disposition. Rather it is a harmony that arises through diversity. Even if Christian love and sacrifice animate all the denizens of Paradise, the dwellers in the City of God still have different functions and roles to perform. Dante's Paradise is an epic-poetical rendering of the Neoplatonic *nous* (mind). It is a realm where perfection is achieved through the medium of diversity. Paradise is composed of differentiated spheres:

(1) *The Moon.*[27] Those who inhabit the Moon attempted a religious life but failed. They gave up their vows and returned to the world. Yet they are reconciled with their own limitations. In moral terms, in one way they are failures: they lacked the courage or character to maintain their religious vows. But, on the other hand, they had the self-knowledge to realize this, and so do not blame their failures on others. Thus they manage to live without rancor and bitterness.

(2) *Mercury.*[28] Those who belong to Mercury are what the pagans called glory seekers. That is, they actively pursue fame and honor, but they also serve a greater cause (God), so that their glory seeking is tempered by devotion.

(3) *Venus.*[29] This is the realm of lovers. Human (sexual) love might be thought to have no place in a chaste Christian *kosmos*, but Dante observes that sexual love, where it is properly directed, enlarges its scope — it becomes a compassionate and charitable love. It becomes the kind of unselfish Christian love that ties families, kingdoms, regions, and offices together.

(4) *The Sun.*[30] In the Sun are to be found scholars — philosophers, theologians, natural scientists, legal scholars, grammarians, historians, and others — all busily engaged in a selfless pursuit of truth.

(5) *Mars.*[31] The inhabitants of Mars are warriors. Again, they are not obviously exemplars of the Christian spirit. Yet, says Dante, these are the warriors whose fighting is conducted in the spirit of self-sacrifice. These are the warriors, or crusaders, whose love of God inspires them to sacrifice themselves in the spread and defense of the Christian faith.

(6) *Jupiter.*[32] Rulers belong to the sphere of Jupiter. Their function is

to uphold order, right, and justice. A Roman-style empire best achieves this, in Dante's view. Imperial rule is the best form of rule, and his model emperor is Justinian, who stood for a clear differentiation of secular and spiritual power — church and state. To confuse the two, in Dante's opinion, only leads to the corruption of each. Imperial Roman-style government is superior to other forms of government. When Christ died under Roman jurisdiction, God in effect sanctioned Roman imperial authority. And the reason for Dante's admiration of imperial Rome is his belief that the "one government" of empire overcomes the factiousness of parties and cities. It offers one jurisdiction over all of humankind, and it alone has the authority to discipline bad kings and corrupt churchmen.

(7) *Saturn*.[33] In Saturn there are to be found religious figures and spiritual guides. Notably, we do not find there representatives of the institutional church hierarchy, but rather leaders of monastic communities, in particular religious leaders who spurn wealth and power and who insist on devotion to prayer and contemplation. Their concern is only with spiritual life; they stay out of matters of earthly government.

Dante has a strong sense of the differentiation of human capacities and roles. This places him squarely in the humanist tradition. Yet the question he has to answer is: *What makes the world?* What is the binding force/power that draws all those different roles, capacities, and offices together in order to make a coherent, meaningful whole? What gives form to an otherwise formless differentiation? In the classical humanist tradition, this binding force is the power of the public. The public place/space is the common thing that makes of a diversity, a union. So in Dante, also, there is a place — the heavenly garden — where all the different functional traits and tendencies, roles and offices — all the diversity of a good human society — come together. The passively accepting soul, the active glory seeker, the warrior, the scholar, the ruler, the religious — each with different talents and capacities are drawn together. Jews and Christians, men and women, children and adults, are all alike represented in this diversity. Variety is central to human existence. The society of Paradise is based on differentiation. Metaphorically, the garden of Paradise is a gathering together of individual flowers.

> Unequal voices make sweet tones down there.
> Just so, in our life, these unequal stations
> make a sweet harmony from sphere to sphere.[34]

Each contributes to a common good according to a specific ability. But what force brings harmony to the disparate elements? From each according to their capacity, to each according to ... what? What the warrior (scholar, lover, and so on) gives in accordance with their distinctive capacity is clear, but what motivates the giving? For Dante, it is Christian love. Mary is the center of the garden. Mary is the destination of Dante's journey. And through the love symbolized by the figure of Mary, *the ideal society forms itself as a single rose* — in which each soul is a petal of the one flower; each is distinct but made one by a love that is symbolized by the stream of heavenly light whose radiance bathes, engulfs, and merges everything into the original formless and infinite *archê* of things — into a divine oneness.

THE MONAD

The original One toward which the Christian poet-traveler journeys is a state of undifferentiated unity through which both sensuous physical imagery and conceptual thought are derived *and* transcended. The aim of the individual is a mystical union with the unity or Monad.

There is a powerful classical streak in Dante's work, as I have suggested. Yet this sits uneasily with the Neoplatonic and Christian mystical desire to transcend form and limit; in other words, to transcend what the classical Greeks viewed as perfection. What we see here is a reiteration of the dilemma of Neoplatonism in late antiquity. Like the Dantean vision, the Platonism of Plotinus was a kind of compromise,[35] forged in the declining days of Rome, between Greek thought and Christian other worldliness. The coincidence of Plotinus's life and the chaotic phase of Roman politics between the time of the death of Marcus Aurelius (180 C.E.) and the accession of Diocletian (284 C.E.) is significant. This is a period when the Roman, worldly order of things was being torn apart. Under the pressure of fragmentation, there was strong inducement to think kosmopoietically — to think how the world is ordered/arranged. For Plotinus the principle of reality is *formless*, and notably, he rejects Greek attempts to conceive spiritual reality in *spatial* terms. Correspondingly, he rejects the assumption of limiting conditions for the *archê*, the One — in sharp contrast to the view of (say) the Pythagoreans that the One was the limit (*peras*): that the principle (*archê*) of things, or in Pythagorean terms the principle of numbers, was the limit of things — and that what "made" things was their form. For the classical Greeks, goodness and power and greatness consisted in form. The power of creation was the craftsman-like power to shape matter. By contrast, Plotinus employs the metaphors of "flow" and "light" — Eastern metaphors — to describe the Monad. "Flow" and "light" are *indivisible streams*. Such metaphors are directly counter to the spatial metaphors employed in the Greek-Roman world to describe creation.

In Plotinus's treatment, an *outflow* from the One — an overflow from the golden river, an emanation from the light of the Monad — creates two lower levels of reality: the realm of the soul and the sensible realm of corporeal matter. The corporeal bodies (on the lowest level of reality) produced by the overflow of the indivisible Monad are extended in space and therefore spatially divided and, as a result, imperfect. The contained body cannot receive the full power of incorporeal reality. *Its limitedness is its imperfection.* Less imperfect than the body, but still imperfect, is reason (soul) — the second level of reality. The objects of reason are not corporeal shapes (bodies) but discursive shapes (forms) — i.e., geometrical shapes, ideas of beauty, truth, and so on. In Dante's terms, ideal conceptions of the self-sacrificing warrior or lover, the scholar or religious leader, are the objects of reason. Yet as distinct entities, these objects of reason are imperfect. Reason — as we have observed of the Greeks — lays things together. It moves *from* one object *to* another. Reason deals with what is not yet a unity. And in moving successively from one object to another — ever-restless, the Neoplatonists argued — it exists *in time*, another sign of the imperfection of reason. By contrast, on the highest level of reality — the *intelligible world* — each part or member of that world identifies, not with a specific form, but with the whole order of things. *Subject and object are identical.* In the intelligible world, each part is *distinguishable without separation* — without division, without any drawing of the line (the limit) so characteristic of the Greeks. In Plotinus Greek thought becomes its opposite.

In the intelligible world of the Neoplatonist, the intuitive person can comprehend the whole world and everything in it. By mystical union with the Monad, that person can enter into the self-contemplation of the One. The ambition to comprehend the whole world is consistent with Greek thought. The classical Greeks, through their cosmology, sought to produce, in the act of *kosmopoiêsis*, a rounded world capable of being taken in at a glance. But for the Greeks this occurred at the point of intersection of counterposed intellectual and corporeal shapes as they tested each other's limits in the central space of the city. Out of this clash appeared an intelligible form. This comprehensible form of the city signified an intelligible unity, but at the same time a paradoxical one. The space of the city center is limited. It draws to it all different types and kinds of social forces. The central space — not any one of the "types, kinds" — is the unity of the society. This central space, moreover, is the antithesis of the indivisible Monad. It is the central space because it has been marked out as such—by boundaries, limits, architectural markers, and so forth. What has been marked out is a space that belongs to all (however this is defined) of the agonistic forces of the city. It is, in Roman terms, the *res publica*. This *initial (archê) division* of space prefigures the *union of parts* of the city. This is not a *union with a unity*. It is not a mystical union—the entering of the self into the self-contemplation of the One. It is not a homogenizing of parts or the intimation of an indivisible union. Rather it is the unity of a point (without extension)—the Pythagorean *archê-number one*. It is the point of equilibration, the *fulcrum point on which the scales of justice are balanced*.

In both Neoplatonic and Dantean treatments, the One is infinite, rather than finite. It is not the equilibrium point at which each force learns its limits; rather the One is an entity free of all external limitation, but which nonetheless gratuitously emanates and disperses the forms that the soul reasons about and, in doing so, might be said to impose limits on itself and to create an imperfect finitude in contrast to perfect infinitude. From a Neoplatonic perspective, finitude is a disqualification for anything to be considered as belonging to the highest reality. Limitation (even in the guise of the forms of beauty, truth, or justice) is a deficiency. The One is infinite and formless and undifferentiated. Soul and matter are steps down from this perfection—the supreme object of aspiration—which human beings can really only comprehend in a mystical union: a *union with a unity*. The pluralization and differentiation created by the overflow (plenitude) of the One is a fragmentation of the indivisible perfection of the highest reality, and thus less than it. What is perfect emanates what is less perfect. There is a procession (*proodos*)—a formless, everlasting, infinite stream of life—flowing from the One. It can be compared to an outflow of light from the sun, like the light flowing into a Gothic cathedral. It is the overflow of a superabundant, infinite, undiminishable power with inexhaustible energy. The self-contemplation of the Monad is creation, and it creates without will, need, affection, concern, or movement. Creation is a gesture of divine generosity. The Monad has no need of its products. Creation is an act of pure uselessness. The Monad creates without temporal beginning or end, producing a pluralization of *logoi*, and a worldwide soul (*logos*), corporeal bodies, and so on. Spiritual (human) beings, though, partake in something of the nature of this creation. They are creatures who, in the overflow of creation, *create themselves*. These beings are self constituted. They are the souls who turn back upon themselves and imitate the perfection of their source to the best of their powers through self-contemplation and the mystical union with the One.

Yet the overflow of creation is also a descent, a fall. Spiritual beings are self constituted; they choose who they are, yet plunge from the heights of the universe downward through the intermediate level of the planetary spheres (the rational soul, the forms), further downward to the realm of sensuous materiality — the realm of physical bodies, bodily emotions, sexuality, appetites, passions, bodily pleasure, anger — or, to anticipate the Neoplatonizing Christians, to the greed, lust, and so forth, of irrational souls. What is wrong with life lived on the lower level is that it is unwholesome. The body (sensuous matter) in particular is unwholesome, because bodies of necessity are divided, plural. Bodies in themselves do not even have speech/reason to gather themselves together. Bodies are fragmented, limited, particularistic. Like the souls in Dante's Hell, each body is isolated and uncommunicative; each body is attached through affection to itself, cut off from other bodies. Such separateness is the source of evil, imperfection, and disease (natural evil). This is quite unlike the pre-Socratic/Pythagorean account of evil, where one part oversteps the limit and overwhelms another part. Instead, in the Neoplatonic scheme of things, to be apart is the source of evil. The body intimates evil because it is the prison-house of separation, the temple of self-regard. In contrast, to do well, to be well, the individual has to overcome self-regard. Intellectual and moral acts occur, Plotinus suggests, when we are *least aware of ourselves*. (The person whose foot "goes to sleep" on him while reading — completely concentrating on ideas — is a case in point: that person has forgotten himself.)

Evil arises from the awareness of the particular self (body) — the interest in the particular self, the assertion of the particular self, the fear of loss of the self. How far this takes us away from the Greeks and Romans, who saw evil not in the assertive self but in the unlimited self, the excessive self that was stimulated, perhaps by appetite or pride, fear or anger, to overstep the mark, to act immoderately and thereby destroy the shape or form (the character) of one's part in the drama of life. For the Greeks, good conduct required that each part (self) remained well-proportioned in relation to all the other parts — in other words, that each was a beautiful part of a beautiful whole. For Plotinus even the best formed shapes — the forms that the rational soul can contemplate on the middle level of reality — are partial in a way that suggests deficiency. True, the rational soul can become absorbed in the contemplation of these forms, which is a step toward self-forgetting, but true self-forgetting lies first in the contemplation of the self as self constituted in imitation of the creativeness of the Monad as a step toward the mystical union with the Monad and the self-contemplation of the indivisible One. This unity is not beautiful—radiant perhaps but not beautiful—at least in the Greek sense of something well formed and shapely. It is rather a golden stream, a procession, a flow: fluid, indeterminate, and formless.

In one crucial and powerful dimension, this is what Dante's journey is—the return to the One. He learns about infernal self-isolation; he learns to control it with purgatorial self-sacrifice. As he ascends Mount Purgatory and enters Paradise, he encounters different but reasonable forms of life, and in a final beatific vision he sees them united by spiritual love in the radiance of creation.

Yet, for all of the power of its Neoplatonic-styled Christian conclusions, Dante's humanism equivocates as to what is the force of *kosmopoiêsis*—the force that orders or arranges the diversity of things of creation. Radiant love is one (the Christian) answer to this question. But there is also *character*, the pagan answer to the question. Characters are figures of reliability, trustworthiness, and constancy—figures of classical reason—and on that basis form bonds with one another. In Roman terms, such figures have *fides*. They are capable of faithfully carrying out promises and commitments.

Dante is not insensitive to this Greco-Roman way of seeing things. Indeed, many of those assigned to Dante's Hell are there because they lack character. And Dante reflects at some length on the Christian extension of this idea—the notion that the promises we make are made by us as a matter of free will. The freedom of will is, in the Christian reading, a gift of God. But gift of God or not, the point Dante makes is that a vow, made freely and continuously adhered to, is the basis of a civilized society. But Dante also observes that such promises need to be made *rationally*. In making a commitment we each need to take into account *our own capacity to fulfill the commitment*. To make a commitment rationally means to anticipate whether we have the capacity, in the face of life's pressures and vicissitudes, to adhere to the commitment. Rationality involves, in other words, considerable self-knowledge.

The breaking of promises, as Dante was painfully aware of from the Italian politics of his time, leads to chaos and traumatic instabilities. Those who have a moral character are those who do not capitulate to pressure (external or internal), and thereby betray their promises (or at least if they do, they own up to their weakness, like the souls on the Moon—they admit they were frail, that they made foolish promises in excess of their capacities or their character).

This is the paradox of the *Divine Comedy*. So much of its surface is Christian. Yet certain pagan themes are present beneath the surface. Dante's philosophical poem stands midway between the Greco-Roman world and the Christian world. It speaks to both. The very epic journey of the *Comedy* is a revival of Greco-Roman themes. The poet-wanderer, like all epic heroes, begins in the middle of things. The thiry-five year old Dante, all of a sudden, strays and is lost in the woods, plunged into a midlife crisis. This disorienting beginning of things is a metaphor for the life of the citizen of the *kosmopolis*. The epic wanderer is one who possesses the strength of character to begin a long journey that makes sense of all of the things of the world in spite of such an arbitrary beginning. The wanderer has the courage to accept responsibility for finding his way, and has the resolve to undertake the arduous journey.[36] At this point the wanderer commits to the difficult journey that will be his destiny. From that moment, and as long as the wanderer's character holds up, he makes of the fragments of the world a *kosmos*.

Correspondingly, the citizen of the *kosmopolis* begins in the middle of things—in the city center—amidst a sometimes bewildering amalgam of factions, interests, and personalities. The good citizen has the strength of character to deal with all of the human diversity that gravitates to the city center—to not be frightened by it or swamped by it, to not run away from it or be lost among it. In the middle of the apparent randomness of this human comedy, the citizen discovers something shared with other citizens: character. All actors in the human comedy—warriors and scholars, lovers and rulers—can be characters. Character, not love (*agapê*), binds human beings together in the good city. Or, if one prefers a less Roman, more Greek way of putting things: reason (*logos*) binds human beings together. The person of character is the person of *logos*. Character, *logos*, signifies that which endures in the face of the pressures, flux, arbitrariness, randomness, and vicissitudes of the world—that which stands in the face of the pressures of overweening appetites: greed, envy, pride, factious violence, and all the rest of human frailty and malignity.

Logos is what gathers the parts (of the city) together—in the central *choros* of the city, the common place. The *logos* is the "*betweenness* of places"—it is that which *relates* the parts of the city. *Logos* is not any one part of the city; rather it is the tie, the bond, the connection, the relation, the middle, the interchange between contrasting forces of society. It is this conjunction (syntax) that creates the meaning of the whole, that permits the synoptic "seeing of things together," and that permits the judgments that hold together in thought and action the different parts of the city.

FLORENTINE HUMANISM

Dante's confluence of Christian love (*agapê*) and Roman character is the first great construction of Renaissance humanism, even if the terms of Dante's synthesis of Christian and Roman are also at odds with classical humanism. Cicero's *humanitas* was the culmination-synthesis of all of the learning of the classical world — Aristotelian and Platonic, Stoic and Latin. In his lucid prose, he found a place for almost everything. To read Cicero we can indeed take in the classical world at a glance. But to read Dante we stand precariously between two worlds that do not fit easily together. Christian *caritas* and Roman *honestas* are not made for each other.

Dante's synthesis was certainly not idiosyncratic. It was not the construction of a truculent exile spinning a private fantasy. It is in fact a thread in the fabric of a twelfth- and thirteenth-century Roman-Christian synthesis, exhibited elsewhere in the attempted fusion of canon law with a partly resuscitated Roman law. In law this fusing was guided by the humanist precept that it was possible to *derive harmony from dissonance*. The task was to take two dissonant legal systems and reconcile them. The take-off point for this enterprise was Lombard Italy and the formerly Byzantine regions of the Italian peninsula that had preserved portions of Justinian's Code (*Codex Justinianus*), his elementary *Institutiones*, and an abridged version of his *Novellae*.[37] Stimulated by the rediscovery of Justinian's Digest around 1070, a new school of jurisprudence took shape in Bologna and spread to other centers in northern Italy, the Rhineland, and England. The task of bridging the imperial Rome of Justinian's *Corpus* and the Apostle's Rome of canon law was done by a methodical assembling of references (*allegationes*) to parallel or adversative texts. The intention was to provide solutions (*solutiones*) to conflicting references (*contraria*). Working from antinomies in the sources, the aim was to offer elegant, dialectical *solutiones contrariorum*.

Roman law was more suited to the needs of the city than canon law, and the growth of scholarly interest in Roman law must be accounted a response to the revitalization of urban life in the Mediterranean and the North Sea littoral. Of course, the Roman Empire was looked to for more than its law. As Lombard and Tuscan cities overthrew the rule of bishops and feudal lords, the political model of imperial Rome was postulated as an alternative to clerical and patrimonial authority.[38] Imperial Rome was, after all, an imperial *city*. And given the virtual disappearance of any reference to republican Rome in the Christian thought of the Middle Ages, it is unsurprising that city protagonists should cite the imperial city as a model. The program of *restauratio imperii Romani* operated on the cheerfully optimistic premise that the emperor was "son and minister" of the city and the title *Augustus* was a free grant by the city, its "senate and people." This empire, moreover, was ruled by laws, and was universalistic in character (a point manifest in Dante's *Monarchia*).[39] Admiration for imperial Rome was at the same time admiration for a *humana civilitas* that was putatively made up of Moslems, Jews, and pagans as well as Christians, drawn together in a manner reminiscent of polyglot imperial Rome. This humanism tended to look, at first, to the period of late antiquity and the empire of the Christian emperors from Constantine to Justinian, not the empire of Augustus. By the end of the fourteenth century, paralleling the decline in the authority of the church, Augustan Rome was openly propagated as a political model for cities like Florence.[40] This shift was an expression of the fact that humanism's reconciliation of Christianity and Rome was unstable. The rediscovery of Augustan (pre-Christian) imperial Rome was an important acknowledgment that the synthesis involved too many unresolvable antinomies.

The rediscovery of the classical past culminated in a reacquaintance with republican Rome, a civic model that was not explicitly imperialist, or ridden with Neoplatonic and Christian disenchantment with the city, and whose constitutive value was the *res publica* — the public space at the center of the city where the diverse forces of society engage politically with one another, where they speak frankly of their concern, be it that of *caritas*, righteousness, excellence, or otherwise. The *res publica* is the political common place, where the diversity of society is represented. This *common place* plus the *aretê* of the city dweller (the drive to render beautiful all deeds and things), plus the *character* required by a person for frank speech (in the Greek: *parrêsia*) in the face of opposition (Jew against Christian, imperialist against papist, stoic against epicurean) are *co-constitutive of the city*. Acting on these principles (*archai*) is the only thing required of *all* city dwellers. Republican Rome was the *model* of such a *civitas*. Like all models, it was to be imitated — not slavishly, not without ingenuity, and not without adaptation to radically changed social and economic, technological, and physical circumstances. Yet *to imitate a model, even ingeniously, falls short of kosmopoiêsis*. And here we confront one of the problems of the city tradition: its failure after the pre-Socratics to postulate a *kosmopoiêsis* in advance of the founding of the city-republic. Cicero's great *De republica* appears in the transition of Rome from *civitas* to *imperium*, while Machiavelli's *Discourses* appears after the city-republic of Florence has succumbed to Medici rule. The next great work in the tradition, Shaftesbury's *Characteristics*, is likewise an owl of Minerva. Its stoic cosmopolitanism solemnizes the fact that there will be no English republic but only another Augustan age of gifted humanists, empire, and colonial gubernatorial cities. This (British) empire, of course, prompted into existence an (American) republic. But while the American founders—notably Jefferson—studied closely classical and Renaissance works, the American Republic also lacked a kosmopoietical conception of itself at its birth. And when, two hundred years later, the work of the American founders finally received an adequate philosophical self-representation in Hannah Arendt's *On Revolution* (1963), the question she had to pose at the same time was of "the crises of the republic"[41] that, as in Cicero's or Machiavelli's time, were tearing at the fabric of the republic.

Models are a necessary, but not a sufficient, condition of civic and republican creation. Florentines in the fourteenth century discovered in Roman republicanism a model of a city-republic sufficient for a time to stabilize their republic—to provide it with some collective character—but not sufficient to provide it with real durability. Coluccio Salutati (b. 1331) and Leonardo Bruni (1370–1444) contributed decisively to the discovery of the Roman republican model. Both were Chancellors of Florence (Salutati: 1375–1406; Bruni: 1427–1444). Salutati promoted a Ciceronian republicanism that depicted man as "un animale civile," that stressed the importance of activity compared with contemplation[42] and the citizen's capacity for *amicitia* in place of the medieval *domus* and the cloistered withdrawal from the world. He spoke in his letters of Florence as governed by an aristocracy of *deeds*—the merchants and the artisans—rather than an aristocracy of birth.[43]

Here, indeed, was a Roman republicanism—*a city of deeds*. But would deeds translate into *character*?

This question was answered when the Florentines had to deal with the threat of the tyrant Giangaleazzo Visconti. Visconti was one of a new style of prince-tyrant that had started to appear in northern Italy in the thirteenth century. In the power vacuum of towns torn by factionalism emerged *signoria* (lords). In the period 1250–1350, all the major communes except Venice and a handful in Tuscany became dominated by local *signoria*—"princes" of the republic, who turned the office of *podestà* or the captaincy of the *popolo* into a perpetual office, and gained the freedom (*arbitrium*) to suspend and amend the legal statutes of the commune.[44] Over time, *signoria* became hereditary, and councils—where they continued to meet—became a legal fiction, although perhaps a necessary fiction, because the *signoria* came to power through council votes or acclamation, and upon this their tenuous legitimacy rested. The *signoria* mobilized popular support through networks of family-based parties that dominated city politicking. This, again, indicated the lack of a fully artic-

ulated civic identity in the cities. The Visconti in Milan were a typical
family-party. Magnates played a leading role in such parties, although
the web of family connections spread far beyond their magnate core. The
signoria bore all the marks of the worst kind of medievalism—cruelty,
lust, volcanic anger, and bloody deception. Yet both their ambitions and
their dynamism were modern in tone. Giangaleazzo Visconti is typical of
this modern prince. In 1385 he audaciously usurped his uncle's power in
Milan, and by 1390 had seized Verona, Vicenza, and Pavia, and had
turned his attention to Florence. This Visconti had ambitions to empire.
He even worked up a fantastic family tree that had him descended from
Aeneas. (Even tyrants grasped the importance of *kosmopoiêsis*, if only to
give themselves the dynastic legitimacy they lacked.) Giangaleazzo had
a large, well-trained army. Florence, by contrast, had to get by with unreliable mercenaries. It had no standing army, a consequence partly of the
classical republican view that fighting was properly done by the citizen-
soldier, not by standing armies which could be maintained only by imperial bureaucracies. Also the Florentine citizenry—who were, after all,
merchants and artisans—were not known for their fighting spirit. They
had mercenaries do their fighting. To compound Florence's difficulties,
her traditional allies, the papal state and Venice, refused to intervene on
her side against Milan—underscoring once again the tenuous nature of
any concept of alliance in the late medieval Italian context.

Given all of this, the prognosis for the survival of Florence as an independent republic was not good. In response, Salutati, in a series of public
letters to his fellow-citizens, made the case that the Milanese prince could
be resisted by republican/Roman/Ciceronian/Stoic steadfastness, that
arms could be matched by moral character, that Florentines were "new
Romans." Here was an answer to the question of what was the identity
of the Florentines—not imperial, not ecclesiastical, not familial, but
republican. The moral ideals of ancient republicanism offered Florentines
both a common bond, greater than their familial allegiances, and one
capable of carrying them through a time of difficulty. In 1399 the Florentine situation was perilous. Pisa to the north and Siena to the south
turned to the Milanese side. Florence was effectively blockaded. An apocalyptic religious fervor swept Florence. In 1402, after Bologna had fallen
to a massive Milanese army, Giangaleazzo surrounded Florence, and
expected to starve the city into capitulation. Again Salutati responded by
eulogizing the ideal character of the republican city, playing an effective
waiting game. The strategy worked. Florence outlasted Giangaleazzo,
who died of the plague shortly thereafter.

In this ethico-political intervention a growing circle of supporters, including the young Leonardo Bruni, joined Salutati. Some years later (in 1403–1404), after the threat of Milan to Florence subsided, Bruni wrote a *Laudatio* to Florence that explored the constitution (in all senses) of Florence, and that explained the survival of Florentines collectively as being due to their classical character.[45]

The *Laudatio* was evidence of a retrenchment of Christian and imperial interpretations of the past. In Florence, earlier, the trecento humanism of Petrarch (1304–1374) had idealized the stoic sage aloof from society, enjoying the contemplative existence that a universal and imperial city might afford. Trecento humanism was, naturally enough, colored by a medieval Christian perception of the world as *campus diaboli*, a place of tribulation, misery, and vanity. Quattrocento humanism, in contrast, exhibits an *amor mundi*, a propensity to see the world as a source of joy, pride, and serenity. Part of this resuscitated worldliness was a renewed readiness to idealize the citizen carrying out public duties in place of the stoic sage. Rather than emphasize, as Dante had done, the model of *Imperium Romanum*, quattrocento humanists like Bruni turned to the model of *Respublica Romana* and also to the inspiration of Greek works (notably, in Bruni's case, Aristotle, whom he translated). Bruni's *Laudatio Florentinae Urbis* criticized the enervating effect of empire on the brilliant minds of Rome. In the eyes of the quattrocento humanists, the greatness of Augustan Roman civilization was due to a generation—Virgil, Horace, Livy, Seneca—who were born and bred while the Republic was still alive. In this view great energies were not released but stifled by the universal and imperial city. So what, then, was the condition for cultural greatness?

On one level the view was that intellectual energies were released when human beings *played an active part* in their city—in the *vita activa civilis*. But the argument of Bruni and the civic humanists of the fifteenth century was not simply that political participation equaled cultural greatness. The argument was subtler than this. A citizen's republic, it was thought, embodied a balance of contestatory forces that an imperial city destroys, and it is *this balance that is both the principle of the republic and the source of cultural greatness*. This was true, in Bruni's eyes, not only of republican Rome but of ancient Athens as well, and both were comparable with quattrocento Florence. Bruni makes a topographical demonstration of this. Inspired by Aelius Aristides's praise (in his *Panathenaicus*) of *Athens* for upholding the golden mean between the disadvantages of plain and mountain-steepness (and their extremes of climate), Bruni lauds *Florence's* position on the Arno plain in between the Apennine mountain slope and the hills of Tuscany.[46] The claim of the Greek orator that the constitution of Athens was a perfect blend of the three forms of

government is likewise paralleled by Bruni's demonstration of checks
and balances in the workings of various Florentine offices and councils.
Bruni wrote that the city had nine elected magistrates, not just one, and
that the terms of their office were short in order to curb the insolence of
power.[47] Moreover, the city was divided into four quarters so that no section would lack representation among the magistracy. Each section chose
two magistrates, and a further chief magistrate was chosen on a rotational basis from the same quarters — and was clearly meant to act as a
fulcrum for a balanced order.[48] *Liberty was the consequence of this balance of
forces.* The relationship between the different offices and councils in Florence had to be understood as a system of measures to prevent, by
mutual checking, any of the agencies from arrogating tyrannical powers.

Bruni's topographical metaphor for balance was not a "grounding."
It did not evoke a "rootedness" in the soil. Bruni's writing of place, his
graphe of the *topos*, was really a "writing" about a relationship *between*
places. The Arno is written about almost as if it were a dialectical *solutiones contrariorum* — the solution (*solutio*) to conflicting references (*contraria*). In Bruni we also see a resurrection of the greatest of all of the
images of ancient *harmonia*. Bruni eulogized the *ordo rerum* (order of
things), the *elegantia* (grace), and the *concinnitas* (the elegant/skilful
joining of several things) of Florentine institutions, and described them in
terms of the Pythagorean simile of musical harmony.

> There is proportion in the strings of a harp so that when they are tight-
> ened, a harmony results from the different tones; nothing could be
> sweeter or more pleasing to the ear than this. In the same way, this very
> prudent city is harmonized in all its parts, so there results a single great,
> harmonious constitution whose harmony pleases both the eyes and
> minds of men. There is nothing here that is ill-proportioned, nothing
> improper, nothing incongruous, nothing left vague; everything occupies
> its proper place which is not only clearly defined but also in the right
> relation to all elements.[49]

Liberty was the consequence of the musical harmony of forces in the
city, and the city, in its turn, was like a castle in its defense of reason and
liberty, a shelter for freedom against the despot, and this was possible
because of the boldness and indifference to danger of the Florentines —
qualities that they had inherited from the Romans. Also, in Greco-Roman
style, Bruni portrays Florence as a liberal city, open to all those exiled from
their homelands, uprooted by seditious plots or dispossessed on account
of the envy of their fellows.[50] As long as the city of Florence existed,
nobody would be cityless. Bruni's Florence was in effect the *apoikia* of all

Italians rendered homeless by domestic tyrannies and other troubles. Florentine liberalism extended into the realm of international diplomacy. Florence had in the past used its authority to reconcile opposing views in other cities and had encouraged the negotiated settlement of differences between parties caught up in civil strife. As well as their courage and liberality, Bruni's *Laudatio* also cites the faithfulness of Florentines (quite the opposite of Dante's view). Whenever Florence entered into a league or alliance with another city, it did so with careful consideration. It looked at whether the cause of the alliance was just and whether Florence could deliver its side of the bargain. But once the city agreed to something, it never went back on its promise.[51] In Bruni's words, nothing could be judged more proper to the dignity of a state than a reputation for observing all its commitments. Conversely, nothing was worse than betraying its promises. Here Bruni draws the political lesson of Dante's invocation of the Roman ethos. As Bruni expressed it, a good city ought always to make its commitments only after due consideration. And once it had committed itself to something, it should never consider permitting anything to be changed except for those things that are not in its power.

Courage and constancy were the qualities mobilized prospectively and retrospectively by Salutati and Bruni against the Milanese. But, crucially, they were qualities that were summoned not in an inward-looking or narrowly patriotic way, but in the spirit of a generous cosmopolitanism by which Florentines thought of other Italians as citizens of Florence as much as citizens of their own towns.

Salutati and his circle called upon the character of the Florentines—their courage and their constancy—as the weapon against the Milanese. This character, Salutati judged, would enable the Florentines to outlast their enemy. The Florentine leader understood the mercurial nature of tyrants, and that with Roman perseverance—a propensity to dig in and wait—they might see Florence outstay the Milanese prince. As it happened, this wager proved the right one. Giangaleazzo Visconti's death in 1402—it is said from the stresses of his promethean effort at conquest—saw his empire disintegrate into factions and his generals grab individual towns for themselves. Florence had found a *model* that served her well. But whether such a model alone could continue to *sustain* the city was another matter altogether. Could a model, alone, do the work of *kosmopoiêsis*? The Florentines certainly learned a lot from Aristotle and Cicero. But without a Florentine Aristotle or Cicero, Homer or Virgil, it was not clear that the citizens of this city could form a clear and indelible impression of themselves. And without such a clear and indelible impression, it was not at all certain that the Florentines could achieve for their city what Ovid, in the closing lines of his *Metamorphoses*, expected for his own work of creation:

Now stands my task accomplished, such a work
As not the wrath of Jove, nor fire nor sword
Nor the devouring ages can destroy . . .

If truth at all
is stablished by poetic prophecy
My fame shall live to all eternity.[51]

NOTES

1. For a discussion of the idea of the constitution of society out of its division, and the difficulties thereof, see Claude Lefort, "Permanence of the Theologico-Political?" *Democracy and Political Theory* (Cambridge: Polity, 1988); Jean-Pierre Vernant, *The Origins of Greek Thought* (Ithaca, N.Y.: Cornell University Press, 1982).

2. The same century saw a reassertion (in 1020) of Byzantine authority in Greece after centuries of Slav domination. Byzantine hegemony was subsequently broken by the Fourth Crusade (1204), resulting in various European knights (the "Franks") establishing feudal domains in southern Greece. The fluidity of domination continued when Greece was conquered by the kingdom of Aragon (1311–1386). Later Athens fell into the controlling hands of Florentine and Venetian interests (1386–1456), while the Peloponnese was recaptured by the Byzantines who established a gubernatorial center at Mistra (1349–1460).

3. Paul Oskar Kristeller, *Renaissance Thought and Its Sources* (New York: Columbia University Press, 1979), pp. 152–54.

4. *Inferno*, Canto 6. The Cantos cited here and below can be consulted in any standard edition of *The Divine Comedy*. Specific lines of Dante's *Divine Comedy* quoted below come from the translation by John Ciardi. Dante Alighieri, *The Divine Comedy*, rendered into English verse by John Ciardi (New York: Norton, 1970 [1954]).

5. *Inferno*, Canto 7.
6. *Inferno*, Canto 15.
7. *Inferno*, Canto 13.
8. *Inferno*, Canto 30.
9. *Inferno*, Canto 24, 25.
10. *Inferno*, Cantos 32, 33.
11. *Purgatory*, Canto 6, Lines 148–153. Ciardi translation, p. 217.
12. *Purgatory*, Canto 6.
13. *Inferno*, Canto 21.
14. *Inferno*, Canto 19.
15. *Inferno*, Canto 14.
16. *Inferno*, Canto 7.
17. *Purgatory*, Cantos 5 and 6.
18. *Purgatory*, Canto 12.
19. *Purgatory*, Canto 16.
20. *Purgatory*, Canto 13.
21. *Purgatory*, Canto 18.

22. *Purgatory*, Canto 19; cf. *Paradiso*, Canto 27.

23. *Purgatory*, Canto 15.

24. *Purgatory*, Canto 20.

25. *Purgatory*, Canto 22–24.

26. *Purgatory*, Canto 25.

27. *Paradise*, Cantos 1–5.

28. *Paradise*, Canto 6.

29. *Paradise*, Canto 8.

30. *Paradise*, Cantos 10–13.

31. *Paradise*, Cantos 14.

32. *Paradise*, Cantos 18–20.

33. *Paradise*, Cantos 21–22.

34. *Paradise*, Canto 6. Lines 124–26. Ciardi translation, p. 427.

35. Plotinus, *The Enneads*, trans. Stephen MacKenna (Harmondsworth: Penguin, 1991).

36. *Inferno*, Canto 2.

37. Stephan Kuttner, "The Revival of Jurisprudence" in *Renaissance and Renewal in the Twelfth Century*, eds. Robert L. Benson and Giles Constable [with Carol D. Lanham] (Oxford: Clarendon Press, 1982).

38. Robert L. Benson, "Political *Renovàtio*: Two Models From Roman Antiquity," in Benson and Constable, *Renaissance and Renewal in the Twelfth Century*.

39. Dante, *Monarchia* trans., ed. by Prue Shaw (Cambridge: Cambridge University Press, 1996); see also Walter Ullman, *Medieval Political Thought* (Harmondsworth: Penguin, 1975), chap. 7.

40. Hans Baron, *The Crisis of the Early Italian Renaissance* (Princeton, N.J.: Princeton University Press, 1966).

41. Hannah Arendt, *Crises of the Republic* (New York: Harcourt Brace Jovanovich, 1972).

42. See, e.g., "Letter to Peregrino Zambeccari," in *The Earthly Republic*, ed. Benjamin G. Kohl and Ronald G. Witt (Philadelphia, Penn.: University of Philadelphia Press, 1978).

43. Marvin Becker, *Florence In Transition*, vol. 1 (Baltimore: Johns Hopkins Press, 1967), pp. 35, 178.

44. J. K. Hyde, *Society and Politics in Medieval Italy: The Evolution of Civil Life 1000–1300* (London: Macmillan, 1973), pp. 141–42.

45. See the Benjamin Kohl translation as *Panegyric to the City of Florence* in *The Earthly Republic*, ed., trans. Benjamin G. Kohl and Ronald G. Witt, with Elizabeth B. Welles (Philadelphia: University of Pennsylvania Press, 1978).

46. Kohl, *Panegyric to the City of Florence*, p. 137.

47. Kohl, *The Earthly Republic*, p. 169.

48. Elsewhere, in an explanation of the Florentine Constitution, Bruni painted a picture of a constitution that evenhandedly excluded certain noble families from the highest offices in the state and the lowest class from participation in governance. This was a city that was governed by two councils: one of the people (300 large) and one of nobility (200 large). For measures to have the force of law, they had to pass through both councils. Such arrangements were established to

avoid extremes. Florence looked to the mean, which Bruni described as the best and the wealthy (after all this was a mercantile republic) but not the overpowerful. See "On the Florentine Constitution," in *The Humanism of Leonardo Bruni: Selected Texts*, eds. G. Griffiths, J. Hankins, and D. Thompson (Binghamton, N.Y.: SUNY Press, 1987), pp. 171–74.

49. Kohl, *The Earthly Republic*, pp. 168–69.

50. Ibid., 159.

51. Ibid., 161.

52. Ovid, *Metamorphoses*, trans. A. D. Melville (Oxford: Oxford University Press, 1987), p. 379.

7

THE SCALES OF JUSTICE

CITIZENS AND PATRICIANS

Humanism has flourished where the city, as opposed to the locality or the nation, is the chief locus of identification for human beings. The city is the meeting place of people with different ways of life. It gathers them together at its center, and finds the ways and means of equilibrating them. The notion of a constitutional balance is one expression of the city's power of bringing together, in a *concilium*, different social classes, forces, and orientations. A recurring idea of civic humanism is the *balancing of opposites* to yield a beautiful resolution of contesting powers and forces. The ideal underlying this is *beauty*. This beauty is not an aesthetic ideal in the modern sense, but a public-political one.

In the classic humanist sense, a constitutional order is an order of beauty. Beauty is the effective and powerful resolution of contradictions, the merging of contraries into a union. Such unions do not last.[1] Achieved balances invariably are upset by unbalancing elements, and when that happens the task is for the city to achieve a new equilibrium in a new setting.[2] It is in its nature that the city, as a social and political arrangement, eventually will be torn apart by time, necessitating its being rebuilt in another place or time. The constitutional order of quattrocento Florence—Bruni's Florence—is typical of this story. It became upset by "unbalancing" elements—i.e., forces that it could not contain. Yet, while the city cannot endure immortally like a work of art, the city can create enduring works of art through which it will be remembered. So it was in Florence that, through the fifteenth century, the power of the city was displaced by the familial power of the Medicis. But not before Filippo Brunelleschi (1377–1446) and his successors Leon Battista Alberti (1404–1472) and Michelozzo di Bartolommeo (1396–1472) had found a way of expressing the humanism of the city in stone, and thereby memorializing it. In their

works of art, the image of the city and the humanist republic were to survive the Medicis' eventual destruction of the Florentine constitution.

Cosimo de Medici (b. 1389) established a principate—a type of personal rule—in Florence around 1434, at the end of Bruni's life and chancellorship of Florence.[3] The civic form of power (the balancing of powers)
could not stabilize itself sufficiently to eclipse the familial form of power.
Even prior to the rise of the Medici family, the Albizzi (a family of rich wool
merchants) had acquired inordinate influence in Florentine politics.
Although growth in the power of the Medicis was irrepressible, Cosimo at
least had respect for the idea of the *civitas*. Despite the urging of his friend
and ally Francesco Sforza, the Duke of Milan, he resisted assuming explicit
power over Florence. Instead Cosimo remained a citizen—one of six thousand out of the total male population (over twenty-five) of fourteen thousand. Yet he was a citizen with enormous wealth (based on banking) and
incalculable influence, who was able, because of this, to initiate a series of
alliances between Milan, Venice, Naples, and Florence that were the cause
of an unprecedented peace between these disputatious cities. Cosimo's
directing hand in Florentine politics kept factionalism and conspiracies to
a minimum. Wealth is one thing, but to acquire (as the Medicis did) enormous informal political power requires more than wealth. A crucial factor
in the rise of the Medicis was their talent for peacemaking. The Medicis
appeared in the guise of the patrician peacemaker. Lorenzo, Cosimo's
grandson (1449–1492), engaged in extensive diplomacy, and on at least
seven occasions arranged peace between major Italian powers. Through
the agency of the Medicis, Florence extricated itself from much of the
infighting that had plagued it both internally and externally, even if this
meant in effect the ultimate dominance of one (the Medicean) faction in
political life and the waning of the *civitas*. What all this demonstrated was
not so much the virtues of the patrician peacemaker, but the poor peacemaking and diplomatic skills of the city. This deficiency was age-old. It had
plagued city governance since the time of the Greeks.

It is unsurprising, then, that Machiavelli, in *The Discourses*[4]—his
bitter-sweet allegory of the decline of republican Florence—should single
out weakness in foreign policy as being at the center of a conjunction of
factors that undermined the republic.[5] Machiavelli alludes to the slow-
ness in republican decision making because of the balance of powers,[6] the
enriching of citizens rather than the public,[7] the corruption of supposedly
independent officials by the powerful,[8] and the envious and imprudent
opposition to Cosimo (which backfired badly),[9] as all contributing to the
decline of the republic. These factors, though, played themselves out
against the background of a fiercely divided Italy and the general

Florence, Italy (painting) ca. 1500. Anon.

inability of the Florentine republic to effectively navigate these divisions. For Machiavelli what Florentines lacked was virtue—in the classical (Roman) sense of that word. They suffered from a lack, or rather from a *corruption*, of character. No republic could survive, as Florence attempted, by relying on mercenaries to fight its wars for it, for such troops were inherently unfaithful.[10] Nor could a republic rely on exiles in political matters.[11] They were also unreliable. But the fault of character lay not just with foreigners in Florentine employ, but with the Florentines themselves. Machiavelli (contra Bruni) insinuates that they had difficulty maintaining their oaths and promises,[12] and that the mass of the populace was fickle and inconstant.[13] In such an environment, a firm patrician would appear attractive, and his steadying hand would inevitably translate itself into the power of a prince.

For a long time, even the most egalitarian of Italian cities had recognized the diplomatic role of the patrician. Through a combination of skill, wealth, and fortune, the early Medicis parlayed this into political influence. Initially this did not mean a constitutional counterrevolution—the erection of an oligarchy or anything of its kind. Instead, the constitution of Florence was outwardly preserved and inwardly corrupted—e.g., the drawing of lots for the Florentine assemblies was manipulated to ensure that only names loyal to the Medicis were drawn. Cosimo's chief constitutional ambition for Florence was the introduction of a body modeled on the old Roman Senate—an ambition that remained (however loosely) within the parameters of republicanism. Cosimo initiated the *Concilio Maggiore*, an elected body to which the Councils of Florence delegated powers of taxation and security. The *Concilio* lasted for two terms, from 1438 to 1441 and from 1443 to 1458, and then having grown unpopular (or rather the Medicis having grown unpopular) was replaced by a weaker Council of One Hundred (loyal supporters of the Medicis), the *Cento*.

Cosimo's overriding desire for Florence was "peace and leisure" (*pax et otium*). In pursuit of the latter, much of the Medici wealth was directed toward the endowment of art and architecture. The classically educated Medicis returned to the ancient idea of liberality: viz., that the justification of wealth is the spending of it on works of beauty, especially on works that can make the enjoyment of that beauty widely available. The Medicis were also sensitive to the view of the ancients that, because great beauty is timeless, great art and architecture could immortalize the memory of its patrons as much as its creators. Aware, in particular, of the Romans as great builders, Cosimo commissioned Brunelleschi to build the church of S. Lorenzo, to work on the Sagresta Vecchia and the rotunda of S. Maria degli Agnoli—and for Michelozzo to build the Convento di S. Marco, the Medici chapel at S. Croce, and the chapel at S. Miniato. In the cosmopolitan spirit of the Florentine merchant, Cosimo also funded the renovation of S. Spirito in Jerusalem and a college for Florentine students in Paris.[14] Impelled by a classical-leaning ethos, even private spending acquired public overtones. In 1444 Michelozzo was commissioned by Cosimo to design the Palazzo Medici. Michelozzo based his design on the Pythagorean-Vitruvian notion that the circle and the square were perfect shapes. The arcaded courtyard of the Palazzo forms a perfect square, while the windows and doors on the street are framed by semicircular arches.[15] What was created in this way was not just a private house but also a work of public art, built to be looked at and admired for its civic character. Notably, Cosimo rejected an original design for the house by Brunelleschi that promised a grandiose building that would have stood like a despot's castle isolated from its neighbors. In Michelozzo's realized design, the house sat on the street. Its geometrical shapes gave it a grace and a sense of completion, clarity, symmetry, and proportion that were not in the least forbidding or intimidating to the eye, and that signified an orderliness and restraint that was neither tyrannical nor monstrous. This was neither the quasifortress of a feudal family nor the lurid and ostentatious fantasy-palace of the modern prince.

Cosimo's grandson Lorenzo carried forward the program of *pax et otium*, but in a way that saw its civic overtones became more dissonant

Palazzo Medici Riccardi, façade, Florence.
Designed by Michelozzo, 1444.

and less clearly sounded. Lorenzo's manner, while shaped by a classical education and the example of his grandfather, acquired an increasingly mystical quality. In constitutional matters, Lorenzo (who "ruled" Florence from 1469 to 1492) at least notionally preserved the form of the Florentine constitution—as Cosimo had done—but under Lorenzo familial patrician rule became more and more entrenched in practice. While seeking to use constitutional methods as much as possible, increasing signs of independence caused Lorenzo in 1471 to purge the *Cento* and to strip the Florentine assemblies of their financial powers. He repeated the purge of the *Cento* in 1478, creating the Council of Seventy, after a conspiracy of a rival banking family (the Pazzi) failed. Lorenzo was caught in the Augustan dilemma of being the prince of a notional republic, and whatever his protestations or even intentions, the regime became gradually, even imperceptibly, more and more regal in nature. Following a French invasion directed by King Charles VIII, the Medicis were expelled in 1494 and the Florentine Republic was temporarily restored.[16] It survived precariously until 1512, when a conquering Spanish army helped the Medici family regain power and establish an unambiguously ducal regime (a Tuscan monarchy in effect) that gave up any pretence of coexisting with or accommodating republican or constitutional forms.

THE FLORENTINE COMMENTATORS

With the decline of the Florentine republic after the age of Bruni, and the increasing assertiveness of the Medicis, the orientation of the humanist idea shifted. Florentine philosophy moved from a civic toward what might be described as a mystical humanism—recapitulating the Neoplatonism of Dante's humanism. The Florentines Marsilio Ficino (1433–1499) and Giovanni Pico della Mirandola (1463–1494) exemplify this shift.

At the Council of Florence, convened in 1439 to repair the schism between the Eastern (Greek) and Western (Latin) churches, Cosimo met George Gemistos (Plethon),[17] a Byzantine-Greek authority on Plato who followed in the tradition of Michael Psellos.[18] Between council sessions Gemistos gave a revelatory series of lectures on Plato—revelatory, first, in the sense that he talked about a monumental figure of ancient philosophy only sketchily known in the West.[19] In the late Middle Ages, of Plato's writings, only the *Timaeus*, the *Phaedo,* and the *Meno* had been available in Latin, in sharp contrast to the extensive translation of the Aristotelian corpus.[20] (The disinterest in Platonic works is at least partially a reflection of an equal disinterest on the part of Arab scholars in Plato.) Bruni had added to the knowledge of Plato with his translations of the *Apology, Crito, Gorgias, Phaedrus,* and *Phaedo.* But still, in 1439, the reception of Plato remained hazy. Cosimo was also impressed with Gemistos's Platonic argument that the divine world possessed perfect order, harmony and economy, and the implication of this—viz. that God was to be found in beauty. Such was Cosimo's interest in these Platonic, or more properly speaking Neoplatonic, ideas that in 1459 he adopted a young Greek scholar, Marsilio Ficino (the son of the Medici family doctor), gave him a house and an income, and commissioned him to translate all of Plato's writings into Latin. Out of this emerged a Platonic commentary with a distinctive Renaissance twist.

Ficino's major philosophical work, *Platonic Theology* (1474), emphasized the remarkable ambit and mediational qualities of the human being.[21] According to him the human being, unlike other creatures, passes through all parts of the universe, is related to all of them, and has a share in all of them. More particularly, the human soul is directed both toward God and toward the body, that is, toward both the intelligible and the corporeal world. The human soul stands in between these, and thus can participate in both time and eternity. It can mediate between the upper and the lower halves of reality. The soul, observed Ficino, is the greatest of all miracles in nature. All other things beneath God are always one single being, but the soul is *all things together*. Therefore, argued Ficino, it may be rightly called the *center of nature, the middle term of all things*, the series of the world, the face of all, *the bond and juncture of the universe*. In Ficino, in this way, the idea of Man as the mean resolved itself into a religio-mystical conception. Thus Man was unique among created beings in possessing the ability to enter into the intellectual essences of all other creatures so that he *could identify himself with them* and in turn *take them into his own nature*.[22] Human beings, in other words, had a God-like quality to unify all natures within one nature. (The parallels with Dante's Neoplatonic treatment of the intellect are unmistakable.)

In his *Commentary on the Philebus*, Ficino emphasized that the principle of all things is the one (God), which is outside the multiplicity of all things.[23] The one and the good are the same thing.[24] The explicit assumption is that there is *one ultimate end* of human action. Note the gulf between Ficino's *Commentary* and Plato's *Philebus*. In the original dialogue, Plato asks the question: What is the cause of the good life? Is it reason or pleasure? Plato's answer is not that there is one good that makes for a good life, but rather that the good life is the result of the mixing of pleasure and reason. The good life is a mixed life. What interested the Greeks was *how* things mixed well together. To achieve a life that was well formed, the elements of that life had to be combined in a way that achieved the effect that each part was determinate, that each part limited the others, so that no part would be indeterminate or endless. For the Greeks, including Plato, "the one" was the *archê* of all things inasmuch as "the one" was the Pythagorean symbol of limits or determinacy. Plato identifies "the one" as the source of all goodness because "the one" is the limit (*peras*), and the limit is the source of all geometrical shapes. In Pythagorean-Platonic usage, a life lived badly was a life that lacked limits or determinateness—that lacked shape—which is also to say one that lacked form or beauty. As Plato, following Pythagoras, observed in *Philebus*, in certain kinds of mixtures, elements have a proportionate relationship, and are therefore properly integrated. They exhibit due measure and proportion in their relationship.[25] Limit (the Pythagorean "one") contains a plurality of things—whereas indeterminacy (unlimitedness) generates only more of the same thing,[26] rather than conjoining a variety of things. In contrast, for Ficino reason and pleasure are goods only so far as there is *some one nature that they share in common*,[27] something that contains, in the sense of incorporates, both of them, rather than (in the Pythagorean-Platonic sense) gives limit and shape to each of them, leaving them related but distinct. Thus in Ficino's eyes, when reason and pleasure are joined together, they have one thing in common, and because of that one thing they are good.[28] The "one thing" (the common nature) is not reason, nor is it pleasure: it is the unity shared by the one.[29] It is this *unity* (the divine "one") that joins things together well—by purifying things, measuring them, moderating them. Things are joined together well not by virtue of an impersonal, mathematical ordering of things (not by virtue of ideal proportions, shapes, and spatial relations), but by a divine agency that imparts truth as well as beauty and proportion to things, and that generates determinacy out of indeterminacy.

It is in this manner that Ficino transforms Platonism into Neoplatonism. Yet interestingly Ficino's comments also pointed to an increasingly *modern* view of things. The specifically modern implications of Ficino's arguments are spelled out by Ficino's student Pico when he puts together two of Ficino's key propositions: (a) that Man has a godlike nature, i.e. Man takes all natures into his nature, and (b) that God ("the one") is not form, but gives form. Pico concluded, in a radical gesture, in his *On the Dignity of Man* (1486), that Man has a plastic nature, one not restricted to some limited form, and that Man gives himself his nature— that the excellence or dignity of the human being lies in the fact that Man *chooses* his own nature.[30] This proposition departs radically from the classical Greek preoccupation with the limit, shape, and form of things.

Ficino's Neoplatonic understanding of Plato ought not surprise us, given that Platonic thought had come to Florence via Byzantium. Still, this was not just a matter of the contingencies of scholarly influences, either. There was a *disposition* in Florence, on the part of the Medicis and their circle, to receive a certain kind of Plato in a certain kind of way. The case of Cosimo's grandson Lorenzo helps us understand this.

Ficino tutored Lorenzo, and in turn Lorenzo was close friends with Ficino and Pico. Lorenzo was a happy and hospitable person who, very much in the classical manner, cherished friendships. His patronage of the philosophers, though, had a meaning that transcended close friendship. It provides a barometric reading of Florence itself, or rather of the gradual disintegration of its civic idealism. The Florence of Lorenzo's time was a less wealthy city than in Cosimo's heyday. (Among other things, Florence faced the stiff competition of English wool producers.) Also the Medicis were less wealthy. Lorenzo could not endow the city like his grandfather. In comparison with the twelve buildings Cosimo erected, Lorenzo built three. So in the place of *city building* — the work of the *demiourgos* — comes Medicean support for the *interpretation of texts*, and the endowment of the search for texts to interpret. In exemplary fashion, Lorenzo commissioned Giovanni Lascaris to go to the East, notably to Mt. Athos, to search for manuscripts. (Lascaris brought back two hundred of them to be researched, at Lorenzo's expense.) Lorenzo did not initiate this kind of activity. It was Cosimo who had begun a methodical search for ancient manuscripts (in the Latin West and the Greek East). But under Lorenzo the weight of this activity increases, and as it increases it brings to the surface a tendency present even in the heyday of Florentine civic humanism. Instructively, even the epitome of the civic humanist, Bruni, was, as an intellectual, primarily an interpreter and commentator on classical texts, not an architect of the city in words, although his youthful *Laudatio* was an important exception to this.

Here is the essence of the matter — *the city requires builders, not commentators*. These builders might, like Plato, Aristotle, or Cicero, be architects of the city in words. But like the geometrical numbers that give shape to space, so their words give shape to the living city. The intellectual protégés of the Medicis, gifted as they were, were not builders in this sense. They were commentators on the "great" books, the "divine" books. Whether these books were Greek or Arabic, Judaic or Christian in origin meant less than the operations of commentary performed upon them, operations deeply rooted in the monotheistic religions of the Middle East. The task of the learned person in these cultures was to interpret the book of divine revelation. This style of commentary stands in radical contrast to the pre-Socratic epigram, Odyssean epic, Platonic dialogue, Aristotelian lecture, or Ciceronian exposition. The greatest philosophy of the ancient Mediterranean world reenacts the speech (*logos*) of public places. It can be read aloud. In contrast, the theology/literature of Middle Eastern origin esteems the scripture, the book, the written word — and especially commentary on the written word, *writings on writings*. When Ficino employs the mode of commentary — of writing upon writing — the aspiration of the citizen of the *polis* to objectivate and to build the city becomes displaced by the aspiration to fathom the mystery of the word of God through interpretation, commentary, exegesis, and so on.

Pico, indicative of a declining humanism, pursued the project of combining all the given cultural heritage of the Mediterranean world (Platonic, Aristotelian, Christian, Hebrew, Arabic, and so on) into one great synthesis.[31] For Pico, Jewish, Christian, and pagan thinkers all had insights into the truth.[32] Indeed each had a share in a common universal *truth*. This was so despite the fact that the monotheistic cultures of the Middle East were hermeneutical, while Greco-Roman civilization was objectivating (reifying) in nature. In the case of the former, the source of the culture was a holy or canonical book subjected to ongoing interpretation—*the one truth engendering a multiplicity of interpretations*—while the center point of Greco-Roman civilization was the building of civic places and spaces in which public action could unfold and be immortalized, and where the multiplicity of things and deeds could find their limit and form. While thinkers in these different traditions seemed to contradict one another, by including propositions from all of them in his "Nine Hundred Theses," Pico's intention was to show the essential harmony of their doctrines. Such a synthesis resembled outwardly the *humanitas* of Cicero: the effort to combine all the learning of the Greco-Roman pagan world. But to suggest, as Pico does, that the Judeo-Christian-Islamic conception of meaning (the generation of meaning through interpretation) and the Greco-Roman conception of meaning (the generation of meaning through making/acting in the world and the memoralization of that making/acting), could be synthesized, and not simply that they could tolerate each other (the old Roman position), was far more radical than Ciceronian humanism. It was also far less successful, at least in the hands of Pico. Indeed, today, centuries after the Renaissance, it is still not clear that the hermeneutical and objectivational, the interpretative and the "craftsman," principles of meaning can be fully reconciled.

THE WISE RULING OF SPACE

While Pico turned outward, beyond Florence, to develop a philosophical humanism that aimed to synthesize the greater part of the intellectual currents that had crisscrossed the world of the Mediterranean in the previous centuries, and in doing so to forge a union of interpretative and objectivational cultures, the great architects of quattrocento Florence, who persisted with the principle of objectivation and immortalization of the city, gave concrete expression to Bruni's vision of a city where nothing is ill-proportioned and nothing is incongruous.

The classical humanism of Florence's architects continued a quiet but insistent resistance to the entrenchment of Medici family power in the ducal era. The growing *hubris* of this power was the antithesis of the play of contradictory (intellectual, symbolic, social, material) forces that the classical humanist sought to represent in an objectivating manner. Yet such was the *spiritual* power of the humanist architects—such was the resonance of their civic vision, their ability to take the dramatic tensions of Florentine life (the struggle of classes, qualities, powers, and ambitions) and find a way not just of symbolizing those forces but of equilibrating them in their architecture—that the echo of their civic vision long outlasted the death of the city-republic and the rise of the ducal Tuscan state dominated by Medici descendants and orchestrated by foreign powers (most notably the Austrians). The strength and durability of this civic humanism was such that the later Medici rulers' love of the exaggerated and the bizarre—their passion for the fantastic and extravagant—was restricted to the interior decoration, gardens, and zoos of their palaces. As Mary McCarthy observed of the Medicis of the cinquecento and later, in the *decorative* arts, all restraints were lifted, and human scale rejected, as a proclamation of the license of the ruling family. In place of humanist decorum and elegance, they looked to monstrosities, typified by the special art collection maintained by Cosimo III (1670–1723) in the Villa Ambrogiana near Empoli, which contained portraits of unusual or monstrous flora and fauna, including two-headed calves and sheep and colossal trees.[33] The Medicis collected zoomorphic curiosities, decorated the interiors of their palaces after hideous fantasies, and embellished their gardens with tortured topiary work—yet, for all of this torporous decadence, their architects, as McCarthy notes, remained true to the old way of building.[34] And somehow Florence itself resisted their lurid fantasies.

When Goethe, then aged thirty-seven, finally visited Italy in 1786, he observed of Florence that it appeared to be the very image of the ideally governed city—an architectural representation of justice, equity, proportion, order, and balance. One of the chief tasks of an ancient hero, like Theseus, was to be a city builder, and in the eyes of Goethe, Florence had the air of having been constructed by an ancient hero and lawgiver to be the home of virtue and civil peace. Seen from a distance, in a bird's-eye view, the city, drawn up for inspection on either side of its green river, radiated a sense of good government in its orderly distribution of verticals and horizontals, in the planification of its surrounding hills and slopes—marked off by dark cypresses and measured by yellow villas—while Florentine painting, in its government of space, made every masterpiece a little *polis*. McCarthy comments that the Florence which Goethe had come to had suffered two and a half centuries of conspicuous misrule under grand dukes,[35] and the evidence of wise rule that Goethe thought he perceived was the *wise ruling of space*—the only kind of government, McCarthy opined, that the Florentines ever mastered, but crucially (and

paradoxically in certain respects) one that was passed on to later generations, like a Magna Carta, by the great builders of the Republic and their
successors. While the city that Goethe visited was to a considerable extent
a grand ducal construction—the Trinità bridge, the Uffizi, the extensions
of the Pitti Palace, the Fort of the Belvedere, the palaces of Via Maggio
and Via de' Ginori and Corso degli Albizzi were all done under Cosimo I
(1519–1574) and his deplorable successors—it held firm to the old way of
building, to the republican tradition of lucidity, order, and plainness.[36]
While the republic no longer existed as a political fact, it continued as
longing and nostalgia for good government that broke out in poems and
histories, architecture, painting, and sculpture.[37] This is perhaps the
greatest testament to the spiritual power of the Florentine humanist
architects: that their preference for the economy and restraint that comes
from the balancing of opposing forces—their desire for a city of art, and
an art of perfect balance—should, long after the humanist republic was
interred, continue to contain the spread of the lurid fantasies and extrav-
agances of the new rulers of Tuscany.

The architects were able to do what none of the philosophical interpreters and commentators were able to do: viz., to achieve the *kosmopoiêsis* of Florence. That they did this under the patronage of the
Medicis and their successors is one of those ironies that political life
throws at us. Under their guiding hand, Florence, like classical Rome and
Athens before it, was given the shape of a *kosmos* of justice. This *kosmos*
was made by the *archi*tects. They were the *archê* of the *kosmos* of justice.
That architects—artisans in the eyes of the Renaissance—should be able
to achieve this work of foundation ought not to surprise us. After all, at
the center of the greatest of the philosophical cosmologies of the ancient
world was the idea of the *creator-artisan*. Plato's term for the *via media* of
the creation of the *kosmos* was the *demiourgos*, craftsman.[38] Plato portrayed creation in this way: At the beginning, the *kosmos* lacks equipoise.
It sways; it is chaotic. While it is filled with "powers," these powers are
not balanced. The *demiourgos* orders this turbulent and incoherent welter
by arranging the relationship of powers according to a mathematical proportion and measure.[39] Plato's demiurge works from a *paradeigma* or pattern—a term also used by Herodotos to denote an architect's model or
plan of a building. In realizing its creation, the *demiourgos* copies the
paradeigma, just as the builder copies the architect's plan. The pattern, not
the craftsman, is the source of the order of things. But where does this
plan come from? In the classical cosmological conception of things, it is
most definitely *not* an outpouring of the genius of the architect. Such a
modern-romantic conception of things—perhaps first hinted at in the late

Renaissance in the persona of Michelangelo—is alien to the classical humanist cosmology. Rather what the architect, the beginner of the plan, does is to work with numbers that are shapes (geometrical numbers) and with proportions (ratios of numbers) that are "divine." The ones who possess the skill, even excellence, at working with such numbers create forms that are pleasing to the eye and to the human sense of rhythm and rhythmic flow (*rhuthmos*).[40] These forms—the forms of the *kallipolis* (the beautiful city)—balance the ebullient forces of creation and contestation.

SYMMETRY AND PROPORTION

The rediscovery of the notion of the balance of forces—both as specific to artistic practice and as a metaphor for politics—came when the architects of the Florentine Renaissance turned to antiquity. Vitruvius (Marcus Vitruvius Pollio), the Roman architect and theorist (active 46–30 B.C.E.), while obscure in his own time, proved enormously influential in the Renaissance.[41] Vitruvius's treatise *De architectura* (dedicated to Augustus and rediscovered ca. 1414 C.E.) confronted, theoretically, the problem of the relationship between the parts and the whole. Vitruvius called this the question of *dispositio*. For Vitruvius the aim of the architect was to achieve the "congruity" of all parts of a building. "The congruous" is a relationship between parts. "The congruous" is achieved where there is an accordance, harmonious relationship, or mutual correspondence between parts. "The disposition" of anything (be it building, city, or state) is its arrangement. A principal question for the architect is: *How can we arrange things so that they are not "incongruous"?*

For Vitruvius, and following him, for the Renaissance, the answer to this question lay in the image of a *well-proportioned* human body. The well-proportioned human body was a model of congruity, and the proportionality of that body was exactly what militated against incongruity. Vitruvius described how the well-proportioned human figure with extended arms and legs fitted into the perfect geometrical figures of the circle and the square. Through Vitruvius' discussion of perfect geometric forms, the Renaissance rediscovered a classical and urbane conception of form—quite different from the principle of *hierarchy* that had such a pervasive influence in the landed medieval world. Fra Luca Pacioli (mathematician, pupil of the mathematician-painter Piero della Francesca, and friend of Alberti and Leonardo) summarized this in a striking fashion in his treatise *De divina proportione*: "First we shall talk of the proportions of man because from the human body derive all measures and their denominations and in it is to be found all and every ratio and proportion by which God reveals the innermost secrets of nature." The human body is the starting point, the *archê*, because it embodies all of the ratios and proportions that are the key to the right arrangement, the "disposition," of things. In *De divina proportione*, Pacioli defines "proportion" as the mean between two extremes.[42] Proportionality in the antique sense meant the happy mean (the golden mean) between excess and deficiency, between the too large and the too small.

A further way the Renaissance had of imagining a good arrangement of parts was via the principle of *symmetry*. Alberti, in this connection, developed what he called the principle of duity or "mobile numbers." Such numbers were akin to Pythagorean pairs. A mobile number can be divided in a tripartite way. The number 9 can be written as 4 1 4 or 3 3 3 or 2 2 1 2 2. The mobile number is written as a sequence with an axis, with equal entities or pairs of numbers distributed on either side of the axis. As Pacioli put it, all rational qualities are divisible in this tripartite way. Applied to architecture, this becomes a principle for the symmetrical distribution of openings and rooms. The arrangement (or "count") of such artifices, for Alberti, demanded the positioning of equal entities on either side of a real or imagined axis. Alberti wanted to match solid for solid, void for void, window for window, and so forth. In an early version of his treatise *Ten Books on Architecture*[43] he wrote: "It seems to me that one of the most excellent arrangements that a building can have is the concordance and conference [*conferenzia*] of each thing, as one tribune to another, windows to windows, chapels to chapels, columns to columns, one member to another, void over void."

This conference of equal pairs does not tell us anything about the relationship between *different* parts. What is the proper relationship between window and column, window and door, council room and dining room, bedroom and kitchen? What, in other words, is the relationship between "opposite" parts? In particular, what is the proper relationship between opposite pairs: mobile and stable, female and male, rich and poor, odd and even, visible and invisible, light and dark, square and oblong? The Renaissance architect answered such questions by invoking the idea of *proportionality*. Different parts were expected to be well proportioned in relation to each other—neither too large nor too small. Proportionality involved *the equalization of two relations or ratios*. When Alberti designed the Palazzo Rucellai (1446–1451) in Florence, he did so by employing the classical humanist principle of good proportions (for example, the ratio of height to width in the rectangular parts of the windows of this building is equal to the relation of height to width in the bays of the building).[44] In such compositions, large and small windows could be arranged around an axis—large against small—and yet the large would not overbalance the small, thus destroying the symmetry of the whole, because the large and small were proportionately "equated."

As it detached itself from the medieval gothic ideal, the Renaissance offered its own ideal conception of the world: a world that exhibited a kind of mathematical order, much like the *kosmos* of the Pythagoreans. This order was meant to contain within itself many distinctive, well-articulated parts ordered in such a way as to achieve a whole whose effect was that of classical grace. Even when an early Renaissance architect like Brunelleschi, in works like the Foundling Hospital (designed 1419, constructed 1421–1445) or S. Spirito (1436), borrowed freely from historical sources (the Romans, the Tuscan proto-Renaissance, and so forth), [45] by drawing the various historical motifs together in a mathematical order of proportional requital, the Renaissance architect gave these buildings an extraordinary sense of serenity.[46] The appearance of such buildings was *kos*-metic. Their appearance was meant to induce in the viewer, or in the city dweller, a sense of harmony or contentment—of being at ease with the world. The gothic structures of the Christian Middle Ages also promised contentment, but in this case contentment of an *unworldly* kind. The earthly city was, after Augustine, a place of evil, sin, division, and discord. The earthly city was a place to be transcended, and the architecture of the Gothic church was intended to lead the eye toward heaven, leaving behind the discordant mundane order for the mystical light of the celestial kingdom. The Renaissance, in contrast, offered a much more worldly conception of harmony.

This worldliness is apparent even in the design of the Renaissance church, which departed from the asymmetrical composition of Romanesque and Gothic churches in the direction of a highly symmetrical centralized plan. The Roman Pantheon was an influential model for this, as was, in a more abstracted way, the Pythagorean-Platonic notion that the circle was a perfect shape. Brunelleschi experimented with the circular shape. He built the Pazzi chapel[47] (1442–1457) in the form of a squared circle, and designed a centralized chapel for S. Maria degli Angeli[48] (1434–1437), which was not completed because of lack of funds. Actually, no church was ever erected in Florence that was, *in toto*, a centralized/circular building—although such structures were built in other Italian cities. It was not an incidental factor in this that clerical opposition to circular structure was considerable. The rotational symmetry of the completely centralized church of the Renaissance[49] was unmistakably *humanist* in its spirit:

The prime function of the medieval church had been to lead the faithful to the altar. In a completely centralized building no such movement is possible. The building has its full effect only when it is looked at from one focal point. There the spectator must stand and, by standing there, he becomes himself "the measure of all things." Thus, the religious meaning of the church is replaced by a human one. Man is in the church no longer pressing forward to reach a transcendental goal, but enjoying the beauty that surrounds him and the glorious sensation of being the center of beauty.[50]

The "focal point" from which the spectator can "take in" the church interior as a whole is not a bench mark to which everything must be raised. Rather it is a kind of fulcrum, a point of equilibrium — the point at which contending forces meet and balance each other. "Man as the measure of all things" is not the imposition of a law on all these forces. Measurement in the classical humanist conception meant neither equality before God's law — a *law* that is natural, universal, that applies in all places and times, nor was it the work of a *ruler*, as in Plato's *Republic*, who lays down a standard to which all must measure up.[51] *The measure is not a ruler.* It is neither a human nor a divine lord. For the humanist, that which is measured represents a *balance of forces.* All that a human being does is stand in the center of things and observe the beautiful relationship between things so balanced. The spectator stands in a three-dimensional space — be it a space covered by a dome, an atrium, a courtyard, lawn, city square, polygonal central chamber, or whatever — and looks around at all the multifarious forces that intersect — gracefully, beautifully, resonantly — at that point.

Man is not "the center of things" or even "the measure of things," but rather the "ideal man" is an image of *centeredness*, of measured action, of *sôphrosunê*. For the Renaissance, the idealized human body was a source (a model) of measurement. Inches (*"onci,"* thumbs) and feet were supposedly derived from the ideal human figure; the dimensions of columns imitated human dimensions (their width a sixth of their height, a schematic of the "perfect" body; their depth a tenth, modelled on the distance from navel to kidney). In Vitruvius's schema, the ideal man is six feet in height, the foot is one-sixth of a man's height, and six is a "perfect" number because it is the sum of its factors.[52] But the human body represents *measure* in another sense — it is measure in the sense of *moderation*, of acting in a measured way, of *being balanced*, of *being centered*. This is measure in the sense of weighing (measuring) things in a balanced way on the scales[53] — the *bi-lanx* in Latin, the "two" — "plates, pans." This is measure in the sense of the Latin *modus*, signifying a limited quantity or extent.

Modus first entered the English language as a word meaning "architects' plans." It had connotations of "size," "limit," "method," "way of proceeding," — of something that set *bounds* (limits) for others to follow, in the sense that the fashion conscious (the modish) might today follow influential models. *Modus* was closely related semantically to the Latin *moderare* — to reduce, control — as in the sense of "keep within the limits." A measure is a moderate quality. A measured person possesses the quality of moderation. Such a person avoids extremes. Measure in the sense of the Latin *metiri* comes from the same Latin stem *mat-*, *met-*, or *med-* as mediate, moderate, modest, and modify. Measure shares semantic space with the Mediterranean (literally, the *middle* of the earth), with the idea of a medium (as in intermediate agency), and so forth. In the imagination of the humanist architects of the Renaissance, the human body superimposed on the ideal geometrical figures of the circle and the square was a symbol of measure. Vitruvius had provided a description of the "ideal man" whose navel was the center point of the square and the circle. Alberti reworked this to make the base of the pelvis (the actual midheight of man standing erect) the center point. Leonardo (in his famous Venice Academy drawing of 1485–1490) reworked the theme yet again. In his version, the center of the circle remains — as for Vitruvius — the umbilicus, while the middle point of the circle is the pelvis base. He achieves this by superimposing one image of the "ideal man" with raised arms and legs spreading apart over another image of the "ideal man" erect (legs together) and with arms horizontal. Unlike Vitruvius or Alberti, in Leonardo the square is no longer pictured as being within the circle but as overlapping it. In this imagery the body appears as a symbol not of rulership but of equilibrium — the naval or the pelvic base is a point that *mediates* all the bodies' (and by implication all human, all natural, perhaps all heavenly) motions and elements. It is not "Man at the center," but a "centered Man" — and this image of a "centered Man" is a symbol for all kinds of "centering," as for example, Francesco di Giorgio (1439–1502), whose vision of the city likened the parts of the city to the parts of the body, and who imagined the city square as the "umbilicus" of the city.[54]

The Renaissance "returned" to something that had deeply interested antiquity: the idea of a whole that is a well-proportioned, balanced way of relating opposite parts. The distinctive take of Renaissance thinkers on this idea was the notion that opposite parts could be *symmetrically arranged*. This suggested, further, the notion of a *symmetrical reciprocity* among the parts of the city. Symmetry meant the grouping of opposites around a central axis so as to produce a balanced effect.[55] As Heinrich Wölfflin (1864–1945, the great art historian and student of Jacob Burckhardt) suggested, not only the architecture but the art of the Renaissance as a whole rested on the idea of the symmetrical *contrast of opposites*. The Renaissance loved to work things out as oppositions, e.g. the opposition between horizontal and vertical, the oppositions of colors, and so on.[56] These oppositions were organized in an even-handed manner, and artworks were symmetrically built-up. Picture elements were grouped around a central axis, so as to produce a perfect balance of the two halves of the picture. There is nothing more natural to the Renaissance, Wölfflin suggests, than the juxtaposition of two equivalent figures,[57] or else the symmetrical composition with a central figure and an equal distribution of figures on both sides of the central figure. In Leonardo's *Last Supper*, Christ sits as the central figure positioned in between symmetrical side-groups. Underlying such compositions is the principle that *every direction has its counterdirection*, and every part has its *counter*part.

Artistic form, like social form, has to relate parts so as to achieve a meaningful whole. Renaissance art does this while at the same time maintaining a strong sense of the *independence* of the parts. Independence is maintained artistically by the clear definition of parts.[58] Each part (each figure) is sharply outlined. Clear lines separate part from part. The eye is led along lucid boundaries; the hand is induced to feel its way along sharp edges. Line has a superior value to light and shadows. The Renaissance style is objective—epitomized in the work of Albrecht Dürer (1471–1528), where the contour line is the essential element, and where everything is boundary and tangible surface. It is this objectivity that allows for the distinctiveness of parts. (In this specific sense the Renaissance is "an age of multiplicity.")[59] At the same time that an independence of parts is evoked by definitive boundaries and sharp contours, "the whole" is achieved through the coordination and balancing of opposites. Renaissance art, as Wölfflin observes, achieves its sense of compositional unity by *coordinating* these *independent values*.[60] The unity it achieves is a *multiple unity*. Opposites are coordinated so that no one of them overpowers or overbalances the other. Coordination rather than subordination, symmetrical reciprocity rather than hierarchy, is the key to the artistic form of the Renaissance.

This coordination of independent values is nowhere more exquisitely represented than in Raphael's *Disputa*.[61] Around an altar sit four doctors of the church, the formulators of doctrine—Jerome, Gregory, Ambrose, and Augustine. Their dispute is in no way rancorous. It is carried on in a spirit of peaceful coexistence. The four doctors represent four styles of Christianity—intellectual, contemplative, millenarian, and administrative. Raphael depicts a polyphony of voices, each with its own audience, each a distinctive voice, yet each part of a coherent whole. Each of the parts is independent, yet, as Wölfflin argues, ultimately the *meaning* of the picture lies not in its details but in its *fugal effect*, the dovetailing of all the elements. So that while the art of the Renaissance is one of strong contrasts, the gestures of any one individual motive can develop its fullest expression only in combination with its opposites—the great is surrounded by small things, the simple is juxtaposed with complexity, calm is opposed to movement—so that each restrains the other.[62]

HELLENISM AND THE VENETO

The Renaissance believed implicitly in the principle of *moderation*. Not moderation as a watering-down of strong distinctions, but rather the moderating of powerful forces in conflict so that they may coexist. In his copy of an Italian translation of Plutarch's *Moralia*, the English architect Inigo Jones marked with special approval a passage in which the author draws an analogy between music and medicine.[63] The composer, says Plutarch, does not achieve perfection by doing away with sharpness and flatness, nor does the physician achieve health in a body by eliminating heat or cold. Rather, the extremes are to be reduced to that moderation within which harmony and health are to be found. Just as in medicine so also in architecture, there is hot and there is cold. Neither should be eliminated. Neither should dominate.

The greatest Italian exponent of this ethos, and Inigo Jones's inspirer, was Andrea Palladio (1508–1580), the provincial Vicenzian architect whose work represents the most perfect and purest rendering of the Renaissance's preoccupation with order, proportion, and harmony. Palladio's architectural designs are an unsurpassed expression of the idealized mathematical order that lay at the heart of the civic humanist imagination. His work was both a continuation and a summation of what had been started by the classical humanists of the Florentine quattrocento. While the ducal regime of the Medicis gradually reduced the vigor of civic humanism in the Tuscan world, the opportunities for its expression persisted in the cities of the Veneto, where the hegemonic city of Venice retained its republican character.

Palladio's personal story is well known: born into an artisan family, his exceptional talents were recognized by such aristocratic patrons as Giorgio Trissino (1478–1550) and later Daniele Barbaro (1514–1570), who educated him and promoted his work. Palladio transformed the face of the city of Vicenza, and its surrounds, designing palaces and villas (for the Vicenzian city nobility) that displayed in their layout a powerful understanding of the humanist aspirations that had percolated through the Italian city-republics, and which, interwoven with the very idea of the city, had come down from the Greco-Roman period. The social form of the city had never completely died out on the Mediterranean littoral and its immediate hinterland, neither in the time of the long decline of the Roman Empire nor during the Middle Ages. One of the centers where the city ethos survived was in the university city of Padua. During the Middle Ages and into the Renaissance, the University of Padua was a key center of Aristotelianism — though not of the Thomist type that had accommodated Aristotle to the demands of princely, hierarchical, and regal government.

Part of the exceptionalism of the cities of the Veneto — cities like Padua and Venice — can be explained by Byzantine influence. The long connection between the Veneto, its imposing civic power Venice, and Byzantium meant that a *Hellenized* Aristotle was present in the atmosphere. This Aristotle was received as one of the classic Greek authors rather than as an imaginary dialogue partner of Augustine.[64] Although interested in Greek scientific writers, the medieval European world had little interest in the broad gamut of classical Greek literature. In contrast, the study of this literature was cultivated in the Byzantine Empire throughout the late Middle Ages.[65] After the middle of the fourteenth century knowledge of this corpus of literature began to spread in the West, through the efforts of Byzantine scholars who went to the West, temporarily or permanently, or through Italian scholars who went to Constantinople in quest of classical Greek learning.

As a result of this, in the late fifteenth and sixteenth centuries ancient Greek commentators on Aristotle (Alexander of Aphrodisias, Themistius, Simplicius) became available, thereby balancing the interpretations of Arabic and Latin commentators relied upon by Thomistic Europe. Humanists published editions of such authors, wrote commentaries on them, and engaged in grammatical, philological, and historical studies of Greek literature.[66] (Ermolao Barbaro, for example, provided a complete translation of Themistius.) The efforts of the Venetian philhellene Aldus Manutius (born Teobaldo Manuzio, 1450) were exemplary in this respect. An assiduous publisher of classical texts, Aldus tracked down manuscripts and founded the Aldine Academy (in 1500), which met once a week to discuss (in Greek) literary questions and to identify texts that deserved publication. The Academy published a number of important editions of Greek authors.[67] When Aldus's press started, only four Greek authors had appeared in print in Italy; by the time of his death (1515) he had published editions of more than twenty, including Aristophanes, Herodotus, Pindar, Plato, Sophocles, Thucydides, and Aristotle. Hellenized Renaissance Aristotelianism found its most original voice in the work of Pietro Pomponazzi (1462–1525). Trained at Padua, and professor of philosophy at Bologna, Pomponazzi's views reflected the latitude of the typical humanist, freely mixing an Aristotelianism influenced by Greek commentaries on Aristotle with Stoic and even Platonic inflections. He also echoed the general humanist view that Man occupied *a middle place in the universe*. As Pomponazzi argued, Man is not of a simple but of a multiple nature, and is placed "in the middle" between mortal and immortal things.[68] In Pomponazzi's mind, the ancients rightly placed Man between eternal and temporal things. Man is neither purely eternal nor purely temporal, because he participates in both natures, and existing in the middle, he has the power to assume either nature.

Pomponazzi was a beneficiary of the Hellenic revival of the late fifteenth century, and of the dedicated translating, publishing, and commentating of Greek originals by humanist scholars. But even before this — in the more Latinized world of fourteenth-century Padua — a Greek inflection is evident. Paduan Aristotelianism was exemplified by the early fourteenth century work of Marsiglio of Padua, who in *The Defender of the Peace* (1324) postulated that it was the role of a "congregation of citizens" to deal with the mundane matters of this world (to make laws, institute governments), and not the "congregation of faithful" whose concern was strictly with the afterlife, and whose obedient subjection to God (and by analogy to clerical and princely superiors) was relevant only to their salvation, but not to their earthly life or governance. The effect of this kind of argument was to help open up a space for city life independent of seigneurial and clerical powers. Quite notably, by the sixteenth century it was quite a normal thing for young nobles of both Vicenza and Venice to be educated at the university in Padua. By the mid-1550s, a third of Vicenza's City Council were *dottori*, usually graduates from Padua, just as in the 1530s many of Palladio's future patrons — among them Antonio Valmarano, Pietro Godi — were either attending or had graduated from the Paduan university.[69]

Having soaked up antique intellectual sources in their law and other studies, the young graduates of Padua sought a civic art to match the civic-accented philosophy that their professors taught them. In what way could they build the public buildings, the churches, and their own (semipublic, semiprivate) palaces so as to escape the grip of the medieval gothic, and reinfuse the shaping power of geometric form into their city? The answer to this question lay in Vitruvian ideals. The intersection of the Roman Vitruvius and the Greek Aristotle seems distinctly Vicenzean. Typically, both Palladio's first patron, Giorgio Trissino, a diplomat and refugee from the sack of Rome (1527), and his second, Daniele Barbaro were Aristotelian scholars, and both made a close study of Vitruvius. Barbaro also was trained at the University of Padua; and in 1544, four years after graduating from that university, he published a commentary on Aristotle's *Rhetoric* and an edition of the *Nicomachean Ethics*. In 1556 he published an edition of Vitruvius's *De architectura*, with an extensive commentary, and illustrated by Palladio.

METRICAL JUSTICE

Like all interesting commentaries, Barbaro's on Vitruvius extended itself beyond the original. Antiquity may have been a model for the late Renaissance humanist, but it was antiquity with a distinctively sixteenth-century twist, one that expressed the classical idea of the balance of opposing forces in terms of a *symmetrical grouping of opposites around a central axis*. Indeed Barbaro (and others) tended to project a concern with symmetry back into antiquity. Vitruvius, for example, in the third book of *De architectura*, specifies geometrical or proportional rules for temples only, yet Barbaro in his commentary suggests that Vitruvius had meant the same rules to apply in house design as applied in the case of temples.[70] (Cesare Cesariano made a similar interpretative leap in his 1521 edition of Vitruvius.) In fact, the typical Roman house was not at all symmetrical. Palladio's interpretation of Vitruvius was even more radical. As George Hersey has pointed out, Palladio's *domus Romana* is really a Vitruvian temple with six columns across the front.[71] Rarely in fact were Roman houses ever as decorative as this. For Romans, exterior beauty and decorum were proper to temples but suspect in private houses.[72] But authenticity was not the point for the Renaissance humanists. They were not replicating the classical past, but revitalizing something of its *spirit* of dignity, restraint, balance, and harmony. Whatever else, the temple portico, which Palladio grafted onto the villa form, offered an antique precedent of symmetry, one of the few. If this conveyed the spirit of classical form better than the practices of the classical world, then the interpretative latitude of Barbaro, Palladio, and others was entirely justified. And what is more, it indicates the difference between the stultified revivalist, who appeals to the letter of a given "classical" period, and the humanist, who is more interested in the spirit of an order of things that instantiates a balanced union of opposites.

This union of opposites was achieved by the Renaissance architect through a *symmetrical* grouping of elements around a central axis. *Symmetry* entails the same measurement on either side of an axis. In a symmetrical building, a room (or window or column) of a given shape and dimension will correspond to an identical room (window, column) across an axis. One side (one part) is the mirror opposite of the other. They represent equal and opposite parts. In this schema a corner dovecote tower balances an identical dovecote tower opposite and equidistant from the axis; a large room balances an equally large room; a small room is the counterpoise of an identical room; the weight of a Corinthian column is matched by the equal and opposite weight of another Corinthian column, and so on. Six columns are distributed—three on either side—at equal intervals on either side of an imaginary axis that intersects the apex of a pediment. And so forth.

Symmetry for the Renaissance was a powerful device. Symmetry represented a congruent relationship between *the same things in opposition*. Yet, like Renaissance painters, architects and architectural theorists also concerned themselves with the more difficult question of the relationship between *different things*—between a large room and a small one, between column and bay. How are such artifices brought into a congruent relationship? A union of opposites cannot be merely the repetition of identical parts in contrary and equally divergent directions. That really applies only when opposing parts grouped around a central axis are *mirror* images of each other. The axial identity (equality) of parts was perhaps the simplest method of achieving the harmony of opposing forces that the architects of the Renaissance aspired to. Over and above this *symmetrical reciprocity* between parts, another kind of reciprocity was tried out. This second kind of reciprocity was based on *proportionality* rather than *axial equality*.

If we compare these two models of equilibrium, we find that in both cases reciprocity implies a mutuality of parts. It represents a state in which no part overwhelms or crushes or subsumes the other part. Each part is conditioned by (and limited by) a *counter*part. Yet where that counter part is not simply the *same* weight or size or shape as the first part, what then holds the parts in balance obviously cannot be the fact that their respective "weights" ("forces," "sizes," etc.) are one for one. What creates equilibrium in the case of unequal quantities is that the *ratios* of the parts are equal rather than the fact that the parts are equal. To achieve reciprocity via proportionality, what is important is not that room A is the same size and shape as room B facing it across an axis, but that (for example) the ratio of the length and width of room A is equal to the ratio of the length and width of room B.

Palladio was a master not only of symmetry but also of proportionality. It is a commonplace in Palladio's work that the ratio of the length to the width of the rooms of buildings he designed stand in a relationship

Palladio, S. Giorgio Maggiore, Venice.

of proportionality to the ratios of the length and width of other rooms. His Villa Malcontenta exhibits geometrical proportionality.[73] In the case of his Villa Sarego an arithmetical proportionality[74] is the key to the building, while in the example of his Villa Emo a "harmonic" kind of proportionality[75] dominates. The concern to achieve proportionality extends to the dimensions of individual rooms as well. In his *Quattro libri dell'architettura* (*Four Books of Architecture*, 1570), Palladio recommends that in houses the height of rooms should be either the arithmetic, geometric, or harmonic mean between the extremes of room length and width. What is at stake here is not simply artistically pleasing design. Rather there was a definite *ethical* spirit that underlay the Palladian conception. The house was an exemplar of this spirit. Or, if you prefer, it was a material embodiment of this spirit. At any rate, the ethical lessons of antiquity were not ignored by the Renaissance architect. Above all, the lesson that the good, and with it justice in both its broad and narrow senses, was concerned with the middle, with the mean.

This was a lesson that the Pythagoreans first imparted, and it was a lesson that Plato and Aristotle both reiterated. For the Pythagoreans the good was always epitomized by the mean. The good was that which stood in between extremes. A good life implied moderation, temperance — the moderating of opposing forces, qualities, and things. Palladio sought to realize this ethic in the ordering of architectural space.

For the Pythagoreans the ethics of the mean could be expressed mathematically. Ratios expressed the mean between extremes.[76] Such ratios were employed by Palladio to ensure the pleasing proportionality of a building. But these ratios, so employed, were also the prefiguration and the partial realization of an ideal society where proportionality governed the relations between its parts. To grasp the wider ethico-political implications of this, let us take the hypothetical example of wealth and its distribution in a *modern* setting. If we take contemporary social relations as our starting point, we can easily conceive of a model social arrangement where the working class (A) stands in relation to the middle class (B) as the middle class (B) stands in relation to the wealthy (C) in matters of taxation. Under this "moderate" tax regime, A:B = B:C. This is a case of geometrical proportionality.

This tax regime is scalable. The difference between richer and poorer does not disappear, but it is moderated. Take the following case: Say a worker today earns $40,000 per annum, a member of the middle class $100,000 per annum, and a wealthy person $1,000,000 per annum. If each person were taxed 30 cents on the dollar, the worker would have a net income of $28,000, the middle class income earner would have a net income of $70,000, and the wealthy individual would have a net income of $700,000. In this case, the rich person has 10 times the net income of the middle class person who in turn has 2.5 times the net income of the worker. This distribution of income is ill proportioned. To achieve geometrical proportionality, the worker would have to be taxed at 30 cents on the dollar, the middle-income earner at 40 cents on the dollar, and the wealthy person at 87 cents on the dollar. In such a case, $28,000:$60,000 = $60,000:$130,000, or A:B = B:C.

Let us take another case: that of arithmetical proportionality. Again a theory of just proportions allows us to imagine acceptable (ethically justifiable) departures from strict equality (the rule of identity) in society. Let us consider the example of the possession of wealth in a just society. Where arithmetical proportions regulate the social distribution of wealth, a second term (a middle term B = possessions of the middle class) will exceed a first term (A = possessions of the working class) by the same amount that a third term (C = possessions of the wealthy) exceeds the second term (B). Where such proportions do not apply we get distributions such as the following: in a society of 100 persons with a total wealth of $100,000,000, 5 percent of this population possesses 90 percent of the wealth (= $90,000,000); 15 percent of the population possesses 7 percent of the wealth (= $7,000,000); 80 percent of the population owns 3 percent of the wealth (= $3,000,000). The possessions of the wealthy in this case exceed the possessions of the middle class by $83,000,000; the total wealth of the middle class exceeds the wealth of the working class by $4,000,000. In contrast, a social arrangement regulated by arithmetical proportions would look something like this: the wealthy 5 percent of the population would own 40 percent of the total social wealth (= $40,000,000); the middle-income 15 percent would own 33 percent of the wealth (= $33,000,000); while the remaining 80 percent of the population would own 27 percent of the wealth (= $27,000,000). In this case the total possessions of the middle class would exceed the possessions of the working class by the same amount that the possessions of the middle class in turn are exceeded by the wealth of the upper class.

There is nothing to suppose that we should think of the distribution of tax burden between classes in terms *only* of a geometrical proportionality any more than we should *only* think of the distribution of wealth in society in the terms of an arithmetic proportionality. The point really is that *qua* thought experiments there are a number of ideal proportions — "divine proportions" — that might help us to answer those eternally pressing questions of the just relations between different parts of society. Geometric and arithmetic proportionality are two ways of conceiving of *good proportions*. Another way is that of harmonic proportionality. Harmonic proportions exist where the mean (B) exceeds one extreme (A) by a fraction (e.g. one third) of that extreme (A) and in turn is exceeded by the other extreme (C) by the same fraction (one third) of that second extreme (C), as in 6:8:12 where the mean 8 exceeds 6 by one third of 6 and in turn is exceeded in the case of 12 by one third of 12. This may be, again, another possible model of the acceptable departure from strict equality; a model that allows for variations of quantity but in a manner that is well proportioned — that is, to use a variety of metaphors, not ugly, or dissonant, or bloated. It is a departure from strict equality that is *scaled*.

This was the ethico-political message of the Renaissance architect. It was also what the age of the Renaissance most deeply admired: a well moderated arrangement of things. This was the promise of a good society — one that was not deformed either by the extremes of wealth and power or by the delusional dream of absolute equality.

NOTES

1. Jack Lindsay, "A Note on My Dialectic," in *Culture and History*, ed. Bernard Smith (Sydney: Hale and Iremonger, 1984).
2. If it does not, it becomes "stupefied into an inert acceptance of the existing world, with all its unbalances, injustices, falsifications." Ibid., p. 365.
3. Bruni's chancellorship lasted from 1427 to 1444. Despite Cosimo's wholesale purge of anti-Medicean forces in 1434, Bruni remained in office undisturbed, until his death.
4. Niccolò Machiavelli, *The Discourses*, edited and introduced by Bernard Crick, trans. Leslie J. Walker, revised by Brian Richardson (Harmondsworth: Penguin, 1970).
5. Machiavelli held senior diplomatic and military posts in the restored Florentine republic of 1494, and was thus well versed in the practical realities of what he wrote about.
6. *The Discourses*, I.34.
7. Ibid., I.37.
8. Ibid., I.49.
9. Ibid., I.33, I.52.
10. Ibid., I.43, II.10.
11. Ibid., II.31.
12. Ibid., I.11.
13. Ibid., I.58.
14. Vincent Cronin, *The Florentine Renaissance* (London: Plimico, [1967] 1992), p. 108.
15. Ibid., p. 207.
16. On this episode, see Christopher Hibbert, *The Rise and Fall of the House of Medici* (London: Penguin, 1974), chap. 15.
17. Born 1355, died 1450/52.
18. C. M. Woodhouse, *George Gemistos Plethon: The Last of the Hellenes* (Oxford: Clarendon Press, 1986).
19. Ibid., pp. 148–51.
20. Gemistos's lectures were later embodied in a summary version entitled *On the Differences of Aristotle from Plato*, known also as *De differentiis*. There is a translation of *De differentiis* in Woodhouse, *George Gemistos Plethon*, chap. 11.
21. For an English translation of a selection of *Platonic Theology*, see Marsilio Ficino, "The Soul of Man," in *The Portable Renaissance Reader*, trans. J. L. Burroughs, ed. James Bruce Ross and Mary Martin McLaughlin (New York: The Viking Press, 1953). See also Paul Oskar Kristeller, *Renaissance Thought and Its Sources* (Columbia University Press, New York, 1979), pp. 173, 188–91.
22. For another version of this argument, see Ficino, "Five Questions Concerning The Mind" [1476] in E. Cassirer, P. O. Kristeller, and J. H. Randall, *The Renaissance Philosophy of Man* (University of Chicago Press, Chicago, 1948), especially paragraphs 3–6.
23. Marsilio Ficino, *The Philebus Commentary* (Los Angeles: University of California Press, 1979 [1975]), p. 92.
24. Ibid., p. 102.

25. *Philebus* (Harmondsworth: Penguin, 1982), 25e–26a.

26. Ibid., 26c–d.

27. *The Philebus Commentary*, p. 348.

28. Ibid., p. 348.

29. Ibid., p. 354.

30. Pico della Mirandola, *On the Dignity of Man* (Indianapolis, Ind.: Bobbs-Merrill, 1965).

31. Agnes Heller, *Renaissance Man* (London: Routledge, 1978), p. 96; Paul Kristeller, *Renaissance Thought* (New York: Harper, 1961), pp. 60, 132.

32. Having spoken of the Arabs, the Christian Fathers, the Hebrews, the Pythagoreans, Plato and Zoroaster, Cicero, Aristotle, and Thomas, Pico put it this way in *On the Dignity of Man*: " . . . I have resolved not to swear by anyone's word, that I may base myself on all teachers of philosophy, examine all writings, recognize every school."

33. Mary McCarthy, *The Stones of Florence; and Venice Observed* (Harmondsworth: Penguin 1972), p. 149.

34. Ibid., pp. 147–48.

35. Grand ducal rule began in 1569.

36. McCarthy, *The Stones of Florence; and Venice Observed*, p. 143.

37. Ibid., p. 142.

38. On the ancient parallels of cosmological creation with artisanship, see Jack Lindsay, *The Origins of Alchemy in Graeco-Roman Egypt* (London: Frederick Muller, 1970), and *Ballistics and Blast-power: Concepts of Force and Energy in the Ancient World* (London: Muller, 1974).

39. *Timaeus*, 52d, 53b.

40. The Ionian word for shape.

41. In contrast, the model of *Greek* architecture began to make itself felt only at the end of the 1400s, due to the efforts of Ciriaco de' Pizzicolli (b. 1404) who began, at the age 30, a long series of travels to the Eastern Mediterranean — to Dalmatia, Greece and the Greek Islands, to Crete, Cyprus, Asia Minor, and Egypt. Florentine patrons, who were thereby introduced to Greek marvels such as the Parthenon, financed these trips.

42. G. L. Hersey, *Pythagorean Palaces: Magic And Architecture in the Italian Renaissance* (Ithaca, N.Y.: Cornell University Press, 1976), p. 29.

43. Ibid., p. 73.

44. Nikolaus Pevsner, *An Outline of European Architecture* (Harmondsworth: Penguin, 1963), p. 193.

45. Ibid., pp. 177–78.

46. In S. Spirito, as Pevsner notes, "(the) nave is just twice as high as it is wide. Ground floor and clerestory are of equal height. The aisles have square bays, again half as wide as they are high . . . Walking through the church, one may not at once consciously register all these proportions, but they contribute all the same decisively to the effect of serene order which the interior produces" (p. 179).

47. Adjacent to the monastic church of S. Croce.

48. For the Camaldolese monastry in Florence.

49. Brunelleschi designed the first one — the church of S. Maria degli Angeli, begun in 1434 but discontinued three years later.

50. Pevsner, *An Outline of European Architecture*, p. 182.

51. Hannah Arendt, *The Human Condition* (Chicago: University of Chicago Press, 1958).

52. Robert Tavernor, *Palladio and Palladianism* (London: Thames and Hudson, 1991), p. 37; Hersey, *Pythagorean Palaces*, p. 88.

53. The English word "scales" derives from an old Norse word, *skál*, for drinking-cup, plural weighing-scale.

54. Hersey, *Pythagorean Palaces*, pp. 93–94.

55. See, e.g., George Hersey and Richard Freedman, *Possible Palladian Villas* (Cambridge, Mass.: MIT Press, 1992), chap. 1.

56. Heinrich Wölfflin, *Principles of Art History* (New York: Dover, 1950), pp. 125–27.

57. Ibid., pp. 130, 133

58. Ibid., pp. 18, 19, 54, 65.

59. Ibid., chap. 4.

60. Ibid., pp. 159–61.

61. Wölfflin, *Classic Art* (London: Phaidon, 1953), pp. 88–89.

62. Ibid., pp. 258–59.

63. John Summerson, *Inigo Jones* (Harmondsworth: Penguin: 1966), p. 71.

64. For a discussion of the Byzantine Greek influence on the Renaissance, see Part 3 of Kristeller, *Renaissance Thought*.

65. Judith Herrin, "A Christian Millennium: Greece in Byzantium" in *The Greek World*, ed. Robert Browning (London: Thames and Hudson, 1985), pp. 215–52.

66. Myron P. Gilmore, *The World of Humanism 1453–1517* (New York: Harper, 1952), chap. 7.

67. Cronin, *The Florentine Renaissance*, pp. 180–83.

68. Pomponazzi, *De immortalitate animae* (Bologna, 1516), trans. as "On Immortality" in *The Renaissance Philosophy of Man*, ed. E. Cassirer, P. O. Kristeller, and J. H. Randall (University of Chicago Press, Chicago, 1948); see especially chaps. 1 and 2.

69. Travernor, *Palladio and Palladianism*, p. 24.

70. Hersey and Freedman, *Possible Palladian Villas*, p. 35.

71. Indeed, Hersey and Freedman, ibid., add, the house plan could have been traced from the temple plan that Palladio drew to illustrate Vitruvius 3.2.1.

72. As Hersey and Freedman, ibid., observe:

[Palladio's] design proposes to illustrate Vitruvius' Roman house with a type of facade that, at the very most, is rare in ancient Roman architecture. Most Roman houses, even the most luxurious, had little or no architectural ornament on the exterior walls, however gorgeous the interiors. Simple columned porticoes were fairly common. But the addition of the triangular pediment or *fastigium*, creating what looked like the front of a temple on the facade of a private house, was highly unusual, and indeed could be considered suspect and pretentious.

73. 12, 16, 24, 32.

74. 12, 18, 24, 30 (=10x10x10), 36.
75. 12, 16, 27.
76. On what follows, see Rudolph Wittkower, *Architectural Principles in the Age of Humanism* (New York: Norton, 1971), chap. 4.

8

THE FIRST MODERNITY

NORTH SEA HUMANISM

T he classical image of the balance of opposites fell into disrepute with the advent of the age of the baroque. The seventeenth century brought to the fore a new kind of social signification: *dynamis*, and with it a new way of conceiving the relationship of the parts of society. This is not to say that all that went before was erased. The interest in the classical persisted, but with decreasing returns. There was an emaciation of Greco-Roman ideas. Often they were driven into not altogether satisfactory marriages with reformed Christian and Gothic ideas. Other times they became the sterile object of scholarly revival. Important works of art and thought continued to be conceived in a classical humanist vein, but very few possessed the lucid power of a Machiavelli or a Raphael.

The philosophy of James Harrington (1611–1677) is a case in point.[1] Disturbed by the destructiveness of seventeenth-century English politics, Harrington looked to the model of the Venetian republic, and imagined England as a *new oceana*. Stressing republican moderation, Harrington proposed the doctrine that balance was the principle that made politics.[2] He imagined an England that had the equipoise of the Venetian republic but also an agrarian flavor that was peculiarly English.[3] Harrington had traveled to Venice, and had studied the legacy of the humanist republic first-hand. In the seventeenth century this legacy was in decline. But, because of the vigor of the Renaissance experience, its echoes were still audible to the attuned listener. Harrington understood that city culture thrived on the watery margins — that the coasts of the Mediterranean and the waterways of Europe had kept city life vital. Yet, at the same time, Harrington's "new oceana" was rooted in the gothic tradition of England, and idealized the armed landed freeholder (the yeoman) as the source of citizenship and republican virtue.[4] His chief device to guarantee a strong political balance was an agrarian law that had as its aim the turning of the "whole people" into landlords (by means of rules limiting the amount of property any person could acquire or else leave to a child).

A parallel ambiguity afflicted late sixteenth-century and early seventeenth-century Dutch republicanism, although in the Dutch case the attempt was made to blend the idea of the watery city not with the heritage of the independent gothic warrior-farmer, but with the legacy of reformed Christianity. Dominated by its waterways and the omnipresent sea, the Netherlands enjoyed a powerful civic tradition going back to the twelfth century. Although impeded by the rule of the Spanish Habsburgs (the Netherlands had become a province of Spain in the early sixteenth century) the Dutch nonetheless developed a strong late Renaissance strand of classical humanism. Among the notable figures contributing to this dyked classicism was the Flemish humanist Justus Lipsius (1547– 1606), who produced editions of Tacitus and Seneca, and who wrote a theory of politics, *Politicorum libri sex* (1589), based on Tacitus, and an ethical treatise (*De constantia*) based on Seneca. Lipsius's influence remained considerable in the seventeenth century. By the time of his death, *De constantia* had been reprinted in twenty-four Latin editions and translated into seven modern languages.[5] Lipsius's Roman stoicism was not antithetical to the mentality of reformed Christianity (after all, Seneca was a favorite of Calvin's). Yet, it was a temporizing influence on its rigidities and zealousness. The stoic acceptance of the world was a corrective to the activism of the Calvinist anxious to demonstrate affiliation to the elect — to the community of those predestined to live in God's grace. The interlacing of Calvinism with Stoicism was best exemplified in the work of Dirck Coornhert (1522–1590) and his pupil Jacobus Arminius (1560– 1609). Coornhert was a religious poet and dramatist interested in theological questions, who translated Cicero's *De officiis* and Seneca, as well as Boethius and the *Odyssey*. His work, like that of Lipsius, was a break from an unyielding Calvinism, and his defense of a loving and tolerant Christianity ultimately realized itself in Arminius's rejection of the doctrine of predestination.

The effect of sixteenth-century Dutch humanism at first was to temper the power of orthodox Calvinism, and to contribute to the relative air of political and religious tolerance in the new Dutch Republic of the United Provinces, which had won its freedom from Spain in 1579. Yet, ominously, Arminius's rejection of the doctrine of predestination led to a politico-theological dispute that deeply divided the newly created Republic. The latent polytheism of the humanist and the doctrinal demands of Christianity were difficult to reconcile, even if the attempts of Dutch humanism to achieve conciliation were heroic. Symptomatic of the declining space afforded to humanist eclecticism was the eventual imprisonment and later exile of Hugo Grotius (1583–1645) because of his criticism of the doctrine of predestination and his defense of Arminius's rejection of the sectarianism of the Calvinists.

The influence of the Dutch Renaissance humanists lingered into the baroque age of the seventeenth century, especially in the writings of Grotius and Johannes Althusius (1557–1638). Drawing on the experience of city leagues and commune governments, Althusius developed a model of politics based on ideas of federalism and *concordia*. (His principal work was *Politica methodice digesta atque exemplis sacris et profanis illustrata* [*Politics, Methodically Arranged and Illustrated with Examples Sacred and Profain*], 1603, enlarged 1610 and 1614.)[6] Grotius's 1625 treatise *De jure belli ac pacis* (*The Law of War and Peace*) offered a stoic version of natural law as the basis for a modern international law. Among other things, Grotius defended free access to the oceans for all nations, a *mare liberum*. Grotius's work reflected a broad taste in classical, Christian, and even gothic ideas. He wrote a history of the Dutch Republic's revolt against Spain, *Annales et historiae de rebus belgicis* (*Annals and History of the Belgae* [i.e., the Dutch]) that was modelled on the work of Tacitus. He edited the *Phaenomena* — a work on astronomy by the third century B.C.E. Greek Aratus of Soli — as well as the work of the Roman epic poet Lucan. Grotius published a Latin translation of the Greek pastoral poet Theocritus. He also wrote a volume of sacred poems (*Sacra*), a commentary on the Bible (*Annotationes in libros evangeliorum*), an introduction to the history of the jurisprudence of Holland, and a history of the Goths, Vandals, and Lombards.

For all its far-ranging intellectual interests, Dutch humanism lacked the strength of its Italian Renaissance predecessors to absorb all the conflicting currents of its environment into a *systematic* vision of the world. While it influenced events, it did not *define* them. We see this also across the North Sea, where figures like Robert Baillie, influenced by the Dutch, furnished Scotland with a mix of Aristotelianism and Calvinism, and a jurisprudence based on Roman-Dutch law that was fundamentally different in character from the feudal-derived Common Law dominant in England, and which provided the underpinning for an independent Scottish system of law that survived Scotland's 1707 Treaty of Union with England.[7]

In such ways Greco-Roman ideas survived, but only precariously, in the interstices of the seventeenth century. The network of extraterritorial power created between North Sea-facing Edinburgh and the ports of Amsterdam and Rotterdam is typical of such intervallic spaces. These belonged neither to the agrarian-feudal domain nor to the new territorial-absolute states that were appearing over the horizon of the seventeenth century. Extraterritorial power was nodal in character. It was a kind of junction power, the switching point of an alternating current between oppositional forces. If classical ideas were deployed as a symbol of this junction power, it was because these ideas provided images of ambidexterity, not least of all the ambidextrous condition of tragedy, apposite to the forward-and-backward rhythm of great entrepôt, riverine, and coastal cities.

The case of seventeenth-century France provides further examples of interstitial classicism. There a monumental process of state-building was underway, spearheaded by Henry IV and orchestrated by Cardinal Richelieu. The kernel of a centralized sovereign-bureaucratic state, the forerunner of the modern nation state, was being created. It was only when this state-building process temporarily faltered, that the classical seemed relevant—as in the years between 1630 and 1650, a time of protracted resistance to the newly centralizing French state. Revolts by towns, threatened with the loss of their independence, were common. Bordeaux, Paris, and Lyons, amongst others, challenged royal power—as did the many semi-independent fortified towns of the Huguenots in the south and southwest of France. The resistance by both towns and provinces to the protobureaucratic centralization of the French monarchy ended in defeat. But the challenge to the baroque power of the French monarchy provided a climate in which classically framed art momentarily flourished. The neoclassical drama of Pierre Corneille (1606–1684) attracted great attention in France at this time. In plays like *Horace* (1640) and *Cinna* (1641), with their Roman settings, Corneille lionized strong characters that acted with lucidity and courage to overcome enormous obstacles. But with the consolidation of Louis XIV's regime—and the end of challenges to the baroque state—Corneille's drama declined in popularity. Its sense of moral greatness was at odds with the official grandiosity of Louis's solar absolutism. But it set a precedent for the employment of classical themes as a critical measure of modern governance.

BAROQUE ART AND SOCIETY

The dominant mood of the baroque age—whether expressed in democratic movements or in the aspirations of monarchical absolutism—was hostile to any kind of classical temper. Both the puritanical extremes of the English Revolution and the political architecture of Louis XIV's Versailles palace, the grand extravagance of French absolutism, are testaments to the interior spirit of the baroque: its contempt for limits.

The effect of this on the visual arts was profound. The greatest art-historical description of the interior spirit of the baroque—that of Heinrich Wölfflin (1864–1945) in his *Renaissance and Baroque* (1885), *Classic Art* (1899), and *Principles of Art History* (1915)—brilliantly depicts the spirit of an age that was compulsively restless. In baroque art, Wölfflin observed, light and shadows dominate pictorial space, not the line.[8] This is so as to create an impression of *plasticity*. The effect is quasi-indeterminate. Baroque art lacks the classical stress on boundaries. Unlike classical art or architecture, the form of the baroque artwork no longer involves interplay, or movement, *between* distinct parts. Rather, in the baroque artwork, form *is* movement. Each part shades into another part. Each part is a transition to another part, and everything is enlivened and animated by this shifting. This is dynamic form *par excellence*. The whole of the artwork takes on the semblance of a movement that is ceaselessly emanating, and never ending. Everything in the artwork is endlessly deferred. The attitude of the baroque is subjective rather than objective. Under its auspices pictorial form becomes elusive. The world, as represented by baroque art, shimmers, rustles, and ripples. (Even in the court portraits of Diego Velásquez [1599–1660] the stiff costumes of his subjects shimmer.) Surfaces are broken up. Walls crumble. Edges become restless. Geometric lines disappear. Twilight displaces light and dark contrasts. Restlessness displaces calm. Distinct parts dissolve into amorphous, indistinct masses; lines are broken, dispersed; edges are unsteady; figures are disfigured. In Rembrandt (1606–1669), broken lines replace the contour lines of Albrecht Dürer (1471–1528)—color is not separated, as in the case of Hans Holbein (1497–1543), but flashes here and there out of a mysterious depth. In the baroque sculpture of Gianlorenzo Bernini (1598–1680), the folds of garments are restless, plastically indeterminate.

The baroque form is open.[9] It opens onto infinity. It is constantly moving. It constantly refers us to "what is coming." Finished figures are replaced by the apparently unfinished, limits by the apparently limitless. The tense, the unsatisfied supplants the harmonized repose. The vibrant, shimmering character of the baroque anticipates something emergent. This is an art of becoming rather than of being or of balance. (Even its mathematics is the mathematics of variation.)[10] In the classic art of balance, as Wölfflin notes, everything is boundary, tangible surface, separate object; in the baroque, everything is in transition. Classic art respects boundaries; the baroque negates outlines.[11] One represents definite, tangible values; in the other, transition and change are the primary values. In the baroque, the eye is led beyond the edge; everything is arranged with a view to change. Everything looks adventitious, shifting, becoming.

Movement bursts through the classical tectonic scaffolding. Nothing is substantial or tangible. When Holbein designs a tankard, it is a determinate figure; in contrast the late seventeenth-century rococo vase is an indeterminate work: it settles into no tangible outline. Baroque beauty is the beauty of movement, and this movement is one-sided.[12] That is to say, in the baroque, the symmetrical arrangement of oppositions, and the movement (back and forward) between opposites, disappears. The baroque conceals oppositions and upsets balances. It consciously *emphasizes one side*. It is a committed, rather than skeptical or classic humanist, art. Whereas every direction in the typical art of the Renaissance has a counterdirection, the baroque *delights in the predominance of one direction*. The unity it creates is *an absolute unity, rather than a unity of multiplicity*. Diverse values, as they are tied together, lose their independence. Parts are subordinated to a single motive.[13]

It is the same in the baroque building. Parts are handled in such a way that they are fused into a whole, creating a mass effect: windows blend with pilasters, pilasters with cornices, and so on. A form that "flows" (like time) in one direction supplants tectonic form:[14] it appears to be *going somewhere*. Independent values within the frame disappear, and so does the *relative equality* of those diverse values.[15] The baroque erases the very thing that maintains independent values in equilibrium with each other — viz. the presence of limits. The baroque architect is fascinated with limitlessness, or with the ambiguous disintegration of limits. We see this in the very way that the contours that clearly defined both the parts and the whole of the Renaissance building disappear in the baroque age. Elements that previously had been used to frame buildings or parts of buildings became a complex of lines that made it difficult to identify the actual contour of the building or decide where forms began or ended. Pilasters were superimposed on pilasters,[16] and the lines of the cornice were echoed several times over. Whereas in the Renaissance wall surfaces would commonly terminate with a simple pilaster, in the baroque the pilaster was moved inward, leaving the bare wall to form a corner by itself, or else corners were marked by quoins whose alternating sizes made the contours of the building seem agitated and restless.[17] The effect of such practices was to blur contours — to make them transitional rather than definitive, inconclusive rather than terminal. This served a more comprehensive intention of reducing the clear articulation of independent parts, and with it the sense that the specific qualities of each part had to be respected, and that the building as a whole was an equilibrium of parts.

The baroque architect did not work through individual forms, figures, and motifs, but via large masses.[18] Buildings were composed in terms not of contours, but of areas of light and shade.[19] This determined the visual effect of the composition on the viewer, and thus the meaning of the building. The eye of the viewer could not rest on specific parts because parts were not definitively bounded and because composition in terms of a mass of light tends to a movement of dispersal — the eye is led to and fro. The eye registers the building as elusive. It no longer absorbs specifics, but rather the generalities of motion. The eye is caught up in the motion of the building, and that motion is unending. Feelings of movement and transition were simulated by the baroque architect by the use of ellipses rather than circles or semicircles,[20] or the oblong rather than the square,[21] and by replacing sharp edges and hard angles with opulent and curved lines, and the use of soft and fluid moldings, convex and concave walls, and luxuriant and uncontained ornament.[22] Guarino Guarini's chapel of the Holy Shroud (1667–1694) in Turin represents what is practically the apotheosis of this. The interior drum of the chapel's dome is festooned with rapidly repeating raised and lowered ornamental surfaces, an effect which sets in train a sense of movement that is magnified as the eye is drawn up into the vault of the dome where the hatched effect of the ribs of the vault creates the appearance of frenetic movement all the while bathed in the ethereal light pouring through the vault windows that diffuses any clear and distinct perception of form. Seen from below, the elliptical shapes of the ribs (echoed in the ornamental motifs applied to the dome's drum) appear to hover somewhere in between straight lines and circles, in a state of linear ambiguity. At a glance, the interior of the vault seems to spin. The sensation of movement throughout the dome is underpinned by the squeezing together of pilasters, cornices, window frames, pediments, and ornamental designs to create an overwhelming feeling of busyness. Gone is the sense of the Renaissance that forces could, and should, be restrained (in the sense of moderated). The meaning of restraint changes from a positive to a negative value. The restraint of the Renaissance building implied that the building or its parts were contained in their relations with other buildings or parts. They did not need to colonize, intrude on, or overlap other parts, forms, and spaces. They did not need to constantly extend themselves, develop, or go beyond what they already were. Each part conveyed or insinuated a satisfaction with what it was. The identity of each part or form was self-assured. Its identity was not the nonidentical identity of something in transition to something else. It was not the nonidentical identity of becoming.

The baroque building took on the nature of the baroque personality: the nonidentical identity that wants to be something that it is not, fueled by dissatisfaction with itself. The restlessness of the baroque building is a

Interior dome, Chapel of the Holy Shroud.
Built 1667–1694 to the design of Guarino Guarini.

symbol of the forces of dissatisfaction that permeate seventeenth-century European society, and, indeed, seem to characterize all *modern* societies.[23] The satisfied person says: I am happy with things, this far, this size, this way. I do not want to become something other than what I am. Dissatisfaction, on the other hand, drives persons to continually change what they do, who they are; to expand, exceed, and overcome themselves. For the dissatisfied person restraint is not a positive but a negative value. It represents a punitive discipline in the face of their impulsion to be what they are not. *Baroque architecture was an architecture of dissatisfaction.* It set aside the quality of contentment for a sense of agitation. Like the dissatisfied person, the baroque building is riddled with tension—it is "on edge." This tension is simulated by architectural techniques such as holding columns back into recesses in the wall,[24] overcrowding ceilings and decorative fillings so that they overflow their allotted space,[25] squeezing niches between pilasters in spaces too small for them, and pushing pilasters up from the center of bays into the zone of the capitals.[26] The quality of being at ease with the world that characterizes the Renaissance humanist building is replaced in baroque composition by a pervading uneasiness.

The baroque, however, conveys something more than restlessness and tension. It also conveys a sense of massiveness. This is partly an effect of the loss of independence of parts—e.g. the distinct window shape is eroded: where in the Renaissance each window had its own sill, in the baroque the tendency is to place all but the most important windows on string courses;[27] the window also loses the frame (*aedicule*) which had given it the character of a house within a house[28] with the consequence that the part (in this case the window) is subordinated to the mass of the wall. Such massiveness was pursued not simply for aesthetic effect. Massiveness was a *social and political value*, a metaphor for a kind of power: *absolute power*—the power of an absolute unity in society. This was not the power of a balanced order (the balance of powers). It was not a humanist arrangement of power, but a baroque arrangement—epitomized in the idea of grandeur. In architecture, various techniques were used to simulate such grandeur: facades consisting of a series of equal stories became unacceptable,[29] so that either one story of a building became predominant[30] or the facade became a unified body,[31] held together by (for example) a single order of giant pilasters. Facades were designed as magnificent showpieces,[32] to overawe the viewer—even if such facades were sometimes just counterfeits of paint and plaster that hid insignificant buildings behind them.[33] Steps were stretched across the whole widths of facades.[34] The human scale of the Renaissance building disappeared, as did the lightness of those earlier buildings. Heaviness was suggested via shallow steps or the depressed pediment, while the pervasive sense of depression and melancholy of the seventeenth century world was suggested in turn by this architectonic weight.

SPACE AND SPEED

Corresponding to the changes in the design of the facade, there is a key change in the plan of buildings in the baroque age. The centralized building of the Renaissance disappears. The centralized church, with the four arms of the cross in perfect balance, gives way once again to the longitudinal plan.[35] In the palace, the formal courtyard (the enclosed central space) is eliminated.[36] The light, airy bounded form of the arcaded courtyard is replaced by the *galleria*, a longitudinal space that functioned to draw the eye into a long perspective—a perspective that insinuated the extension of space into infinity. Correspondingly, rooms were reorganized so that they no longer opened onto each other or onto a central space but were grouped along a corridor, as houses in turn were grouped along corridor streets.[37]

**Piazza di San Pietro (1656–1666), Vatican, Rome.
Designed by Gianlorenzo Bernini.**

This is not to imply that the notion of a center disappears in the baroque. Far from it. Rather the very meaning of "centering" changes.

The notion of the civic forum, or city center, which had been revived in Italy in the thirteenth century, and had served as a material symbol of a union of social opposites, was displaced as a principle for arranging urban space. Piazzas like Florence's Piazza della Signoria or Venice's San Marco were centers for mixed neighborhoods and mixed activities. In their space, contestation and festivity, tragedy and lyrical celebration coexisted. Rich and poor rubbed shoulders, and often lived in the same buildings that surrounded the city squares. Law, commerce, official business, pleasure, and art were all conducted in close proximity to each other. People lived and worked in the same immediate locale, often in the same building. Life was centered in a place, not dispersed along a radial axial.

The baroque age also built urban squares. But their nature differed markedly from their Renaissance predecessors.[38] Gianlorenzo Bernini's fountain-obelisk (1657), with its Egyptian markings, gave Rome's Piazza Navona its uncanny sense of infinite space, producing the illusion that it receded beyond the limits of the surrounding buildings into the heavens. Bernini's design of the Piazza of St. Peter's (1656) intimates a grandiose space: oval rather than square, it is surrounded by monumental columns rather than by the embrace of lived-in buildings. Such space was brilliant and majestic, but not especially convivial—a space to walk through but not to linger in.

The English in the age of the baroque also reconceptualized public space. Numerous squares laid out by English commercial developers—including Covent Garden (1631), Leicester Square (1635), and Lincoln Inn's Fields (1638)—were intended as purely residential developments, and ones reserved to an upper class. This was typical of the modern imperative to decenter, and thereby separate, work and residence, business and hearth, pleasure and home, and to segregate classes and other social groups spatially. The English were not alone in this. Henry IV's development of the Place Royale (Place des Vosges) was also dedicated to upper-class residences. The repetitive palatial facades of Hardouin-Mansart's Place Louis le Grand (Place Vendôme) in Paris (1699) epitomized the grand residential development and its baroque one-dimensionality. Still, the intention of designers is one thing; usage is another. Over time, behind the facades of such buildings, residences were converted into businesses, offices, and hotels, or in the Covent Garden case, used as a marketplace. In Aveline's eighteenth-century engraving of Hardouin-Mansart's Place, we see a square filled with the inevitable carriages waiting for their owners and masters. But we also see a square filled with people talking, looking, transacting, meeting, greeting, strolling, pleading, and indicating. The square thus remained a magnet for lively human activity, although with no law courts or municipal offices, and a greater social homogeneity, the range and color of this activity was something less than that of the Italian Renaissance piazza. Civic character persisted in spite of the imperatives of modernity. Public places for mingling, trading, talking, adjudicating, or for simply watching passersby, remained popular.

Still, these were *survivals*—persistent, tenacious, but survivals all the same. Indicative of this, the key central space of the baroque is neither the multidimensional city square nor the centralized church; rather it is a space (polygonal, orthogonal, or circular) from which radials fan out, and from which the meaning of society is disseminated. It is a space normally occupied by a single building of public power (e.g. a royal palace) or some public monument. The radials (typically avenues) cut diagonally across the urban fabric, a willful slash across the face of the city.[39] The baroque center is not a point of intersection for all that is human, but a vantage point from which to view the infinite. It is an outgoing rather than incoming center. Or to put it another way: the king commands all approaches. In the baroque schema, the radials, emanating from the center, are long, wide, straight avenues, boulevards, or malls that either extend further than the eye can see or else form a vista marked at the opposite distant end by some monument (obelisk, triumphal arch, commemorative column) or by the lantern of a public dome, which provides the eye with a "vanishing point" on the horizon, and an entree into infinity beyond. The *straightness* of the radials and the repetitive regularity and uniformity of dimensions of the accompanying urban block provide a material critique of feudal irregularity — the pattern of irregular growth ("organic" growth) of feudal urbanism and the feudal body (*corpus*) — while the *diagonality* of the radials is at odds with the symmetry of the classical grid pattern of streets of Greco-Roman origin. The fact that baroque radials *cut across* the urban fabric is significant in another way. The angular slash of the radial symbolizes the *cutting of time* by using the most direct (quickest) route across the city. It is a symbol of modernity — of the desire to speed up travel, to communicate immediately.

Unsurprisingly, in pursuit of such speed it is the urban planners of the baroque age who separate traffic thoroughfares from pedestrian ways.[40] In the baroque conception the city becomes subordinated to the vehicular thoroughfare. The beauty of the building that the passerby admires declines in value and significance in contrast to the functional value of quick passage through the city. In the spirit of great avenues, streets begin to take up more and more of the space of urban areas. The physical dominance of the street moreover has a psychological correlate. The desire for speedy passage — no longer a journey — is best satisfied by grand avenues or thoroughfares where the passenger glimpses nothing more than the horizontal lines of cornices and string courses merging together, heightening the sensation of being catapulted into infinity and belonging to a space of uninhibited movement and acceleration. In this way the idea of space comes to be dominated by the idea of time. Space becomes something to be passed through quickly, as a person moves from point to point. Speed rather than space is the signifier of modernity, and the emblem of modern rationality. To do a task, or convey a message with the least investment of time, is a sign of modern rationality at work. In contrast, in the classical (Greco-Roman) conception space, not time, is the leading signifier. Space is a source of meaning independent of time. Even before stories are told, or books or plays written, the central spaces of the antique city are sources of meaning. Their beautiful architecture and their ordered arrangement encompass all the forces of the city, and endow those forces with a common point of reference. For the carriage riders of the baroque, or the servants dashing across the street dogging their onward rush, there is no center in the Greco-Roman sense. What there is, is movement. It is *dunamis* that imparts meaning. It is from *dunamis* that the denizens of the emergent modern society draw meaning and make some sort of sense of their world.

Rather than the journey of Odysseus or Aeneas, with all its risks and vicissitudes, moderns exhibit the desire for a kind of absolute movement free of all obstacles and encumbrances: a *"freeway"* — from the perspective of which all the features of landscape and cityscape blur into indifference. Place, under these conditions, becomes displaced. The preoccupation with speed is unequivocally modern. Sometimes this preoccupation reduces itself to merely utilitarian considerations. Speed, then, means little more than the quick transport of goods and people. But *dunamis* usually signifies more than this. In the baroque schema, *dunamis* was also *grand*. Grandeur was created by virtue of the monumental scale of radiating avenues (their comparatively great width) and the imposition of uniformity along these radials (uniformity of facades or trees lining avenues, uniformity of pavements, cornices, and string courses), and by the use of such avenues as ceremonial thoroughfares for the great rituals of state. Baroque planners typically were military engineers who suffered little hesitation in clearing the ground of historical encumbrances so that vehicles could move constantly and without impediment. To cut avenues through existing cities (against the grain of the city), to recut the urban fabric around these radials, to ensure mass conformity to building codes so as to achieve uniform facades and streetscapes required a new kind of power. Schemes as the *Friedrichstrasse* and the *trivium* of the Rondell in Berlin, the French monarchy's "city residence" at Versailles, the house of Savoy's transformation of Turin in the seventeenth century from a medieval to a baroque city, and the scheme of the Pontificate of Sixtus V (1585–1590) for three great avenues to radiate from the Piazza del Popolo in Rome were all testaments to this new power.

DYNAMISM AS THE SELF-IMAGE OF THE AGE

The age of the baroque felt itself reaching out for a new world of unlimited horizons, not just moving between the parts of what existed. I do not want to suggest that the world of the Renaissance, as an age of multiplicity, was somehow an anemic, pacified world. Renaissance politics had no shortage of ruthlessness, strife, and intrigue. It was in no sense a safe world. Yet it did have a profound sense of equipoise. The baroque age, by contrast, possessed little of the classical and Renaissance intuition that *every direction has a counterdirection*. This revealed itself not only in the absolutism of monarchs, and their drive to remake the world along rational lines, but also in the enthusiasm of democratic and reformation movements. The zeal of the puritans in the English civil war, and the grandiosity of Louis XIV and his ministers are equally expressive of the age and its indifference to limits, especially to the limits that come from the counterposition of forces. The baroque is a troubled and turbulent age.[41] It is permeated by an atmosphere of unrest and anguish, agitation and disturbance. Mutinies, revolts, separatist uprisings, banditry, and civil turmoil color the picture of Europe throughout the epoch. Indeed the seventeenth century borrows the term "crisis" from medicine to describe what it is experiencing, and the derivative term "critic" starts to be used to describe the person who diagnoses the disturbed condition of the age. The iconography of the age is macabre; its energy is restless; its sense of itself is dynamic.

The idea of *movement* is all-important to the *self-understanding* of the age. Its writers and thinkers spoke endlessly of a world in motion. They recommended poetry and literature that was *moving*, passions that *moved* people.[42] Notions of change, decay, transformation, and mutability provide the self-image of the age. Montaigne: "Our life is nothing but movement." Pascal: "Our nature is in movement." Hobbes: "That which is really in us, is only motion." Gracian: "Moving is the definition of life." Bernini: "A man is never so similar to himself as when he is in motion." For the baroque, something has identity only when it is changing. Life is a course of unceasing modifications. The human being is a succession of states, and is caught in a flux of changes that cannot be arrested. In this world the human condition is turbulent. Existence is a whirlwind, a storm, choppy seas. Such an existence, of course, cannot produce happiness — the *eudaimonia* of the ancients. It is not happiness that the dynamic personality seeks, but excitement, wonder, astonishment, surprise, and suspense, and it finds these qualities represented in artworks that are obscure, difficult, distorted, strange, and complicated. The art of the baroque is dynamic. It is an art of movement, and the baroque artist engages in the attempt to capture instability, transitoriness, variability, uncertainty, or indeed, as the prominent theme of ruins in baroque art suggests, disintegration. Baroque art had all kinds of ways to suggest instability and transitoriness: techniques like painting in splotches and smears (to suggest the incompleteness of the artwork); *anamorphosis* (leaving the viewer to complete the picture); the leaving of imperfections in the work; the promotion of carelessness as an aesthetic quality; and the creation of irregular constructions.

Not much of a society can exist in the midst of prolonged crisis and instability, it might be thought. But all societies, even the most traditional or static, have their divisions and their agonies. Modern societies are not unique in being torn apart. What distinguishes them, however, is their fascination with the idea of being torn apart. The baroque age inaugurated the modern attraction to the symbolism of disintegration and ruination, but it also suggested to moderns the idea that they could draw meaning from chaos, that they could extract sense from senselessness. Where disintegration and crisis were driven by the imperatives of change, or were the effects of resistance to change, a world torn apart would still make sense to its denizens. The storm of transformation would be as much meaningful as it was agonizing. The principle of coalescence in a torn world was *dynamism*. *Dunamis*, in creating tears in the world, justified them at the same time. It did not matter whether a person's sympathies lay with the Counter-Reformation, or with Protestantism, or indeed with the ancients. Subsuming all of these was the image of *dunamis*. Most of the great intellectuals and artists of the seventeenth century, irrespective of their particular sympathies, pay homage in one way or another to *dunamis*.

Dunamis is what in effect Pietro da Cortona painted in *The Triumph of Divine Providence* (1633–1639) on the ceiling originally of the Palazzo Barberini in Rome. *Dunamis* fills the scene. The eye is caught up in a restless, swirling cascade of ceiling figures, many of which reach out and over lines that frame the sections of the painting. Similarly, *dunamis* is what the great Flemish artist Peter Paul Rubens (1577–1640) paints in *Christ Bearing the Cross*, with its motif of an agonizing, upward movement—a procession of figures that overlap and meld into an almost undifferentiated plastic power of stress and strain. This is the spirit of the age. The surge of movement that suffuses Rembrant's *Blinding of Samson* (1636), the restless, almost chaotic action of *The Night Watch* (1642) with its bold play of light and shadows, the urgency of the *Polish Rider* (ca. 1655), are drenched by this spirit.

For all these artists, and for their age, meaning was an endless, anxious, writhing movement that drove humanity forward, upward, outward.

Naturally, an age that sees itself as caught up in a ceaseless movement—that supposes restlessness, turmoil, and instability to be the human condition—will have problems defining or recognizing limits and bounds. Such an age will lack a developed sense of proportion, moderation, or self-restraint. The art, culture, and politics of the baroque were, to put it mildly, exuberant. Grandiosity, enormousness, exaggeration seeps into every facet of seventeenth-century European life. At the heart of this lay the grandiose self-presentation of the baroque monarchies. This style worked to exalt monarchy, to underline its majesty, its magnificence, its radiance, and its triumphal character. One key element of majesty creating was the development of capital cities. At the same time cities systematically lost their autonomy as the power of the monarchy extended itself. They became parts of the centralized administration of the baroque state—the forerunner of the modern nation-state. Monumentality was what was admired in the baroque cities. The height of buildings increased; houses grew more luxurious; fountains and churches became more magnificent; plazas larger, streets wider, banquets more opulent. So also a kind of hallucinatory quality was induced, as people milled and swirled in the city, at times almost in a delirium. The aim of majesty-creating efforts on behalf of the baroque monarchies was intended to impress and overwhelm others. Hobbes's image of Leviathan captures this perfectly. Leviathan holds those it rules over in awe, in a state of almost unbearable tension. Awesomeness is a technique of power.

Unrestrained behavior, caprice, outlandishness, and "oversizedness," are ways to impress and overawe, as is really any kind of breaking of human limits. If there is a distinctive seventeenth-century technique of power it is this: paralyze and control others by engaging in actions that have some terrible or extreme quality, something that will make a shocking impact on their psyche. Baroque personalities took pleasure in the terrible; they cultivated the extreme; they exalted violence in order to intimidate and subdue. All kinds of temperate emotions were thereby deemphasized in this atmosphere—nonviolent, nonpassionate emotions: emotions of happiness, the feelings of pleasure in beauty, the love of the world, cheerfulness, calmness, and optimism. In their place reigned the emotions of pessimism, bitterness, melancholy, disaffection, gloom, distrust in the world, confusion, disorientation, and senselessness. Rather than equanimity in the face of the world, the baroque personality felt furor. The baroque body was inflamed with anger, and out of this anger grew a furiousness with the world, a furor in which the person was literally "beside himself," shaking, trembling, uttering incomprehensible rants that mirrored the distortions and obscurities of the baroque world.

COVENANTS AND CREATION

During the Renaissance, city-republics in Italy, and free cities elsewhere in Europe, had been the leading edge of European society, possessed of a remarkable energy and spiritedness. With the onset of the seventeenth century and the rise of baroque culture, the energies of the city falter. The city imagery of *concordia*, of a harmony of powers, diminishes in its authority over European minds. In its place appears the imagery of *dunamis*, of directional rather than relational virtue—the imagery of a "world turned upside down." The city, of course, had always competed with a hierarchical conception of society. This hierarchical conception had recolonized Europe during the Dominate period of the Roman Empire and had been the prime source of social meaning during the Middle Ages. The hierarchical view conceived of society as divided into ranks (superiors and inferiors). Ideally—and like all ideals, these were departed from—superiors were "fathers" or "parents" to those below them. Superiors were the protectors of the weak and vulnerable. They pledged to feed their dependents, to defend them against attack, to benefit them. In return—and there is a kind of asymmetrical reciprocity at work here—those who were dependent pledged to serve and obey their superiors. This was not a despotic relationship (even if it could, on occasions, degenerate into despotism). Justice required that servants (of whatever rank) were not treated as slaves. Superiors were expected to act protectively toward their charges. This protective ethos was meaningful for all those in "the great chain of being," no matter how high or low—no matter whether one was a servant or a seigneurial lord, a peasant or a prince of the church. The civic paradigm resisted the hierarchical view of the world. It did so in antiquity against the claims of tribal and patrimonial hierarchies, and later on against the clerical and feudal hierarchies of the Middle Ages. The free city banned feudal relationships within its perimeters.[43] It offered instead the freedom of the city—independence from the control of secular princes and archbishops. Justice in the city was a kind of fitting or joining, a tie or concordance, of diverse capacities and powers in the state achieved by proportionality and symmetry rather than hierarchy.

In the age of the baroque, interest was maintained, but less intensively, in the literature and ideas of the Greco-Roman world. The civilization of the antique and the Renaissance city-republics had little to offer the building of the absolutist sovereign state that dominated the political atmosphere of seventeenth-century Europe. At the end of the seventeenth century, Latin was abandoned as a common language of learning,[44] while the study of the Greeks was destined, with the rise of romantic Hellenism in the eighteenth century, to become a model of personal cultivation—the *bildung* of an autonomous personality[45]—and a model for the idea of a *national* culture,[46] a culture stamped by the impress of national uniqueness, one whose greatness was equated with uniqueness and autochthonous development—for which Periclean Athens was to serve as a model. The baroque era also saw a flowering of interest in nonclassical cultures. There was great interest in Egyptian hermeticism, exemplified by the work of the German Jesuit Athanasius Kircher, who argued that the Egyptians were the source of Platonism and Pythagoreanism.[47] Likewise, in the work of the Cambridge Platonists Henry Moore and Ralph Cudworth, Egypt figured as a *prisca sapientia* that the Greeks only partially assimilated and transmitted.[48]

Just as seventeenth-century philosophers turned from the image of antiquity as the crucible of learning, so a Hebraic model of politics displaced the classical model that had captivated Bruni, Machiavellli, and their ilk. The image of the city was replaced by that of the covenant. The idea of the covenant was central to the Hebraic model of social formation.[49]

In the biblical metaphor, the deliverance of the Israelites from Egypt was followed by their entry into an antinomian state of nature. Social formation begins with the experience of the asocial. After fleeing the oppression of Egypt's patrimonial rulers, the old tribal bonds of the Israelites no longer sufficed for social cohesion. The confrontation with God in the wilderness provides the crucible in which a new kind of society is created. In the covenant story, everyone's natural right in the wilderness is freely and equally transferred to a community based on biblical law. In the covenant made between this community and God, God promises the Israelites a bounteous land and they promise to obey the moral law. A *community* of God's beloved children is formed out of the covenant, a "we" committed to God and God's commandments. The covenant is a founding act that creates, in place of old tribal affiliations, a new nation composed of willing members. As Michael Walzer argues, the Israelites in Egypt were a people only insofar as they shared tribal memories, or more potently the experience of oppression. Their identity before deliverance was something that happened to them. Only with the covenant do they make themselves into a people in the strong sense, capable of both resistance and obedience.[50] Covenantal politics functioned in the seventeenth century as a model for the creation of an abstract community—a nation or a commonwealth—in a manner analogous to the way the ancient Hebrews became something more than tribes. Freedom from dynastic rule was equated with freedom from Egyptian rule.

The Hebraic covenant, notably, was not a pact in the Roman sense. It was not a pact between tribes *to come together*—"the unity of two altogether different entities"[51]—but rather the willingness of all the people, and each individually, *to answer together*:[52] to promise that what God has spoken, "we the people" will do. In return for doing what they promise, God confers the benefits of freedom and plenty on "a people." The mosaic trek of deliverance, depicted in the Exodus story, is *through the desert*, quite unlike the classical odyssey *across the sea*. The promise of exodus is not the *kallipolis* of the Greeks or the refounding of Troy as Rome—the work of *kosmopoiêsis*—but a land of bounty and of freedom from the oppression of pharaohs and masters. The promise of God is *land* that can be freely farmed. In the biblical conception, the first founder of a city was a murderer, and the city (Davidic Jerusalem) was the seat of the monarch. Where kings rule justly (as in the Davidian case), they do so by maintaining laws that are tribal in spirit and a way of life that is predominately agricultural and pastoral, not commercial and urbane. Consequently, a city that is separated from the soil can never be just. The promised land will be reached as long as those who have promised to obey God's law do so. If divine law is not fulfilled, God's promise is deferred, and the search for bounty and freedom has to be renewed.

In the seventeenth century this story is radicalized. What began as the idea of a whole people who freely commit and individually bind themselves in a covenant to be the upholders of a law handed down by God in exchange for God's benefaction, became in modern times, under the modernizing impetus of the baroque age, the idea of an activist community of saints (Protestant dissenters). Infused with the breath of God, filled with the expectation of religious grace, plenty, and liberty, they believed that laws and institutions were an obstacle to living in God's grace, and thus they sought to transform the world accordingly. Yet they still saw themselves as a community capable of answering together and moving in one direction, indeed so much so that the communal process of emancipatory journeying/migration (out of all of the metaphorical Egypts) became its own kind of immanent law, a kind of modern law of nature.

Eventually Protestant dissenters were to find even the bonds of the exodic community too much to bear, so fierce was their antinomianism. In the course of time, dissenting communities split apart; churches broke down into sects. Eventually individuals, by themselves or with their families, were to set off alone to find the promised land. They still swore to uphold the word of God—but separated from their fellows, not as a people-in-exodus. They became responsible to God alone. If they could settle on the land outside of the reach of corrupt government and oppressive officials, they could be free. Having moved in imagination from exodus to exile, they were free to live on the basis of a universal moral law written in the scriptures rather than among a nation of fellow believers. Scripture alone was sufficient. It was not until the late eighteenth or early nineteenth century that the Hebraic antinomianism of the seventeenth century yielded a consistently radical individualism of this kind. It was, to be sure, implicit in the sectarianism of seventeenth-century dissenters. But even when sects hived off from existing communities, they did so in the beginning as groups. Promises to God still had a communal significance, or in more secular terms, while the community of believers saw the world as oppressive, the future held a promise of the good, the promise of migrating and entering collectively into a New Jerusalem. The community looked expectantly to the future, and invested its hope in the long passage through the wilderness to find paradise, the promised land.

It was the appeal not for a Rome reborn but for a New Jerusalem that was convincing for seventeenth-century ears. The Israelitism of English dissenters was typical of this.[53] There was an easy identification between reformed congregations and the elect nation of Israel,[54] and an enthusiasm for the idea of a nation resisting (as a nation) dynastic princes and their commands.[55] There was a hunger for a New Jerusalem, the kingdom of the saints on earth. In this kingdom, persons would not live under the law, but in God's grace. The power of God, the King of Israel, the Messiah, among men would make the need for the power of the monarchy, as well as the clergy, the nobility, and institutions of all kinds, redundant, and if the old European world was intractably resistant to this, then it was supposed that a new Israel would be founded in the New World.[56]

It was such beliefs that spurred the puritan Separatists to cross the Atlantic in 1620—an ocean, not sea, crossing, and thus unimaginable to Hellenic odysseans—and which took the puritans to the shores of Massachusetts Bay where they covenanted and combined themselves into a body politic that was congregational rather than institutional. This body politic was self-governing, able to manage its own affairs in the congregational meeting and the town hall set around the green or common that was the sign of paradise in the midst of the inhospitable wilderness of New England, and a locus of meaning for the Puritan villagers. Just as the plain white houses they lived in signified the ascetical restraint, thrift, and diligence of their religious morality (God's law), the green was the sign of paradise regained, a green and pleasant land that justified all of the Puritans' exodic hardships. Whether they lived in a state of grace was a moot point. In a community, laws and ordinances could not be done without. It was not until the transcendentalism of the New Englanders Emerson and Thoreau two hundred years later that individualism without community was consistently conceived. But the first New Englanders at least could claim this much of the antinomian dream: that self-government through their own town assemblies and congregations did away with the state, as if the spirit of the ancient mosaic tribal league had triumphed over the Israelite kings.

In this sense the Protestant-Hebraic model sat well with the general antinomian tone of the baroque age. This was an age in which apocalyptic and millenarian mentalities flourished. The image of Jerusalem as a paradisiacal place on earth was an inspiring force for baroque personalities. It was to be found at the core of much of the burning religious faith and mania of the age. The obsessive, fixated search for the New Jerusalem is no better exemplified than in the story of the Iberian explorer and pilot Pedro Fernandez de Quiros, whose imagining of the Hebraic *topos* of promise became identified with a search for the great southern continent that had been speculated on by Europeans since the days of Herodotus and thought, by the time of the seventeenth century, to extend south of Cape Horn to somewhere not very far south of Java. Sailing from Peru in 1605, de Quiros discovered what he thought to be South Land or "Terra Australia del Espirito Santo" (Australia of the Holy Spirit). He named the largest island—of what he deluded himself, in a half-mad state of religious delirium, was a continent—the New Hebrides, and with his three hundred colonists set about creating utopia. He named the capital of his colony New Jerusalem and the river on which it was situated, Jordan. The colony lasted a month before the colonists forced de Quiros to return to Acapulco.[57]

DYNAMIC JUSTICE

It was not only dissenters who relied on the covenant story for their politics, or rather their antipolitics. The most influential theory of the new seventeenth-century European state was the theory of the social contract. The story of the covenant proved well-suited to legitimating the power of the new sovereign state being created by absolute monarchies. The biblical image of the covenant was radically reworked for this purpose. But the setting of the covenant outside of the city—in the "state of nature"—remained unchanged. The moderns to whom this story was addressed were not conceived of as town dwellers. They were not like Odysseus, returning home to punish those who had violated the norms of hospitality; they were not like Aeneas—with his home city (Troy) burned—destined to journey through Africa, Crete, Sicily to Italy where the confrontation and eventual union of the wandering Trojans and the Latins would lay the foundation of Rome. The moderns to whom the covenant story was addressed—most powerfully by Thomas Hobbes—neither knew the fundamental civic norm of hospitality nor were driven by destiny to found a city anew.

Moderns were *anomic*. They were born not with obligations but with *rights* to do as they pleased with whatever powers they had. Moderns were *ateleological*. They had no destination. In the story of the social contract, the brutish life that anomic behavior caused pushed individuals to strike a compact among themselves. They ("the people") would mutually agree to convey some of their rights and powers to a sovereign whom they would agree to obey. In return, the sovereign would guarantee them safety and peace. But in this story neither the people nor the sovereign have a destiny. *There is no point of arrival which is also the foundation or beginning of the city — the end which is the beginning.* Instead of destiny, there is *dunamis*. Originally, the impulsion of individuals is to freely, willfully exercise their rights and powers without any preconception of a common end; subsequently, when the sovereign acquires rights and powers in the social covenant, these are rights and powers to impose law and order for the sake of the common end of preserving life. But this common end is no destiny. It is not a *place* to which one goes. It is not a place of arrival; it is not the *termination* of a journey that signals the beginning of a new life. It is an end — in the sense of a *purpose* — that is *served by the making of laws rather than the making of a city* (with its beautiful things and deeds). It is an end that is not a boundary or limit (*peras*). It is an end that defines no place. It is an end that is open-ended, and the laws (of the sovereign state) that guarantee this end are likewise open-ended. The end they serve is capable of growth, expansion, extension, and thus to serve this end well the laws must be *dynamic*.

The good, the just law in the sovereign state is dynamic. It is law that is erasable by the state. Repeal, abolition, replacement, substitution, correction, amendment of the laws — to stimulate and keep pace with the *dunamis* of society — is the imperative of the sovereign state. Consequently, in the seventeenth century the paradigm of civic justice was overtaken by the conception of *dynamic justice*. The immediate vehicle for the spread of this conception was the newly emergent absolutist states in Europe (notably France, Sweden, and Prussia), and those states with absolutist pretensions (England). It is, on the face of it, a seemingly odd thing to speak of justice in the same breath as absolutism. But remember: only the most debased states — and the most desperate societies — make no claim for themselves that what they do is just.

The most powerful argument for this new kind of justice came from Hobbes. In Hobbes's view, what was just and unjust was determined by the command of the ruler, the sovereign authority in the state. The fluctuation of the sovereign's commandment replaced the permanence of customary law (of feudal society).[58] In the traditional regime, seigneurial lords of course ruled on what was just. So what was different about absolutism? In the landed hierarchical order, a lord or prince ruled (dispensed benefices, punishments, and protections) on the basis of custom, or else on the basis of natural law — in other words, there was a fixed standard of succor that it was the duty of the prince to bestow on the obedient (or disobedient as the case may be). The new authorities of the seventeenth century, bolstered by the political and philosophical doctrines of sovereignty, did not govern (and did not claim to govern) anymore according to fixed standards but rather *fixed the standards*, and *in that sense* what was just and unjust was determined by *the command of the sovereign*. In other words, the new powers of the seventeenth century acted more as legislators than judges, and, even more importantly, the laws that the sovereign commanded could be repealed, reworked, reversed, and reformed. In this conception, the laws specified what was just and unjust in a society. If the laws changed then so did the notion of what was just and unjust. In other words, the substantive content of justice became fluid, dynamic, and open-ended. Arrangements recognized as just one day could be dismissed as unjust at some later time. Social arrangements were now assumed to be plastic and changeable. But does this not make justice something arbitrary? Not necessarily if — as for the baroque seventeenth century — *justice is what promotes movement or change*. In the view of their defenders, the new sovereign powers of Europe were just because they promoted movement in economic, social and governmental affairs. Traditionalists might be horrified at "the world turned upside down" by interfering royalists, but royalists found a justification for the new regal system precisely *because* it was capable of turning the world upside down. Sovereign power *altered* inherited social arrangements with the aim of making them *more dynamic*. Where the city was *energetic*, the new sovereign powers were *dynamic*.

Where the energies of city dwellers (ideally) complemented each other in a prudential if precarious balance of forces, the social forces of the seventeenth century were "driven" in a *single* direction, and the growing centralization of state power in this period expressed this very well. The new states that began to appear — in Prussia, France, England, Spain, and so on — justified their power with the doctrine of sovereignty. This was the view that there was legitimately only *one* authority in the state, and this authority was indivisible, final, and supreme. This meant that royal (sovereign) authority could not be shared with either seigneurial or civic authorities. The sovereign power of the new monarchs could not coexist with either city-republics or with patrimonial and feudal arrangements of power. So consequently when the French monarch Louis XIV assumed *personal* control of the state in 1661, he moved against the French *parlements* (the high courts of Paris and other cities). Traditionally royal edicts had to be registered by the *parlements* before they could acquire the force of law. In 1673 Louis annulled their ability to remonstrate against laws that they did not like. Similarly, over time provincial estates lost their power to bargain over taxes with the French Crown, while in the towns mayoral power was circumscribed, and military garrisons were established in recalcitrant cities. The higher nobility was exiled to Versailles, to live a life of splendid vegetation away from their base of power in the provinces. The development of Prussian absolutism followed a similar pattern, and even earlier. From the 1650s onward the Prussian estates lost their power to veto new royal taxes. (The Swedes, who invaded in the 1630s, had set a precedent for this by collecting taxes during the occupation in defiance of the estates.) The landed aristocracy lost political power, although in exchange they gained economic privileges (tax immunity). Prussian cities did even less well, and the cities that resisted the extension of royal power were coerced into submission. In 1674 Königsburg, a former Hanseatic city particularly unbending to the new regime, was occupied by the military and deprived of its autonomy. From the 1680s the Prussian state imposed punitive taxes on the cities, deliberately enfeebling them. In England the new Stuart dynasty tried much the same tactics, though with less ultimate success.

For the new sovereign states it was not only their ability to crush rival powers that counted; what also mattered was their new way of conducting the business of the state. The state became modernizing or rationalizing. This was expressed in a number of ways. It set about destroying the parochialism (the economic and social barriers) and the rigid status system of the old hierarchical world of the European countryside. Out-of-the-way hinterlands were absorbed — via roads or canal building — into a new, enlarged economic order. Petty feudal principalities were integrated into larger state structures that displayed an increasingly bureaucratic rather than feudatory structure. The old "nobility of the sword" was displaced by a "nobility of the robe" that owed its place in the world more to its ability to carry out the functions of its office (and the commands of the sovereign) than to its inherited status. Decisive in the French case was Cardinal Richelieu's use of the *intendant* system of offices — appointed directly by the monarch (rather than the local country nobility) and revocable by the Crown. What such actions pointed to was the fact that the new sovereign state was not a "natural" state. It was not a *corpus*. Indeed its most astute defenders portrayed it as the *artificial* creation of a social contract. It is fitting to call this the *liberal* aspect of the sovereign state. Liberals could sympathize with this side of state building that put a squeeze on the old "natural" hierarchical order, with its paternalism, patriarchy, and parochialism built in. Yet the sovereign state was not a liberal construct by any stretch of the imagination. Liberals like the English philosopher John Locke (1632–1704) found themselves at odds with both the old patriarchal *and* the new absolutist conceptions of the world (although they never managed to elaborate a coherent alternative conception of the state to rival the civic paradigm). The liberalism of the emergent sovereign state consisted in its releasing energies from feudal fetters. But the protagonists of the new order wanted to mobilize and direct those energies in a concentrated manner. The sovereign state was determinedly centralizing. It absorbed principalities and cities into protonation-states. To achieve such incorporation, the sovereign (no longer Machiavelli's prince) needed the capacity (power) to do so, and the empowerment of the sovereign came via the creation of rationalized bureaucracies and the creation of permanent standing armies, so as not to have to rely on intrinsically unreliable mercenaries or on politically unreliable citizen's militias — the armed force of the city — or on the service of armed vassal loyalists.

The sovereign state organized itself through offices rather than statuses. Its nature was, and is, bureaucratic, not traditional. Even at the very time Louis XIV asserted personal control of the state, and built his residential palace at Versailles, the building of bureaucratic offices was firmly in train.[59] The modern sovereign could not administer the state with a household staff alone. Thus, gradually, and sometimes with difficulty, household and public responsibilities — the purse of the king and the public treasury — were separated. Eventually, in the course of the eighteenth and nineteenth centuries, sovereignty was impersonalized, and the most powerful forces in the state came to occupy public offices that were institutionalized. Such public offices were not the bureaus of cliché — slow and dilatory. If they came to seem so, or were satirized as such, it is because of the underlying cultural demand for *dunamis* in all modern societies. "It is not done quickly enough." In truth, the sovereign state (and later on, the bureaucratic company) moved with speed and concentrated force.

Dunamis is the modern touchstone. Moderns conceive of themselves and their arrangements as dynamic. Moderns obsessively strain to push beyond the limits of their society. They experience the arrangements of things as unjust because these arrangements are limiting. Moderns find the limits of wealth or income, time or space, power or ability, esteem or recognition to be sufferances that they do not want to live with. From antinomian dissent to liberal choice, from the images of crossing the Jordan to the dreams of endless opportunity, moderns imagine an infinite horizon of life. Moderns resent boundaries. They want to exceed themselves. So they create movements that promise to change the world, "to turn the world upside down." But they find always that these movements exhaust themselves and are subsumed by bureaucracies which, in their own peculiar way, are also driven by the need for expansion and change. The state institutes offices, organizations, and rules in answer to the demands for change. Liberals and dissenters alike find reason to object to this, for it conflicts with their purer antinomian impulses. And yet they seem unaware of the more troubling irony that all of this represents. Moderns seem able to effect only one kind of social change: *the cre-ation of new offices and organizations.* In the end, no matter how antinomian their starting point, no matter how fiery or furious their rhetoric, no matter how powerful the *dunamis* they summon up, the road of change seems to lead moderns eventually, inexorably, to more and different, larger and newer, public and private offices and bureaus. The more stren-uously moderns assert themselves, the more conclusive is their fate.

NOTES

1. Harrington insisted that the doctrine of balance was the principle that makes politics. See Felix Raab, *The English Face of Machiavelli* (London: Routledge, 1964), p. 201.

2. James Harrington, *Works*, ed. John Toland (London, 1771), pp. 35–72.

3. This marrying of the "Polybian city" with the countryside was to influ-ence, a century later, Thomas Jefferson's agrarian-inflected republicanism.

4. J. G. A. Pocock, *Politics, Language and Time* (Chicago: University of Chicago Press, 1989), p. 113; Paul A. Rahe, *Republics Ancient and Modern*, vol. 2 (Chapel Hill: University of North Carolina Press, 1994), pp. 179–96.

5. Peter Gay, *The Enlightenment: An Interpretation, The Rise of Modern Paganism* (London: Weidenfeld and Nicolson, 1966), p. 300.

6. For a discussion of Althusius's work, see John Ely, "Libertarian Feder-alism and Green Politics: A Perspective On European Federation," in *The Left in Search of a Center*, ed. Michael Crozier and Peter Murphy (Champaign, Ill.: Uni-versity of Illinois Press, 1996).

7. Alasdair Macintyre, *Whose Justice? Which Rationality?* (London: Duck-worth, 1988), chap. 12.

8. Heinrich Wölfflin, *Principles of Art History* (New York: Dover, 1950), pp. 19, 22, 52, 57. As well as Wölfflin's classic art history, see also R. Wittkower, *Art and Architecture in Italy 1600–1750*, 3d ed. (Harmondsworth: Penguin, 1973); J. R. Martin, *Baroque* (Harmondsworth: Penguin, 1977); John Varriano, *Italian Baroque and Rococo Architecture* (New York: Oxford University Press, 1986).

9. See, e.g., Gilles Deleuze, *The Fold: Leibniz and the Baroque* (Minneapolis: Uni-versity of Minnesota Press, 1993), p. 3; Wölfflin, *Principles of Art History*, pp. 149, 152.

10. Deleuze, *The Fold*, p. 17.

11. Wölfflin, *Principles of Art History*, pp. 50, 54, 57, 59–60, 67.

12. Ibid., pp. 66, 126, 130, 159, 161.

13. This is strikingly illustrated by Rembrandt's etching of the *Virgin's Death* where—in contrast to Dürer's Renaissance woodcut of the same—the arrange-ment of opposites is replaced by a single motive.

14. Wölfflin, *Principles of Art History*, p. 153. See also Deleuze's comments on the fluidity of the baroque in *The Fold*, p. 5.

15. Wölfflin, *Principles of Art History*, p. 161.

16. The pilaster was flanked on each side by a receding pilaster and later by

a further quarter pilaster, as Heinrich Wölfflin notes in *Renaissance and Baroque* (Ithaca, N.Y.: Cornell University Press, 1966), p. 53.

17. Ibid., pp. 55, 134.
18. Ibid., p. 34.
19. Ibid., p. 30.
20. Ibid., p. 45.
21. Ibid., p. 62.
22. Ibid., pp. 47–48, 55.
23. Agnes Heller, "The Dissatisfied Society," in *The Power of Shame* (London: Routledge and Kegan Paul, 1985).
24. Wölfflin, *Renaissance and Baroque*, p. 63.
25. Ibid., p. 56.
26. Ibid., p. 98.
27. Ibid., p. 135.
28. Ibid., p. 134.
29. Ibid., pp. 40–41.
30. Ibid., p. 127.
31. Ibid., p.135.
32. Ibid., p. 93.
33. Lewis Mumford, *The City in History* (Harmondsworth: Penguin, 1966 [1961]), p. 433.
34. Wölfflin, *Renaissance and Baroque*, p. 97.
35. Ibid., p. 91.
36. Ibid., pp. 136–38.
37. Mumford, *The City in History*, p. 439.
38. Mumford, *The City in History*, pp. 451–56; Michael Webb, *The City Square* (London: Thames and Hudson, 1990), pp. 84–97.
39. Spiro Kostof, *The City Shaped: Urban Patterns and Meanings Through History* (London: Thames and Hudson, 1991), chap. 4.
40. Mumford, *The City in History*, p. 442.
41. What follows is indebted to Jose Antonio Maravall, *Culture of the Baroque* (Manchester: Manchester University Press, 1986).
42. This emphasis on movement was prefigured in certain late Renaissance figures. Leonardo da Vinci (1452–1519) is certainly one such figure. Leonardo's early sixteenth–century *Notebooks* demonstrate an awareness of movement exceptional for the time. Images of rising, falling, expanding, revolving, dragging, flowing, ebbing, pouring, and penetrating abound in his writings. [Cronin, *The Flowering of the Renaissance* (London: Pimlico, 1992), p. 136.] The fascination with dynamic movement is reiterated in Galileo Galilei (1564–1642), the Paduan mathematician who rejected Padua's Aristotelianism for a view of the world in which movement was dynamic rather than teleological.
43. Daniel Waley, *The Italian City-Republics* (London: Weidenfeld and Nicolson, 1969).
44. Vassilis Lambropoulos, *The Rise of Eurocentrism: Anatomy of Interpretation* (Princeton, N.J.: Princeton University Press, 1993), p. 44.
45. Ibid., pp. 38, 53.

46. On the later development of this, see P. Murphy, "Romantic Modernism and the Greek Polis," *Thesis Eleven* no. 34 (Cambridge, Mass.: MIT Press, 1993).

47. Gay, *The Enlightenment*, p. 77. See also Martin Bernal, *Black Athena: The Afroasiatic Roots of Classical Civilization* (London: Vintage, 1987). The thrust of Bernal's work in *Black Athena* is to reiterate, with the aid of twentieth-century scholarship, the seventeenth-century turn to Egypt.

48. Ibid., p. 166.

49. On the nature of Hebraic covenant politics, see Michael Walzer, *Exodus and Revolution* (New York: Basic Books, 1985), especially Part III. On the centrality of covenant politics in the political theory of the seventeenth century, see Paul Harrison, "Border Closures" in *The Left in Search of a Center*, ed. Crozier and Murphy (Champaign, Ill.: University of Illinois Press, 1996).

50. Walzer, *Exodus and Revolution*, p. 76.

51. Arendt, *On Revolution* (Harmondsworth: Penguin, 1973 [1963]), p. 187.

52. Walzer, *Exodus and Revolution*, p. 80.

53. Lambropoulos, *The Rise of Eurocentrism*, p. 35.

54. Ibid., p. 36.

55. G. P. Gooch, *English Democratic Ideas in the Seventeenth Century* (New York: Harper and Row, 1959), p. 5.

56. Ibid., pp. 63–78; see also Hannah Arendt's discussion of the role of the Hebraic model in the New World in *On Revolution*, pp. 189–90.

57. Russell Ward, *Finding Australia: The History of Australia to 1821* (Richmond, Victoria: Heinemann, 1987), chap. 3.

58. Deleuze, *The Fold*, p. 19.

59. The first purpose-designed bureaus were in the Uffizi in Florence, designed by Giorgio Vasari in 1560.

9

COMMONWEALTH AND CONTINGENCY

SOCIAL CONTINGENCY AND CIVIL WAR

The ideal character of the sovereign state was realized nowhere in the seventeenth century. Indeed, failure was more common than success; yet the examples of failed absolutist ambitions — and the reasons for those failures — are often as interesting as the successes, and as important. Sometimes failure meant the reassertion of a quasi kind of traditionalism. Austria is a good example: the Habsburgs relied on an old semi-patrimonial, multinational idea of empire, in contrast to a state like France that moved increasingly to eliminate linguistic and cultural differences within the state (e.g. between north and south; or through the integration of the semi-Iberian Navarre). Sometimes failure meant the reassertion of a civic ethos: the case of England is a very peculiar, and complicated, instance of this.

The assertion of royal power began relatively early in England.* The Tudors (Henry VII, Henry VIII) were successful in ending the private wars of feudal magnates and their armed retainers. Henry VII abolished feudal tenure. The Tudors started to enlarge a central bureaucracy, and ended the power of seigneurs to appoint justices of the peace. Henry VIII abolished the monasteries. But the Tudors still relied on a landed militia system for military power: they had no standing army. The English militia system arose out of the military service provided by armed vassal loyalists. With the abolition of explicit feudal ties, militias acquired something of the character of a citizen army capable of defending the state in times of crisis, although militias continued to be led by local gentry and notables, albeit freeholders, and were thus never completely free of feudal overtones. The

---

*The reigns of the monarchs mentioned in this chapter are as follows: Henry VII (1485–1509); Henry VIII (1508–1547); Elizabeth I (1559–1603); Charles I (1625–1649); Charles II (1660–1685); James II (1685–1688); William III (1689–1702); and Anne (1702–1714).

very ambiguousness of this state of affairs had consequences: by the time of the death of Elizabeth I, Ireland had been militarily annexed by England, but the militia system limited the Crown's ambitions for further overseas expansion, and Parliament would not consent to taxes for a standing army. Neither Henry VII's refusal to call regular parliaments nor the later Stuart dynasty's contempt of parliament altered this. In the end, the conflict between the Crown's attempt to extend its power and the Parliament's resistance to this led to the English Civil War (1642). One of the key triggers for the Civil War was the attempt of Charles I to circumvent parliament and institute a standing army.

This was no ordinary power struggle. It was a struggle about the nature of power. The standing army was not just an expression of the modernization of the state by the Crown; it was also an expression of the *spirit* of modernity. The classical (Epicurean) maxim advised human beings not to live in fear or hope. Moderns not only rejected this maxim, but also found themselves living in both fear and hope at the same time. This was fear and hope of future contingencies—fear at what the future *might* bring and hope that the horrors of the future *might* be avoided. A standing army was an army standing in readiness to act—against future contingencies. These contingencies had a special quality. These were *imagined* possibilities. The modern mind was preoccupied with the future, and what alternative prospects and courses of action the future might present. But what was imagined was often the worst, for the baroque mind—the paradigm of the modern mind—allied the imagination less with reason than with prerational passions of fear, panic, anxiety, loss, melancholy, and so on. And as the possibilities that the modern mind imagined were often dreadful ones, so the institutional imperative was to prepare *against* those contingencies. As Thomas Hobbes recommended in *Leviathan* (1651), it was necessary to accumulate powers (arms, riches, and so on) against future possibilities.

The baroque imagination was phantasamagorical. It saw everything through *the mirror of the future*, and what was imagined looking into this mirror was a world of dark dreams and extravagant desires about to be born. The thought of *future contingencies*—the desired, hoped for, or feared events that *might* come to pass—had a galvanizing effect on human action. For baroque personalities the nightmares of the present were the future. These personalities could almost reach out and touch the future. Who they were was difficult to distinguish from what they *wanted* to be or *hoped* to become, and such hopes and desires were the flipside of fears and horrors. The future was at once promising and dreadful.

In fear of death, moderns armed themselves against future threats.

And in hope of reward, moderns traded on the future. New (future-orientated) financial markets (credit, stock, and property markets) were created in the seventeenth century. They offered the fantasy of a "golden future," and as such were traps for the credulous and unrealistic. Speculators learned to prey on those who imagined that great wealth was around the corner only if they invested in this scheme or that company. In speculative scheming—and this a great age of speculation—commerce became a kind of fantasy.[1] The speculator helped induce in others, and usually in themselves as well, the fantasy of wealth and success—a wealth or success that existed in the imagination: unreal, yet almost tangible; always "about to happen." Credit did the same as speculation. To live on credit meant that one could acquire all kinds of property, but, if one could not repay the debt, this meant living in a phantasmagorical world (a world of one's desires that *seemed* attainable but that was, in fact, fantastic and illusory). It is, of course, not only individuals who were capable of such delusions. Governments which built enormous standing armies, or which thought that they could wage endless wars, or build colossal empires on the basis of credit (debt) were equally credulous. National, as much as private, debts can create a fool's paradise. Debt is a correlative of the imagination: it can make present what is absent (the desire for national prestige, for might in defending one's interests, or for the expansion of trading monopolies.) It gives the designs and anticipations—the hopes—of governments a semblance of reality. Yet it is a fantastic reality if the money borrowed cannot be repaid, and repaid without bankruptcy or mortgaging the future earnings of the nation.[2]

The Hobbesian imperative, to accumulate (riches, arms) against future contingencies, expressed as well as anything one of the core self-understandings of modern life. But as much as this imperative was a shared semantic for moderns, it was also a source of division, for the question that it begged was: *Which contingencies matter*? Puritan opponents of the English Crown regarded the state building of the monarchy as being preoccupied with contingencies that were inconsequential. Religious dissenters, the puritans, lived in the face of "absolute contingency." Their God was an elector God who might or might not select them for salvation. They did not know whether they would be selected—their future was contingent. Yet God's choice was absolute. It was already predestined whether or not they would be saved. Yet they were denied the fatalism that one might have expected to accompany a doctrine of predestination. Their election was still, at least as far as their knowledge of the event was concerned, a contingent matter, and so they sought to prove the unprovable—that they had been elected to live in the grace of

God. The puritans developed an ascetic discipline—frugality, economy, methodicality, and severity—to manage the fact of living in the face of the dreadful paradox of absolute contingency. Their displays of ascetical "goodness" were "proof" of their election—proof of the unprovable. In other words, to prove the unprovable, the puritan was forced to go to extremes of "goodness." The ascetic drive of the puritan inevitably clashed with the expansive drive of the Crown. The Crown hedged its bets against worldly contingency with a large treasury, a growing bureaucracy, and a standing army; the puritan saints hedged their bets against absolute contingency with ascetic discipline. The court was all lace and finery; the puritan simplicity and plainness.

The puritans, who forged an "enthusiastic" antinomian mode of politics, believed in the immanent transcendence of all institutions and furiously rejected the law of the established church and of the state. The revolutionary saints, driven by passionate conviction and alienated from inherited laws, sought, in an apocalyptic moment, to overturn all human authority. The conjunction of traditional opponents of royal power with dissenting religious antinomians fueled the English Civil War. The antinomians, though, pushed the conflict beyond compromise, and drove the warring factions into chaos and exhaustion. In the consequent vacuum, Oliver Cromwell imposed his dictatorship. That the antinomian movement ended, in the English case, in the despotic, law-despising world of the Cromwellian dictatorship is not a surprise. For the dynamic of the modern baroque imagination seeks to escape all forms, all meaning-imparting structures. It is driven by sense of *reform* but at a certain point this becomes a desire for *formlessness*, and politically speaking, the vacuum of formlessness/destruction always appears as the personal dictate of the tyrant, who imposes *order without form*. While the dictatorship of Cromwell ended the English Civil War, it did so inconclusively. That the conflict—between the protagonists of a modernizing state with a bureaucratic structure and the opponents of this state—was not settled by the Civil War was clear when the Crown was restored in 1660 with Charles II on the throne. Charles's brother and successor James II* fell into dispute with Parliament because it (again) refused to allow the Crown to build a standing army, and this proved a trigger for James's expulsion and the invitation for William and Mary to accede to the throne in 1688–1689. The Glorious Revolution of 1688, however, still did not resolve the fundamental issue between the Crown and its opponents. Far

---

*In his time as lord high admiral, James directed military campaigns against the Dutch. Among other things, he was successful in removing New Amsterdam (New York) from Dutch control. James was the King of Britain from 1685 to 1688.

Aerial view of Blenheim Palace, Oxfordshire, UK.
Palace buildings designed by John Vanbrugh, and built 1705–1724.

from it. The logic of modernity is to build bureaucratic institutions, and this modernizing process was difficult to thwart. The expansionary significations of modernity survived the simple change of monarch.

Indicative of this, the years between the Glorious Revolution and the death of Queen Anne (1714) are the heyday of the English baroque. Somewhat more restrained than the continental baroque, it reflected simultaneously the reassertion of the expansionary power of the Crown and the obstacles that it faced. The precarious compromise between the two is reflected in the architecture of Christopher Wren (1632–1723), who created a baroque version of the classical. Sir John Vanbrugh (1664-1726), on the other hand, was less modest. Vanbrugh's most famous design, Blenheim Palace (1705), was "planned on a colossal scale. . . . The *corps de logis* has a massive portico with giant columns between giant pillars, and a heavy attic above. The same baroque weight characterizes the side elevations, especially the square squat corner towers of the wings. Here is a struggle, mighty forces opposing overwhelming weights; here are fiercely projecting moldings and windows crushed by thick-set pilasters placed too close to them; here is the deliberate discordance of the semicircular window placed against a semicircular arch right above, and higher up again a segmental arch. Everything jars, and the top of the daring composition has nothing of a happy end either."[3] *Eudaimonia*, the happy medium, is missing from these buildings. Vanbrugh's baroque expresses the tension and struggle of forces that *defy* balance, and that are highly directional in character. Yet the English baroque was never as frantic as its continental counterpart. "Spatial parts never abandon their separate existence, to merge into each other, as they do at S. Carlo or Vierzehnheiligen. The individual members, especially the solid round detached columns, try to keep themselves to themselves. English baroque is baroque asserting itself against an inborn leaning toward the static and the sober."[4] Suspicious of the enthusiastic excesses and rhapsodic possession that led to the Civil War, there is a distrust of the baroque's lack of reserve. Yet at the same time, the expansionary significations of modern life remain compelling, and difficult to resist.

COMMONWEALTH AND BUREAUCRACY

Nowhere was this appetite for expansion more evident than in the English Crown's attempt to become a continental power, an effort that led to the largest commitment of English military forces since the Middle Ages. Both William III and Queen Anne pursued a strategy of continental wars. England was at war with France (and France's allies) from 1689 to 1697 and 1702 to 1713. Both Whig and Tory cabinets were caught up in the war spirit, and both faced significant internal opposition from Parliament. The Whigs, from 1704 to 1710, prosecuted the war against France, and then in the face of national war weariness, lost governmental power to the Tories (1710–1714), who promptly split between those who wanted peace and those who wanted to continue the war. Whig ministers under William III were berated by Whig stalwarts for betraying the "Good Olde Cause" — forcing the growing differentiation of "Old Whigs" from court Whigs.

The last years of William III's reign saw a rerun of public arguments (first articulated prior to the Civil War and again in the restoration era) against a standing army. In the view of the critics, a standing army was a threat to liberty (once armies were paid for by taxes, those taxes would be collected by armies); the armed citizen was morally superior to the professional soldier (military service by a property-owning citizenry was an expression of civic virtue); the professional soldier was a lifelong dependent on the state rather than a free and independent person; the standing army was capable of enforcing royal power — it was the vehicle for the Crown to become a continental potentate instead of a power reciprocally dependent on other powers in the state (estates, parliament, etc.). The pioneers of these kinds of arguments were the "commonwealthmen" — followers or associates of James Harrington. They recognized that the end of feudal tenure had severely weakened the English grandees, and had thereby eroded feudal constraints on the monarchy. The commonwealthmen saw a threat from a despotic centralized patrimonialism, and wondered who would fill the shoes of the feudal grandees in forestalling such a state. Because they often sympathetically invoked examples of city regimes, and because they held dear the idea of the yeoman-soldier, the commonwealthmen are sometimes thought of as republicans. But their practical aim was in reality a *gothic limited monarchy*, not a republic.

Examples of city-republics were cited in order to suggest that it was not at all unusual in the European tradition for the power of monarchs or of an executive-magistracy to be limited. Henry Neville (1620–1694) in his *Plato Redivivus, or a Dialogue Concerning Government* (1681) makes effective use of this discursive strategy.[5] He cites the cases of republican Rome where the Senate proposed, the people resolved, and the magistrates executed; the aristocratic commonwealth of Sparta where the *aristoi* played a major role in administration; and Venice, where a hereditary nobility (plus "men of talent" adopted into it) managed the state. There were also the examples of the German Empire, which was composed of free towns as well as princes, and the Dutch government of the United Provinces that followed the model of the ancient Greek federations with a states-general made up of seven city-provinces that could act only with the concurrence of the whole seven. These provincial assemblies were composed of deputies sent by several cities of each province, and the cities in turn were governed by councils. Even in the French monarchy, Neville observed, towns were represented in the system of estates. The collective point of such examples was that monarchy was not the only viable or long-lasting kind of power. However, the English critics of monarchy were fundamentally of a "country," not of a "city," disposition. They sought to remodel England not as a city-republic, but as a commonwealth, which meant a gothic limited monarchy. The commonwealth, like the city-republic, was an alternative to the patrimonial state in which the monarch's household dominated all social relationships. In the original gothic structure of power that had replaced the power of Rome, other patrimonies (lords, the church) had acted as a counterweight to the power of princes. European feudalism was a special, decentralized kind of patrimonialism, and the idea of a commonwealth owed much to it.

Neville described how a limited monarchy had been "introduced by the Goths, and other Northern peoples" after the barbarian conquests of Rome.[6] Both princes and "great men" shared the lands of the conquered territories, and both acquired a hereditary right to their estates. Princes and nobles kept to themselves part of these lands as demesnes; the rest were granted as feuds to "freemen" tenants who performed services for lords such as following them to war. On the condition that these services were performed, tenancies were hereditary. Neville distinguished between this gothic yeomanry and other tenants (*villeins*) who performed servile offices for a lord and whose estates were the lord's to dispose as he pleased. What distinguished a gothic monarchy from other patrimonial monarchies was that the king did not possess all the property. Property (land) was distributed between kings and lords, whereas in a patrimonial monarchy, everyone in the state ultimately was a vassal or tenant of the king; all power lay in the hands of one person.

The consequence of unlimited monarchy was despotism. As Neville put it, such a prince could make, break, and repeal laws when he pleased, and dispense with them when he saw fit. The monarch could play favorites in adjudication; take away the life or estate of a person without formal trial process; and appropriate the revenue of towns and parishes, and administer them by employing appointed officers. England in the feudal age had successfully resisted such despotism. The reason for this was that the English Crown did not possess all lands, and because landed property was the foundation of power—so Neville argued—the English Crown therefore was not all-powerful. Barons and peers had successfully extracted from the Crown charters and laws protecting their rights, and had successfully entrenched a parliament from which the Crown had to seek authorization for many of its acts. This parliament, true, was summoned and dissolved by the Crown, but the law still determined how and when the king could do that, and peers in the counties had the power, if pressed, of calling together their vassals for war.

Since gothic times,[7] however, there had been a property revolution in England. Feudal arrangements had been altered or abolished. There was now a yeomanry no longer dependent on lords, but without political power. Meanwhile the lords, who had once interceded to ensure the assembling of parliament, were without feudal tenants, and their political power now rested on the memory and sentiment of feudal obligation rather than on its legality. "[The] people are kept from the exercise of that power, which is fallen to them by the law of nature; and those who cannot by that law pretend to the share they had, do yet enjoy it by virtue of that right which is now ceased. . . ."[8] The government of England, consequently, was broken. With the lords having lost their feudal hegemony, there was no longer an effective check on the Crown. This meant that monarchs were more and more ready to exercise their prerogative powers — such as to call and dissolve parliament — without consultation. Neville identified four crucial prerogative powers of the monarch: making of war and peace, treaties and alliances; ordering the militia, raising forces, garrisoning and fortifying places; nominating and appointing officers of the kingdom; and employing the public revenues of the kingdom. The question for the commonwealthmen was how — after the demise of the feudal arrangement — the prerogative powers of the Crown could be checked. Neville rejected the idea of divesting the monarch of these powers. Instead he argued that they should be exercised only with the consent of four councils appointed by parliament. These councils would act like the ephors of Sparta.

Such commonwealth arguments had a practical effect on the course of English state-building. The commonwealthmen were never numerous, and never constituted a party. But their propositions nonetheless found followers amongst both Whigs and Tories. Broadly speaking, the Tory party in parliament was proroyalist and the Whig party proparliament. But the structural arrangement of the Restoration state, as well as the general confusion of English society, contributed to a muddying of clear allegiances. In the English state there was no clear separation of powers. The Crown was "in Parliament." It recruited ministers from parliament; it had forms of patronage to manage parliament and induce its cooperation. Under these circumstances, Whigs could become "courtiers" and Tories could become backbench opponents of the Crown. Meanwhile, gentry supporters of the Tories often had reason to object to the Crown's buildup of bureaucratic military power because their taxes paid for it, while monied interests that might have been Whig in sympathies found the readiness of the Crown to borrow money to pay for its armies a pragmatically attractive thing. Thus, laid over the division between Whig and Tory was a division between country and court ideologies. Perhaps we could say that Whiggish principles were corrupted or that Tory stalwarts looked to their own interests. But in truth individual consciences were divided between the pull of modernity and the push of gothic liberties. On the one hand, the modern state offered, via its institutions, an expansion of activities that was remarkable, and if not actually irresistible, certainly compelling. On the other hand, the bureaucratic state threatened to overwhelm the independence of the parts of the old gothic society with its *dunamis*.

For all its real effects, the commonwealth argument did not go to the heart of the English difficulties. What it missed was that property, and in particular landed property, was not the only foundation of government. In this respect the commonwealth argument was indelibly gothic. In ancient cities (like Rhodes or even Athens), in Renaissance Italian cities (Florence, Venice), in French and German free towns, in the United Provinces, commercial wealth was a major force in city councils and social assumptions. Yet to read the commonwealth argument, it would seem that the fate of the city — indeed of all kinds of government — was shaped by agrarian laws. Nor was it true to say that property of whatever kind was the only foundation of government. In modern bureaucratic societies, nascent in the seventeenth century, offices were becoming as significant as property in determining a person's position in society. True, the commonwealth argument disapproved of the spread of "placemen" (officeholders) financed by taxes levied by the Crown. But at the same time the commonwealthmen believed that legal constraint, or the oversight of the committees of parliament, would obviate the power of the government of officers. A limited monarchy — a legally circumscribed monocratic administration — could regulate the spread of placemen. But such measures did not contest the nature of this office-power, or even its extent, only its potential abuse or misuse. Indeed such public oversight helped the Crown in its more speculative activities, such as public borrowings to finance its wars abroad. For it helped bolster public confidence. It boosted the faith of borrowers that they would be paid what was owed to them, despite the fortuitous outcomes of the wars and other imperial adventures that their money financed.

Bureaucratic offices in the English state expanded tenfold in the period between the 1660s and 1720s. These were offices of the Crown, not the personal retinue of the king or the retainers of the grandees. Of course, this was a bureaucracy in formation, and many of the features of the old regime still persisted. For example, patronage remained a key to getting appointed to office in the first place, and, to some extent, an influence in securing elevation to a higher office. Yet the features of a new structure of administrative power were also quite evident. Boards and departments of government were established or reorganized to employ a new class of officeholders. These officers were generally paid salaries, although some were still remunerated according to the fees they collected (which was, in effect, a form of feudal privateering). Bureaucratic offices were organized hierarchically, but the hierarchy was not a traditional or feudal one. It did not imply personal loyalty to those in command. Bureau-holders were not clients or vassals. From 1688 until the time of Queen Anne, a neofeudal system of ministerial patronage still flourished. Officeholders often lost their positions as ministerial power shifted from Whigs to Tories or back again. But even this ministerial patronage largely, if not completely, disappeared under Anne. Henceforth officeholders were assumed to be permanent, at least if they possessed a basic honesty and competence. Corruption and graft occurred, but the bureaucratic norm was that the officeholder subsist on a salary alone, and not accept private payments or use public monies for private benefit. This did not, however, preclude systemic corruption: the practices of officeholders occupying sinecures (for which they were paid, but did no work) or more than one office at a time (pluralism) or "deputizing" others to do their work for them, or department heads paying officers out of their own pocket as if they were clients, were commonplace enough. Yet such systemic anomalies occurred against a background—especially after the 1690s—where the duties of office were being regularized, and where a bureaucratic discipline of work was being created by reformers. This was done by techniques of rationalization. Offices were grouped into specialized departments or boards, each with a specific focus or area of competence. Rules were drawn up for each office. These established times of arrival and departure, specific tasks to be done by the officeholder, routines of daily and weekly business, procedures for handling business, making rulings and decisions, and so on. Out of the turbulence of the preceding century a new kind of order was being created. The order was achieved not by a balancing of powers or by a gothic arrangement, but by methodical practices: the careful, if unimaginative, following of organizational rules. The rationality of the officeholder was displayed in exact, precise ways of working. (The devil was now in the details.) The good officer was the efficient officer who had a knowledge of the rules of office and a methodical persona capable of following them with precision. By the end of the reign of Queen Anne (1714)—by which time the bureaucratic system had attained some stability—such a person could expect, once appointed, to serve in a department or board for a lifetime, and to be promoted within the hierarchy. Old patrimonial bonds of patron and client and family still influenced promotions, but the tendency was for these to be overdetermined by questions of the officeholders' specialist knowledge and experience and identification with departmental ways of working and of the seniority (length of service) of the officeholder.

This system was an answer to the disorders of the baroque age. But it was a very peculiar kind of order. It was far removed from the order of classical reason. It substituted rationality for reason. So then, was this system despotic? Perhaps, but not in the sense that the commonwealthmen and the advocates of the country ideology feared. What they had anticipated was the emergence of a centralized patrimony, something like the Ottoman Empire, where the will of the monarch determined everyone's life, property, and position. Critics of the monarchy saw the repeated efforts of the English Crown to create a standing army as the chief symbol of this. Yet a *permanent* army *could not* be patrimonial. A patrimonial prince employed vassals—together with contract soldiers (organized by feudal entrepreneurs)—who were mobilized as the occasion demanded. A standing army was something quite different. It possessed organizational continuity. It was an administrative entity that persisted over time. Its core was composed of commissioned officers (not vassal loyalists or irregular mercenaries) who were subject to codes and rules of conduct like their civilian counterparts. And like their civilian counterparts, their loyalty was not to a particular monarch or dynasty, but to the impersonalized Crown or sovereign. The behavior of such officers, as it became apparent, was not inherently despotic in the sense that they did not carry out measures giving effect to the angry whims or cruel pleasures of the monarch. Their behavior was codified, regularized, and disciplined by a bureaucratic (regulatory) law—and even, in the English case, additionally subjected to civil law.

The particular nature of this codification was influenced by commonwealth arguments. We see this in the regulation of the royal army. Some of the constraints on the English royal army included: (1) insistence on the supremacy of civilian law over military law and the rejection of the proposition that the wearing of the king's uniform provided any immunity from the reach of civil courts; (2) refusal to give the Crown the right to billet troops in private residences; (3) refusal to allow the Crown to quarter troops in barracks, on the premise that soldiers should intermingle with the general populace, and not associate together exclusively; (4) the prohibiting of troops from towns where an election was being held, unless with the express permission of local authorities; and (5) the requirement that troops be transported within England exclusively by *private* contractors. These constraints on the army were consistent with both the ideas of limited gothic monarchy *and* bureaucratic regularity.

As a standing army, the bureaucratic army possessed organizational continuity. As uniforms were introduced, the soldier bore an organizational identity. To stand no longer signified, as it had in the traditional (landed) order of things, a place in the chain of being. Nor did to stand signify the standing quietly, free of panic or rage, of the classical citizen. The standing of things was rather an ongoing readiness to meet contingency head-on. The standing army stood in preparation for contingencies. It planned for contingencies of threat or reward, invasion or discovery. Such organized action promised to master contingency and to control fortune. Traditional hierarchy had provided some protection from contingent events (plague, invasion, factionalism, and so on). Classical virtue shaped characters to both stand up to malign contingencies and not get carried away with fortunate events. Modern organization offered neither asylum nor fortitude but instead the prospect of controlling future possibilities by acting methodically. Contingency (the uncertainty/ambiguity of the future) could be mastered by accumulating power (the power of arms, riches, etc.) in a methodical way, via offices, and deploying that power systematically to meet the threat or exploit the possibilities of the future.

Moderns opened up the future. An expansive (transoceanic, transcontinental) drive accompanied a desire to explore unknown, uncharted, and boundless reaches. The classical sense of *acting with both destination and limit in mind* was dispelled. At the same time, moderns sought to control the future—first by anticipating it (imagining it, predicting it) or by subduing it with rationally organized power—with the planned deployment of agents, offices, rationally budgeted materials, and so on. This rational organization involved a kind of modern asceticism. Rational—i.e., effective and efficient—organization did not waste energies, materials, or time. This asceticism, however, was quite unlike that of the citizen-farmer of the old Roman republic. The asceticism (the vernacular stoicism) of the ancient citizen-farmer of Rome did not insure against the contingencies of the future. Unlike moderns, the Romans assumed that one could not master such contingencies. (It was only at the tail end of the Renaissance that such a thing was thought of.) Rather it was supposed that fortune would upset the best-laid plans. The virtue of the citizen-farmer was a way not of controlling fortune but of *adapting* to it. For the citizen-farmer, the climate was an uncertain thing, as was politics. Bad luck could visit the farmer in the form of poor seasons or the volcanic eruptions of politics. The citizen-farmer could not master this fortune, but nonetheless could attain a certain independence from it via the possession of arms, property, and the vote, and an ascetic moral character—all of which provided a type of stability, a "standing firm" in the face of the fluctuations of fortune.

SHAFTESBURY'S SYSTEM

Modern asceticism was the correlate of an order of rationality. This order of rationality shared certain features with the classical order of reason. Systemic organization persisted over time and it unified disparate social parts, functions, and powers. But whereas in an order of reason this durability was an effect of individual and collective *character*, such character was lacking from rationalized modern organization.

Was an order of reason still possible in English society? Anthony Ashley Cooper, third earl of Shaftesbury (1671–1713), thought so. Through works that he wrote at the turn of the eighteenth century, he was to have a profound influence on Alexander Pope, Francis Hutchenson, and Immanuel Kant, among others. Shaftesbury was born to the world of the aristocratic farmer-citizen. But by inclination, he was drawn to the world of the maritime city. In Rotterdam and Naples he was to write his most challenging works[9] — in the guise of the stoic philosopher removed from the demands of English parliamentary life and estate management. On the surface of things, Shaftesbury was a member of the country party of Old (anti-court) Whigs, but his "country" was also the world of coastal Dorset.[10] Judging the world from the vantage point of a place halfway between Commonwealth parliamentary politics and a maritime stoicism that came to a head in his periods of self-exile in Rotterdam and Naples, Shaftesbury was to challenge many of the key premises of thought in the baroque age, principally that:

(1) Virtue (or justice) had no other measure, law or rule than fashion and custom;

(2) The dominant emotions are prerational ones including fear, frenzy, and anger; the greatest fear is the fear of death; the highest good is the good of life; the imagination imagines the worst; and reason devises methods and institutions for avoiding the worst;

(3) God is a punitive and commanding figure, a deity of power.

Against these baroque assumptions, Shaftesbury postulated that:

(a) The purpose of human acting, feeling, and reflecting is to serve a larger system (a harmonious order) of things, ultimately the cosmic order.[11] This cosmos is made up of a vast collection of systems or natures — inanimate and vegetable, animal and human, which together comprise a universal nature. The good or end of a creature is that creature's relationship to the system to which the creature belongs. To put it another way: nature is order in the universe.

(b) The nature of being human is that a person is capable of behaving rationally, which is to say morally. An individual is capable of acts or emotions beneficial to the whole. Virtue is a relationship to the whole; virtue is synonymous (in a manner of speaking) with order. A human being is capable of natural affection, a love of harmonious wholes. Conversely, if natural affections are absent, disharmony results.

(c) Nature is reason in action, feeling, and reflection. All human beings have a *sense of right and wrong*, of rational reflection, action, and emotion. Nature in this way resides in the hearts of human beings. But the development of this internal sense may be distorted or restricted in a number of ways.

The internal sense may be opposed by nonrational ideas of divinity — of a nonrational God who punishes those who do not sin, or a God who threatens sinners with hellfire, or an unjust God who plays dice with the salvation of believers. To ground morality in the fear of punishment or the hope of reward in the afterlife is to corrupt morality. Shaftesbury's deity, by contrast, is benevolent and punishes no one. Rather, there is a beneficial necessity at work in the universe. Like the Stoics, Shaftesbury thought of the universe as one living creature or living soul, encompassing all things with a single purpose — ordering them or patterning them to a beneficial end. Each part of the universe was interdependent on all other parts, and these elements were combined via the (Pythagorean-Platonic) principles of order, symmetry, regularity, union, and coherence, or else (Shaftesbury alternatively explained) they were united together by a (Stoical) common sense or feeling — *sympathy*.[12] There is an all-knowing, all-intelligent nature that is sympathetic to all the parts of the universe. This nature is a deity — what Shaftesbury variously called a presence, an eternal and infinite mind, an intelligent principle that is inherent in everything and that makes each thing contribute to the whole.

The internal sense may be opposed by nonrational emotions (passions). Such emotions as fear and panic may swamp natural affections or cognitive feelings. In such cases perturbations will dominate the mind and will render the individual incapable of pleasure. Feelings of fear or guilt or melancholy will supplant feelings of calmness, steadiness, or constancy.

The internal sense may also be corrupted by the operation of flux — a species of cosmic rot — that erodes the stability of systems, corrodes them so that nothing is fixed, so that all is change and succession, and eventually cataclysm.

(d) Human beings are free insofar as they partake of Nature — insofar as they *follow Nature*, to use the old Stoic maxim. They are free because they can act, feel, and reflect rationally. Like the Stoics, Shaftesbury believed that human beings cannot control external events—they are unable to *master* contingency. They cannot make the elector God choose them; they cannot anticipate every military contingency, every possible threat, every twist and turn of fortune and misfortune. Does that make human beings the victims of events? of chance? the hostages of fortune? playthings of fate? Not at all. Human beings are still *free* because they possess reason, and through reason they can achieve order—both *internal* and *external* order. Internal order frees the human being from the despotism of the passions. This is the stoical inner freedom. External order (the shape of things) frees the human being from the despotism of arbitrary events.

Thus, through their ordering, forming, patterning capacity persons can in a stoical manner *adapt to the contingent, chance, unpredictable events that lie in the future,* or in a Pythagorean-Platonic manner they *can create hospitable worlds for themselves that are not simply random or arbitrary or accidental but that have something of the cohesion and harmony of ultimate beauty.*

A person can achieve *internal order.* To do this, the Stoics had recommended *ataraxia*—disinterest in those things we have no effective control over. As Shaftesbury put it, God has put some things under our control and others not under our control. Those individuals who do not disconnect from what they have no control over will be perturbated—upset, frightened—and will easily fall into frenzies, rages, tumult, and commotion. The passionate person is a disordered person, and such internal disorder is imprisoning. The person who emotionally invests in what he or she has no control over becomes a captive of that event. The person who is detached, in contrast, displays emotional calm in the face of chance, contingent events in the world. Contingency will not faze this person; it will not disturb this person's tranquility, and will not trigger fury, commotion, tempers, or trepidation.

A person can achieve *order outside of the self.* Because all persons share reason, all are members of a larger community of humankind—members of what the Stoics called the *kosmopolis* or what they otherwise referred to as *to koinon* or the fellowship of humankind. This human order or (in Shaftesbury's terms) human system is universal. There is a social reason or natural affection that binds human beings together. The operation of this reason may be impaired by other factors (passions, etc.), but human beings can act and feel and reflect dispassionately; *they can invest their energies in pattern creation, and can draw intellectual pleasures from the results of this form giving.* They can enjoy the intellectual pleasure of stepping back, in tranquility, from the order they create and admire it. The mind grasps the splendor and variety of the world, at the same time as it grasps its under-lying coherence and harmony.[13] Human order is exhibited in *graceful* actions, *beautiful* human characters, *well-proportioned* minds and bodies, and *sociable* feelings.[14] The internal sense recognizes the patterns, order, symmetries, and harmonies of the whole. It recognizes *decency* in human company, *justice* in society, *order* in the cosmos, and *truth* in the patient, steady observation of the world. The search for human order (for form) culminates, in Shaftesbury's eyes, in the arts. The internal sense (the pat-tern recognition sense), when it is directed toward artistic objectivations, is called *taste*. The tasteful person has a well-developed sense of the form and harmony of artworks. (Music with its connection to harmony is the art that is the closest to the *nature* of things.) With the corruption of taste comes the stagnation of arts.[15] In particular, courts (court patronage) corrupt the arts—exemplified, for Shaftesbury, in the English court's patronization of the barbaric (the gothic) and the unharmonious (the baroque, the French princely style). Taste counters this by turning to *Italy*, to the example of the Italian city-republics, especially to the example of Raphael. Good taste rejects the embrace (by seventeenth-century artists) of the grotesque and the distorted. Where the baroque unites fearful passion and imagination, Shaftesbury argues instead for a uniting of reason and imaginative trans-port, something that the Italian Renaissance artist had achieved.

In all of this, Shaftesbury returned to the Greek-Ionian idea of *kos-mopoiêsis*. In this conception, *politics is the creation or ordering of the world*. The first act of politics is the creation of the just order of things. Politics, after this, is the attempt to reiterate that order of things—to recreate a just ordering in the midst of the struggle, sometimes the terrible struggle, of competing forces. This ordering is achieved by bringing powerful diver-gent forces into equilibrium. With time and its contingencies these forces will eventually tear apart. But where the equilibrium of forces has been attained, it can be reiterated. Such reiteration is not a return to the past, for each reiteration is played out in different circumstances, with a dif-ferent constellation of forces. What is reiterated is not the conditions of the past, but the form, the image, of a beautiful arrangement of opposing powers—a way of harmonizing opposites so they lose nothing of their spirit, energy, or vigor, but rather mesh together in a just rather than vio-lent, ordered rather than chaotic, way.

Shaftesbury's significance is that he returns to the premise of classical politics, to the question of *kosmopoiêsis*. He in effect asks how is order (*kosmos*) possible? Just as Plato had looked to the model of the artisan to answer this question, Shaftesbury invokes the model of the artist. The artist creates a *kosmos* by the exercise of taste. Morality, ethics, and politics are like art in this respect. Different impulses and motives, aims and ambitions, interests and values are put together so they do not clash violently and resolve into chaos. This does not obliterate differences or conflicts or antipodal natures; rather, it orders them so they do not end up alienating each other, so that differences and conflicts do not end in violent estrangement.

THE AUGUSTAN AGE

Shaftesbury's importance is his preparedness to take seriously the legacy of Hellenism and its understanding of the importance of *kosmopoiêsis*. Shaftesbury's contemporaries and successors, however, were less attracted to this legacy. Indeed the key point of reference for the English eighteenth century was Augustan Rome, not Hellenism. That this should be so is not surprising. For what the English settled upon after the troubles of the baroque age had more than a passing resemblance to the socio-historical arrangement instituted by Augustus. The imagery of Augustan Rome and the Principate resonates in the politics and culture of eighteenth-century England.

A sense of Augustan resolution, indeed relief, came with the death of Queen Anne (two years after the death of Shaftesbury). With the Tory party sorely divided, the Whigs invited George of Hanover to become king in 1715. In the protracted course of the Hanoverian settlement, the political ferment of the seventeenth century gave way to an atmosphere that accommodated both the pull of modernity and the push of the gothic. The Georgian Crown continued, as its predecessors had, the process of modern state-building, but its administrative and military efforts were focused abroad and oceanically, not domestically or continentally. Regal ambitions for a continental monarchy were replaced by the ambitions for an oceanic empire, first of all in the Atlantic basin, then in the Far East, the Pacific, and Africa, while imperial expansionism abroad was tempered by a constitutional order at home. Naval bases were established at Gibraltar and Minorca, Jamaica and Antigua, Boston and Nova Scotia. This strategy was quite disarming to the gothic-commonwealth critics of the power of the Crown, which they identified with *landed military* forces (the army). There was no precedent for criticizing a royal *navy*. Indeed the gothic monarchies that had originally broken the back of Roman power established an identity in the European mind between monarchy and land-based armies. Sea-borne powers were city (or city-based) regimes like Venice or the Dutch republic's United Provinces (i.e., thalassocentric republics). The seas, the classical, and the city were reciprocally identified. Now the British Crown broke the mold, as a monarchy that looked to the seas — or rather the oceans, with a blue-water policy and a vision of a transoceanic trading empire that had no equivalent (or precedent) among the continental European monarchies. The critics of the standing army could not match this shift in approach. They were either disinterested in the seas — as a country party — or, if they were of a more classical disposition, the odyssean sea had an enduringly positive connotation. The Shaftesburyians were no better prepared than the Goths to meet this challenge. Even the very late Augustan figure of Jane Austen, a female Aristotelian and an inheritor of Shaftesbury's legacy, succumbed to key gothic assumptions — that city life was wicked (the site either of the court or of moneymaking) and soldiers were dangerous, while navy personnel were to be treated with affection.[16]

One of the paradoxes of Augustan England is that the classically-minded absorbed gothic ideals, while the Crown appropriated (and transformed) the peripatetic vision of the ancients. The fall of the Tories from government and the installation of the Georgian monarchy were accompanied culturally by the decline of the English baroque and an upsurge of interest in classical humanist ideas of a *Caesarist* kind. The point of reference of the latter was not the republican but the imperial city of Rome, the Rome of Augustus. The English Augustan age took as its model the literature of the first Augustan age — the works of Horace, Virgil, Ovid, and the writers of the first two centuries of the Empire, including Juvenal, Longius, and Martial, when imperial Rome was culturally most vital. Its towering work of history was Edward Gibbon's *Decline and Fall of the Roman Empire* (first volume 1776). The interests of eighteenth-century Augustans, like the Romans themselves, were cosmopolitan. They embraced the Syrian philosopher-satirist Lucian, the Spanish rhetorician Quintilian, and the Greek essayist Plutarch. From this starting point Augustan humanism cast its net wider, drawing into itself the work of Roman stoics, epicureans, and eclectics of both the republican and imperial epochs.

The model of the Augustan-Roman architect Vitruvius was also deeply felt (filtered, of course, through the experience of the Italian Renaissance). Indeed, the Whig ascendancy of 1715 coincided with the publication of the first volume of *Vitruvius Britannicus*[17] — an illustrated compendium of classical architecture in Britain by the Scottish architect and Whig Colen Campbell (1676–1729). Campbell criticized the baroque "excesses" of Wren and High Church Toryism, promoting instead the classicism of the English Renaissance, especially that of Inigo Jones. The same year that *Vitruvius Britannicus* was published, Richard Boyle, the third earl of Burlington (1694–1753), returned to England from a study tour in Italy and began to renovate Burlington House, located in London's Piccadilly, in the classical style of Palladio and Jones, in collaboration with Campbell. Campbell also designed such buildings as Wanstead House (Essex, 1717), Stourhead House (Wiltshire, 1721), and most importantly Houghton Hall (Norfolk, 1722) for the Whig Prime Minister Sir Robert Walpole. For Houghton Hall, Campbell drew heavily on the ideas of Jones's English classicism, while Burlington's design for Chiswick Villa (1725) utilized the proportions of Palladio and the architectural vocabulary of Vincenzo Scamozzi (1552–1616), a follower of Palladio and Sebastiano Serlio. Burlington's Assembly Room in York added Jonesian ideas to this mix. Burlington and his collaborator William Kent designed Holkham Hall (Norfolk, 1734) for Thomas Coke, the Whig earl of Leicester, basing their design on Palladio's Villa Trissino and his Villa Mocenigo. These different projects expressed a common political (or rather ethico-political) ideal: that of moderation. Their classicism aspired to a classical equilibrium and a putting to rest of political extremism: a preference for what Oliver Goldsmith (1730–1774) called "the warmth of candor" in place of the "virulence of hate" — a rejection of the fanaticism and civil warring of the mid-seventeenth century in favor of a temperate worldliness. Artistically, this meant a preference for beauty over grandeur. Robert Morris, in his *Essay in Defense of Ancient Architecture* (1728) and his *Lectures on Architecture* (1734), argued for a return to the "beauty and harmony" of the ancients as opposed to the "irregularity" of the "modern" school of Vanbrugh, Hawksmoor, and their ilk.

None of this neoclassicism, though, possessed anything like the vigor or strength of its Italian Renaissance predecessors. It is as though the English were grand tourists when visiting with the ancients. With the important exception of Shaftesbury, they could not match the kosmopoietical force of the Hellenes. Neoclassicism meant, in principle, a return to the system of harmonic proportions of Pythagoras and Plato. The Augustans spoke in the same breath of the well-proportioned building and the just proportions of a good society. But in practice the English could not realize this. After Shaftesbury the radicalism of the Greek-Ionian conception was diluted. For all its latitude, the humanism of the age remained indubitably Augustan in its tone. Britain was not a city-republic; it was a monarchy and an empire, and one that was still based on status distinctions. Yet it was a monarchy and an empire that modeled itself not on an agrarian patrimony like ancient Egypt, but on the urbane and civil society of Rome.

The English Augustans admired writing that was economical and that avoided excess. The ideal verse, like the ideal society, exhibited clarity and order, and achieved beauty by hitting the exquisite mean.[18] The Augustans distrusted the extravagant and the disorderly in culture, and the political and religious counterpart of this: fanaticism. The calm spectator was preferred to the enthusiastic meddler. The Augustan was not an earnest crusader or a belligerent social isolate, but a cheerful, good-tempered person, at ease with the world, accepting of its ways. This did not mean that the Augustan humanist was indifferent to suffering or injustice, but rather that he was disinclined to rant about such things, or believe that the world should be turned upside down to redress injustice and alleviate suffering. Indeed, the Augustan belief was that to subvert the world like this would cause more misery and injustice than it eradicated, and that restraint (order) in action might more often be the cause of justice between persons than fantastical attempts to do away with all human structure, or to locate an immanent *nomos* in an enthusiastic activism that proved itself by more and more extreme, or fanciful, actions.

This sense of restraint did not mean that the English Augustans were narrow-minded or provincial in their politics or in the literatures they championed. On the contrary, they showed interest in a remarkable range of classical sources and models, and in this exhibited an attitude, typical of the classical humanist, that goes back to the Scipionic Circle and its readiness to include figures as diverse as the Greek historian Polybius and the North African comic dramatist Terence. The classical (Greco-Roman) values of order and clarity (and brevity) were not at all antithetical to diversity and breadth of learning and character, only to extravagance and excess. The belief was that a great variety of parts could be united in a social structure, on the condition that the design was regular, that it manifested order, economy, and just proportions. The Augustan humanists exhibited a skeptical detachment that allowed them to mix different styles of thinking (e.g. stoic and epicurean).[19] No single set of beliefs had absolute validity. The Augustans were ready to recognize the (partial) truth in different systems, and to combine those truths in order to create a composite design—a *composition*. Intellectual dexterity and versatility were admired. The religious counterpart of this was a latitudinarianism that rejected warring sects, sectarian zeal, and vehemence.[20] The intellectual counterpart of this was toleration. The governmental counterpart of this was a constitutional monarchy. However, all of this betrayed a certain *weakness of thought*. Latitude and toleration are attractive antidotes to enthusiastic dogmatism. But the satirical, wry, skeptical, even comedic tone of the Augustans papers over in many cases a lack of serious ideas. Shaftesbury aside, the thought of the Augustan age lacks depth. It is mocking, witty, acidic, but not *strong*. The struggle of kosmopoietical creation, the strain of competing forces, the effort required to order those forces, does not resonate in Augustan writing.

The Augustan more readily *identifies with the the observer of creation, rather than with the artisan or artist of creation.* Thus the sense of a tremendous, aching struggle of creation is lost. In the Augustan conception, *order is not produced but observed.*

COMMON SENSE

Commenting on Vanbrugh's Blenheim Palace, Alexander Pope, one of the great spokesmen of the Augustan age, remarked of its colossal scale and the extravagance of Vanbrugh's architecture: "Something there is more needful than expense/And something previous even to taste—'tis sense."[21] *Taste* and *sense* encapsulates the spirit of the Augustan age. Conservatives and radicals alike drank from the same well—a well not of enthusiasm or inspiration, but of cautionary balance and moderation. Yet it was also a spirit lacking in greatness or immortality.

In the language of the age, *taste* represented the mean between extremes; the union of antitheses. Taste never conceded much to agonizing or ecstatic intensities. The Augustan attitude, unlike its baroque predecessor, was objective, not subjective; reflective, not passionate; urbane and fluent, not hectoring and angry; assured and judicious, rather than dissatisfied and turbulent. Consequently anything colossal, unlimited, or one-sided was not in "good taste." What *was* tasteful was the balanced, symmetrical presentation of different states—values, emotions, and deeds. To achieve "good taste," the artist or the politician had to be an *observer* or *spectator* of the "diverse natures" of humanity.[22] And for such taste to be possible, it required the artist or politician to possess *common sense.*

At the beginning of the eighteenth century, common sense was closely allied to reason. *Common sense was a faculty that formed or shaped things.* It was a sense that ordered the diverse impressions provided by the external senses. It arranged impressions into a coherent whole. It did the work of reason (or of rational intuition). In this view, common sense was a cognitive faculty—a sense that we have for apprehending and ordering the diversity (and complexity) of the world by creating patterns.

On the simplest level, an inward or common sense combines the information we have from our different outward senses. What we *see* in the world around us is often contrary to what we *hear.* We constantly "check and balance" the information of one of our senses against the information of some other. The combination and checking for consistency of sense data is a primitive (everyday) version of the operations required to "check and balance" different sets of norms, values, and feelings that are encountered in the world. The sensible person is the one who can move judiciously among countervailing expectations and practices. Common sense *orientates* us in a complex world. The cognitive (yes/no) judgments that we make on the basis of common sense register relations amongst things, events, and actions in the world. These judgments make sense of the world by discovering its patterns, its systems. At the core of such systems is reason. The common sense is the organ for perceiving — *recognizing* — the connective (formative) power of reason in the world. We judge something positively because it corresponds to a pattern or shape of things. We approve of an action because it fits an order of things. When our action is consistent with other actions that we undertake, our life (over time) acquires shape, and with it significance. It exhibits reason. On the other hand, if judgments are not based on common sense/reason, then we live in fear or hope; we judge from the depths of melancholy or from the heights of fantasy; and a life lived this way will be chaotic or incoherent.

The idea of a common sense was the great philosophical discovery of the Augustans. Yet, for all of their distaste of chaos or incoherence, *the Augustans could not turn their notion of common sense from a receptive to a productive faculty.* Thus Augustan reason was incapable of producing a beautiful world. The basis of art production — and also of the creation of the *kallipolis* — is the externalizing (objectivating) of the pattern (the "mental pictures") perceived by common sense. Augustan common sense, however, lacked productive force. It was capable of *appreciating* fine form, even of copying it, but not of creating it. It could not manage the work of *kosmopoiêsis*. And as Augustans came to a self-recognition of this, they gave up even the pretence to it, and *common sense and reason became separated.* The common sense became thought of as akin to a particular sense — most often the analogy was drawn with the external sense of taste. A person of good taste was good at discriminating (say) sweet and sour, fruity or piquant, even at appreciating the subtle combination of tastes. Taste could be cultivated, educated, instructed, and refined. But as the inner sense was separated from reason, it was no longer productive or thought of as productive. It no longer *ordered* the materials and sensations of the world; it just appreciated them.

This meant that eventually even the nature of appreciation changed. If reason was separated from the inner sense then form could no longer be the basis of appreciative judgments. Other qualities — ranging from engagement to chaos, transgression to sensationalism — would have to be substituted for form. But when this happened, *the consideration of art was transformed into the consideration of aesthetics.* To inquire into art is to inquire into the artist's creation of shape or form. The appreciation, wonder, and enjoyment of art are responses of the inner sense when it recognizes the form of the artwork and all of the energies, materials, forces, and themes the artist has drawn together in the artwork. Yet in an aestheticized world — in which judgment no longer rests on reason — appreciation can be as much of the artist's *failure* to give form as it is of the artist's success in creating a form.

To turn the question of art into one of aesthetic appreciation is to take away from the consideration of art the most important issue: *How is it possible to give form?*

LEGISLATORS AND OBSERVERS

The power to give form is also the first question of politics. And just as the Augustans aestheticized art, so did they astheticize politics.

A sensible politics was one where executive, courts and parliament, land and commerce "checked and balanced" each other. But in the English Augustan world, the image of the *agôn* of social forces was interlaced with images of hierarchy and stratified social order. At the same time, common sense, exhausted by the battles of the preceding century, conceded much to modern rationality. Consequently the eighteenth-century English constitution was animated less by the idea of a classical order of reason and more by a tenuous accommodation of hierarchy and protobureaucracy, tradition and modernity, country and court. Thus, from the *demiourgoi's* point of view, the state that the English built was a rather ramshackle thing: a cobbling together of gothic, lordly, and imperial significations. This was less a balanced constitution than an eclectic accommodation.

The English through the eighteenth century consolidated what was a partially rationalized state. They rapidly expanded the apparatus of offices at home and a blue-water empire abroad under the auspices of the Crown. This was achieved at the same time as parliament asserted itself as a legislator and an overseer of government. English common sense permitted the coexistence of strong vestiges of traditional amateur administration, gentrified independence, family connections, status lines, and personal recommendation — in short, traditional "country" behaviors — alongside the new discipline of office power. There was indeed an accommodation of contending forces — one prompted by the stalemate of the preceding century. Thus an English monarch might preside over the growing state machine and still pretend to be a mere "farmer." But if "country" and "court" were reconciled, the English were singularly lacking in any classical notion of "city." There was no city center around which the contention between office and estate was modulated. The English parliament, true, was functioning increasingly as a public forum where opposing sides were heard (instead of where social estates petitioned the Crown and the Crown summoned their services). The English successfully established a model of government and loyal opposition. However, parliamentarians were not city builders but legislators. They were members of the houses of parliament, not of the councils of the city. They assumed responsibilities for laws and budgets, not for the city's public spaces of appearance.

In telling contrast, the making of laws had been regarded by the ancient Greeks as a secondary aspect of politics—important but not primary. Even the Romans still held as the chief signification of their politics the idea of the city (of Rome). While the English parliamentarians stood and spoke in a public space—though one still thought of as a "house" — their deeds were not centrally directed to the public thing: to the defense and enhancement of the *res publica*. The ancient politician was concerned with *kosmos* (order) before law. Law was a derivative of *kosmos*. *Kosmos* was in the first place a function of *logos* (reason). *Logos* ordered things, events, actions, and feelings, and achieved the good ordering of things by its formative power. This *logos* was something more than merely speech, as it came to be thought of later. The idea that "the word" gives rise to good order (*eunomia*) or that reason is "the word" is fallacious. If the contrary were true, laws alone would prevent social disintegration, collapse, and catastrophe, which in no century have they done. Neither legal—nor for that matter moral—commandments create eunomic states. The ancient citizen knew that *eunomia* was a function not of words but of the *res publicae*—the public places and spaces of the city. These *res publicae* were a function of reason—of the quality/force that united the different parts of a thing in a beautiful form. It was the *res publica* that exhibited the pattern of ancient society — and that provided the all-important boundary for human activity and ambition.

Thus the beautiful order of things was displayed—so far as ancient politics was concerned—in the form of the city. The *eunomia* (good ordering) of the city was the first and highest responsibility of the ancient citizen. To carry out this responsibility required the *power to give form*. It required the capacity to shape the city—to be the *demiourgos*, the craftsman, of the public places of appearance. The English *legislator* lacked this faculty. The greatest of their breed in the eighteenth century, Edmund Burke, demonstrates this very well. Though he was a brilliant polemicist and speechmaker, no work of material creation is associated with his name. Rather, what he is remembered for is a series of devastating critiques of English (colonial) and French (revolutionary) politics—*the judgments of the observer par excellence*. It is also no accident that Burke was one of the first theorists of aesthetics. In his remarkable philosophical pamphlet on the beautiful and the sublime, he marked out in the middle of the eighteenth century—and, incidentally, well before Kant—the shift of interest of moderns away from the creation (production) of the beautiful to the reception (appreciation) of the sublime.[23] The very shift of preoccupation away from reason to aesthetic judgment signaled the fracturing of the classical idea of politics. The consequence was the *aestheticization* of citizenship. Rather than the citizen being the producer of the *order of things*, and participant in the making (*poiêsis*) of a civic order, the citizen gradually came to be thought of as no more than the evaluator—the *observer*—of legislators and ministers. *Ergo modern citizenship*. That Burke should turn in disgust when the new French citizens—born of the French revolution—took pleasure in the horrors of the guillotine is simply ironic. For the subject of modern (sublime) aesthetics was *the observer*—the observer of barely imaginable horrors or sensational events.

Modern democracy grew out of the idea of citizen-as-observer. Once the citizen was thought of as an observer, it became much easier to begin universalizing citizenship. It was easier to draw the conclusion that everyone possessed the faculty of taste than to have to contend that everyone possessed a forming/patterning faculty. It was easier to imagine everyone as an art critic than everyone as an artist. Anyone (eventually, with the spread of literacy and so on) could give an account of their distaste (for governments, leaders, factions). Everyone had an *aesthetic sense*, an inner sense or *sensibility*, through which they could express like and dislike, approval and disapproval, and if necessary reconcile the evidence of their eyes and the evidence of their ears, the odor of government corruption and the silky feel of the prime minister, when making their electoral judgments. Everyone possessed this *common (aesthetic) sense*. The modern citizen eagerly awaited something, anything, to horrify this new sense. Outrage and shock became the natural sentiments of the modern citizen, while protestation and enthusiasm (feelings of the ethical sublime) became a common affinity between citizens whatever their differences.

THE SUBLIME

Aesthetic sense proved to be a halfway house between the modern version of classical form and the romantic sublime. The idea of the sublime identified the boundless and the amorphous as the proper object of art, in the place of form. As romantic currents surfaced in the late eighteenth century, the boundless and the amorphous were equated with the nature of modern society. Such claims were a self-fulfilling prophecy. They announced a new signifying core of a society dominated by mood—captive to atmosphere, to the play of light and shadows, to waves of panic and enthusiasm, anxiety and impulsiveness. A sensationalist, amorphous ("painterly") society was possible only because moderns—against the advice of the ancients—were prepared to live in fear and hope. In the classical conception, reason *modulated* fear and hope, pre- and post-rational experiences. Classical reason laid things together in a way that gave those things shape or form. The shape of things was their limit or boundary. It gave things a certain self-containment or independence (*autarkeia*). The shape of things persisted over time; it had continuity; it gave a *character* to things. Human action was rational when it did not exceed the end (*telos*) or boundary of things. Reason ruled where post-rational feelings of imaginative transport (hope, dreams, ecstasy, fantasy, "forgetting," reverie, longing, free associating, curiosity) did not get out of bounds; where they did not transport a person or a society into an infinite, overflowing cascade. Likewise, human action was rational where neither person nor society was transfixed by fear or any other prerational affect or passion (desire, despair, grief, jealousy, panic, vengefulness, melancholy, greed, rage, appetite, disgust, anger).

Reason, through virtue (self-control), establishes boundaries. Actions, feelings, and thoughts that arise out of reason are concerned with "orientation" and "contact." Reason orients by the creation/recognition of patterns in the midst of disorder. Reason both creates and recognizes relationships, linkages, and contacts between different things (persons, events, activities). The person (society) of reason forms patterns and maintains the limit (*peras*) of those patterns, and the independence of things that this *peras* creates. The actions of the rational person (society) are constant, not passionate. They do not erupt but persist, and they are persistent in the face of threat, scourge, and death. The rational person is not easily discouraged or intimidated. This is partly because of the rational virtues of courage, constancy, or fortitude. It is also because the rational person is confident, a confidence that comes from a firm knowledge of self that is possible only because the person is a self-contained entity, unwavering in its essential orientation over time, and therefore knowable with confidence.

In the modern age *reason is replaced by rationality*. Reason therefore decreasingly modulates fear and hope. To achieve this, moderns jettisoned the idea of the limit. Fascinated by boundlessness and infinity, they came to believe themselves the masters of infinite space. Moderns believed that there was a nature (*phusis*) of things, but not a shape of things, which bit by bit led them to eliminate necessity from the idea of nature. Nature was, as it had also been for the ancients, growth—but without limits. The modern *phusis* was growth, development, and expansion without *peras* or final cause. Growth without shape has no internal necessity, no *logos*. Growth without shape tends to the indefinite, the enormous, the vast. Such growth produces the unexpected, the surprising, the astonishing, the unfathomable. It spreads out into terrain that is beyond the boundary, that is uncharted, unknown. It transports human beings into wild and chancy and obscure territory: *terra incognita, terra nullus*. Exploration of the continent of *terra nullus* tends toward a state of pure contingency. Whatever happens next cannot be anticipated with any certainty or even probability. Much about this exploration is fortuitous, chancy, surprising, eventful, riddled with "perhaps" and "maybes," governed by luck, and so on. Yet moderns, at the same time, wish to master this contingency. They do so because of its *phusis*, which pushes and transports it and them beyond the boundaries of the known world into barely imagined continents whose strange terrain, even for the bold and adventurous, has a topography of dark abysses. This nature is sublime, and it triggers fear in those who look upon it or imagine it. The fear of sublime nature is terror. Moderns seek to master this terror (their fears of plunging into the abyss to their death) by rational calculation (rationality). Yet at the same time they are fascinated by the sublime and hope to abandon themselves to the abyss (to plunge freely into its depths).

The great English eighteenth-century exemplars of this were the fictional characters of Daniel Defoe (ca. 1660–1731): the adventurer-calculators like Robinson Crusoe. The adventurer-calculator is the modern Odysseus—the one who follows the imperatives of the imagination in search of the promised land, the place of exilic hope, or simply fortune; encountering on the way the unexpected and the undefined, which terrifies by its strangeness or enormity. The modern Odysseus survives by infinitesimally careful calculation, rationing, budgeting, and hoarding in the face of catastrophic contingency. It is not calculation *per se* that is the modern quality. The first Odysseus also was a calculator—a devisor of clever ruses to escape danger. Classical reason is calculative as well—the

Pythagorean-Platonic sense of structure is mathematical in nature. Or to evoke a more mundane example: If we turn to the cosmopolitan elites of Renaissance cities, we see the role that practical mathematics played in portal trade—in the ambidextrous transactions and logistics involved in the transshipment of goods. Something of this ambidexterity is continued with Gottfried Wilhelm Leibniz (b. 1646) and Sir Isaac Newton (b. 1642) when they redefine calculus as a calculation of the rate of change of one variable with respect to another. This was represented technically by differential equations, and socially by a growing sense of the need to master the relationship of multiple streams (or logics) in modern society. None of these cases (mythic, philosophical, or pragmatic), however, has the specific quality of the modern calculator of contingencies who, in the shadow of fear, tries to figure out how to control an unforeseeable future. It is this ambition that is the specific Crusoe-like quality of the modern calculator.

The true hero of Augustan England in the end was not the Shaftesburyian stoic but the Defoean adventurer-calculator. Initially in the Augustan setting there was a sense in which the stoic injunction not to live in hope or fear was taken seriously at the social level, and *worldliness was valued above dread or fantasy*. Yet anxiety and trembling asserted themselves. Protestant dissenters remained fearful for their election. Servants and tenants stood before their masters in trepidation, and their masters worried about riots and the power of crowds. Society was haunted by images of political turbulence and rebellion, and the sovereign's sword was wielded against the internally colonized Irish and Jacobites to ensure a pacified United Kingdom. And if dread remained socially prevalent, so did fantasy. The commercial revolution—the shift from market*place* to market *society*—that the seventeenth century had ushered in was not reversed. Augustan humanism was ultimately at a loss as to how to deal with modern commerce, which stressed the need for economic endeavor to be linked to happiness. As far as the individual was concerned this meant that those in business lived in the present, and looked to the pleasures of the present, rather than to the ecstasies of the imagination. This did not mean that the ideal Augustan personality was uninterested in change or development; nonetheless, this was an age that spoke of "happy changes" and "pleasing improvements." Commerce was thought of as a vehicle for bringing nations into cooperation and harmony, a vehicle for universal peace, a way of fostering a cosmopolitan interchange between states. Yet, in truth, the discontents of modernity were never dispelled, nor its expansionary significations contained. An apostle of the market society like Adam Smith (1723–1790) saw no contradiction between the stoicism he defended and the idolization of market *dunamis*.

He saw no contradiction between his profession of the rational ordering of the stoic and the nervous ordering of the generalized market that increasingly stretched across continents as well as across the seemingly endless oceanic expanses occupied by the world system (the modern mercantile empire) of the English type.[24]

As the century progressed, speculative venturing came more to the fore, in episodes like the South Sea Bubble (1720). Expansionist, imperial appetites were whetted by the explorations of Samuel Wallis (1766-1768), Captain Cook (1768–1771, 1772–1775, 1776–1779), and others. This exploration was executed in the spirit of enlightened curiosity, but it stimulated a romantic fascination with the exotic and the strange. Dutifully the explorers took their copies of Homer's *Odyssey* with them; but, far from sailing by the shoreline like the ancient Greek sailors, eighteenth-century navigators plunged into the oceanic immensity. Both kinds of sailing demanded skill and daring; both were dangerous. But the oceanic explorer had to contemplate a seeming boundlessness that could intoxicate the imagination while terrifying the body.[25]

Augustan belief in the centrality of beauty and harmony retreated in the face of new theories of the sublime. Interest in the sublime was accompanied by a fascination with the power of the *untamed*. The sublime encapsulated *both fear and hope simultaneously*. It induced a dread that was ecstatic and a terror that excited. Under its auspices true intellectual power came to be identified with arbitrary arrangement and wild behavior, true emotional power with passionate intensity, true economic power with infinite accumulation, true political power with revolutionary explosion. *True power broke through all barriers, limits, and boundaries.* It crashed through, or crashed. True power was an unanswerable force; it swept all before it. If that required resort to terror, so be it. Bounded, limited, balanced power was power that did not live up to its name—*potentia*. It was not sheer potential, sheer promise. *True power was promise*—the promise of knowing more, earning more, seeing more. Nobody in the unfolding world of modernity thus could legitimately limit promise or restrict opportunities (without courting the accusation of causing injustice). Moderns lived in the expectation that what the world of tomorrow promised would be delivered to them. Power was *dunamis*—the capacity to transform what is into what could be. The *potentia* of modern power was potentiality itself.

The *reductio ad absurdum* of this was that what power could potentially bring into existence was power itself, though not all versions of the modern idea of power were quite as abstracted as this. Some moderns believed *potentia* to be the promise of a promised land, a land of plenty.

(The image of a land of opportunity stands somewhere between the these two versions of *potentia*.) In yet another version — or rather inversion — it was no longer the promise of returning from the wilderness to the promised land that beckoned; instead, the wilderness itself became the image of power and promise. Wilderness became the promised land of modernity. For its very sublime condition — the awesome, terrifying, seemingly infinite expanse of the wilderness — signified an infinite *dunamis*, a power that *could break all bounds*. Gradually the classical belief in the *self-disciplined* power of the *independent person* was displaced by an image of power as wild and untamed. Side by side, sometimes at odds with this, sometimes in a curious symbiosis with it, was the inclination to control (master) the untamed. This was represented in a new, and what was eventually to be a far-reaching and enormous power: *the power of industry*. Inventors like John Kay, Thomas Newcomen, James Watt, and others began to translate artisanal ideas into practical machines that would replace human labor power, and that would harness the energies of a nature whose *phusis* was endless growth. These inventors were methodical and rationalist. Many began as clock and instrument makers, and many were dissenting Protestants with the habits of a lifetime of "mechanical" discipline, exactitude, and precise calculation. Theirs was the planned-out, scrupulously regulated life of the rational ascetic who disdained the substitution of sumptuary expenditure or ecstatic abandonment for sober and careful calculation, and who by the 1780s had begun to organize a system of factories and factory employment that demanded even of unskilled laborers that they acquire some of the regular and exacting habits of their employers.[26] Yet the first clocks and instruments which this nascent class of industrial manufacturers made were nautical, created for the navigational needs of Britain's navy. Like so much of modern rationalist calculation, the careful, cribbed instrument makers served, at the behest of Adam Smith's hidden hand, the purposeless purpose of infinite development. In a way that (at best) they could only half-understand, their organizing ability yielded ever-growing companies, their sobriety realized ever-growing savings, and their precision manufacture produced machines which unlocked the infinite nature dreamed of by scientists since Leonardo da Vinci.

The dynamic and boundless image of nature that modern science professed was made true by the world-transforming Industrial Revolution. As moderns moved out, pushing back the frontiers of settlement and science, what followed them was the locomotive of science and technology, harnessing the potentials of nature and simultaneously opening up the promise of infinite movement across continents, the globe, even the heavens.

NOTES

1. J. G. A. Pocock, *The Machiavellian Moment* (Princeton, N.J.: Princeton University Press, 1975), p. 471.

2. Public debt grew prodigiously during the eighteenth century. By the 1780s, 40 percent of Britain's wartime expenditure was financed by public borrowing. (John Brewer, *The Sinews of Power* [New York: Knopf, 1989], p. 114), and 30 percent or more of British state income during most of the eighteenth century was required to service interest on this debt.

3. Nikolaus Pevsner, *An Outline of European Architecture* (Harmondsworth: Penguin, 1963 [1943]), p. 339.

4. Ibid., p. 342.

5. *Plato Redivivus*, in *Two English Republican Tracts*, ed. Caroline Robbins (Cambridge: Cambridge University Press, 1968).

6. Neville, *Plato Redivivus*, p. 112. See also pp. 92–93, 97, 114.

7. For Neville, a period of early, true feudalism. Such periodization does not necessarily bear any relation to modern historiography.

8. Neville, *Plato Redivivus*, p. 145.

9. Notably the *Exercises* which he began during his first stay in Rotterdam (1698–1699) and *Second Characters, or the Language of Form* which he wrote in Naples at the end of his life (1711–1713). See "Excercises" in Benjamin Rand (ed.), *The Life, Unpublished Letters, and Philosophical Regimen of Anthony, Earl of Shaftesbury* (London: Sonnenschein, 1900), and Shaftesbury, "A Letter Concerning the Art or Science of Design" in *Second Characters, or the Language of Forms* (Cambridge: Cambridge University Press, 1914). On Shaftesbury's life, see Robert Voitle, *The Third Earl of Shaftesbury 1671–1713* (Baton Rouge: Louisiana State University Press, 1984).

10. Shaftesbury was for a time vice admiral of Dorset, responsible for the administration of naval matters for the coastal county. "Country" in this context implied independent landed proprietorship as a counterweight to the power of the Crown.

11. Shaftesbury [Anthony Ashley Cooper, Earl of, 1671–1713], *An Inquiry Concerning Virtue, in Two Discourses* (London: Bell, Castle, Buckley, 1699).

12. "Exercises," in *The Life, Unpublished Letters, and Philosophical Regimen of Anthony, Earl of Shaftesbury*, ed. Benjamin Rand (London: Sonnenschein, 1900).

13. Shaftesbury, *Characteristicks of Men, Manners, Opinions, Times*, 3 vols., 2d ed. (London: J. Darby, 1714 [1711]).

14. Shaftesbury, *Characteristicks*, I: 135–36; III: 161.

15. Shaftesbury, "A Letter Concerning the Art or Science of Design," in *Second Characters, or The Language of Forms* (Cambridge: Cambridge University Press, 1914).

16. John Ely, "Jane Austen: A Female Aristotelian," *Thesis Eleven* no. 40 (Boston: MIT Press, 1995), pp. 93–118.

17. The final, third volume was published in 1725.

18. On such Horatian ideals in poetry see Norman Callan, "Augustan Reflective Poetry" in *From Dryden to Johnson*, ed. Boris Ford (Harmondsworth: Penguin, 1957); A. D. Hope, "The Middle Way," in *The Cave and the Spring: Essays in Poetry* (Sydney: Sydney University Press, 1974).

19. Peter Gay, *The Enlightenment: An Interpretation* (London: Weidenfeld and Nicolson, 1966), pp. 124, 162, 164–66.

20. A. R. Humphreys, *The Augustan World* (London: Methuen, 1954), chap. 4.

21. Alexander Pope, *Essay on Man and Other Poems* (New York: Dover, 1994).

22. See, e.g., *From Dryden to Johnson*, ed. Boris Ford (Harmondsworth: Penguin, 1968).

23. Edmund Burke, *A Philosophical Enquiry into the Origin of Our Ideas of the Sublime and Beautiful* (Oxford: Oxford University Press, 1990 [1757]).

24. The former in *The Theory of Moral Sentiments* (1759) and the latter in *An Inquiry into the Nature and the Causes of the Wealth of Nations* (1776).

25. In this atmosphere, it was easy for Whig politicians to abandon old Whig ideas about countervailing powers, and become, over time, increasingly subject to the patronage of the Crown. Symbolic of this shift, Colen Campbell was dismissed before the building of Walpole's house was completed, and he was replaced by the baroque architect James Gibb (1682–1754), who promptly erected baroque-style high octagonal domes on the unfinished end towers of Houghton Hall, instead of the gabled "houses" Campbell had proposed.

26. Christopher Hill, *Reformation and the Industrial Revolution* (Harmondsworth: Penguin, 1969 [1967]), 250–52; Max Weber, *The Protestant Ethic and the Spirit of Capitalism* (London: Allen and Unwin, 1976 [1930]).

10

THE REPUBLICAN EMPIRE

A CHRISTIAN SPARTA

In pursuit of its baroque ambitions, the English Crown during the eighteenth century built a mercantile empire around the Atlantic basin. Its
possessions stretched from Newfoundland down the east coast of America
and across the Caribbean to the west coast of Africa. The empire represented
an impressive expression of sovereign power. But it was also in the colonies
that a far-reaching challenge to this sovereign power would arise.

The trigger for this challenge was the question of taxation. The business of maintaining a blue-water empire was very costly. England had to
defend its overseas territories against other European powers, and to do
this, became heavily indebted. The pressure of this came to a head after
the Seven Years' War (1756–63) with France. The war had been a military
success for Britain, but at the cost of running up a massive national debt.
The problem was how to discharge the debt. The answer: tax the colonies.
The English introduced the Stamp Act—a tax on legal and commercial
transactions, and on newspapers and printing in the American colonies.
The Americans rebelled against this, and after a long campaign of protest,
the English withdrew the Stamp Act, only to replace it with the equally
hated Revenue Act. The American mood of rebellion grew, finally, into a
war of independence against the English Crown.

While the question of tax *triggered* the American Revolution
(1776–1783), the spread of the rebellion was *nourished* by a peculiar
amalgam of beliefs. The Americans were legatees of both antinomian religious attitudes and classical ideas of balanced power. Both played roles
in the development of the American political psyche, and both were
called upon freely in the course of the birth of the American republic.

Americans considered that they were being taxed without their consent to support Britain's professional military apparatus and to redeem

the debt financing of this military force. Old commonwealth arguments against standing armies, government debt, and the "placemen" who administered the system were recycled in the North American colonies in the 1760s and 1770s. The question about tax imposts became in turn linked to the question of the moral decline of Britain. In this view the British monarchy, in its spending on war, was profligate, and through its use of patronage had ensnared Parliament in its designs.

What alternative could be offered to this? When James Harrington and the Commonwealthmen criticized the power of monarchy, they invoked an idealized gothic past and argued for the idea of a gothic commonwealth. But no such past existed in the seaboard colonies of North America. True, the majority of colonists were small or middling freeholders, settled on the land, akin to a gothic yeomanry. Even the planters of Virginia and the Carolinas might have been compared to an aristocracy, or at least a gentry. But the mobility and the newness and the religious dissidence of the immigrants contrasted sharply with the "station," the strong social bonds, the communal sense of duty, the stability, and even immemorial character of the gothic-style estates. So Americans necessarily looked to another past: to the example of the Roman and Spartan citizen-soldier-farmer. It was not the gothic commonwealth but ancient Roman and Spartan republics that interested the Americans in the 1760s as their dispute with English power grew.

The type of republicanism that Americans were first drawn to was *anti-humanist* in nature. This kind of republicanism was, in a Greek vein, *Spartan*, or in a Roman vein, *Catonian* — the latter in the tradition of the Roman politicians Cato the Elder (234–149 B.C.E.) and his great-grandson, Cato the Younger (95–46 B.C.E.).* In the American setting, Spartan or Catonian republicanism was subtlely Puritan in inspiration. That it to say, via the neoclassicism of the republican idea, many theological concerns of the seventeenth century, particularly those having to do with moral reformation, were carried on in a secular guise in eighteenth-century America. The world of the ascetic citizen was one that sat well with Calvinist values of the simple life, frugality, and hostility to adornment. In the Catonian model, Calvinism's equation of luxury and moral corruption could be wrapped up in a republican robe.

It has been suggested with some plausibility that this in fact was not republicanism at all, but rather a politicized Calvinism.[1] A figure like Samuel Adams (b. 1722) is a case in point. In his own words, he envisaged America as a "Christian Sparta." He entered Harvard in 1736 intending to become a minister of religion. But once he began reading Plutarch, Cicero,

---

*The source of so much of the American image of the Catos came from the portrayal of them by Plutarch in his *Lives*. See *Plutarch's Lives*, trans. Aubrey Stewart and George Long (London: G. Bell, 1914–24).

Virgil, and Sallust, his interests turned to politics. Adams's view of the good life was basically that of a seventeenth-century Puritan for whom a good person was one who distrusted elaborate ceremony, luxury, extravagant decorations or displays—who was, in sum, plain-living. A low regard for private ostentatiousness had been commonplace in the ancient world also, but with entirely different effects. In the old Hellenic world, the wealthy were expected to endow the public places and spaces of the city rather than build extravagant pleasure palaces for themselves with their fortunes.[2] The Puritans, in contrast, had little regard for the glorification of the city. Instead they assumed that moral persons would use their wealth to "do good" in the community—either by charitable schemes or by investing in productive enterprise. Avoidance of conspicuous consumption was equated with public good. There was little impetus, then, to spend wealth on civic glorification. Churches and theological colleges were appropriate recipients of superfluous wealth, as were institutions like universities that brought the practice of inward moral reflection (exemplified by the Protestant-Hebraic model of "reading the book") into the secular domain. *Display*—in the sense of drawing meaning from public appearances—was forbidden to the Calvinist.

Protestant theology had little sense of civic virtue in the classical sense. It emphasized serving God by working methodically and hard at a vocation. The classical idea of leisure—of time spent in public spaces and places, absorbed in music, dance, and drama—was a harbinger of idleness, and was disapproved of. Public display was a sign of evil, of a superfluity that offended the Protestant, and modern, sense of economy. An individual who worked hard, and who was frugal and temperate, could accumulate wealth. Prosperity was a sign of God's blessing of morally charged labors. But to *display* that wealth extravagantly was sinful. Superfluous wealth was wealth not employed productively—wealth spent on conspicuous consumption: on luxuries, fineries, and indulgences, on adorning one's house, on ostentatious flaunting, on vanities. (Calvin advised that such wealth should be given away to the deserving poor.) The puritanical republican shied away from the consumption of things that flattered the senses or stimulated the taste for living or were used for the purposes of ease and elegance.[3] A thin diet and mean clothes were regarded as virtuous, whatever one's circumstances.

Political conclusions were drawn from these moral premises. In the mid-eighteenth century, especially in those colonies permeated with Puritan or Quaker influence, conspicuous consumption was seen as a sign of a despotic monarchy and of a declining empire. Ostentation was pointed to in order to explain why the British imposed taxes on the colonies.

Oppressive taxation was the result of the superfluous expenditures of the Crown. Tax imposts subsidized a standing army and the patronage paid to members of the British Parliament by the Crown to garner support for its blue-water empire. Tax imposts on Americans were viewed as the consequence of the intemperateness, proclivity for luxury, waste, artifice, dishonesty, idleness, sensuality, and veniality of the English political class, court, and Crown. Through the medium of reformed politico-theology, Americans found themselves resisting English taxes in the name of virtue. Even if by the mid-eighteenth century the descendants of the original Puritans and Quakers had not only prospered, but had themselves acquired a taste for luxury—this was especially true of the merchant classes in port towns like Boston—still the ideal of reformed theology retained enormous cultural power, and its ascetical undertow helped to stiffen resistance to the British. Both the economic boycott of British goods, the first line of resistance against the English, and later the Revolutionary War, required living in straightened circumstances. Reformed theology invested rebellious and sacrificial political strategies with meaning, and fortified the colonists to persevere in the face of hardships. Yet of necessity this theological spirit was forced to take on a secular form. When the Calvinist resisted Caesar, it could not be in the guise of a Calvinist—for lots of reasons. For one thing, many of the colonists were not Calvinists. Calvinism itself was divided into numerous sects. Furthermore, the antinomian substratum of Protestantism rejected the idea of a state religion. Its covenantal politico-theology could justify the creation of congregational and communal bodies, but not a body politic. Thus, reformed theology had to take on a neutral form—so it wrapped itself in the robes of a classical republicanism of an ascetic kind.

Ascetical republicanism was not an invention of the eighteenth century but had a long historical lineage. It formed part of a broader palette of republican ideas that had accumulated over the centuries. As already stated, among the Greek states it was not Athens that caught the attention of Americans but Doric Sparta.[4] The example of Crete (similarly Dorian) was also invoked.[5] Especially powerful was the appeal of the early Roman Republic of the fourth and third centuries B.C.E. The frugality of its farmer-soldier-citizens and its moral exaltation of agriculture appealed to many Americans. This was the world of Cato the Elder—a world of simple tastes, hard work, and piety. Its exemplary personalities and heroes were censorial, austere, and prohibitionist. The republican ascetic was careful with money, vigorous, uncompromising, priggish, and hostile to self-cultivation as well as to the conspicuous accumulation of wealth and to luxury.[6] Eighteenth-century Americans, especially New Englanders, responded well to the portrayal of this kind of republicanism. They read Thomas Gordon and

John Trenchard's *Cato's Letters* (1720–24) avidly,[7] while Addison's *Cato* (1713) was very popular with American audiences.[8] The public voice of this kind of republicanism was a kind of asceticized moralizing that condemned luxury in the name of virtue, identified moral activism with citizenship, and denied self-love in the name of the public good.[9]

The image of the hardworking farmer was knitted into this moral tapestry. Americans regarded employment in agricultural pursuits as virtuous.[10] The Puritan's search for God's promised land, of course, had already given a moral coloring to the land. But a comparable view of things also reached back to ancient republicanism—particularly to the time when the Roman people, the mainstay of the Republic, were predominantly smallholders. The invocation of the smallholder as the backbone of a republic had made its appearance in James Harrington's *Oceana* (1656), read a century later in America alongside other seventeenth-century English republicans like Algernon Sidney. The life of the yeoman farmer (Harrington's husbandman) was virtuous because he owed allegiance to no master, yet lived a life that was simple and frugal. In a society where there were large numbers of such husbandmen, it was supposed that a lid could be kept on ambition and wealth.

Not all the American founders, however, regarded classical models, Catonian or otherwise, with enthusiasm. The nationalist Alexander Hamilton summed up one skeptical strand of opinion when he said: "We are laboring hard to establish in this country principles more national and free from all foreign influences, so that we may be neither Greeks nor Trojans, but truly American."[11] Still, in the period when Americans were constructing a new order, the classics were widely and sympathetically read in a search not so much for exact answers, but for instructive moral lessons and suggestive historical examples.[12] America was to be a new order of the ages. The past, Americans believed, offered both a model of the future (in the sense of a working precedent or analogue for a non-monarchical form of government) and a basis for understanding why the existing arrangements of government and society were *morally* flawed. They were also drawn to the classics because the classics seemed to provide models of moral heroes struggling against a world gone wrong. The theological assumptions of American Calvinism encouraged this kind of reading of the classics. Republican heroes were thought of as similar to Christian saints fighting against a corrupt, licentious, improvident, ostentatious, wanton, dissipated, and extravagant world.[13]

Side by side with the moral condemnation of the British, the Americans engaged in a legal critique of English rule. In sum, the two most powerful aspects of the American political character were evident from the mid-eighteenth century: the *moralizing* and the *legalizing* propensities. Moral condemnation and legal remedy always were more attractive to the Americans than the *kosmopoietical* and city-building sides of historical republicanism. In American arguments with British colonial power, classical natural law was frequently invoked against British law.[14] Aristotle, the Stoics, and notably Cicero's *De legibus* were cited in this connection, while James Otis and John Adams proposed the relations between the Greek cities of antiquity and their colonies as an ideal model for British colonies in North America.[15] Otis argued that the British Empire was following the brutal example of Roman imperialism instead of the humanitarian example of Greece. Adams, on the other hand, held that even Rome gave her colonists equal rights with her citizens. In their dispute with British power in the colonies, most often cited was the example of Rome. The behavior of the British—for example in quartering their troops with colonists—was seen as a repeat of Roman imperial behavior. Americans understood Imperial Rome as being basically a military despotism. What they counterposed to that despotism most often was republican Rome. Republican figures who had fought against the rise to power of the Caesars were particularly admired—Cicero especially, but also Brutus and Cassius.[16] The most commonly cited classical authorities in colonial tracts, speeches, and correspondence were Cicero and Tacitus.[17] The most popular classical author was Plutarch.[18] Almost every American library had a copy of Plutarch's *Lives*, a book that served as a republican analogue of *The Lives of the Saints*. The Roman Stoics Marcus Aurelius and Epictetus, and the Roman lawyers, were paid reverential attention, while Lucretius, the Roman Epicurean, also had a good reputation.[19] Of the Greeks, only Aristotle had real appeal (at least if we assume that Polybius and Plutarch belonged to an essentially Roman literary world). Pythagoras, Xenophon, and Isocrates were paid some attention.[20] Plato was largely dismissed.[21]

Whatever reading the colonists did, the practical relevance of classical sources to Americans was limited by one crucial and irreducible fact: *the American colonies were territorial states, not cities*. The classics that the Americans read were concerned with cities, not sovereign states. Even the Roman Empire, with its enormous territorial span, was anchored in the life of cities, most crucially Rome itself. In contrast, the political class of the American colonies came from, and were identified with, states— Virginia, Pennsylvania, Rhode Island, and so on. The character of the American states was defined by their *territorial extent* and *land borders*, whereas the character of the city was defined by its *center*—or in the case of the port-city, by its littoral or riverine location (and its primary affiliation to liquid networks rather than to a territorial expanse).

The majority of the American settlers, and the nascent American political class, identified with the countryside, not with the city. The Quakers of Pennsylvania, the Puritans of Massachusetts, and others who settled in the Northeastern colonial states were deeply influenced by Protestant-Hebraic notions of coming to the promised land, while the dominant social force in the Southern states of Virginia and North Carolina — although Episcopalian and less theologically radical — was a *planter* class. While in one aspect this early planter class had a riverine aspect — in the tobacco states of the South the planter class lived (in handsome villas) on tidal creeks and rivers — in another aspect, this class was indelibly agrarian, utilizing as it did the labor of chattel slaves, and reliant on the products of the fields. When the Virginian planters turned themselves into a *tidewater* "aristocracy," they forged a tragic way of life torn between urbane manners and rustic cruelty.

Americans established cities, and significant ones at that, like Philadelphia. But their image of the virtuous life was pastoral. If, as in the classical world of the Mediterranean, the early American settlers were coastal dwellers — living along, or close to, the *peras* of the Atlantic — the ambition of subsequent settlers was continental, and they could not be limited to the seaboard. Symptomatically, when the American colonies joined together in rebellion against England, they organized themselves in a *Continental* Congress — whose name betrays unmistakably the scale of American ambitions. Even in the prerevolutionary period there was a persistent movement of settlers westward, across the mountains into the Ohio Valley, over the "Indian Lands," and down toward the Mississippi River. What was already envisaged, however uncertainly, in the midst of the War of Independence against Britain, was the political organization not of city dwellers but of farmer-settlers.

Montesquieu (1689–1755) had argued that republicanism was suitable only for the city,[22] and that monarchy was the political form of an extended territorial state. Americans — having rejected both the city as the material basis of their society and monarchy as its political form — set out to disprove Montesquieu (whose ideas were widely disseminated among the American political class).[23] They set about to create *the first extended republic* — the first modern and continental republic. To help themselves in this effort, they returned to the classics — yet knowing these could not be applied without significant adaptation to the American situation. In practice, the lessons of antiquity were transformed beyond all recognition.

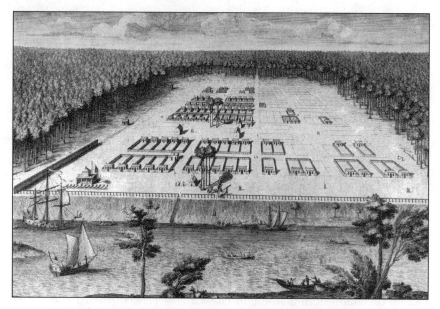

Savannah, Georgia. 1734 engraving by Peter Gordon.

A CONTINENTAL EMPIRE

The Protestants who came to America considered themselves an elect people. Their ministers told them that God periodically chose a people for deliverance from bondage into the promised land. The ancient Israelites, the children of Abraham, were the first such chosen. The American Protestant settlers, their spiritual descendants, had a divine obligation to fulfill: to journey into the wilderness, tested along the way by trials of temptation and purification, until they reached the land of deliverance. Theirs was a God-given mission to settle the Western lands and to establish the New World Israel.[24] The American wilds were vast and dangerous, inhabited by Indian tribes who fought against the intruders on their lands. But the American Israelites—with a conviction in this aspect more Augustinian than Old Testament—believed themselves a providential people, subject to divine providence. God, they were convinced, would watch over them in the midst of the howling wilderness.[25] God would guard them and build a wall of fire around them. They knew, whatever the danger, they had God on their side. This was a powerful theology, and one at odds with a civic or classical order of things. Ideas of providence, redemption, the protection of an all-powerful God, and the journey into the wilderness were all foreign to the classical (Homeric or Virgilian) spirit.

Providence was more attractive to the American soul than the *peras* of the ancients. Providence drew Americans away from the shoreline and the coastal seas of the ancient topographical imagination on a journey into the wilds of the vast American interior. It drew them into an unchartered Continental expanse. While the roots of this journey were religious, its idea was quickly absorbed into popular mythology. The figure of Daniel Boone (1734–1820), the son of Quaker parents, represents a secularized version of this American exodic quest. Brought up on the Pennsylvania border, Boone was an exemplar of romantic restlessness. Lured by the dark woods, he was an indefatigable searcher of the wilderness. A creator of Fort Pitt (Pittsburgh), a trail blazer across the Appalachians and down into the Kentucky bluegrass region (1769), a pioneer of what is now the state of Missouri (1798), and an explorer of the Missouri and Platte rivers up into the Wyoming and Yellowstone territories, he could never settle down with his family or establish legal title to any of the lands he helped open up.[26] Fixture was not in his nature. The romance of the pristine, lonely wilderness — its grandeur spiced with danger and antinomian freedom — was an unconquerable allure, but one which also chartered the way for a massive influx of settlers into the frontier lands. Such was the tidal force of this quest for the new country that in 1784 the loose confederation of states represented in the Continental Congress agreed upon a land ordinance drafted by Thomas Jefferson in order to regularize the surveying and sale of western lands. (The subsequent [1787] North West Ordinance provided, in turn, an orderly procedure for the step-by-step emergence of new states to the west and their integration in the anticipated federal Union of states.) In effect, the various states gave over their claims on these lands to a confederal authority, and American migration into the back country west of the Appalachians was subjected to a loose common authority. The ever forward-looking Jefferson wanted, by virtue of this measure, to ensure access to the then French-controlled Mississippi, so that crops could be transported for export down the river to the port of New Orleans, guaranteeing that Americans would not be isolated from the Atlantic commercial system.

As the early settlers moved across the Appalachian Mountains and down the Ohio Valley, they found a certain ascetical — "Spartan" or "Catonian" — virtue of service as a supplement to their radical Protestant Hebraism. In the Old Testament the tribes of Israel had joined together as a people to make a covenant with God. The covenant required them — as a people united — to obey God's commandments. God's promise was that if the moral commandments were obeyed, the chosen people would reach a land of bounty and free soil. If they were not moral, the promise would be deferred. The Protestant Reformation, especially its radical wing, drew heavily on this Old Testament imagery, but at the same time transformed its meaning in an antinomian direction. Protestant Hebraism emphasized the direct relationship between individual and God, rather than mediation through a people or a community. Moreover, wilderness (the state of nature) acquired a positive connotation. Nature represented emancipation from corrupt institutions and worldly powers (from all the metaphorical Egypts). It was expected, in the more radical Protestant theologies, that the elect could live outside law or authority in the grace of God. Even divine law (central to the theologies of Augustine and Aquinas) was swept aside in favor of the individual being filled with the breath (spirit) of God.[27] Yet "amazing grace" did not completely suffice to steer the settlers in their journey. They sought out a supplement of classical ideas. The state of nature was a powerful inspiration to them, a place that was numinous. Yet it was also dangerous. Physical hardship, attacks from Indians fighting displacement from their traditional lands, the unneighborly "independence" of the average settler, and the outlaw mentality of many whose appetite for social and legal transgression was encouraged by the antinomian atmosphere of the backwoods—all these loomed before the settler on the frontier. To master these dangers, the settlers drew firstly upon a stock of old puritan images. The methodical, planning, saving, rational-ascetic self idealized by Puritanism helped the settler survive and prosper in the absence of community. Overlaying these were classical republican ideas that had been popularized in mid-eighteenth century seaboard America. An image of a resistant, hardy, independent farmer, armed and settled on free soil, was derived very loosely from a reading of classical republicanism. Alongside the Bible and the Protestant hymnbooks, images of ancient Sparta and Crete—and the early Roman Republic—entered into common currency. These, it was supposed, had been republics of sturdy, free farmers. A republic, it was imagined, was a state where the soil was owned not by a monarch or pharaoh, but by citizen-farmers who were armed and able to defend the freedom of their soil, and whose free status derived from the fact that they bore arms. In dealing with the hazards of war, drought, flood or civil division, these farmers exhibited the virtues of courage, fortitude, and tenacity. But, in American eyes, Calvinism always colored these models of classical character. The classical persona was imagined to be ascetical and methodically independent. Sparta's Lycurgus and Rome's Cato the Elder were admired for seemingly puritan-like qualities.

The classical model was in many ways, whatever its popularity, inapplicable to the American settler condition and mentality. In the American wilds, neither Doric Sparta (or Crete), nor, for that matter, early Rome could be a model of governance for the settlers. After all, Sparta was a small state harboring no expansive ambitions, and most definitely none of a continental imperial kind. Moreover, Sparta, despite the fact that its wealth was agrarian, was a *city*-state.[28] The focus of Spartan existence, especially of the citizens, was city life, not frontier life or the wilderness. The same applied even to expansion-oriented Rome. The center of existence of the Roman citizen-farmer was the city. Roman freedom was the experience of the *res publica*, not the cradling of a weapon, standing in solitude against the world with one eye on the impositions of government and neighbors and the other eye on threats from original inhabitants[29] and outlaws.

All Americans were outlaws in some sense. American freedom was freedom from law and government. Yet paradoxically such freedom, the European Enlightenment had taught Americans, could be secured only through the creation of institutions of law and government. The modern (Lockean) Enlightenment rewrote the Old Testament covenant. The Enlightenment view supposed that the most basic freedom was to be found in the antinomian state of nature, but that not all individuals could live out this freedom securely or gracefully. Thus there was a need for institutions of government and law. A people would form themselves by agreeing (contracting) to give up some of their freedoms, and thereby subject themselves to a civil state, but only on the condition that government and law protected other, inalienable, prepolitical freedoms. The civil state was legitimate and tolerable only insofar as it served the end of antinomian freedom. This state was not a "public thing" in the classical sense. It was not a city or polity [a *civitas* or *polis*], but a set of *institutions*.

True, when Americans came to create such a state—in their constitutional conventions of the 1780s—they invoked the notion of a constitutional balance of powers borrowed from the ancients. Outwardly the American constitution looked quite Roman—a Senate offset a people's assembly (the House of Representatives); the legislative branch was a counterweight to the executive (the Presidency); the power of states balanced a federal power, and so on. But the ultimate purpose (*ratio*) of the constitutional arrangement was not the augmentation of the city and its brilliant shining forth. The offices of the 1789 constitutional union of states did not serve a civic *end*. There was no "final end" of the city to anchor institutions and offices. Citizenship, in the classical sense, was the life of the city dweller—a life that included office-holding along with many other public roles and activities. In the 1789 Constitution, office-holding became a specialized representative function, while citizenship became little more than the right to select key officeholders. The consequence was that citizens had to spend little time in the public space and officeholders had few responsibilities to augment or enrich that public space. Rather the ultimate *ratio* of the Constitution was the building of a nation across a continental expanse, or, in the language of eighteenth-century Americans, it was the building of a continental empire. Protestant divines agreed that God's plan for America was an empire. Thomas Brockaway, in a 1784 sermon, even foresaw that American settlement would expand westward to the Pacific.[30] David Tappan, Hollis Professor of Divinity at Harvard University, called upon Americans in a 1783 sermon to see themselves as a continental people and to extend their "benign influence" to the utmost bounds of the vast continent whose margins they occupied. Americans, who protested English imperialism, began to see themselves as creators of an alternative empire — *an empire of liberty.*

This empire was to be created out of an amalgam of images of the Catonian citizen-farmer, Protestant rational asceticism, a promised land politico-theology, and Enlightenment know-how. As George Washington stressed in his Circular Letter to state governors after the end of the War of Independence, the foundation of this American empire was "not laid in the gloomy age of ignorance and superstition."[31] Americans on the whole, even those of strongly Protestant-Hebraic or Classical disposition, regarded themselves as children of the Enlightenment. The useful arts, mechanics, science, and technology were to be used to turn — as the Old Testament prophet Isaiah had envisaged — the wilderness into a fruitful land. Modern science was yoked to the fulfillment of America's providential mission. In doing so, the countryside would be transformed from inhospitable wilds into a Garden of Eden. The "vast forests void of inhabitants"[32] were to be turned into cultivated soils and pleasant habitations by the alliance of religious purpose, virtue, and scientific learning. Religious purpose was the divine mandate of settlers to spread across the face of the land. Virtue was the fortitude needed to face the dangers of settlement, a virtue that managed to be Plutarchian and Christian at the same time. Science was the science of mechanics and engineers, needed to make the land more productive and easier to farm. In short, the purpose of America was realized in a providential empire, virtuous endurance of the trials of the wilderness, and enlightenment science to speed the conquest of an untamed nature and to turn the wilderness into a pleasing garden.

The final element of this picture was the commerce and trade that could distribute the fruit of this garden far afield. Americans debated the model of the self-sufficient farm, and here classical opinion was divided. While the ancient Spartans had isolated themselves from the Mediterranean trading system, history provided Americans with reassuring examples of commercial republics—Rhodes, Venice, Florence—and the large-scale trade of later Rome. The example of the self-sufficient gothic freeholders[33] who had come after the collapse of the Roman imperial trading system was weighed in the American mind against the commercial breadth of the ancient world. The War of Independence against the English Crown freed the Americans from the exclusive grid of British imperial trade, but not from the Atlantic trading system. As it evolved, the trend of American opinion was for integration with this oceanic trade. The Spartans might have disowned commerce, but not the Americans. "All the world is becoming commercial," Jefferson advised Washington in 1784.[34] It was impossible to keep "our new empire" isolated. "Our citizens have had too full a taste of the comforts furnished by the arts and manufactures to be debarred use of them."[35] The new Republic being created in the 1780s could not and ought not to be isolated from the Atlantic system. American settlers would sell their harvests to Europe and the Europeans "in return would manufacture and send us in exchange our clothes and other comforts."[36]

All the same, there was a sensitivity to the fact that modern commerce generated excess wealth which the rational-ascetic Calvinist theology of the Pilgrim fathers warned against.[37] The market was a corrupting influence on morals. American Calvinists and their eighteenth-century Catonian republican heirs saw avarice and greed, luxury and dissipation as problems of successful commerce. Consequently agriculture was endowed with a moral aura, while commerce (particularly the banking and credit system) was regarded as unvirtuous. Even the most honest commerce brought with it the dangers of luxury. Eighteenth-century Scottish political economists like James Stewart and David Hume had explained how—when all the land a society has is taken, and that society moves into the stage of commerce—the interchange of goods, peoples, and ideas stimulates inventiveness and a taste for finer things. Commerce, the political economists suggested, led to a love of luxury and, the Catonian republicans added, to corruption and vice. Commerce, they believed, encouraged the consumption of things that were superfluous.[38] The ascetically-minded saw self-cultivation and luxury (in a word, culture) as signs of the corruption of the body politic.

At the same time, accumulation of wealth was the sign of God's providence and protection, a proof of the election of the American Israelites. How then were settlers to deal with the question of (excess) wealth? One way was through self-discipline. The theological advice was not to indulge in luxuries—the buying of "fripperies" and "superfluities."[39] The good life, even for those who became rich selling the fruit of the garden, was a *simple* life. But given the powerful Atlantic market system, this could not be enforced by sumptuary laws (as the ancient ascetic republican preferred). An alternative technique was to *tax* the wealth created by prosperous freeholders and employ it for civic purposes. In the classical world the wealthy had been *expected*, as a *duty beyond duty*, to employ their wealth for civic ends—to build theaters, fora, memorials, and so on.[40] The sect communities (Anabaptists, Congregationalists, Quakers, Moravian Brethren, Pietists, Seventh Day Baptists, and so on) who settled in America levied members for community purposes, but the intense antinomianism of the Protestant sects meant that, with time, individuals or individual families rebelled against the rules of the sect and struck out on their own. The search for the promised land became increasingly individualized in an anomic sense. These individuals refused any civic virtue, and even any kind of community responsibility. As the eighteenth-century American essayist and doctor Benjamin Rush opined, the self-sufficient yeoman types, with their log cabins in the middle of the wilderness, relying on their own labor or that of a fatigued family, exhibited little social virtue. They were unwilling even to support a church and bear the burden of taxes, and their only social engagement was to spend time attending protest meetings. In effect, they exhibited *an excess of independence*. What Rush thought preferable to these antinomian settlers were communities of farmers who built solid homes, invested in their properties, and looked to the protection of the law, and accordingly paid their taxes.

But this begged the question: What kind of governance would suit such church-going farmers? Obviously it was not the civic form of governance. These farmers were not city or town dwellers. They met together for church services. But that was the expression of a communal, not a city life. The righteous exalteth a nation, not a city. Thus, to them, a state based on the city (or on a confederation of cities) was inconceivable. On the other hand, the fact of having fought a War of Independence against a monarchy made the adoption by Americans of a monarchy (even a constitutional monarchy of a gothic kind proposed by the English "commonwealth men") unlikely. Monarchy to the American settlers was indelibly colored with the reputation of despotism. On the other hand, the antinomian liberty of the first pioneers was suggestive of an unpalatable license. What kind of government would obviate both despotism and license? The answer of educated Americans was a *republic*, but *one that was not based on the city*—a republic whose farmers did not live in town. This republic would provide the frame for some elementary community or social responsibility embodied in law, a focus for common loyalties, a means of providing common economic infrastructure (like roads and ports), but it was a republic that did not expect—of the citizens of the republic—a civic virtue. This was to be a paradoxical republic, a republic without *res publicae* (public things).

THE CONSTITUTION

While eighteenth-century Americans bracketed classical notions of civic virtue, preferring ascetical-moralizing or antinomian-individualistic senses of the moral self, they still drew many positive *institutional* conclusions from the history of republicanism and humanism—conclusions they proceeded to act on with concentrated purpose.

In 1787, eleven years after the final break with Britain, delegates met at Philadelphia to frame a constitution for the new republic. The delegates had absorbed lessons from the tradition of classical humanism and republicanism that had passed down from ancient Rome, through the free cities of the Middle Ages, to the Italian Renaissance, and then on to the English "Old Whigs" and Augustan Humanists.[41] Eighteenth-century colonial Americans studied the experience of the past carefully, and were drawn to the beautiful mechanics and sense of structural equilibrium of the classical humanist tradition. But at the same time as they embraced it, they sought to modify it, to adapt it to the condition of the modern world—with the consequence that the nature of the original was dramatically recast.

Having read Plutarch and Tacitus, supplemented by Livy and Polybius, Americans thought themselves to be like the farmer-republicans they imagined had fought to prevent the rise of the Caesars.[42] The Roman republican constitution was steadily praised.[43] Conversely, Americans like James Otis believed that Rome fell when its constitution failed to secure a perfect separation of powers.[44] In formulating a republican constitution in the new world, as an alternative to Britain's imperial model of government, the Americans sought to overcome such flaws. The fundamental, underlying principles of the American Constitution were derived from the model of Roman government.[45] Americans were also sensitive to the weaknesses of that model, and sought to correct those weaknesses. They were also ready to supplement the model when it was deficient, as when the founders turned to the ancient Hellenic model of federative city leagues as an instructive guide to how they might arrange a republic that extended beyond the bounds of a single city—aware all of the time that when Rome expanded beyond its city bounds, the republic had collapsed. The analogous question they were grappling with was how could various colonial states be united together without the dominance of one state over the rest or the obliteration of the states under the hegemony of an imperial monarchy? The founders were eager not to repeat the failures of Rome. The examples of the Amphictyonic centers of religious worship (Delphi and elsewhere) that organized the sacred truces and periodic games between Greek city-states were invoked as well as examples of Achaean, Lycian, Aetolian, and other Hellenic city leagues.[46] A great interest was shown in how the common councils of the leagues worked, and in questions such as whether each city had an equal voice in the workings of these common councils. Commentators like John Dickinson and James Madison were clear-eyed and frank about the defects of the ancient confederacies as well as their beauties. But the point of their research was to find parallels and suggestive examples of a way of uniting existing states politically without destroying their distinctive capacities, rather than slavishly following a set historical pattern.

The image of politics underlying this conception was of an ordered arrangement—i.e., a Shaftesburyian unity in diversity, a *system* of interlocking parts. Citizens, in acting responsibly, *energized* the arrangement. But the dynamism of the actor (or association of actors) was not the nub of politics. Rather, politics was a systematic arrangement for checking and balancing the power and dynamism of each part of the system so as to realize a harmonious equilibrium. This understanding of politics was republican, but not in the Catonian sense. It was republican in the metricizing sense. This was the idealized republic of Polybius and Cicero. *It was a republic of order, not heroes, an order that was almost mathematical in conception.*

The intellectual root of this idea goes back to the pre-Socratics, and had entered the Roman world via the Scipionic circle and Polybius. The ethico-political conceptions of the Scipionic circle were quite distinctive from those of their Catonian opponents, and what they understood by a republic was not a self-sacrificing citizenry but a balanced constitution. (When Cicero later wrote his *De re publica*, the chief characters of the dialogue were members of the Scipionic circle.) Americans like Jefferson were similarly drawn to the sense of just order and equilibrium of the classical humanist tradition. They wanted an "Old Whig" (commonwealth) order of balance and limits—a constitutional order. But in England the balanced order of the constitution meant a *class* constitution. The constitutional balance of the English state (like the Roman *res publica*) was a *balance of classes*. The Americans rejected the idea of a class society. Aristocracy had little relevance or place in the new world.[47] While many on the other side of the Atlantic supported absolutism as a way of under-mining the class system, Americans wanted to destroy the class system without installing an absolutist state or sovereign power; that is, without betraying the classical ideal of a constitutional order. In the case of a sovereign state there is one person or agency in the state (e.g. the Crown) that has the ultimate authority. This agency cannot be subject to any higher authority, even that of the law, and therefore is not in principle subject to any limits.[48] This notion of an unlimited power deeply repelled eighteenth-century American republicans. "Old Whiggish" Americans wanted to *check* the power of the Crown, and to somehow *balance* the Crown (or executive authority) with *other forces* in the state; that is, they wanted to institute some kind of equilibrium of forces in the state. But the problem was how to do this when the only precedents for it suggested that a balanced constitution meant a class constitution. The problem for the Americans was how to be classical and modern at the same time.

In answering this question, the Americans did several things. The first was to remove classes from the state. They deprived classes of explicit political (decision-making) power. Contrast this with the eighteenth-century English constitution, which was a social constitution. Different classes shared in the power of the state, and people participated in political life as the members and representatives of social classes. The English constitution was composed of the Crown (with its retainers, supporters, servants, allies, etc.), the Lords or nobility (peers), and the Commoners (gentry, propertied). The two Houses of Parliament, the Lords and Commons, were social instruments that balanced the power of the Crown. True, this was beginning to break down in the eighteenth century. A nascent public opinion had begun to emerge, as had forms of social mobility, but the past weighed heavily on the English, and even the most radical among them thought little beyond the gothic dreams of the Commonwealthmen who envisaged that some kind of freeholding agrarian class would provide the social weight (and thus the political ballast) needed to replace the declining aristocracy and to counterbalance the growing power of the Crown. The American republicans, on the other hand, rejected the notion that either Crown or aristocracy would play a part in their political order.

So what did this leave—the commons, the people? The Americans, as they began to design their Constitution in the decade following the Revolution, had to ask themselves the question: Are we creating a popular sovereignty? Are we envisaging the rule of the people—as we have no room left either for the royals or the aristocrats in our Constitution? For the Americans, the very idea of sovereignty of any kind meant a single power in the state, a power that by implication was excessive, absolute, unlimited. The Americans were too "Old Whiggish," and too schooled in a classical culture, to abide such a notion. They were not about to create a sovereign state of any kind, even a popular sovereignty—not even a popular sovereignty dominated, in a late commonwealth manner, by a Jane Austen-style "gentry of sufficient means." They wanted limits, checks, balances, and diversity. So they removed not only the Crown and the aristocracy, but also the people *qua* social class from the fabric of the Constitution, and in doing this the idea of the people changed. The people were no longer a class, but everyone, or at least all those who had the vote which—as suffrage became universal—eventually came to include all adults.[49] The people became the voters, and the voters voted for representatives who no longer acted on behalf of a distinctive class. So what then did it mean to act as a representative? The answer to this came to depend on *what* office the representative held in *which* institution. The Americans created a series of representative institutions—the most important at a national level being the presidency and the two Houses of Congress: the Senate and the House of Representatives. Outwardly this order was modeled on the Roman Republic, but inwardly politics and social class were now separated. A member of the House of Representatives represented voters normally in a county or city district; senators represented voters in a state; the president represented voters across the union of states. In creating this arrangement, the Americans *rejected a single center of power*. Decision-making was divided. *No one person, office, or agency could adequately represent the people.*[50] Thus, there was institutionalized a *separation of powers*.

This separation of powers not only operated between institutions within the state, but also between states—for the American republic was not a state, but a union (or federation) of states. The inspiration for this, as has been noted, was the long-standing tradition of federative leagues of cities—a tradition that included the federative leagues of cities during the late medieval period and the Renaissance, and extended back to the Greek cities of the fourth century B.C.E. Federation provided the advantages of size without the loss of independence of the constituent parts of the union. Where the European absolutist states, via the process of nation-building, laid the foundations for large scale nation-states, incorporating territory through conquest and promoting a common culture over the extent of the nation's territory, the Americans instead set about to construct a college or federation of states. The original thirteen separate colonies that rebelled against England formed a federal union. In forming the union, they gave up some, but not all, of their powers (their capacity to act) to the center. Under the terms of the union, the federal government acquired a specified range of powers, while the states retained the substantial residue of powers for themselves. Yet the seventeenth-century theory of sovereignty had said that there could only be *one* power (one ultimate power) in the state. Now there were *two*: the power of states and the power of the union, and in neither of these cases was power truly sovereign. For in both cases of state and federal governments, power was *divided* between two legislative houses and an executive branch.

The point of dividing power is to have different powers in the state check and balance one another, so that no power has a monopoly in the state; so that each power limits the ambit of each other power. When this works, there will be an *equilibrium of powers*, and such an equilibrium is the essence of a constitutional order. Yet where there is a division of powers, and the greater the number of powers, then so multiplies the opportunities or likelihood for disputes between the bearers of those powers, disputes triggered by the tendency of one power to encroach on other powers. The question the Americans had to address was: How do you settle such constitutional disputes? The answer was to create a *written* constitution, a *legal* document that set out the broad limits of each institution's power. They then created a legal body, the Supreme Court, which could declare acts of state and federal institutions *unconstitutional*, with the intended effect of upholding *the equilibrium between institutions*.

THE ABSENT AGORA

What the founders created was a constitutional structure of great ingenuity. Yet it was also one of an overwhelmingly legal-institutional nature. The problem with this is that institutions alone do not make either a polity or a state. Institutions must be animated by human actions and human psychology.

In the city regime or polity, ideally conceived, action is based on *reason*. Reason is that which draws diverse things together, giving them form and shape, and which gives the parts of an individual life, and the life of a polity, consistency and continuity. In contrast, the expectation in the modern (sovereign) state is that human action is ruled by passion—by fear, ambition, desire, and so on. Reason is reduced to corporeal calculation—the calculation of risks for the fearful and of opportunities for the ambitious. The founders of the American republic, by the time of the making of the U.S. Constitution (1787), in large part rejected the notion that human action could be based primarily on reason. They agreed with the mainstream of Enlightenment philosophy (from Hobbes to Hume) that the primary spring of human action was the passions. Yet, while they assented to this proposition, they did not do so without misgivings. They understood the consequence of extravagant or enthusiastic behavior—the damage caused by the play of zeal or ambition, fear or interest without limit. But they also believed that they had found a republican solution to this problem without having to rely on the rule of reason. Modern individuals, they concluded, were passionate, not reasonable, and a modern republic must be arranged on that premise. Passionate action was expansive—invasive—and where the passions were not checked, the most passionate (zealous, enthusiastic) part of society would exercise dominion over all of the other parts. Yet passion, they believed, could be checked only by other passions. Under the right circumstances, the passions of one individual (or group of like-minded persons) could be balanced by the passions of another individual (or group). Only ambition could check ambition, and only fear could check fear.

Prerevolutionary American thought had supposed that virtue provided at least some check on passion. Americans could never decide—nor did they bother to distinguish—whether this virtue was of a classical, or Augustinian, or Calvinist kind. Somehow, in the prerevolutionary period, virtue encompassed classical self-governance (self-control), saintly resolution (willful discipline over the sinful passions), and the sobriety and diligence of the dissenting Protestant. Virtue variously discouraged sloth, encouraged industriousness, and was an incitement to meet adversity with vigor, fortitude, and perseverance. On the classical side of the balance sheet, virtue was a token of reason. Virtue temporized actions, and from that was to be inferred that there were limits to actions. Reason was the origin of *peras*. Reason was what gave shape to actions. Virtue, in giving shape to human actions, was an aspect of reason. Virtue was what kept passionate actions within bounds. The founders of the Constitution, on the whole, were skeptical of this. Against the ancients, John Adams expressed doubts whether virtue/reason had any real force.[51] Like the Enlightenment *philosophes*, Adams thought that the passions were easily inflamed. With imagination (the force of inflammation) so strong, reason so weak, and wealth and power so enchanting, reason easily became an advocate on the side of the passions. Conversation and contact with one's fellows seemed only to stir the passions and to disrupt rational reflection and calmness, and when passions became inflamed, malice, envy, hatred, pride, fear, rage, and despair overtook human conduct.

By the 1780s this view of human nature was confirmed in Adams and most of the other American founders. The consequence was to exclude the idea of reason from the premise of the 1787 Constitution. The operation of the Constitution was not the work of reason. Reason did not give shape to an American *polity*. Indeed, projects of government founded on the supposition of virtue, Adams concluded, were chimerical. Rather, an American *society* existed that was acquisitive, and whose passions were unlimited. Self-interest, private avidity, ambition, and avarice dominated human conduct. In the midst of this, there was still the need for a "public good" or "public welfare." Yet such a good was not the reason, which is also to say not the virtue or limits, of a classical order. For human nature (the nature of *modern* humankind) *never rested*; once in motion, it rolled like the stone of Sisyphus—at least, until some resisting force constrained it. This resisting force was not the figure of reason that we find in Heraclitus, Pythagoras, Plato, and Cicero. Reason is erased from the picture. For reason *moderates* the passions. It forms them, shapes them, delimits them and the actions that they trigger. Reason gives definition where otherwise indefinition rules. In the classical conception: In collision, different forces find the measure or limit of themselves. They find how far, and no farther, they can go. In the classical conception the conflict of forces is the crucible of reason. In Adams's conception, by contrast, passion is not moderated; rather it is *checked*. Ambition checks ambition, interest checks interest, pride checks pride. None experiences the shaping force of reason (virtue).

The best way to achieve this checking and balancing of the passions, the founders discovered, was by proliferating the interests, parties, and sects in society. James Madison argued that a great multiplicity of sects was the best guarantee of religious liberty in a society.[52] Proliferation would dissipate the force of sectarian zeal. No sect would, in effect, be large enough to plunge society into fractious ruin. Thus America could avoid the ruin of the European wars of religion. Likewise, all kinds of factions, interests, prejudices, beliefs, and bandwagons could be multiplied in a modern republic, and so cancel one another out, negating one another's overweening or invasive ambitions. Anything in modern society could be the object of passion. A person could be passionate not only in religious affairs, but also in pursuit of commerce, industry, and agricultural interest; in defense of community or family; in parochial, regional, or state patriotisms; in fear of foreign enemies or domestic aliens; in moneymaking or in resentment at those with money. However, the larger and more extensive the republic, the greater its scope and scale, the more these passionate concerns would be multiplied, so that no one concern could dominate the federal union of states, the "united states." Every enthusiasm, every fear from the standpoint of the federal capital would be rendered a petty one that had to be weighed against all of the other, multitudinous, clamoring interests and movements in society. No one passion could dominate the national psychology (at least not for very long).

This had more than a passing resemblance to the classical conception of the union of opposing forces in the polity. But still missing from this vision is *the idea of reason*. In the union of states there are diverse passions and enthusiasms. They proliferate, so no single drive is overwhelming in its effect. But, equally, there is no conjunction of those forces, and no reasoned coexistence or limitation of them either. A just union supposes that they can be gathered together in one place, and thus adjusted to one another. This supposes a city center, the signifying core of a polity, where the assembling and relating of diversity takes place. The modern (continental) republic, however, is not a polity. Its symbolic heart is not the city center that draws to itself the diverse forces of a complex society. Instead, the most resounding political aim of social actors in the modern republic is to claim the attention of their fellows, if only for a moment. To cause a sensation is the easiest way to do this. The passionate soul longs for the dramatic moment when the light momentarily shines on it. But the passion that generates the sensational gesture does not last. Without the rule of reason over human actions, the passions that are generated, and that *move* modern society, are not *lasting* forces. Passions come and go in waves. Enthusiasms do not persist. The denizens of the society of passions have no character. Their actions, and what results from those actions, do not endure. Those actions are neither firm nor steady; they are of the moment. They have no time to mature and be perfected, and thus cannot be immortalized. Modern individuals startle with their passion, shock with their enthusiasm, alarm with their precipitousness, and discomfit with the heat of their desire. They are remarkable because of their dispatch. But this passes quickly. It only causes sensations.

Because there are so many enthusiasms in the continental republic (the union of states), no one driving force can be strong or popular enough to persecute others or hold them in subjection indefinitely. Yet, also, none of the passionate movements of citizens of the republic leave behind lasting *monuments* or enduring *works*. They do not leave behind them the lasting *material* significations of a polity. Their actions have no civic meaning. Frederick Jackson Turner was perfectly right: *The real signifying core of the American republic was its westward movement*. Its meaning was its frontiers—or rather the rush to push back those frontiers. Its mythic figures were those who lived in the liminal zones of the frontier between civilization and wilderness, city and sublimity.

The American Revolution produced great characters in Jefferson, Madison, Adams, and others who bequeathed to posterity lasting *institu-*

tions but no great architectonic *places* in which reason and justice (and meaning) might reside. Indeed the American founders spoke little about reason and justice, but much about liberties and rights. They were the heirs of the Enlightenment in this. Jefferson was perhaps a partial exception to this. He wanted to be remembered for three things; the first two being his drafting of the Declaration of Independence with its defense of natural liberties, and his writing of the Virginian statute on religious freedom that ensured the disestablishment of the church and the proliferation of sects. His final claim on remembrance was his supervision of the building of the University of Virginia. In the latter, Jefferson returned his focus to the great spirit of the polity. But his feeling for its objectivating spirit was exceptional among the founders. In large measure they did not believe that the enduring places—agoras, forums, piazzas—where classical antinomies were displayed and played out were more significant than the passing enthusiasms of American antinomianism with its catapulting fervors and busy self-importance.

NOTES

1. John Diggins, *The Lost Soul of American Politics* (New York: Basic Books, 1984), p. 25. See also Forrest McDonald, *Novus Ordo Seclorum* (Lawrence: University Press of Kansas, 1985), p. viii.
2. Or as Montesquieu put it:
The love of frugality limits the desire of having [to procure] necessaries to our family, and superfluities to our country. Riches give a power which a citizen cannot use for himself, for then he would no longer be equal. . . . Thus well-regulated democracies, by establishing domestic frugality, made way at the same time for public expenses, as was the case at Rome and Athens, when magnificence and profusion arose from the very fund of frugality. And as religion commands us to have pure and unspotted hands when we make our offerings to the gods, the laws require a frugality of life to enable them to be liberal to our country. (*The Spirit of the Laws*, trans. Thomas Nugent [New York: Hafner, 1949], I.5, p. 41)
3. McDonald, *Novus Ordo Seclorum*, p. 72.
4. Meyer Reinhold, *Classica Americana* (Detroit: Wayne State University Press, 1984), pp. 97, 156; Gordon S. Wood, *The Creation of the American Republic 1776–1787* (New York: Norton, 1972 [1969]), p. 118.
5. Ibid., p. 145.
6. See, e.g., McDonald's description of this puritanical republicanism in *Novus Ordo Seclorum*, pp. 72–73.
7. Reinhold, *Classica Americana*, p. 96; Bernard Bailyn, *The Ideological Origins of the American Revolution* (Cambridge, Mass.: Harvard University Press, 1967), pp. 43–44.

8. Reinhold, *Classica Americana*, p. 98.

9. For a general account, see Wood, *The Creation of the American Republic*, chap. 3.

10. M. G. J. Crevecoeur, *Letters from an American Farmer* (1782).

11. Richard Gummere, *The American Colonial Mind and the Classical Tradition* (Cambridge, Mass.: Harvard University Press), p. 183.

12. Reinhold, *Classica Americana*, pp. 25, 38–39, 95.

13. On the eighteenth-century American image of corruption, see Wood, *The Creation of the American Republic*, pp. 107–14.

14. Charles F. Mullet, "Classical Influences on the American Revolution," *The Classical Journal*, vol. 35 (1939–40), 92-104; Charles F. Mullett, *Fundamental Law and the American Revolution, 1760–1776* (New York: Columbia University Press, 1933); B. F. Wright Jr., *American Interpretations of Natural Law* (Cambridge, Mass.: Harvard University Press, 1931), chaps. 1–4; Reinhold, *Classica Americana*, pp. 96–97.

15. Mullett, "Classical Influences," p. 95.

16. Ibid., p. 96.

17. Ibid., p. 101.

18. Reinhold, *Classica Americana*, p. 152.

19. Mullett, "Classical Influences," p. 101; Reinhold, *Classica Americana*, chap. 5.

20. Ibid., p. 150.

21. Mullett, "Classical Influences," pp. 98–99.

22. As Montesquien remarked,
It is natural for a republic to have only a small territory; otherwise it cannot long subsist. . . . In an extensive republic the public good is sacrificed to a thousand private views; it is subordinate to exceptions, and depends on accidents. In a small one, the interest of the public is more obvious, better understood, and more within the reach of every citizen; abuses have less extent, and, of course, are less protected. (*The Spirit of Laws*, vol. 1, book 8, Section 16 [p. 120 of the London: Hafner Press, 1949 ed.])

23. Wood, *The Creation of the American Republic*, p. 499.

24. On the notion of America as a New Israel, see, for example, Catherine L. Albanese, *Sons of the Fathers: The Civil Religion of the American Revolution* (Philadelphia: Temple University Press, 1976), *passim*.

25. Michael Lienesch, *New Order of the Ages* (Princeton, N.J.: Princeton University Press, 1988), p. 26.

26. Hugh Brogan, *The Penguin History of the United States* (Harmondsworth: Penguin, 1986), pp. 227–30.

27. The most recent version of this theology, one that combines a post-Protestant antinomian romanticism with a Hebraism, is Derrida's. See, for example, Jacques Derrida, *Of Spirit* (Chicago: University of Chicago Press, 1987). Derrida's impact in North America in the 1970s and 1980s is to be explained, in no small measure, by the elective affinities of his theory with the promised land theology of American Israelitism that is deeply infused in American culture. It must be said, though, that this elective affinity stops at the point where Derrida offers a more traditional Judaic messianism, as he does in *Spectres of Marx* (New York: Routledge, 1994) with

its promise not of freedom that is coming but justice. Justice plays little role in the theological politics of American Protestant Hebraism. What is often mistaken for justice by Americans (viz. law) is ultimately suspect in the eyes of American politico-theologies. Law is understood by these influential theologies as corrupt. Justice (good law) is the law (the lawyer) that resists the corruptions of the world. The end of this good law is not justice, but antinomic freedom. It is not even the endlessly deferred end of messianic justice, but the liberties beyond law of the liminal frontier.

28. Even the early Romans, who were expansive, did not trek into a great wilderness, but conquered and then allied themselves with the villages, towns, and cities of other peoples.

29. Because the ethos of classical Greek antiquity required settler cities to be established on the *peras* of the Mediterranean, the question of the large-scale displacement of tribes or indigenous inhabitants did not arise, quite in contrast with the Americas, Australasia, and South Africa where European settlers had continental ambitions. The Roman pattern, of course, was one of much more sweeping expansion and conquest. But, even here, the Roman ethos was one of establishing treaties after conquest in order to turn enemy into ally. There was an echo of this Roman practice in the American proclivity for signing treaties with Indian tribes/nations defeated in war. But, unlike the Romans, the Americans were not sticklers for honoring their treaty obligations.

30. Lienesch, *New Order of the Ages*, p. 29.

31. Ibid., p. 23.

32. A description coined by the indefatigable publicist Benjamin Franklin, in his 1782 "Information to Those Who Want to Come to America." Cf. Lienesch, *New Order of the Ages*, p. 91.

33. Invoked by the seventeenth-century English "commonwealthmen" like James Harrington, to whom Americans owed a certain intellectual debt.

34. "Letter to George Washington, 15 March 1784" in Julian P. Boyd (ed.), *The Papers of Thomas Jefferson*, vol. 7 (Princeton, New Jersey: Princeton University Press, 1953), p. 26.

35. Ibid.

36. Letter to Jean Baptiste Say, 1804. Cf. Rahe, *Republics, Ancient and Modern*, vol. 3, p. 195.

37. Lienesch, *New Order of the Ages*, pp. 30, 88.

38. Banking compounded this. To the "imaginary wealth" of luxury goods (whose value lay in the eye of the beholder) the banker added the "false wealth" of credit. Credit was money not earned by industry but resting on the promise of the borrower. It was "false wealth" in comparison to the "real estate" of land. Credit allowed and encouraged speculation—investments in fanciful or risky schemes using other people's (the bankers', the creditors') money. Thus, it was only after a fierce political battle, in the early decades of the Republic, that the nationalists, led by Alexander Hamilton, were able to establish a modern banking and credit system. But populist opposition to the banking and credit system remained an enduring thread in American political thinking. One of the innovations that Hamilton introduced was the regularizing of public borrowing by guaranteeing regular interest payments to creditors. A credit system, Hamilton realized, depended on the main-

taining of faith and confidence in the system, and such "government guarantees" could help to obviate the problem of false promises or confidence tricks by the borrower. In connection with this, Hamilton saw that governments could not be allowed to borrow endlessly (as the British government had) without destroying the credit system. Loans had to be repaid, and Hamilton insisted that at the time of floating a loan, governments commit themselves irrevocably to the payment of the interest and retirement of the principal. Cf. McDonald, *Novus Ordo Seclorum*, p. 139.

39. Lienesch, *New Order of the Ages*, p. 90.

40. The Greek term for such public giving was *leitourgia* (from which the term "liturgy" derives). The city assigned to wealthy persons "liturgical" tasks, for example, the construction of a temple or underwriting the performance of a tragedy. This was a duty. But the liturgy was not simply a legal compulsion or tax burden. It was characterized by being a competitive (agonistic) activity. The wealthy competed to expend money on the *leitourgia*, and often would do more than legally required for the honor of having accomplished a great or memorable work. On this see, M. I. Finley, *The Ancient Economy* (London: Penguin, 1992 [1973]), p. 151.

41. J. G. A. Pocock, *The Machiavellian Moment* (Princeton, N.J.: Princeton University Press, 1975).

42. Mullett, "Classical Influences," p. 96.

43. Ibid., p. 97.

44. Ibid., p. 98.

45. R. A. Ames and H. C. Montgomery, "The Influence of Rome on the American Constitution," *Classical Journal*, 30 (1934–35), pp. 19–27.

46. Gummere, *The American Colonial Mind and the Classical Tradition*, pp. 179–83.

47. For a very good account of the American detachment from the assumptions of a class society, see Gordon S. Wood, *The Radicalism of the American Revolution* (New York: A. A. Knopf, 1992).

48. The great seventeenth-century argument for this is proffered by Thomas Hobbes in *Leviathan*.

49. The fifteenth amendment to the U.S. Constitution in 1870 guaranteed that no one could be denied the right to vote because of race or color or previous servitude; the nineteenth amendment in 1920 prohibited states from denying the vote to women.

50. Dick Howard, *The Birth of American Political Thought*, trans. David Ames Curtis (Minneapolis: University of Minnesota Press, 1986).

51. John Adams, Diary, February 9, 1772; Letter to Mercy Warren, January 8, 1776; Letter to Mercy Warren, April 16, 1776; Letter to Abigail Adams, July 3, 1776; *A Defence of the Constitution of the United States*, in *The Selected Writings of John and John Quincy Adams*, ed. Adriene Koch and William Peden (New York: A. A. Knopf, 1946).

52. *The Federalist*, p. 51.

11

THE CITY BEAUTIFUL

CICERO'S VILLA

One of the earliest meanings of civic virtue in the classical world was a willingness to risk death on behalf of the city-republic. Courage was expected of the citizen. But this courage was not that of a tribal warrior, nor for that matter did civic courage imply the self-sacrifice expected later on of a Christian. Rather it was a courage that grew out of the public life of the center of the city. Courage, daring, or fortitude was demanded of the city dweller, and this was the price of participation in the public spaces (the gymnasia, theaters, forums) that made the city what it was. Courage in battle — in facing an opponent — was an extension of the (theatrical, artisanal, athletic, rhetorical, and philosophical) contestation (*agôn*) that was a recurring feature of classical civic culture. To be courageous was to be prepared to die for something more important than life itself — viz. public things (*res publicae*).

The citizen did not die to ensure the survival of the tribe. Nor did the citizen die "sacrificing" what he took to be the highest good (viz. life) in the name of the sacred representation of that good (God), and thereby playout a theological paradox. The citizen both lived and died *for the city*, for it was the city that gave form (and thus meaning) to each city dweller. The city formed the citizen through the ethos of, and participation in, the public festivals, drama, music and dance, philosophizing, rhetoric, and athletics of the city. Yet the American republic, as it was conceived, was a republic without the *res publica*. How could its citizens then be formed? One answer was through the reading of the Bible. When the antinomian Protestant did this, the effect was to be the conquest of space (in the name of the promised land) and a perpetual protest against government and *nomos*. When the more conventional church-going Protestant (e.g. the Episcopalian of Virginia) did the same, the effect was a certain neighborliness and law-abidingness. Yet neither was the stuff of civic greatness nor immortality. What a republic without the *res publica* promised was republican governance without civic ethos, and *public institutions without public life*.

America was founded on the book.[1] The Pilgrims began with the book (the Bible). The American republic was also based on a foundational document (the Constitution of 1789), sacred in its own way. The material-constructivist ("building") metaphor of the ancient Roman idea of foundations was recast beyond recognition in the American setting. The American image of the republic was different from that of the classical humanist image of the republic. The difference lay in the urbanity of the humanist ideal and the fact that its sense of citizenship was not premised on a reading of a sacred text, but rather on a love of the world and of public life. In the classical humanist eye, the republic was a place, not a text; its "common" was an architectonic public, not a religious culture.

This is not to say that the humanist idea of the republic had no influence in America. Thomas Jefferson, the most significant of all of the American founders, was indebted to a classical humanism. Yet, instructively, classical humanism was a civic humanism precisely in the sense that city building and civic ethos were inseparable, whereas Jefferson displayed a pronounced hostility to the city ("cities are sores on the body politic"). On the other hand, reminiscent of the classical humanist, Jefferson put into practice a certain kind of materialist ethos. But it was the country villa, not the city center, which was the focus of Jefferson's materialist humanism. In contrast, for the ancient founder or politician, to suggest that the central material signifiers of society were to be placed *outside* of the city was a contradiction in terms.

The ancient founder or politician was a city builder. This was true as much for the imperial as for the republican politician. The *telos* of the antique polity was the city and its public spaces of appearance. Thus, when he was forced to retire from politics and turned to writing philosophy, Cicero experienced life away from the public sphere with great ambivalence. "The book" was not the central signifier of the *civitas*. True, the philosophy of the Greeks that Cicero cast into Latin was prestigious, and acquaintance with it was a sign of a cultivated personality. But the life of the mind was conducted away from law courts and councils. To redress this, the Greeks had conceived of their philosophy as dialogues or lectures arising out of the settings of stoa, gardens, and social gatherings. *Logos* (reason) was not inwardly turned or isolative. Thought required the *presence* of others. To write was to imaginatively represent a public engagement with others; to read was to speak aloud. Julius Caesar was the first person recorded who read silently to himself instead of the normal antique practice of reading aloud. After centuries of Christian inwardness, it is easy to forget that the prized antique life was outward looking, and the chief duty of the citizen, and especially of the influential politician, was to augment the city form in which an active, outgoing life might be contained. As Cicero put it on behalf of his fellow Romans: the whole glory of virtue is in activity.[2] Certainly, Cicero admitted, the search for truth was a characteristic of the human species. "When we have leisure from the demands of business cares, we are eager to see, to hear, to learn something new, and we esteem a desire to know the secrets or wonders of creation as indispensable to a happy life."[3] But withdrawal from civic life — to write, to contemplate truth in isolation from interlocutors and friends — had troubling connotations for the ancients. The philosophers did it, but for a lawyer, rhetorician, and officeholder like Cicero, such retirement from life was forced on him. Men of extraordinary genius who devoted themselves to learning could be excused for not taking part in public life, Cicero proposed.[4] Likewise, those who had ill health or "some still more valid reason" (e.g. disgust at the conduct of the state) might retire without disgrace. But otherwise there was no justification for withdrawing from the active life, and those who did seemed to Cicero only to dread the toil and trouble, and perhaps also the discredit and humiliation, of political failure.

Here we need to appreciate the context of Cicero's views. The substance of civic duty for the Roman was quite different from the modern idea of official duty. Office holding was not tantamount to carrying out a bureaucratic routine. Rather office holding was premised on active virtue, such as the "kind service" (*pro bono* work) of the lawyer who used the gift of eloquence to help those of slender means,[5] or else the liberality of the well-positioned who used their wealth to enhance public life, or the charity of the well-off who were prepared to ransom prisoners or relieve the poor.[6] Cicero, the newcomer to the upper reaches of Roman society, preferred "kind services" to the giving of money for public purposes.[7] Persons too easily overgive money, he believed, and live beyond their means. Moreover, Cicero regarded much of what such money was spent on — public banquets, festivals, games and fights — as "vanities of which but a brief recollection will remain."[8] There was a republican priggishness — a kind of Catonian undertow — in this view. A mildly puritanical distrust of the sensuous impregnates Cicero's writings. Yet Cicero also recognized quite realistically that officeholders had to avoid any suspicion of penuriousness in their public giving, and simply advised that expenditure was better outlaid for *lasting things*: walls, docks, harbors, aqueducts, and all of those works which are of service to the community.[9] Such public improvements, Cicero thought, won greater gratitude with posterity.

Of course, among the most lasting of all Roman things—the monuments that still haunt the modern imagination—proved to be the theatres and arenas that housed the very vanities that Cicero disapproved of for their fleeting nature. Cicero the politician, and Cicero the friend of wisdom (*philo-sophia*), was notably ambivalent about this version of material culture. Out of respect for Pompey's memory, Cicero was diffident about expressing any criticism of theaters, colonnades, and new temples.[10] On the other hand, he thought that the greatest philosophers (the Stoics) did not approve of such *res publicae*. Cicero pointed to the views of Panetius, and to Demetrius of Phalerum, who denounced Pericles for throwing away so much money on the magnificent Propylaea.[11]

Cicero negotiates this ambivalence with some care. For instance in his *Tusculan Disputations* we have the Roman Cicero confronting the heritage of Greek philosophical culture. The issue at stake is Stoic ethics. Such an ethics could be assimilated very easily into a Catonian republicanism. The Stoics' dismissal of worldly goods might easily be read as an argument for austerity. But Cicero does not do this; in his eyes stoicism is to be valued for its contribution to the tranquility of the mind, not to an ascetic life. And even while admiring the Stoic heritage and its notion of the moral good, Cicero at the same time endorses Platonic-Aristotelian arguments to the effect that worldly goods must accompany moral goods. With a humanist broad-mindedness, Cicero seeks to reconcile the various Greek schools of philosophy (even though he cannot sympathize with the Epicureans). Cicero's sense of worldliness extends to the *setting* of his dialogue. The scene is Cicero's villa at Tusculum (near Frascali, outside Rome). This is a retreat from the *negotium* (business) of the city proper—but it is still an urbane retreat, not a rustic one, a retreat where public forms of discussion and life are preserved. The villa life was a kind of halfway point between Pompey and Demetrius. In the villa, some of the more (Eastern) inward-looking, contemplative qualities are catered to. At the same time, the villa is based on the active virtue of hospitality.[12] The hospitable person opens the house to guests and entertains them.

JEFFERSON'S VILLA

This spirit of hospitality is also a striking feature of Jefferson's world. For Jefferson, the villa represented a retreat from the "cabal intrigue and hatred" of political life.[13] Although Jefferson often expressed the desire for peace and quiet, quite evidently what he sought was the tranquility of mind of the Stoic-Epicurean as much as the inwardness or solitude

Thomas Jefferson's villa, Monticello II, Charlottesville, Va. Built 1796–1809.

associated variously with the traditions of Augustinian Christianity, Calvinism, and Romanticism. Certainly in Jefferson's case the search for the tranquil life was suffused with a powerful Epicurean sociability, manifest in his attention to friends, the society of neighbors, visitors, and familial companionship.[14]

We see in Jefferson an adaptation of a classical humanism—and a readiness to learn from the examples of the Greeks and the Romans, certainly, but also from the Renaissance and from the enlightened French, Scottish, and English intellectual traditions. In this respect, Jefferson was a citizen of the world. There was no sign of nativism in his character. He could never have said—as William Vans Murray did in an essay rejecting the analogies drawn between America and antiquity—that America was a "unique society."[15] Jefferson was an eclectic thinker. He drew on an enormous range of sources and influences, and in its scope and antipurism, his thought was a perfect analogue of the New World. Jefferson loved neologisms created by the combination of words.[16] Just as he rejected intellectual purism, he rejected linguistic purism—for example, the attempt of grammarians to legislate a language. He delighted in the variety of dialects and personal idioms that were contained within one language of a given age.[17]

As far as his writings are concerned, Jefferson's sympathetic curiosity manifests itself as a kind of dilettantism. In words alone, Jefferson lacked the unity of vision of the highest kind of thought. Jefferson was no philosopher-*archôn*. He did not have the singer-poet's ability of a Solon.

His writings lack the *kosmopoietical* force capable of uniting the warring strands of creation. With the exception of the foundational document of the Declaration of Independence, no "sacred text" emanates from the greatest of the American founders. Rather, Jefferson's *kosmopoietical* ability was of a more classical, *architectural* kind. It was material signifiers, not words, that enabled Jefferson to gather all the different elements he drew on—republican, Stoical, Epicurean, Scottish Common Sense, Lockean—into something approaching a coherent whole. The core signifier that drew together all the fragments of meaning Jefferson absorbed in the course of his life was the idea of the villa. His lifetime labor of love — the design and building of Monticello—is testament to this. The villa represented a *union* of the Greek, Roman, Christian, Enlightenment, and Romantic sources that Jefferson was acquainted with.

Jefferson modeled the *idea* of Monticello after Pliny the Younger's and Varro's accounts of the Roman villa.[18] The actual design of Monticello was influenced most of all by the late Renaissance classicism of Palladio. Jefferson relied extensively on Palladio's *Four Books of Architecture* in the execution of Monticello.[19] Robert Morris' *Select Architecture* (1755) was also influential. Notably—and for the understandable reason of its association with English dominion—the Anglo-Palladianism of Burlington and his followers, and of Colen Campbell's *Vitruvius Britannicus*, was rejected by Jefferson. (More idiosyncratically, perhaps, Jefferson also often employed the treatises of the baroque architect James Gibbs.) Jefferson was, to say the least, a complex character. He was obsessed with the description of minute physical details and with the design of gadgets—both traits of an Enlightened rational-ascetic. Yet he displayed little of the saving mentality of that type. He had a classical love of spending money on cultivated pursuits (music, gardening, mathematics, architectural drawing, geometry, astronomy, natural philosophy); his mechanical experimenting occasioned the same kind of rational pleasure he gained from building. Like the best of the ancients, it was not passion or enthusiasm that animated him, but the rational-emotional involvement (joy, delight) in ordering, patterning, and constructing. In one respect, though, this generalization is untrue. For Jefferson also had an intense romantic love of nature, and for this reason Monticello was sited—against all classical precept—on top of a mountain. Neither Palladio nor the Roman writers had ever suggested a *mountaintop* as an ideal site for a villa. Jefferson's choice of site was a romanticizing translation of Palladio's recommendation (in his *Four Books*) to build on a small hill.[20] Notably also, Jefferson ignored Palladio's preference for the siting of a villa by the banks of a river. From the summit of his small mountain, the countryside spread out majestically. The view was sublime, and Jefferson often remarked on the constant stimulus this scene gave to the imagination.[21] The effect of taking in the grandeur of surrounding nature was to elevate and expand the soul. [22]

The role of cultivated nature (the garden) was meant to conspire in this. In his gardening practice, Jefferson rejected the classically ordered garden of the Renaissance. The Renaissance villa garden was symmetrically composed, and made up of geometrical patterns or shapes (circles, squares, rectangles, octagons). It was a classical mathematical ordering of space, and was laid out according to the principle of single-point perspective. Untrammeled (wild) nature is deliberately excluded from the Renaissance garden that is enclosed by terraces, walls, or pergolas. The viewer cannot look out onto a scene beyond the garden. The cultivated nature of the garden replicates the harmony and proportion of an ideal mathematical ordering. The best view of the garden is from above, looking down at its patterns. The pleasure of the garden derives from its geometric forms, and it stimulates in the observer the rational emotions of joy and delight. After the Renaissance, baroque designers inflated this classical style, turning it into a huge spectacle, and, using the device of the radiating avenue, sought to penetrate and dominate the surrounding nature beyond the garden. The English in the eighteenth century reacted against both classical and baroque styles, recommending a natural style in place of the formal garden. A garden composed naturally followed the irregularities of topography—the "genius of the place" in Alexander Pope's words.[23] The balance and regularity of the preceding geometrical styles and the geometrically shaped garden walks of the classical and the baroque were rejected in favor of serpentine lines and labyrinthine pathways. In place of the enclosed gardens of the Renaissance, the eighteenth-century English practice was to lay open to view the adjacent countryside.[24]

For Jefferson the landscaping of the Monticello estate was a passage to the natural wilderness, an opening to the exhilaration and sublimity of modern-romantic nature, with its towering mountains and vast woods. The art of gardening provided a graded entry into the infinite, a cultivated passage leading to the untrammeled sublimity beyond. The eighteenth-century English landscape garden afforded him the best model of such a passage. Jefferson's landscape garden at Monticello reached out into nature, incorporating the distant wilderness beyond into the landscape plan[25] (in a way that Jefferson, later in his presidency, was to incorporate the distant wilderness of French territories in his purchase of Louisiana.) Pope had referred to this as "calling in" the surrounding countryside.[26] The *peras* of the Jeffersonian villa did not exclude wild nature, unlike the case of the Renaissance garden. Rather the villa's border (between culture and nature) was its encircling walkways and tracks, serpentine paths and curved drives along which persons ambled in order to view the spectacular prospects of mountains, ridges, and forests in the distance, a romantic experience enhanced by the constantly shifting scene and perspective afforded by such walks—a moving picture, so to speak, that broke with fixed Renaissance perspective.[27]

Villa principles played a role in that other great Jeffersonian design project—his "academical village," the University of Virginia, in which he blended *diaetae*-style pavilions (inspired by Roman villa architecture) with a University Lawn evocative of both the Epicurean garden and the promised green land of the Puritan village common. Villa life was not an urban existence, yet it was not rustic either. Although located out of the city, the villa was the setting for the pursuit of cultivated leisure. Jefferson had little sympathy for the severe republics of Cato or indeed of Montesquieu.[28] He was disinterested in a republic of frugality, simplicity, and mediocre fortunes and abilities (Montesquieu's description), and maintained a respectful distance from the Catonian republican tradition that offered the ideal of the smallholder in the place of the gentrified villa.[29] It was not so much that Jefferson was antithetical to the smallholder (yeoman farmer) ideal, rather that the ideal could not match the ambit of Jefferson's notion of the good life. Jefferson's southern republican imagination often outstripped the realities of America's more puritanical yeomanic democracy, while at the same time the practical politician in Jefferson bended to these realities.

Jefferson the politician encouraged small property owners—at one time supporting a land bill to promote the agrarian smallholder.[30] He proposed smallholding as an *answer to the evils of poverty*, along with exempting from taxation everyone below a certain income level and taxing the higher portions of property in geometrical progression as they rose.[31] Where there were uncultivated lands in a country, Jefferson reasoned, the unemployed poor ought to be allowed to appropriate blocks of land. While the equal division of land was impracticable, he recommended that legislators all the same should experiment with schemes for subdividing land. The earth was a common block for persons to labor and live on. As long as there were vacant lands for wage laborers to resort to, Jefferson argued, there would never be an attempt by other classes to reduce them to a minimum of subsistence, for they could always "quit their trades and go laboring the earth."[32] (Should that earth be all appropriated, then care must be taken that other employment be furnished to those excluded from the appropriation.) Americans should provide by every possible means that as few as possible were without a little portion of land. Jefferson additionally thought that such smallholding was an *answer to the evils of subservience.* The citizen—the republican—was a person who stood outside of hierarchical relationships or arrangements. The citizen was neither a servant nor a dependent of someone else. A person who was a dependent could neither enjoy liberty nor act virtuously. But this begged the question: act virtuously to what end? It was one thing for Jefferson to say, in his *Notes on the State of Virginia* (1787),[33] that into the breasts of the citizen-farmer God had deposited substantial and genuine virtue, and that no age or nation had furnished an example of the corruption of morals in the mass of cultivators. But what was this virtue and what end did it serve? It might have been plainness of manners serving the end of an honest life. It might have been the courage to fight as an armed citizen, or the preparedness to sacrifice one's life or limbs in battles against the enemies of the republic. Yet none of these encapsulates the Jeffersonian ethos.

For Jefferson had a love of beauty and of epicurean hospitality that was the antithesis of puritanical or yeomanic republicanism. His beloved villa's regime of books, arts, and architectural building was far removed from the life of the Catonian farmer-solider. Villa life was not an overtly political existence. Indeed, it was a place of retreat from the grind of politics—a place to recollect and reorder one's thoughts. Yet it could not be equated with a private domestic existence either. The villa was a place of friendship, sociability, discussion, entertaining, reflective solitude, and physical exercise (dancing, riding, walking). In this respect, villa life had something of the character of a "little republic"—though not a Catonian or Calvinistic republic. Indeed, in his embrace of villa life, Jefferson surpassed the Ciceronian rejection of Catonian morality. Jefferson, in particular the older Jefferson, was deeply attracted to Epicureanism (a doctrine Cicero was repelled by). The person who in the name of republican virtue denies himself all pleasure and joy in the world was far from the republican of Jefferson's imagination.

FROM HOSPITALITY TO BUREAUCRACY

The Catonian (yeoman) republic was in so many ways the antithesis of the classical (humanist) republic. In the world of the smallholder, with dawn to dusk farm work, there was no time for cultivated leisure. Conversely, one of the greatest weaknesses of the humanist republican tradition was its inability to find an economic basis for the republic commen-

surate with its cultural superstructure. The Italian city-states during the
Renaissance had come closest to doing this. The importance of skilled
artisan industries to the economy of the Italian cities suggests something
of a correspondence between art and economics in these city-states. But
the example closest to hand — the Venetian model — held little attraction
for eighteenth-century Americans. (For instance, Thomas Otway's
restoration play *Venice Preserved* [1682], popular with American audiences, depicted Venice as a wretched, corrupt oligarchy.)[34] No correspondence between economics and culture can be found in the world of the
villa created by Virginians like Jefferson.

In Jefferson's world, as it had been in Cicero's, the city-in-the-coun-
tryside atmosphere of the villa came at a price: viz. that of slavery. Jefferson, like Cicero, shared the Stoic's belief in a common humanity. Such
a belief could not ultimately be reconciled with slavery, yet the existence
of the gentrified world of the villa depended on forced labor. Slaves
maintained the little philosophical republic — the garden of friends.

The Southern gentry, in the longer term, were unable to justify
slavery against the Calvinist abolitionists, although try they did,
invoking among other things both federalist arguments and a romantic
reading of Aristotle and the Greek *polis*. The relationship between master
and slave was brutal and despotic. Slaves could not share in common
humanity. They had no personal liberty. They were subject to the despotic
will of the master. They had no right to acquire property. They were chat-
tels — property in human beings; property to be secured and returned to
masters, should the slave flee. Measured against Stoic universalism,
Christian natural law or Enlightenment natural rights, slavery was indefensible. And the attempt to defend the indefensible brought the hospitality ethic of Jefferson and his fellow Southerners into general disrepute.
Not only that, it *corrupted* that ethic. This was one of the tragedies of
slavery. The Southern gentry knew that the institution of slavery was
unnatural ("peculiar"), yet the Southern way of life threatened to collapse
without it.[35] Slave labor was justified as a "terrible necessity."* The fruits
of plantation labor maintained villa life. Jefferson put it this way: "We
have the wolf by the ears and we can neither hold him, nor safely let him
go. Justice is in one scale, and self-preservation in the other."[36] Perversely
typical of "enlightened" moderns, self-preservation won the day, with
debilitating consequences. The Southerners expected something of the

---

*"Terrible necessity" is the animating force of ancient tragedy. It can be argued that the
American Civil War was the tragic outcome of the "terrible necessity" of slavery, though no
American dramatist, to my knowledge, has ever portrayed the Civil War in this fashion, or
America as the "tragical" Republic.

cultural glory of the ancients as the fruit of slavery. But over time mastery failed to make the Southern plantation owners more reasoned or more graceful. Indeed it coarsened them, made them more capricious and less interested in learning. In truth, slavery did not explain the cultural greatness of the ancients. Rather the decisive fact was that the classical economy had been geared to conspicuous consumption (to put it in Calvinist terms). In the ancient economy, money lending was primarily for nonproductive purposes[37] — for temple-building, public amenities (like baths), theaters, villa construction and the like — as opposed to investment in agriculture or manufacturing.

Of course, to think the ancient economy in terms of being geared to consumption rather than production is highly loaded. To say that a chair is produced, but a temple building is not, is specious. Both are made, both are objectivations. The real difference is that the latter is constitutive of the public sphere, while the chair may be either a private commodity or else a public thing, depending on circumstances. The key point is that the premium in the classical world was spending on public things (*res publicae*). In contrast, the Southern gentry, when it raised money — and it was often deeply in debt — did so in order to maintain its plantations. So, even if the idea of the plantation, and the appended villa, was modeled on Roman practice, its operative economic assumptions were modern. Production — and not consumption in the sense of public building, festivals, and so on — was the *telos* of economic behavior.

The Southern gentry's ethic was one of hospitality, not one of public endowment. Yet the eventual disappearance of villa life was not an unambiguous triumph of republican virtue, for what was lost, as well as the odious cruelty of slavery, was the myth of a life in which dignified kindness (a kind of adaptation of the Christian virtue of charity to classical virtue), hospitality, and a graceful manner were prominent values, and cultural demeanor was treasured as much as moneymaking.[38] Such a myth is not to be dismissed out of hand — simply as a veil for domination — especially as Jefferson rightly sensed that the emergent Calvinist economy of manufacturing industry in the Northern states would not prove congenial to large investments in the public sphere. Indeed, with a note of self-deceptive exaggeration, he saw the position of the wage laborer in manufacturing industry as much like that of the slave — suggesting that the moral coercion of want subjected the will of the laborer as despotically as the physical coercion of the slave. If in the twentieth century the welfare state corrected this abject immiseration and made Jefferson's equation null and void, modern industrial society still rarely had the effect of creating public artifices of great beauty. And its impact on participation in publics, large and small, was ambiguous to say the least. In the modern industrial society of the North, domestic privacy came to be valued over epicurean sociability (hospitality). This was no gain.

Without the countervailing pressure of the public realm, slavery in America brutalized all concerned in ways not registered in antiquity.[39] The Southern gentry lacked a deep experience of the *res publica*, and thus could not approach the ancients. Graceful manners cloaked violence; political wit was employed for deal-making. Unlike their manumitted counterparts in Rome, who threw off the stigma of slavery in a generation or two and became an indistinguishable part of the general population, the emancipated slave in America continued to be stigmatized because there was no public realm of a classical kind for either freed persons (the Roman *liberti*)* or for that matter even the citizen to join. The manumitted Roman slave joined those who walked, talked, or voted in the public realm, and thus whatever social prejudice attached to being an ex-slave was not enduring, certainly not across generations,[40] or at most was intermittently mobilized as an obstacle to social advancement.† Modern enlightened emancipation worked differently. It promised civil rights to the ex-slave—rights to own property, rights for families to remain intact—or else repatriation to Africa. It did not promise entrance into a modern *agora*. Indeed, such an *agora* did not exist. While citizenship was steadily expanded to all adults, it simultaneously lost the connotation that the citizen was one who filled public spaces and found public life fulfilling, and who temporarily took on public responsibilities and offices in order to ensure the proper provision and maintenance of the "common things" that make appearing in public possible. The citizen became the person who had the *right* to vote but one who was unfamiliar with public happiness—with the joys of speaking and acting in public, and of creating public artifices.

---

*The manumitted Roman slave could obtain three distinct statuses—citizen, Latin, and *peregrini dediticii*. The latter, subject foreigners, were those who had fought a regular war against Rome, had been defeated, and had given themselves up. Any slave who had been put in chains by his master, or had been interrogated by torture, or had belonged to a troupe of gladiators, could not become a Roman citizen or a Latin, but could only obtain the same status as a subject foreigner.

†Those of recent slave origin provoked some social nervousness (snobbishness perhaps) in elite Roman circles, as evidenced by the order of Emperor Claudius to the Alexandrians in 41 C.E. to exclude "those born of slaves" from the ephebate, Alexandria's upper class Greek youth corps. Marcus Aurelius in 175 C.E. instructed Athens to remove from the Council of the Areopagus anyone who was not freeborn in the third generation. At the same time, he expressly permitted sons of freedman membership in the Council of Five Hundred. What these examples (from M. I. Finley, *The Ancient Economy*, p. 77) illustrate is that in ancient times the power of prejudice against those of slave background was circumscribed, and, with sufficient generational distance, would disappear.

Modern office holding correspondingly became bureaucratized. The fateful steps in this direction were taken early in the life of the American Republic. As early as the 1790s, public finances were "reformed" on the English model in order to regularize debt financing of state expansion.[41] Military functions were also gradually professionalized. Both of these were key to the bureaucratization of the state, and were pursued even though Americans were familiar with English Commonwealth (Harringtonian and "Old Whig") arguments against government debt and a standing army. Americans knew debt financing and the professional army to be pillars of the detested monarchical state, but they bowed to these institutions anyway. Jefferson was elected president in the "Revolution of 1800" specifically on a platform of opposition to the National Whig (Federalist) program of Alexander Hamilton, who had worked assiduously (as Secretary of Treasury in Washington's administration) to create a modern system of public finance, which was in essence a stable system of debt financing that would allow the steady expansion of bureaucratic administration. (The cornerstone of this was Hamilton's arrangement that the repayment of the principal and interest on debt would have first charge on public revenues.) Quite notably, once in office Jefferson left Hamilton's system in place. (Indeed it provided the needed fiscal confidence for foreign investors to provide the loans to finance Jefferson's cherished Louisiana Purchase from the French.) The most the Jefferson administration did to confront the National Whig agenda was to put forward a plan to retire all public debt by 1817 (and this plan, of course, came to nothing because of the Louisiana Purchase). In the same manner, Old Whig notions that a citizen army (militia) could effectively defend the Republic faltered. Militias were central in the Revolutionary War, but when the Antifederalist Elbridge Gerry of Massachusetts proposed in subsequent constitutional debates that the Constitution should limit the size of the standing army to two or three thousand men, Washington sank the idea by interjecting that they should also make it unconstitutional for an enemy to attack with a larger force. As President, Jefferson sought to reduce the size of the army,[42] but the War of 1812 with England put an end to the idea that a continental Republic could engage in a modern war—against a powerful sovereign state—without a substantial standing army.[43]

VOLUNTARY ASSOCIATION

Despite all of this, the figure of Jefferson still stood for a Ciceronian sense of public duty—the carrying out of the oftentimes tedious burdens of public office not as an act of self-sacrifice or moral heroism but as a contribution to public happiness. For the Ciceronian republican, while public life in the narrower sense (the life of the law courts and the Senate, etc.) was *dutiful*, duty was not a harsh or austere thing, but the premise of civic happiness (*civilis felicitas*). The republican self was a *happy* person, not a censorious self. Cicero's great work *De officiis* (*On Duties*), popular in eighteenth-century America,[44] saw duty as contributing to the felicity of the citizen. The condition of happiness—unruffled ease and contentment—characterizes the citizen, rather than a Catonian frugality (*frugalitas*). Duty thus simply means contributing to the "common things" that make public happiness possible, rather than being *severus* (stern) with oneself, or censoring, prohibiting, or imposing on people tedious sacrifices of a moral kind. But this Ciceronian image of duty (*a duty beyond duty*) did not compete well with the one styled after the Plutarchian moral hero. Plutarch's *Lives* was the most widely read classical work in eighteenth-century America,[45] and it appealed to the spiritual descendants of the original Calvinist settlers who liked their politics laced with sententious gravity and who preferred political figures to act with great ardor and patriotic zeal.

Like many other southern republicans, Jefferson did not think that public virtue depended on rigorous or censorial private virtue.[46] On the other hand, public virtue in America lacked a proper end. The classical love of spaces and places of public appearance was missing. The Jeffersonian legacy offered the villa as a substitute for the public realm, the city and its civic freedom. But this was a poor substitute, and without an ethos of public performance, participation, and building, governance rapidly became bureaucratized. In the early years of the Republic, there was resistance to the growth of the professionalized state, but there was not the weight of the city to anchor this resistance. Without the presence of powerful cities, bureaucratization was inevitable and unavoidable.[47] True, as de Tocqueville observed in the 1830s,[48] there was a high level of *voluntary* association amongst Americans,[49] something that has remained a constant feature of American life through to today.[50] But voluntary association was premised on the *natural* right of the individual to enter and exit an association (to "contract" in and out). Such an association implied no center—no public artifice—that preceded or succeeded the volunteers, no objectivation that was greater than they, which they held in trust and which they were responsible for maintaining and augmenting. A voluntary association is premised on rights, not responsibilities. Volunteers who form a charity might feel a responsibility to those who are down and out, but this is a prerational sentiment, not a civic obligation, not a *duty beyond duty*.[51]

The voluntary association was not bureaucratic but it also was not "political" in the sense of participating in the making (*poiêsis*) of the city. This was an effect of what Karl Marx had observed in 1843, partly with the United States in mind: the split in modern society between an abstractly political (bureaucratic) state and civil society. The modern state monopolized politics.[52] In the modern social arrangement, things that previously had a political significance (birth, rank, education, occupation) became nonpolitical. Where the political state attained a full degree of development, man led a double life. He lived in the political community (the state), where he regarded himself as a communal being, and in civil society, where he was active as a private individual. Humanness and citizenship were separated. In the profane and immediate world, the individual was depoliticized and separated from the commune (city). An individual could still be a citizen, but "in heaven" — in the fictive community of the state, a participant in "popular sovereignty." The hierarchies of old European society were destroyed by making membership in estates and guilds no longer the prerequisite for citizenship. For traditionally excluded groups (Marx had the Jews in mind) this was a form of emancipation, but also, at the same time, a condemnation to a nonpolitical existence. Modernity erased distinctions between insiders and outsiders of the commune (city) by reducing citizenship to a nominal voting membership of the state, available in principle to all adults. Along with the abolition of the old hierarchies came the abolition of the political character of civil society. Estranged from the commune (the political community of empirical life), the emancipated individual could not appear as a "species being." Rather "species life" now appeared as a framework extraneous to the individual, while the individual withdrew into himself, into private interests and desires. De Tocqueville, puzzling about what drew the American "out of himself," knew that it was not "great affairs" but local matters bearing on the individual's greatest private interests.[53] For these local matters, the otherwise withdrawn personality was prepared to keep in contact with others, to listen and talk with them, and join with them in voluntary cooperative actions. Marx, who had read de Tocqueville, was more skeptical. The rights of man (rights to a career based on talent, education, elementary security, and so on) were the rights of the monad — rights to do or enjoy what does not harm others. The associations of modern civil society — the de Tocquevillian substitute for the city — promote the welfare, education, and religious needs of individuals, but not their political relationship, their association through the media of the commune; their life as empirical, not abstract citizens spent in the public spaces of the university, council, and theater. Indeed, civil society estranges human beings from the commune (city). It sets them apart from their species being, from the *politikos bios* the *vita activa*. The state appropriates the *politikos bios*, and turns it into an unreal reality, a hyper reality. The state presents itself as an emancipator — fighting for universality (e.g. the universal right to a career based on talent) against the old discriminations and hierarchies. But this universality lacks the humanity of city life.

Humanness is experienced when individuals act on their rational obligation — their *duty beyond duty* — to meet and converse, act and build together in the close quarters of the public space of the city. Marx concluded that only when real, individual man resumes the abstract citizen into himself and becomes again a *species being* in his empirical life, would human emancipation be completed. It is exactly the failure of human emancipation, the failure of the excluded to enter into the *vita activa*, the *politikos bios*, that has haunted the United States. The failure of black emancipation (the American equivalent of the failures of Jewish emancipation in Central Europe) exemplifies this.[54] The American Civil War (1861–1865) was fought over the question of whether the American future would be dominated by a Southern slave-based plantation economy or a Northern mix of family farming, "little house on the prairie" agrarianism and wage labor industry. The slaves that President Lincoln's emancipation decree freed had no place in the civil society of the North (at least until the 1920s). Some of the most vicious racism was, in fact, Northern, not Southern. A state like Illinois, Lincoln's home state, was just as hostile to free blacks as it was to slavery. In the eyes of the antinomic white yeomanry that had spread out from New England across the Northwest, the freed black was a competitor for land (free soil). Lincoln's own preference was for repatriation of the ex-slaves to Africa.[55] His vision of emancipation was indubitably Hebraic-Protestant, that is, exodic.[56] Unwelcome in the North, in the South the ex-slaves had no public persona.[57] Thus, the Southern states easily frustrated the exercise by ex-slaves of their nominal civil rights (property, voting, and so on),[58] curtailed their freedom of traveling about,[59] and forced them into a condition of semicoercive tenancy and segregation under the Jim Crow laws. It was only when a fragile surrogate public life had grown up around the black church communities in the South that the prospect of *human* emancipation was opened up.[60] In the 1950s and the early 1960s, when the social structures of the Old South were challenged again, it is of special note that the initial point of explosion was the question of whether whites and blacks could associate or mingle together in public spaces (in buses, restaurants, or elsewhere). The enforcement of the right to vote was secondary to the basic *experience* of freedom. And understandably so, because enlightened emancipation, enforced or not, is not truly freeing unless there are public spaces and places in which those who have acquired the legal right to vote, own property, to speak and associate, can *consociate*—places where, in the simplest terms, they can peregrinate, or freely walk in public. The turning of the antisegregation struggle of the 1950s—the greatest assertion of civic *dignitas* of the American twentieth century—into a civil rights movement in the 1960s was the very cause of its decline,[61] and a sign of the ultimately debilitating power of the idea of natural rights over the American mind.

THE CITY BEAUTIFUL

The condition of peregrination was alien not merely to official Southern society, but to mainstream America generally. The American sense of freedom was unlike the Greek *peripatetic* (the wandering scholar, metic) or the Latin *peregrini* (which carried the sense of those who had gained the freedom to wander in public spaces). The Latin *peregrini* connoted someone from foreign parts, and was related to the condition of traveling, of strangeness, and also, in opposition to the citizen, to a specific status in Roman society, the *peregrini dediticii* (subject foreigner). A freed Roman slave who did not qualify for the status of citizen or Latin* also acquired the status of *peregrini dediticii*, possessing thereby the freedom of the trader and tradesman, along with the freedom of the traveler. Such strangers—both freedmen and foreigners—played a crucial role in Roman trade, and were concentrated in mercantile, port, and caravan cities.[62] They were also prominent in the medical profession.[63] Even if they did not possess citizenship, they often had substantial economic standing, and could accumulate significant wealth. A *peregrini dediticii* had certain legal disabilities—notably such a person could not inherit anything by a will. Yet, at the same time, the stranger possessed the freedom of the market place, trading entrepôt, and mercantile route. This was not so much the freedom of possession (which was subtly limited by the inability to will property) but the freedom of circulation and the freedom of creation. The stranger lived by exchanging things and making things, and by some other professional activities. At the most basic level, one might say that Rome offered two kinds of freedom—the freedom of citizenship and the freedom of denizenship. The stranger—the denizen of the port city or the market city—was excluded from the duties and public

---

*Mainly because of some "offense" that had seen them chained or branded or tortured by their master.

life of the state, yet nonetheless possessed a *sui generis* freedom and considerable scope to move through Roman society.

In contrast to this, American freedom was a freedom based on the Hebraic image of *searching* for the promised land or else on the Enlightenment idea of *possessing* a prepolitical right—the freedom not to be obstructed by one's fellows or by the state in the enjoyment of one's life, locomotion, career, education, property, and so on—in other words, not to have one's *dunamis* impeded. For the peregrinator, or peripatetic, legal rights to act without impediment or to engage in a certain kind of journey are important. But for this person, both movement and journey is *toward the city center*, or else *from city to city*. It is the freedom to appear in public spaces and places, to enjoy the "common wealth." Yet, for there to be such a peregrinational freedom, for it to be possible to walk freely in public sight, there must be in the first place the public spaces and places in which to wander, and a social belief in their importance. It was this very *res publica* that the American republic lacked. Not completely, of course, but in contrast with the city-republics of antiquity and the Renaissance. The American dilemma has been to have given birth to a republic without *res publicae*. The lack of public space was never absolute. Far from it. Yet it is evident, when we compare America's continental republic with the city-republics of Greece or Rome, Florence or Venice that the care with which the city-republics built their agoras, forums, and piazzas is not repeated in the American case.

The foundational act of ancient politics was to create the city center (*agora, forum*). An echo of this persisted even in the Spanish dominions in the Americas. (Even the Spanish monarchy could not shake off the distant trace of Mediterranean antiquity.) For the three centuries of Spanish rule in the Americas, the plaza was the center of political, religious, and commercial life.[64] Around the plaza were concentrated the church, the royal government building, the customs house, the hospital, shops, and mercantile quarters. In the center of all of this was the public space—an inviting place of conviviality and spectacle, authority and proclamation, festival and procession; a place that drew people to the streets, to stroll and chat, sit and play, observe and be seen, mingle and listen to music being performed, or simply enjoy a quintessential human vitality. America—the other, *North* America—never had this, with the important exception of New Orleans, a city that had French and Spanish antecedents.[65] (The ethos of the public square survived New Orleans's incorporation into the American Union as part of the Louisiana Purchase. In the process, the French-designed Place d'Armes[66] was renamed Jackson Square.)[67] Otherwise, the Americans did not build authentic plazas, the "away home" (*apoikia*) of the peregrinator. This points to a curious paradox: unlike the Spanish Americans, the "other" Americans rebelled against royal government, and decided in 1789 on a republican constitution. Yet, they lacked the love of the outside, the exteriorized public place that is central to the spirit of the *res publica*.[68] This was not for want of trying. They created the village common in New England for grazing cows and drilling militia (till the militia were disbanded in 1812). They created central squares in cities in the Midwest and Southwest in the nineteenth century.[69] But these lacked the architectonic depth of the classical city. The square was a planar idea, a variation of the Jeffersonian gridplan. Even when notionally surrounded by buildings, these squares never could evince the three-dimensional shape (the volumetric form and depth) of classical public space. Instead they clung to the open semantics of the two-dimensional grid plan, ensuring that a feeling of emptiness would invariably pervade the heart of the American town.

When Americans did make a concentrated effort at civic building, during the time of the City Beautiful movement (from the late 1890s to the Great Depression), none of the innate American *agoraphobia* was mastered. While some remarkable public buildings were conceived, Americans for the most part continued to imagine and experience public space as empty (planar) space rather than as filled (cubic) space. Symptomatic of this, one of the chief inspirers of American efforts to rebuild their cities, Daniel Burnham (1846–1912), looked to the baroque as a model. His influential city plans for Cleveland, San Francisco, and Chicago were marked by a French-influenced, beaux arts idealism of broad avenues, large parks, and a monumentalism that signified a certain imperial grandiosity. True, for individual buildings, Americans often turned to the rigor and restraint of the classical. (At the turn of the century, Renaissance revival styles were popular; later on, by the 1920s, contemporary forms of the classical such as art deco, epitomized in New York's Chrysler Building [1929], flourished.) At the same time, however, the scale of urban space in which buildings were set was so often imposing, rather than human scale. Civic buildings thus tended to be surrounded by uncomfortably empty or amorphous spaces. What Americans ended up doing was to embed classical republican forms in expansive spaces that mirrored the mentality of a continental empire.

The City Beautiful era was probably the first (and only) time Americans invested a faith and a love in their cities. Many of the greatest and most beautiful civic creations in America date from this period. The spirit of the age had a civilizing quality. Even the industrial barons which the unpleasant post–Civil War Gilded Age had produced (the Fricks, Vanderbilts, Deerings, du Ponts, and so on) began to channel much of their wealth into scholarly

Chrysler Building, designed by William Van Alen. Built 1926–1930.

recreations of Renaissance palaces. They created mansions to house art collections that resembled public buildings, and that were later converted from residences into public museums or libraries, as in the case of New York's Frick Collection or James Deering's Vizcaya in Miami. The faith Americans (temporarily) invested in their cities is evident from the splendor of so much of what they built. This was the time when the great city railroad stations were constructed, such as New York's Pennsylvania Station (1902–1910), designed in Roman Revival style by the architects McKim, Mead, and White (and destroyed in the 1960s to make way for the bland modernism of Madison Square Garden). Throughout America, viaducts, power stations, and dams were built in academic classical styles, as well as the libraries funded by the Carnegie fortune. After decades of neglect, Washington was revived under the guidance of the McMillan Commission Plan (1902) and sponsored by Daniel Burnham and Charles McKim, among others.[70] Over a thirty-year period Washington was rebuilt in a dramatic fashion.[71] Many of the principal signifiers of Washington date from this time. The Mall was restored and lined with buildings in accordance with L'Enfant's original plan. The great Union Station terminal was erected, as were the Lincoln and Jefferson memorials; the Mall's cross axis was landscaped; a system of local and regional parks was created; the White House was restored; the complex of government buildings known as the Federal Triangle was built; the Capitol was expanded; and a new Supreme Court building was completed.[72]

The McMillan Plan served as a model for cities throughout the United States. Under the auspices of the City Beautiful Movement, plans for both small cities like New Haven and Minneapolis and large cities like Chicago and New York were developed.[73] This planification, in turn, generated a great interest in public building. In New York, landmark buildings such as the Richard Morris Hunt-designed Metropolitan Museum of Art (1895–1902); the McKim, Mead, and White-designed Municipal Building (1907–14) and Brooklyn Institute of Arts and Sciences building (1895–1915); and the C. B. J. Snyder-designed public schools were constructed.[74] These were mirrored on the West coast in works like Arthur Brown's distinguished San Francisco City Hall (1915). Importantly, though, the City Beautiful Movement was not restricted to large cities. It was not unusual, as Allen Greenberg points outs, to find small towns like Naugatuck, Connecticut possessing five buildings by McKim, Mead, and White, or Pasadena, California with important buildings by Arthur Brown and Myron Hunt.[75]

The City Beautiful Movement provided civic enrichment in hundreds of cities and towns throughout America.[76] This, however, was inherently contradictory. *Gloria* is a genuine and laudable aspiration of a republic. It represents the ambition for a certain kind of collective greatness. However, greatness is easily confused with grandeur, and civic memory with imperial monumentality. Such confusion is typical in the City Beautiful era. Strikingly, it is only in a handful of *port cities* (New York City and San Francisco primarily) that this confusion is avoided, and then not always consistently. It was avoided because the seaboard provided an inherent *peras* for the city. (The development of Los Angeles, propelled by the arrival of the continental railway, provides a stark example in contrast.) A port provides a natural focus of congregation, a point of human concentration. Where such a center of activity exists (quite unlike the tendency of the railway to disperse human activity along a line), one of the conditions for the existence of convivial public space is met. Only here is there an impetus for public space to fill up—for such space to become a gathering place. Mostly, however, American public space remained empty. It is space occupied periodically by official rituals, processions, and events, but it does not fill up with the jostling, animated, semianarchical crowds that the plaza-type space attracts.

RHYTHMIC FREEDOM

In retrospect what we find quite evidently absent from the central spaces of so many American towns and metropolises is the spirit of carnival—the public reenactment of the shift from chaos to cosmos; the recreation, in a public setting, of the ordering of society. The carnival is enacted in the plaza, beginning with the apparent disappearance of order. This is signified through revelry, ecstasies, commotion, jostling, and self-abandonment of different kinds. In this atmosphere social distinctions are inverted, and society momentarily frees itself from the forms it has established but which it will recreate (through song, dance, and other kinds of public theater). It is through rhythms that the public ordering, the forms of the city, is first created and, each subsequent time later, recreated. Rhythm is an ordering.[77] It is one of the most fundamental of all human orderings. *Rhusmos* is an old Ionian-Greek word for shape.[78] The first shape or form belongs to the person who walks gracefully, whose walk has regular stresses and accents. Rhythm structures the walk. It organizes its timing, orders it in time; it imparts to it regularities, a "beat." From this basic rhythmic organization arise the rhythms of dance and song, and of poetic speech with its "feet" (units) of verse. Song and dance, and later theater, extend the rhythmic ordering of the graceful peregrinator. The basis of public culture, of the performed arts, is the enactment of rhythms that order existence. In the case of the carnival, there is a movement through a cycle of random crowding and crush, descent into frenzy, giddiness, and chaos, and out of this the emergence of rhythmic movements, dance, song, the metered voice, and so on. This rhythmic ordering is not confined to the streets. It may also occur indoors, on the public stage. But the relative paucity of North American theaters and opera houses and the like—until the "American Renaissance" of the late nineteenth century—reminds us how even this transposition of the outdoors indoors did not occur readily in the land of the pilgrims. The American reenactment rather was one of reiterating the foundational texts—as in the case of the readings that took place in the New England meetinghouse or in the interpretations of the laws handed down in Midwestern courthouses, or the aspirations to cultural literacy in the nineteenth-century land grant (agricultural) colleges with their text books. This recreation was rooted in the sacred book, not in the rhythms of the peregrinator.

The one great—and it has to be said, ironic—exception to this was the culture of the ex-slave, from whose ranks (after emancipation) emerged an inevitably harassed but vital public life of musical performance. This culture also had no opera houses or great theatres. It scraped by with bordellos and juke joints, churches and picnic grounds as public spaces of appearance. Yet if we think of the great public spaces of antiquity—the model of all European public space until the rise of Romanticism—these emerged from something very simple, viz. the *choros* or dancing place. Great civic architecture was "frozen music." The culture of the emancipated slave in America was a musical culture that cohered around the traveling performer (the "musical physician") whose peregrinations represented not just freedom from accursed labor but a kind of freedom that most Americans barely understood—the freedom to act, the freedom that comes in and through public performance. The peregrinator travelled to a destination marked by the freedom of a "lawfulness beyond law." In other words, the peregrinator did not travel in search of the promised land of antinomian liberty but in search of a freedom represented by structures that are not imperative, that are an ordering without orders (commands). Music (rhythm, melody, harmony) is such a structure. Architecture (frozen music) is another. Neither operate through the imperatives of the law; neither can be legislated or commanded (at least to any real effect).

There are two kinds of ordering at stake here. One is based on moral law; the other on the regular spacing of things. The moral law originates in the commandments of God. In the modern Enlightenment (Kant), the moral law is superficially secularized. Imperatives that are enunciated by humankind ("Respect the rights of Man") replace God's word. At the same time, the modern age, in the name of freedom, makes any kind of law problematic. Consequently the Americans, a religious people, were also antino-mian. They preferred to live by "the spirit" rather than by the "law of God." They were the first religious people who wanted to live outside the law. The American Calvinists were always antifoundationalists, much to the puzzlement of their Northern European counterparts. They resolved the tension between their moralizing religion and their antinomian faith by making antinomian liberty their law. Their sacred texts set out as law their individual liberty, their inalienable rights.

The other (rhythmic) kind of ordering is the regular spacing of things, as in architecture, music, or in a civic culture. This ordering does not arise out of the written text, although a written text may be rhythmically ordered. The civic ordering of things is the rhythmic composition of ele-ments and parts. These elements or parts are joined together metrically through the regular arrangement of stressed and unstressed parts.[79] Such an ordering is not imperative, but structural. It does not demand that human beings live up to a standard (norm, law). It does not descend into moralizing—as all ordering based on a moral law eventually does. Rather it assumes that there are various patterns that mark the human emergence from chaos and suffering. This ordering is not external to a human being, as a law is to an act (even a "universal law" of a Kantian kind). Beneath the surface of a musical composition or performance is a set of ordering relations (regularities of accent, proportionate relations between tones, etc.). Composition and structuring, performance and ordering are mutu-ally implicated; they are irreducibly part of each other, which also means that such ordering is not a duty in the sense of requiring sternness, cen-sorship or the like to be achieved. The discipline of the composer-per-former is a *duty beyond duty*. It represents an order beyond orders (com-mandments), but it is not antinomian. It is not a liberty beyond law but a lawfulness beyond law. It is motivated not by the human sense of reaching up to the moral heights but by the pleasure, the real delight, of human beings in creating, observing, and enacting patterns, rhymes and rhythms, and the good shape (*euruthmos*) that arises from them.

THE FREEDOM TO PEREGRINATE

The most basic freedom is not something possessed (rights) but some-thing *experienced* in the public realm. It is the experience of being able to wander freely through the public space of the city. This is comparable to the *empeiria* (experience) gathered by Greek citizens and metics as they wandered the *peras* of the ancient Mediterranean—their freedom emerged from their navigating, their experience as they traveled from *emporia* (trading post) to *emporia*, from *polis* to *polis*. As in the paradigmatic case of the merchant-philosopher-traveler Thales, this *empeiria*, and the chance it afforded to observe and compare, was the basis of *logos*, the giving of the account of what was seen.

Experience of this worldly kind is gained only in the public sphere, and in the act of traveling to and from the public centers of performance and seeing for oneself the local practices. In each *civitas*, experience is gained by peregrinating around the sites of performance (including performances associated with exchange, philosophizing, and governance), absorbing the nature of each place, its sights and sounds, textures and tastes — like the *flaneur* of the nineteenth-century French imagination: the one who strolls along, observing. The person who congregates without foreboding in the public space is free,[80] just as the one who strolls in public is freed from the weight of his soul. The *flaneur* experiences — in the act of walking and observing in public — a lightness of being (happiness). Simply so, because in public places persons can move outside of themselves, outside of the vortex of their fears and dreams, desires and jealousies. The walker in public turns outward — away from the enigmas or obscurity of the prerational into the sunny lucidity of the civic place. The Americans, no less than any other society, had to address the chaos of inner nature. But they did so by invoking not the figure of reason, but rather the ecstatic imagination of the Old and New Testaments. In God, they trusted. The legatees of Christianity vividly portrayed the turmoil of the soul racked by desire, envy, vanity, and conceit. Thoughts of wickedness and sin haunted the American mind. God symbolized deliverance from this. But what was the American God? Certainly not the keeper of the heavenly city of Augustine, nor the source of Aquinas's divine law, nor even the object of Calvin's this-worldly piety. Rather, the American God was sublime Nature. Deliverance — from the prison of inner nature, from the obsessive thoughts about immorality and of a soul corrupted by desire — meant to stand alone in the face of infinite Nature, and to immerse oneself in the illimitable wilderness.

Both Nature and city take persons out of themselves — out of their particularistic selves, the selves of fear and anxiety, pettiness and vindictiveness, pain and torment. But they do so in completely different ways. The city (and in this category I would include the humanized Nature of a Horace or a Virgil, the Georgic nature) does this by intimating Reason. Nature (modern sublime Nature) does this by evoking an encompassing vastness. Both city and Nature quiet the torments of inner nature, but in different ways. One has the self flee from the world into infinite solitude;

the other has the self navigate through the world. In the latter case, conscience becomes "civilized" — it takes upon itself the role of rational orientation among the spaces and places of the city.

In the city, the self experiences a rational ordering.[81] Reason *gives shape*
to life. In contrast, inner nature (the prerational) lacks shape. It is tumult —
confused, disorientated. It lacks resolution, determinacy, structure, or legi-
bility. It has power, it is a driving force, but one without form. It exhausts
itself in indeterminacy and the civil wars within; it dissipates itself in the fogs
and shadows of inwardness. But what justifies us in saying that the city, in
contrast, is reason? What makes the city a shaping power? Firstly, the spaces
and places of the city are public. Life in the city (center) is public. However,
simply for something to be "made public" is not by itself the work of reason.
The American compulsion to make public the most private things of life in
the court of laws or the court of public opinion, in newspapers and other
public media, exemplifies this — the mere *revelation* of an inner torment does
not dispel it, or show how it may be dispelled, reasonably. Yet reason *is* a
public thing (a *res publica*). It is not private, not idiosyncratic, obscure, or enigmatic. Reason is something shared, something between persons. Private
nightmares, desires, and delusions might be shared (advertised, exhibited,
communicated) with others, but these affects are not shared *between* persons.
What is *between* persons is the public space. The public space is the *res publica*. The public space (the city center) is the space from which has been
cleared the private dwelling, the domicile. It has boundaries that mark it out
from the private. The space that is opened up at the center is shared by all (of
those who are not in a condition of servitude). Poor and rich, notable and
unnoted, officeholders and householders alike can enter the public space. It
is shared by being maintained by all — through the efforts of governments
and the sense of collective responsibility of civic-minded individuals and
associations. It is shared also because it is the site of conflict, contest, drama,
argument, and game between the denizens of the city. It is the shared space
of conflict and dispute. It unites those who are forever, in a multitude of
ways, always divided. It unites them as the observers and audiences,
cheerers and supporters of disputants and opponents, and of those who act
out, in theater and song, the meaning of the dramaturgical society.

This public space is reason because it is the embodiment of form. It is
space that is well formed. It has definition, contours, boundaries, and
limits. It has symmetries and just proportions. Such shapeliness provides
deliverance from the tumultuous condition of inner nature. This shapeliness is the outline of the world, and the world is external to the self. Yet,
it is not external in the sense of (modern, infinite) Nature precisely
because the world has boundaries. To experience the world is also to

experience boundaries. The self that acquires a sense of boundaries is freed from the debilitating dissemination of the self, from its disintegration. The boundaries of the world of the city are marked by the diagonals of the streets and by the lines (cornices, architraves) of the buildings. The boundaries of the world of the city are three-dimensional. Boundaries are material significations. They exist in the world. They compose the world. And as *material* significations, they are lasting. They endure. The worldly marks of the city are durable, and this also is an intimation of reason. For reason is a kind of steadiness, an unwavering calmness in contrast to the volatility of prerational desires and postrational ecstasies. Reason steadies where ambition and desire drive forward. Reason is lucid persistence, in contrast to the imaginative transport that inflames the human spirit with its blinding light, its lustrous lightning and thunderstorms, its fierce radiance, intense flashes, and edifying uplift. Reason is neither passion nor inspiration; rather it is the ordered connection that fits things together beautifully, and in doing so establishes an equilibrium between things (parts, elements, forces) that allows them to remain joined over long periods of time. The rhythm, the harmony of relations, the proportionate or just fit of things, is a key to the longevity of their coexistence. Law court, opera house, town hall, commercial emporium and the rest are equilibrated—that is, rationally ordered or joined—by the careful spacing of the artful city center.

This enjoining order is the *res publica*, the public thing, the worldly artifice which endures. It is a made thing, assembled from different parts. The parts of the public thing are material. *How* those parts are ordered or composed is the work of reason. Where reason does its work well and an enduring *res publica* is created, then that shared (and artfully composed) space becomes the setting (the stage) for the (real and symbolic) contestations, dramas and conflicts of society. In this worldly setting—with its tables and chairs, capitals and plinths, arches and architraves, vestibules and auditoria—spirited (postrational) and passionate (prerational) as well as rational actions unfold—opponents clash, enemies fight, litigants dispute. And reason, through all of this, endures. Reason is the ballast for all of them. As the figures come and go from the stage, reason is the touchstone for all that happens in the public theater. It ties the memories of the past, the reflections of the present, and the expectations of the future together. Reason is a place, or rather the *ordered spacing*, where things are disclosed, where persons appear, where audiences assemble, where contests are fought and dramas played, where performers gather, and where the stroller, the peregrinator, observes them all, wandering through the streets, the portals, the halls and rooms of the *res publica*. Without such *res publicae*, there can be a republic in name only.

NOTES

1. In the context of the fraught debates of the 1980s in the American academy, Allan Bloom was to bemoan the loss of the common text (the Bible) in American life (Allan Bloom, *The Closing of the American Mind* [New York: Simon and Schuster, 1987]). He asserted this against his "foes," the multiculturalists, who rejected the approach that canonized a text. Ironically, though, both cultural conservatives like Bloom and their radical opponents shared a fervent belief in the importance of texts—in their selection and interpretation. Both assumed that moral goodness descended from reading a text, even if one side approved of the canonized text while the other approved of the marginalized text. No matter, both texts were sacred. In this, the "cultural wars" of the 1980s echoed the fierceness with which seventeenth- and eighteenth-century dissenting Protestants defended their selections and interpretations of biblical passages, and the readiness of dissenters to return to the previously marginalized Old Testament for guidance. A further irony, specifically in Bloom's case, was that the canonized texts he defended against the radicals were classical [Platonic] texts. In his own way, his project was as subversive as his opponents—to turn the public dialogues of Socrates and Plato into sacred (and esoteric) texts to be interpreted by the elect in a manner closely resembling Biblical hermeneutics.

2. Cicero, *De Officiis*, trans. Walter Miller (Cambridge, Mass.: Harvard University Press, 1913), Book I.VI.

3. Ibid., Book I.IV.

4. Ibid., Book I.XXI.

5. Ibid., Book II.IX.

6. Ibid., Book II.XVIII.

7. Ibid., Book II.XIV–XV.

8. Ibid., Book II.XVI.

9. Ibid., Book II.XVII–XVIII.

10. Cnaeus Pompeius Magnus (106–48 B.C.E.) was a Roman general, consul, and leader of the "aristocratic" party against Caesar.

11. Ibid., Book II.XVII–XVIII.

12. Ibid., Book II.XVIII.

13. Anticipating retirement from public life, in June 1793 Jefferson wrote to Madison thus: "The motion of my blood no longer keeps time with the tumult of the world. It leads me to seek happiness in the lap and love of my family, in the wholesome occupation of my farms and my affairs, in an interest or affection in every bud that opens, in every breath that blows around me, in an entire freedom of rest, of motion of thought—owing account to myself alone of my hours and actions. . . . "

14. One consequence of this was that public "rooms of parade" (rooms for guests and entertainment) were as important in the Jeffersonian villa as the domestic quarters.

15. Meyer Reinhold, *Classica Americana* (Detroit: Wayne State University Press, 1984), p. 159.

16. Karl Lehmann, *Thomas Jefferson, American Humanist* (Charlottesville: University Press of Virginia, 1985), p. 81

17. Ibid., p. 103.

18. Ibid., chap. 11.

19. For example, the dome on the villa was inspired by the Temple of Vesta illustrated in Palladio's *Four Books*.

20. William Howard Adams, *Jefferson's Monticello* (York: Abberville Press, 1983), p. 51.

21. Ibid., p. 146.

22. Ibid., p. 151.

23. Alexander Pope, *Epistle to Burlington* (1731).

24. In the words of Charles Bridgeman, the garden—set free from its prim regularity—could "assort" with the wilder countryside without.

25. Adams, *Jefferson's Monticello*, pp. 169–70.

26. And to ensure the sublime view would not be obstructed, the service wings of the villa (i.e., the domestic-working part of the villa economy) were placed underground by Jefferson.

27. Adams, *Jefferson's Monticello*, pp. 171–76.

28. Lehmann, *Thomas Jefferson, American Humanist*, p. 118.

29. Forrest McDonald, *Novus Ordo Seclorum* (Lawrence: University Press of Kansas, 1985), p. 74, incorrectly, I think, suggests that the Southerner's idea of the republic was based on the Harringtonian ideal of the independent yeoman smallholder.

30. In his "Proposed Constitution For Virginia" (1776) he recommended that each adult under the constitution be entitled to 50 acres of land.

31. Garrett Ward Sheldon, *The Political Philosophy of Thomas Jefferson* (Baltimore, Md.: Johns Hopkins University Press, 1991), pp. 74–75.

32. Letter to Mr. Lithson, 1805 cited in Paul A. Rahe, *Republics, Ancient and Modern* vol. 3 (Chapel Hill: University of North Carolina Press, 1994), p. 199.

33. Thomas Jefferson, *Notes on the State of Virginia* (New York: Norton, 1954).

34. McDonald, *Novus Ordo Seclorum*, p. 88.

35. In the words of Patrick Henry of Virginia: "Would any one believe that I am Master of Slaves of my own purchase! I am drawn along by ye general Inconvenience of living without them; I will not, I cannot justify it . . . " cited in Rahe, *Republics, Ancient and Modern*, vol. 3, p. 78.

36. Ibid., p. 94.

37. M. I. Finley, *The Ancient Economy* (Harmondsworth: Penguin: [1973] 1992), pp. 141, 142.

38. Garrett Ward Sheldon, *The Political Philosophy of Thomas Jefferson*, chap. 6.

39. The antique practice of employing slave managers, or slaves working alongside free labor (doing the same work for the same remuneration), was inconceivable in the American setting.

40. In Roman society, sons of freedmen achieved high positions in significant numbers. As M. I. Finley observed, it is difficult to measure the exact extent of this phenomenon, but there are good reasons for thinking that it was substantial: "Now it is a peculiarity inherent in the status of the freedman that it is evanescent, restricted by law to a single generation. A freedman's sons remained slaves if born before his manumission (unless they were also manumitted), but were

fully free if born later. It was on his sons, therefore, that a freedman placed his hopes for those social and political consequences of wealth that the law denied him personally, public office in particular. A close analysis, made nearly half a century ago, of epitaphs from Italy during the Empire revealed that a high proportion of members of the municipal senates were sons of freedman, highest in a city like Ostia, where the figure is estimated to have reached 33% or more, lowest in the more rural district of Cisalpine Gaul, say 12%. The figures have been challenged as too high because of the author's loose tests for determining who was or was not a freedman's son. The criticism of the statistics is correct, but ill-directed. No one is claiming that vast numbers of freedmen's sons became local aristocrats, or that municipal senates were becoming dominated by such men, or that they constituted a new class in Roman society. Even a reduction of the percentages by half would not invalidate the conclusion that a significant number of freedmen had succeeded through their sons in attaining high social and political status." M. I. Finley, *The Ancient Economy* (London: Chatto and Windus, 1973), p. 77.

41. For details of the English model, as it developed under Walpole and Pelham, see John Brewer, *The Sinews of Power: War, Money and the English State, 1688–1783* (New York: Knopf, 1989), chap. 4.

42. Lance Banning, *The Jeffersonian Persuasion* (Ithaca, N.Y.: Cornell University Press, 1989), p. 277.

43. Ibid., pp. 298–300.

44. Reinhold, *Classica Americana*, p. 150.

45. Ibid., pp. 152–57.

46. McDonald, *Novus Ordo Seclorum*, p. 75.

47. Even the great critics of the extended Republic, the Antifederalists, offered only a looser confederation and the protection of states' rights in place of the strong, expansive Continental union and national institutions. (On the Antifederalist vision, see Lienesch, *New Order of the Ages* [Princeton, N.J.: Princeton University Press, 1988], chap. 6; Banning, *The Jeffersonian Persuasion*, chap. 4; and Gordon Wood, *The Creation of the American Republic, 1776–1787* [New York: Norton, 1972 (1969)], chap. 12.) There was no central role for the city in the Antifederalists' prescriptions. The Antifederalists reiterate old republican distrust of the growth of official power, but it is not "the limits of the city" that is presented as the container of power. Rather faith is placed in bills of citizens' rights, in constitutionally guaranteed individual and states' rights. There is no perception of a *topos* that *shapes* individual action, or that anchors the exercise of power. Thus, attempts to resurrect the Antifederalists as a touchstone — to explain the sources and cures of the periodic crises of the American Republic — are not that helpful.

48. In *Democracy in America*. The first volume was published in 1835, the second in 1840.

49. De Tocqueville observed:

Americans of all ages, all stations in life, and all types of disposition are for ever forming associations. There are not only commercial and industrial associations in which all take part, but others of a thousand different types — religious, moral, serious, futile, very general and very limited, immensely large and very minute. Americans combine to give fêtes, found seminaries, build churches, distribute books, and send missionaries to the antipodes. Hospitals, prisons, and schools take shape in that way. Finally, if they want to proclaim a truth or propagate some feeling by the encouragement of a great example, they form an association. (*Democracy in America* [London: Collins, 1966 (1840)], vol. 2, pt. 2, chap. 5, p. 662)

50. The propensity of Americans to join in voluntary associations rates amongst the highest in the world. See the studies conducted by Sidney Verba and his associates. For example, Verba, Norman H. Nie and Jae-on Kim, *Participation and Political Equality* (Cambridge: Cambridge University Press, 1978).

51. On such duties, see P. Murphy, "Classicism, Modernism and Pluralism" in *The Left in Search of a Center,* ed. Michael Crozier and Peter Murphy (Champaign: Illinois University Press, 1996).

52. Karl Marx, "On the Jewish Question," *Early Writings* (Harmondsworth: Penguin, 1975), pt. 1.

53. Alexis de Tocqueville, *Democracy in America,* vol. 2, pt. 2, chap. 4, p. 639.

54. Hannah Arendt rightly saw the problem of the apolitical assimilation of Jews into German society, and the way this deprived Jews (and in fact all groups in German society) of the capacity to politically *resist* the plague of Nazism. (See, for example, Elisabeth Young-Bruehl, *Hannah Arendt: For The Love Of The World* [New Haven, Conn.: Yale University Press, 1982].) Arendt shows us that the intuitions of Marx concerning the limits of Jewish emancipation were realized in the worst of all possible ways.

55. Jefferson also thought in terms of emancipation *and* repatriation (cf. his Letter to John Holmes, April 22, 1820). Lincoln supported the idea of colonization overseas of freed blacks.

56. In a peculiar twist of this story, from the African-American side, later pan-Africanists like the Jamaican-born Marcus Garvey (b. 1887) also argued for the exodic return to Africa ("look to Africa")—to Ethiopia, the promised land.

57. The major, and historically important, exception to this was the public space of musical performance. It is a profound irony that one of the earliest public spaces created in America was the *choros* (dancing place), established by the slaves in the Congo Square in New Orleans, where they were sold to slave owners. Such *choroi* proved to be among the most enduring and significant vernacular public spaces created in North America, and the music created in those spaces among the most important cultural objectivations of the New World.

58. For example, the right to receive a wage was frustrated by the requirement that freed persons hire themselves out by the year; the right to marriage (denied to slaves) was conferred but the newly emancipated were denied the right of marrying whites; the right to vote was frustrated by literacy requirements, and so on.

59. A black person found traveling without his or her employer's permission was liable to be arrested for vagrancy.

60. Taylor Branch, *Parting The Waters* (London: Macmillan, 1990), chap. 1.

61. It became a Washington lobby, lost in the hyperreality of the state, maneuvering between offices and agencies, pressing for "equal opportunity" laws that would have either no effect or a negative effect when legislated in the

absence of any "community" in the civic sense. Those who benefited went on to to enjoy a career open to talents, leaving the rest behind, as the new black middle class made its way from Harlem to Brooklyn to Queens.

62. Finley, *The Ancient Economy*, p. 59; Finley, *Ancient Slavery and Modern Ideology* (London: Chatto and Windus, 1980), pp. 97–98.

63. Finley, *The Ancient Economy*, p. 57; Finley, *Ancient Slavery and Modern Ideology* (London: Chatto and Windus, 1980), p. 106.

64. Webb, *The City Square* (London: Thames and Hudson, 1990), p. 99.

65. In 1699, the French founded a colony (Louisiana) at the mouth of the Mississippi. After the French defeat in the Seven Years' War, control of Louisiana passed to Spain. Bonaparte regained the territory for the French, and then sold it to the Americans for $15 million.

66. "Laid out by a French military engineer in 1721 as a waterfront parade ground facing the Mississippi, and a focus of the 75-block city that is known as the Vieux Carré or French Quarter." Webb, *The City Square*, p. 113.

67. Named for the hero of the War of 1812, and later president, Andrew Jackson.

68. On what follows immediately, see, for example, Christian Norberg-Schulz, *New World Architecture* (Princeton, N.J.: Princeton Architectural Press, 1988), pp. 28–29.

69. Activity was focused on the courthouse, as frontier settlers struggled in their conscience between their antinomianism and the imperatives of written law.

70. Alan Gowans, *Styles and Types of North American Architecture* (New York: HarperCollins, 1992), p. 218.

71. Allen Greenburg, "The Architecture of Democracy" in *The New Classicism*, ed. A. Papadakist and H. Wilson (London: Academy Editions, 1990), p. 71.

72. Ibid., p. 72.

73. Ibid.

74. Robert A. M. Stern, Gregory Gilmartin and John Massengale, *New York 1900* (New York: Rizzoli, 1983).

75. Greenberg, "The Architecture of Democracy," p. 72.

76. It also created a congenial climate for a kind of civic welfare to develop. Unlike later (modernist) programs that dumped the poor into welfare housing, and consequently stigmatized them, the City Beautiful era saw not only a historically unprecedented effort by a nation to house all its citizens, but a federal program of subsidized housing that avoided isolating or segregating the poor. (Greenberg, ibid.)

77. On the role of rhythm in the New World, see P. Murphy, "Metropolitan Rhythms: A Preface to a Musical Philosophy for the New World," *Thesis Eleven* 56 (London: Sage Publications, 1999), pp. 81–105.

78. On the significance of rhythm in classical culture, see Jack Lindsay, *The Ancient World* (New York: Putnam, 1968), p. 113.

79. On rhythmic ordering in architecture, see Alexander Tzonis and Liane Lefaivre, *Classical Architecture: The Poetics of Order* (Cambridge, Mass.: MIT Press, 1984).

80. For an attempt to understand freedom in this sense, and to escape from the weight of the Enlightenment sense of freedom as a possession ("rights"), see

Jean-Luc Nancy, *The Experience of Freedom* (Stanford, Calif.: Stanford University Press, 1993). Nancy, however, finds difficulty in surmounting the *language* of the Enlightenment, specifically of Kantianism, while repudiating its implications. More successful in doing this was Hannah Arendt, who reinvigorated a classical language to talk about freedom, especially in *The Human Condition* and *On Revolution*. Nancy acknowledges the Arendtian contribution, but does not realize the radical significance of her strategy.

81. See also my comments in "The City of Justice" in *Building Cities*, eds. Norman Crowe, Richard Economakis and Michael Lykoudis (London: Artmedia Press, 1999).

82. On this see, Peter Murphy, "Marine Reason," *Thesis Eleven* 67 (London: Sage Publications, 2001) and "Architectonics," in P. Murphy and J. Arnason (eds.) *Agon, Logos, Polis: The Greek Achievement and Its Aftermath* (Stuttgart: Franz Steiner Verlag, 2001), pp. 207–32.

12

CONCLUSION

CONCLUSION

We have traveled a long way in the course of this volume, and, I'd like to think, some way in the spirit of the Greek metic and Roman peregrini. If there is a lesson to be learned from what we have encountered along the way, it is that the history of republics is not just the history of citizenship, or of civic virtue, or political participation, or of country parties and their farmer virtues. The history of republics is also the story of denizenship—the tale of those who make things, not least of all public things, and who trade in those acts of creation, and who often do so as strangers, standing outside the bounds of citizenship, living as denizens amidst the hustle and bustle of port cities, market places, entrepôts, nodes, portals, and the like.[82] Like most citizens, most of these denizens remain anonymous to history. Greek metics, Roman peregrini, medieval journeymen, Renaissance merchants—few of them stand out as names in history. So, in the case of this present story, it has fallen to philosophers (and some poets and architects) to represent the work of the peregrini. If that has been successful, it is only because those same philosophers and poets were themselves at times cast into the role of the stranger—Plato in Syracuse, Cicero in internal exile at Tusculum, Shaftesbury in Rotterdam and Naples, Dante cast adrift from Florence, and so forth.

By listening to the echoes of the peregrini in the works of these writers and in the marvelous architectural legacy of the city-republics, the reader hopefully has come to understand something of the silent, plastic dimension of the *res publica*. This dimension is the work not of statesmen but of artisans, and the work not of legislators but of architects. It is the lynch-pin of a republic—the republic of strangers—composed not of rhetoric and laws but of made things, a three-dimensional republic that both citizens and denizens can walk through, a measured republic, in the double sense of the Latin *metiri*, connoting both the length of things (including immaterial things like meter and rhythm) and also measurement as a passing, walking, or sailing through something. America, which has contributed so much to the history of republics, has also been home to millions of strangers. Yet in its republican self-image this is still to be fully registered. In imagination the United States remains at heart a republic of sturdy farmers and enlightened actors. The role of strangers on the watery *peras* of American life remains obscured by the weight of American continental ambition, just as the activity of *poiêsis* and public construction is overshadowed by the preoccupation with legislation and courts. But self-conceptions and realities of this kind, however resilient, are not necessarily fixed forever. The history of republics is also the history of self-reflection on the nature of republics, and revisions of those reflections. In that sense the history of republics is always a philosophical history. The philosophical history of the American republic of strangers remains to be written. It is a story for another time.

BIBLIOGRAPHY

Adams, John. 1946. *A Defence of the Constitution of the United States*. In *The Selected Writings of John and John Quincy Adams*, edited by Adriene Koch and William Peden. New York: A. A. Knopf.

Adams, William Howard. 1983. *Jefferson's Monticello*. York: Abberville Press.

Albanese, Catherine. 1976. *Sons of the Fathers: The Civil Religion of the American Revolution*. Philadelphia: Temple University Press.

Ames, R. A., and H. C. Montgomery. "The Influence of Rome on the American Constitution." *Classical Journal* 30 (1934–35). 19–27.

Anderson, Perry. 1974. *Passages from Antiquity to Feudalism*. London: Verso.

———. 1974. *Lineages of the Absolutist State*. London: Verso.

Andrewes, A. 1956. *The Greek Tyrants*. London: Hutchinson.

Arendt, Hannah. 1958. *The Human Condition*. Chicago: University of Chicago Press.

———. 1973. *On Revolution*. Harmondsworth: Penguin.

———. 1977. "What Is Authority?" in *Between Past and Future*. Harmondsworth: Penguin.

———. 1972. *Crisis of the Republic*. New York: Harcourt Brace Jovanovich.

Aristotle. 1984. *Athenian Constitution*. Translated by P. J. Rhodes. Harmondsworth: Penguin.

———. 1946. *Politics*. Translated by Ernest Baker. Oxford: Clarendon Press.

———. 1976 (1955). *Ethics*. Translated by J. A. K. Thomson. Harmondsworth: Penguin.

Aurelius, Marcus. 1964. *Meditations*. Translated by Maxwell Staniforth. Harmondsworth: Penguin.

Bailyn, Bernard. 1967. *The Ideological Origins of the American Revolution*. Cambridge, Mass.: Harvard University Press.

Banning, Lance. 1989. *The Jeffersonian Persuasion*. Ithaca, N.Y.: Cornell University Press.

Barnes, Jonathan. 1987. *Early Greek Philosophy*. Harmondsworth: Penguin.

Baron, Hans. 1966. *The Crisis of the Early Italian Renaissance*. Princeton, N.J.: Princeton University Press.

Barrow, R. H. 1949. *The Romans*. Harmondsworth: Penguin.

Benson, Robert L. 1982. "Political *Renovatio*: Two Models From Roman Antiquity." In *Renaissance and Renewal in the Twelfth Century*, edited by Robert L. Benson and Giles Constable, with Carol D. Lanham. Oxford: Clarendon Press.

Bernal, Martin. 1987. *Black Athena: The Afroasiatic Roots of Classical Civilization*. Vintage, London.
Bloom, Allan. 1987. *The Closing of the American Mind*. New York: Simon and Schuster.
Bookchin, Murray. 1987. *The Rise of Urbanism and the Decline of Citizenship*. San Francisco: Sierra Club Books.
Boyd, Julian P. 1953. *The Papers of Thomas Jefferson*, vol. 7. Princeton, N.J.: Princeton University Press.
Bradford, Ernle. 1971. *Mediterranean: Portait of a Sea*. London: Hodder and Stoughton.
Boardman, John. 1964. *The Greeks Overseas*. Harmondsworth: Penguin.
Branch, Taylor. 1990. *Parting the Waters*. London: Macmillan.
Brewer, John. 1989. *The Sinews of Power*. New York: Knopf.
Brogan, Hugh. 1986. *The Penguin History of the United States*. Harmondsworth: Penguin.
Brown, Peter. 1992. *Power and Persuasion in Late Antiquity: Towards a Christian Empire*. Madison: University of Wisconsin Press.
Brucker, Gene. 1969. *Renaissance Florence*. New York: Wiley.
Brunt, P. A. 1988. *The Fall of the Roman Republic and Related Essays*. Oxford: Clarendon Press.
——. 1971. *Social Conflicts in the Roman Republic*. New York: Norton.
Bruni, Leonardo. 1987. "On The Florentine Constitution." In *The Humanism of Leonardo Bruni: Selected Texts*, edited by G. Griffiths, J. Hankins, and D. Thompson. Binghamton, N.Y.: SUNY Press.
Burckhardt, Jacob. 1963. *History of Greek Culture*. New York: Ungar.
——. 1990. *The Civilization of the Renaissance in Italy*. Translated by S. G. C. Middlemore. Harmondsworth: Penguin.
Burke, Edmund. 1990 (1757). *A Philosophical Enquiry into the Origin of Our Ideas of the Sublime and Beautiful*. Edited and introduced by Adam Phillips. Oxford: Oxford University Press.
Burman, Edward. 1991. *Emperor to Emperor: Italy before the Renaissance*. London: Constable.
Callan, Norman. 1957. "Augustan Reflective Poetry" in *From Dryden to Johnson*, edited by Boris Ford. Harmondsworth: Penguin.
Cartledge, Paul. 1993. *The Greeks*. Oxford: Oxford University Press.
Cassirer, E., P. O. Kristeller, and J. H. Randall, eds. 1948. *The Renaissance Philosophy of Man*. Chicago: University of Chicago Press.
Castoriadis, Cornelius. 1991. "The Greek Polis and the Creation of Democracy." In *Philosophy, Politics, Autonomy*, edited by David Ames Curtis. Oxford: Oxford University Press.
Cicero. 1992. *De re publica*. Translated by Clinton Walker Keyes. Cambridge, Mass.: Harvard University Press.
——. 1966. *Tusculan disputations*. Translated by J. E. King. Cambridge, Mass.: Harvard University Press.
——. 1971. *Discussions at Tusculum* (V). In *Cicero on the Good Life*. Translated by Michael Grant. Harmondsworth: Penguin.
——. 1913. *De officiis*. Translated by Walter Miller. Cambridge, Mass.: Harvard University Press.

———. 1914. *De finibus*. Translated by H. Rackham. Cambridge, Mass.: Harvard University Press.

Cronin, Vincent. 1992 (1969). *The Flowering of the Renaissance*. London: Pimlico.

———. 1992 (1967). *The Florentine Renaissance*. London: Pimlico.

Dante. 1969. *The Divine Comedy*. In *The Portable Dante*, edited by Paolo Milano. Harmondsworth: Penguin.

———. 1996. *Monarchia*. Translated and edited by Prue Shaw. Cambridge: Cambridge University Press.

de Tocqueville, Alexis. 1966 (1840). *Democracy in America*. London: Collins.

Deleuze, Gilles. 1993. *The Fold: Leibniz and the Baroque*. Minneapolis: University of Minnesota Press.

Derrida, Jacques. 1987. *Of Spirit*. Chicago: University of Chicago Press.

———. 1994. *Spectres of Marx*. New York: Routledge.

Diggins, John. 1984. *The Lost Soul of American Politics*. New York: Basic Books.

Earl, Donald. 1967. *The Moral and Political Tradition of Rome*. London: Thames and Hudson.

Ehrenberg, Victor. 1969. *The Greek State*. 2d ed. Oxford: Basil Blackwell.

Eisensdadt, S. N. 1969. *The Political Systems of Empires*. New York: Free Press.

Ely, John. 1996. "Libertarian Federalism and Green Politics: A Perspective On European Federation." In *The Left in Search of a Center*, edited by Michael Crozier and Peter Murphy Champaign, Ill.: University of Illinois Press.

———. 1995. "Jane Austen: A Female Aristotelian." *Thesis Eleven* 40. Boston: MIT Press, pp. 93–118.

Ficino, Marsilio. 1953. "The Soul of Man." In *The Portable Renaissance Reader*, translated by J. L. Burroughs and edited by James Bruce Ross and Mary Martin McLaughlin. New York: Viking Press.

———. 1948 (1476). "Five Questions Concerning the Mind." In *The Renaissance Philosophy of Man*, edited by E. Cassirer, P. O. Kristeller, and J. H. Randall. Chicago: University of Chicago Press.

———. 1979 (1975).*The Philebus Commentary*. Los Angeles: University of California Press.

Finley, M. I. 1966 (1963).*The Ancient Greeks*. Harmondsworth: Penguin.

———. 1977 (1956). *The World of Odysseus*. London: Chatto and Windus.

———. 1992 (1973). *The Ancient Economy*. London: Penguin.

———. 1980. *Ancient Slavery and Modern Ideology*. London: Chatto and Windus.

Fisher, N. R. E. 1993. *Slavery in Classical Greece*. Bristol: Bristol Classical Press.

Ford, Boris, ed. 1968. *From Dryden to Johnson*. Harmondsworth: Penguin.

The Federalist Papers. 1961. New York: New American Library.

Forrest, W. G. 1966. *The Emergence of Greek Democracy*. London: Weidenfeld and Nicolson.

Gay, Peter. 1966. *The Enlightenment: An Interpretation, The Rise of Modern Paganism*. London: Weidenfeld and Nicolson.

Garlan, Yvon. 1988. *Slavery in Ancient Greece*. Translated by Janet Lloyd, revised and expanded edition. Ithaca, N.Y.: Cornell University Press.

Gibbon, Edward. 1981 (1776–1788). *The Decline and Fall of the Roman Empire*. Edited by D. A. Saunders. Harmondsworth: Penguin.

Gilmore, Myron P. 1952. *The World of Humanism 1453–1517*. New York: Harper.

Glotz, G. 1930. *The Greek City and Its Institutions*. New York: Alfred Knopf.

Grant, Michael. 1969. *The Ancient Mediterranean*. New York: Penguin.

———. 1997 (1968). *The Climax of Rome*. London: Phoenix.

———. 1991. *The Founders of the Western World*. New York: Scribners.

———. 1990. *The Fall of the Roman Empire*. New York: Macmillan.

———. 1982. *From Alexander to Cleopatra*. London: Weidenfeld and Nicolson.

Gooch, G. P. 1959. *English Democratic Ideas in the Seventeenth Century*. New York: Harper and Row.

Gowans, Alan. 1992. *Styles and Types of North American Architecture*. New York: HarperCollins.

Greenburg, Allen. 1990. "The Architecture of Democracy." In *The New Classicism*, edited by A. Papadakist and H. Wilson. London: Academy Editions.

Griffiths, G. J. Hankins, and D. Thompson, eds. 1987. *The Humanism of Leonardo Bruni: Selected Texts*. Binghamton, N.Y.: SUNY Press, pp. 171–74.

Gummere, Richard. 1963. *The American Colonial Mind and the Classical Tradition*. Cambridge, Mass.: Harvard University Press.

Guthrie, W. K. C. 1962. *A History of Greek Philosophy*. Cambridge: Cambridge University Press.

Halliday, William Reginald. 1923. *The Growth of the City State*. Liverpool: University Press of Liverpool.

Hansen, Mogens Herman. 1991. *The Athenian Democracy in the Age of Demosthenes*. Oxford: Blackwell.

Harrington, James. 1771. *Works*. Edited by John Toland. London.

Harrison, Paul. 1996. "Border Closures." In *The Left in Search of a Center*. Edited by Crozier and Murphy. Champaign, Ill.: University of Illinois Press.

Heidegger, Martin. 1991. *The Principle of Reason*. Bloomington: Indiana University Press.

Heller, Agnes. 1987. *Beyond Justice*. Oxford: Basil Blackwell.

———. 1978. *Renaissance Man*. London: Routledge.

———. 1985. "The Dissatisfied Society," in *The Power of Shame*. London: Routledge and Kegan Paul.

Herodotus. 1954. *The Histories*. Translated by Aubrey de Selincourt. Harmondsworth: Penguin.

———. 1998. *The Histories*. Translated by Robin Waterfield. Oxford: Oxford University Press.

Herrin, Judith. 1985. "A Christian Millennium: Greece in Byzantium." In *The Greek World*, edited by Robert Browning. London: Thames and Hudson.

Hersey, G. L. 1976. *Pythagorean Palaces: Magic and Architecture in the Italian Renaissance*. Ithaca, N.Y.: Cornell University Press.

Hersey, G. L., and Richard Freedman. 1992. *Possible Palladian Villas*. Cambridge, Mass.: MIT Press.

Hibbert, Christopher. 1974. *The Rise and Fall of the House of Medici*. London: Penguin.

Hicks, R. D. 1910. *Stoic and Epicurean*. New York: Russell and Russell.

Hill, Christopher. 1969 (1967). *Reformation and the Industrial Revolution*. Harmondsworth: Penguin.

Hobbes, Thomas. 1968. *Leviathan*. Edited by C. B. McPherson. Harmondsworth: Penguin.

Homer. 1946. *The Odyssey*. Translated by E. V. Rieu. Harmondsworth: Penguin.

Hope, A. D. 1974. "The Middle Way." In *The Cave and the Spring: Essays In Poetry*. Sydney: Sydney University Press.

Howard, Dick. 1986. *The Birth of American Political Thought*. Translated by David Ames Curtis. Minneapolis: University of Minnesota Press.

Humphreys, A. R. 1954. *The Augustan World*. London: Methuen.

Hunt, H. A. K. 1954. *The Humanism of Cicero*. Parkville: Melbourne University Press.

Hyde, J. K. 1973. *Society and Politics in Medieval Italy: The Evolution of Civil Life 1000-1300*. London: Macmillan.

Inwood, Brad. 1985. *Ethics and Human Action in Early Stoicism*. Oxford: Oxford University Press.

Jefferson, Thomas. 1954. *Notes on the State of Virginia*. New York: Norton.

Kahn, Charles. 1960. *Anaximander and the Origins of Greek Cosmology*. New York: Columbia University Press.

———. 1979. *The Art and Thought of Heraclitus*. Cambridge: Cambridge University Press.

Kitto, H. D. F. 1951. *The Greeks*. Harmondsworth: Penguin.

Kohl, Benjamin G., and Ronald G. Witt, eds. 1978. *The Earthly Republic*. Philadelphia, Penn.: University of Philadelphia Press.

Kostof, Spiro. 1991. *The City Shaped: Urban Patterns and Meanings Through History*. London: Thames and Hudson.

Kristeller, Paul Oskar. 1961. *Renaissance Thought*. New York: Harper.

———. 1979. *Renaissance Thought and Its Sources*. New York: Columbia University Press.

Kuttner, Stephan. 1982. "The Revival of Jurisprudence." In *Renaissance and Renewal in the Twelfth Century*, edited by Robert L. Benson and Giles Constable [with Carol D. Lanham]. Oxford: Clarendon Press.

Lambropoulos, Vassilis. 1993. *The Rise of Eurocentrism: Anatomy of Interpretation*. Princeton, N.J.: Princeton University Press.

———. 1995. "The Rule of Justice," *Thesis Eleven* 40. Cambridge, Mass.: MIT Press.

Lefort, Claude. 1988. "Permanence of the Theologico-Political?" in *Democracy and Political Theory*. Cambridge: Polity.

Lehmann, Karl. 1985. *Thomas Jefferson, American Humanist*. Charlottesville: University Press of Virginia.

Lerner, Robert. 1968. *The Age of Adversity*. Ithaca, N.Y.: Cornell University Press.

Lienesch, Michael. 1988. *New Order of the Ages*. Princeton, N.J.: Princeton University Press.

Lindsay, Jack. 1968. *The Ancient World: Manners and Morals*. New York: Putnam.

———. 1952. *Byzantium into Europe: The Story of Byzantium as the First Europe (326-1204 AD) and Its Further Contribution till 1453 A.D.* London: Bodley Head.

———. 1965. *Thunder Underground: A Story of Nero's Rome*. London: Frederick Muller.

———. 1984. "A Note On My Dialectic." In *Culture and History*, edited by Bernard Smith. Sydney: Hale and Iremonger.

———. 1970. *The Origins of Alchemy in Graeco-Roman Egypt*. London: Frederick Muller.

———. 1974. *Ballistics and Blast-power: Concepts of Force and Energy in the Ancient World*. London: Muller.

Lintott, Andrew. 1973. *Imperium Romanum: Politics and Administration*. London: Routledge.

Locke, John. 1965. *Two Treatises of Government*. New York: New American Library.

Long, A. A. 1974. *Hellenistic Philosophy*. London: Duckworth.

Lucretius. 1957. *On the Nature of Things*. Translated by William Ellery Leonard. New York: Dutton.

Manville, Philip Brook. 1990. *The Origins of Citizenship in Ancient Athens*. Princeton, N.J.: Princeton University Press.

Machiavelli, Niccolò. 1970. *The Discourses*. Harmondsworth: Penguin.

Macintyre, Alasdair. 1988. *Whose Justice? Which Rationality?* London: Duckworth.

Maravall, Jose Antonio. 1986. *Culture of the Baroque*. Manchester: Manchester University Press.

Martin, J. R. 1977. *Baroque*. Harmondsworth: Penguin.

Marx, Karl. 1975. "On the Jewish Question." *Early Writings*. Harmondsworth: Penguin.

McCarthy, Mary. 1972. *The Stones of Florence; and Venice Observed*. Harmondsworth: Penguin.

McDonald, Forrest. 1985. *Novus Ordo Seclorum*. Lawrence: University Press of Kansas.

McEwen, Indra Kagis. 1993. *Socrates' Ancestor*. Cambridge, Mass.: MIT Press.

McGlew, James F. 1993. *Tyranny and Political Culture in Ancient Greece*. Ithaca, NY: Cornell University Press.

Montesquieu. 1949. *The Spirit of the Laws*. Translated by Thomas Nugent. New York: Hafner.

Mullett, Charles F. 1933. *Fundamental Law and the American Revolution, 1760–1776*. New York: Columbia University Press.

———. 1939–40. "Classical Influences on the American Revolution." *Classical Journal* 35: 92–104.

Mumford, Lewis. 1966 (1961). *The City in History*. Harmondsworth: Penguin.

Murray, Oswyn. 1993. *Early Greece*. 2d ed. London: Fontana.

———. 1986. "Life and Society in Classical Greece." In *The Oxford History of Greece and the Hellenistic World*. Oxford: Oxford University Press.

Murphy, Peter. 1993. "Romantic Modernism and Greek Polis." *Thesis Eleven* 34. Cambridge Mass.: MIT Press.

———. 1992. "Is The Philosophy of Rights Enough?" *Thesis Eleven* 32. Cambridge, Mass.: MIT Press.

———. 1996. "Classicism, Modernism and Pluralism." In *The Left In Search Of A Center*, edited by Michael Crozier and Peter Murphy. Champaign, Ill.: Illinois University Press.

———. 1998. "The Triadic Moment: The Anti-Genealogy of Hellenist Marxism." *Thesis Eleven* 53. London: Sage Publications.

———. 1999. "Metropolitan Rhythms: A Preface to a Musical Philosophy for the New World," *Thesis Eleven* 56. London: Sage Publications, pp. 81–105.

———. 1999. "The City of Justice." *Building Cities*, edited by Norman Crowe, Richard Economakis, and Michael Lykoudis. London: Artmedia Press.

———. 2001. "Architectonics," in *Agon, Logos, Polis: The Greek Achievement and Its Aftermath*, edited by Peter Murphy and Johann Arnason. Stuttgart: Franz Steiner Verlag.

———. 2001. "Marine Reason." *Thesis Eleven* 67. London: Sage Publications.

Myres, John L. 1927. *The Political Ideas of the Greeks*. New York: Abingdon Press.

Nancy, Jean-Luc. 1993. *The Experience of Freedom*. California: Stanford University Press.

Neville, Henry. 1968. *Plato Redivivus*. In *Two English Republican Tracts*, edited by Caroline Robbins. Cambridge: Cambridge University Press.

Nicolet, C. 1980. *The World of the Citizen in Republican Rome*. London: Batsford.

Norberg-Schulz, Christian. 1988. *New World Architecture*. Princeton, N.J.: Princeton Architectural Press.

Nussbaum, Martha. 1994. *The Therapy of Desire*. Princeton, N.J.: Princeton University Press.

Ortega y Gasset, Jose. 1946. "Concord and Liberty." In *Concord and Liberty*. New York: Norton.

Ostwald, M. 1986. *From Popular Sovereignty to Sovereignty of Law*. Berkeley: University of California Press.

Owens, E. J. 1991. *The City in the Greek and Roman World*. London: Routledge.

Panofsky, Erwin. 1969. *Renaissance and Renascences*. New York: Harper and Row.

Pevsner, Nikolaus. 1963. *An Outline of European Architecture*. Harmondsworth: Penguin.

Pico [della Mirandola]. 1965. *On the Dignity of Man*. Indianapolis, Ind.: Bobbs-Merrill.

Pirenne, Henri. 1952. *Medieval Cities: Their Origins and the Revival of Trade*. Princeton: Princeton University Press.

Plotinus. 1991. *The Enneads*. Translated by Stephen MacKenna. Harmondsworth: Penguin.

Plutarch. ca. 1909. *Alcibiades*. In *Plutarch's Lives*. Translated by Dryden, revised by Arthur Clough. New York: P.F. Collier.

Plutarch. 1914–1924. *Plutarch's Lives*. Translated by Aubrey Stewart and George Long. London: G. Bell.

Plato. 1953. *Gorgias*. In *Socratic Dialogues*. Edited and translated by W. D. Woodhead. Edinburgh: Nelson.

Plato. 1982. *Philebus*. Translated by Robin A. H. Waterfield. Harmondsworth: Penguin.

———. 1974 (1955). *The Republic*. Translated by Desmond Lee. Harmondsworth: Penguin.

———. 1971 (1965). *Timaeus*. Translated by Desmond Lee. Harmondsworth: Penguin.

———. 1975 (1970). *The Laws*. Translated by Trevor J. Saunders. Harmondsworth: Penguin.

Pocock, J. G. A. 1989. *Politics, Language and Time*. Chicago: University of Chicago Press.

———. 1975. *The Machiavellian Moment*. Princeton, N.J.: Princeton University Press.

Polanyi, Karl. 1957. *The Great Transformation*. Boston: Beacon Press.

Polybius. 1979. *The Rise of the Roman Empire*. Translated by F. W. Walbank. Harmondsworth: Penguin.

Pomponazzi, Pietro. 1956 (1516). *De immortalitate animae* (Bologna). Translated as "On Immortality," in *The Renaissance Philosophy of Man; Selections in Translation.* Edited by Ernst Cassirer, Paul Oskar Kristeller, and John Herman Randall Jr. Chicago: University of Chicago Press.

Pope, Alexander. 1994. *Essay on Man and Other Poems.* New York: Dover.

Raab, Felix. 1964. *The English Face of Machiavelli.* London: Routledge.

Rahe, Paul A. 1994. *Republics Ancient and Modern,* vols. 1–3. Chapel Hill: University of North Carolina Press.

Redfield, James. 1995. "Homo Domesticus." In *The Greeks,* edited by Jean-Pierre Vernant. Chicago: University of Chicago Press.

Reinhold, Meyer. 1984. *Classica Americana.* Detroit: Wayne State University Press.

——. 1972. "Greek and Roman Civilization." In *Hellas And Rome,* edited by Robert Douglas Mead. New York: New American Library.

Romm, James S. 1992. *The Edges of the Earth in Ancient Thought: Geography, Exploration and Fiction.* Princeton, N.J.: Princeton University Press.

Rose, J. Holland. 1969 (1934). *The Mediterranean in the Ancient World.* New York: Greenwood Press.

Saint Augustine. 1972. *City of God.* Harmondsworth: Penguin.

Segal, Charles. 1995. "Spectator and Listener." In *The Greeks,* edited by Jean-Pierre Vernant. Chicago: University of Chicago.

Sennett, Richard. 1992. *The Conscience of the Eye.* New York: Norton.

Shaftesbury [Anthony Ashley Cooper, Earl of Shaftesbury]. 1699. *An Inquiry Concerning Virtue, in Two Discourses.* London: Bell, Castle, Buckley.

——. 1900. "Exercises" In *The Life, Unpublished Letters, and Philosophical Regimen of Anthony, Earl of Shaftesbury.* Edited by Benjamin Rand. London: Sonnenschein.

——. 1714 (1711). *Characteristicks of Men, Manners, Opinions, Times,* 3 vols. 2d ed. London: J. Darby.

——. 1914. "A Letter Concerning the Art or Science of Design." In *Second Characters, or The Language of Forms.* Cambridge: Cambridge University Press.

Sheldon, Garrett Ward. 1991. *The Political Philosophy of Thomas Jefferson.* Baltimore, Md.: Johns Hopkins University Press.

Shotter, David. 1991. *Augustus Caesar.* London: Routledge.

Stern, Robert A. M., Gregory Gilmartin, and John Massengale. 1983. *New York 1900.* New York: Rizzoli.

Stobart, J.C. 1965. *The Grandeur That Was Rome.* 4th ed. London: New English Library.

Summerson, John. 1966. *Inigo Jones.* Harmondsworth: Penguin.

Tarn, Willian, and G. T. Griffith. 1952. *Hellenistic Civilization.* 3d. ed. London: Methuen.

Tavernor, Robert. 1991. *Palladio and Palladianism.* London: Thames and Hudson.

Thomson, George. 1955. *Studies in Ancient Greek Society: The First Philosophers.* London: Lawrence and Wishart.

Thucydides. 1972. *History of the Peloponnesian War.* Translated by Rex Warner. Harmondsworth: Penguin.

Tzonis, Alexander, and Liane Lefaivre. 1984. *Classical Architecture: The Poetics of Order.* Cambridge, Mass.: MIT Press.

Ullmann, Walter. 1975. *Medieval Political Thought*. Harmondsworth: Penguin.

Verba, Sidney, Norman H. Nie, and Jae-on Kim. 1978. *Participation and Political Equality*. Cambridge: Cambridge University Press.

Vernant, Jean-Pierre. 1982. *The Origins of Greek Thought*. Ithaca, N.Y.: Cornell University Press.

———. 1982. *Myth and Society in Ancient Greece*. London: Methuen, London.

Virgil. 1958 (1956). *The Aeneid*. Translated by W. F. Jackson Knight. Harmondsworth: Penguin.

Vlastos, Gregory. 1993. "Isonomia." *American Journal of Philology*, 74, no. 4, reprinted in *Studies in Greek Philosophy*, edited by Daniel W. Graham. Princeton: Princeton University Press.

———. 1970. "Equality and Justice in Early Greek Cosmologies." In *Studies in Presocratic Philosophy*, vol. 1, edited by David J. Furley and R. E. Allen. London: Routledge.

Vortle, Robert. 1984. *The Third Earl of Shaftesbury 1671–1713*. Baton Rouge: Louisiana State University Press.

Walbank, F. W. 1981. *The Hellenistic World*. Amherst, N.Y.: Humanity Press.

Waley, Daniel. 1969. *The Italian City-Republics*. London: Weidenfeld and Nicolson.

Ward, Russell. 1987. *Finding Australia: The History of Australia to 1821*. Richmond, Victoria: Heinemann.

Walzer, Michael. 1985. *Exodus and Revolution*. New York: Basic Books.

Weber, Max. 1976 (1930). *The Protestant Ethic and the Spirit of Capitalism*. London: Allen and Unwin.

Webb, M. 1990. *The City Square*. London: Thames and Hudson.

Wittkower, Rudolph. 1971. *Architectural Principles in the Age of Humanism*. New York: Norton.

Wittoker, Rudolf. 1973. *Art and Architecture in Italy 1600–1750*. 3d ed. Harmondsworth: Penguin.

Wood, Gordon S. 1972 (1969). *The Creation of the American Republic 1776-1787*. New York: Norton.

———. 1992. *The Radicalism of the American Revolution*. New York: A. A. Knopf.

Wood, Neal. 1988. *Cicero's Social and Political Thought*. Berkeley, Calif.: University of California Press.

Wölfflin, Heinrich. 1953. *Principles of Art History*. New York: Dover.

———. 1953. *Classic Art*. London: Phaidon.

———. 1966. *Renaissance and Baroque*. Ithaca, N.Y.: Cornell University Press.

Wood, Ellen Meiksins. 1988. *Peasant-Citizen and Slave*. London: Verso.

Woodhouse, C. M. 1986. *George Gemistos Plethon: The Last of the Hellenes*. Oxford: Clarendon Press.

Wright, Jr., B. F. 1931. *American Interpretations of Natural Law*. Cambridge, Mass.: Harvard University Press.

Young-Bruehl, Elisabeth. 1982. *Hannah Arendt: For the Love of the World*. New Haven, Conn.: Yale University Press.

GLOSSARY OF
GREEK AND LATIN TERMS

adikia	the victory of one opposing power over another, injustice
aegritudo	distress
aequabilis	fair
aequatum et temperatum	balanced and moderate
agathos	the valiant (one)
agathos	warrior
agôgê	(Spartan) upbringing
agôn	contest, assembly
agônisma	the meeting of forces from an opposite direction, that with which one contends
agora	assembly, market
agroikos	of or in the country
agros	cultivated field
akropolis	high town, citadel, acropolis
alêtheia	divine revelation, truth
amicitia	political friendship, alliances
andrapodon	chattel slave, slave taken in war
antapodosis	reciprocal giving
aorgêsia	spiritlessness
apeiron	boundlessness
apoikia	away-home, emigrant city, colony
archai	principles
archê	initiative, beginning, principle, origin, first principle, magistracy, office
archein	to rule
archiôtektonikos	builder, maker, founder
archon	chief magistrate, to begin, to lead the way, to rule, to govern
areskeia	obsequiousness

aretê	excellence, virtue
asteios	witty, "citified"
asty	lower town, opposite to an acropolis
atonia	absence of tension
auctoritas	authority, influence
autarkês	self-sufficient, independent, having enough
axia	axis of the earth, like the axle of a wheel
barbarophônoi	non-Greek speakers, barbarians
basileus	king, chief
bilanx	two scales of a balance
boulê	council
caritas	affection, love, esteem
civis	citizen, city dweller
civitas	the condition of a citizen, citizenship, freedom of the city, membership in the community
clientela	clientship
comitia	council, meeting, assembly
comitia centuriata	general assembly of the whole Roman people
comitia tributa	assembly that elected lower magistrates, including tribunes
concilium	a meeting, rendezvous
concordia	an agreeing together, union, harmony, concord
consortia	protective alliances with other families
constantia	steadiness, firmness, constancy, perseverance
demiourgoi	those who worked for the people
dêmokratia	democracy
dêmos	neighborhood, country-district, country, land, people, inhabitants of such a district, hence (since the common people lived in the country, while the chiefs lived in the city) the commoners, common people; all the people
despoteia	tyranny
despotês	arbitrary task master

dignitas	dignity, worth, merit, desert, character
dikaioi	the just ones
dikê	justice, law; law suit
dominus	a master, possessor, ruler, lord, proprietor, owner
domus	dwelling, house, building, mansion, palace
doxa	opinion
dunamis	dynamism, power
eidos	form
ekklêsia	assembly
ekprepês	outstanding, distinguished, preeminent, remarkable
eleutheria	freedom
empeiria	experience
emporion	trading post
emporos	merchant-traveler, one who goes on shipboard as a passenger, trader who makes voyages
en meson	in the middle
energeia	energy, action, operation
ephoroi	(Spartan) overseers
epitropos	steward/slave-manager
eranoi	loans; contributions, favors
eranos	friendly society, friendly loan (without interest), meal to which each contributes a share
ergon	work, function
eris	conflict, strife, quarrel, debate, contention
ethnos	nationality
ethos	custom, way
eunomia	good order
fides	trust, confidence, reliance
finis bonorum	the highest good
frugalitas	frugality
genos	the patriarchal clan, race, stock, tribe
gerontes	the nobility, nobles; elders
gerousia	council of elders
gloria	fame

gnôsis	knowledge, inquiry, investigation (especially juridicial), judgment
harmonia	attunement, concordance
hêgemôn	sovereign power
hêgêmonikon	governing principle
hektemoroi	poorest class of farmers
hetaira	female companion, courtesan
hetairai	companionate associations
hetairoi	male companions, comrades, mates
heteros	different
homonoia	civil peace, concord; agreement
honestum	honesty, integrity, morality, honorable conduct
horkos	oath
hubris	overstepping of the mark, wanton violence arising from pride
humanitas	human nature, humanity
imperium	executive power
isêgoria	freedom of speech
isometria	equality (an equating) of more than two elements, balanced measure
isonomia	balance of norms; equality of rights
isopoliteia	equality or reciprocity of rights guaranteed between two states
isotês geômetria	equality of geometric ratios
iungere	union
ius	justice, that which is binding by its nature
ius civile	law applying to Roman citizens
ius gentium	a mix of Roman and foreign law applicable to foreigners
ius naturale	law applying to the Roman world as a whole
kallipolis	the beautiful city
kalokagathia	nobleness, goodness, the character of a good man
kalos	beautiful, fine, good, noble
kinêsis	shift, movement, motion in a political sense, revolution

klêros	inheritance, estate
koinon	the common thing
koinos	league
kosmopolis	world city, cosmopolitan city, universal city
kosmos	order, the universe
krasis	blending
kratos	power
kurios	sovereign, guardian
latifundia	large landed estates
lex	law
libertas	public life without kings; freedom
lictor	lictor, official attendant upon a magistrate
logos	speech, reason
lussa	frenzy, rage
massa	heap
megaron	great hall, large room
menos	the ardor or might inspired by a god
metiri	to measure
metoikoi	middle dwellers, metics
metoikos	metic, resident worker
metron	common measure, due measure, dimensions
mixis	blending
moderor	reduce, control, to set bounds to, to keep within bounds
modus	limited quality
monarchia	single ruler
nemesis	the personification of retributive justice
nobilitas	the aristocracy
nomas	wandering
nomoi	laws, melodies
officium	dutiful action, official employment
oiketikos	menial members of a household, household servants (not slaves)
oikonomia	management of a household
oikos	household, abode, dwelling
oligoi	the few

optimates	aristocracy
orthos	straight
ostrakismos	ostracism
pactio	an agreeing, agreement, covenant, contract, stipulation, bargain, pact
parrêsia	frankness, candor
paterfamilias	head of the household
patria	home, land, lineage, descent especially by the fathers' side
pax et otium	peace and leisure
peirar	shoreline, boundary, end
peras	limit, periphery
peregrini	freed persons
perimetron	perimeter
perioikoi	fringe dwellers
periploos	coastal voyage
philanthrôpia	benevolence, kindness
philia	friendship, alliance
philos	friend
philosophia	philosophy
philotês	reciprocity, friendship, friendship between states, love, affection
philotimia	love of distinction, ambition
phrateres *or* phratores	warrior bands
phratriai	brotherhoods
phulê	tribe
phulobasileus	tribal king, chief who performs sacrifices
phusis	nature
plebiscitum	resolutions, decree or ordinance of the people
pneuma	breath
poiêsis	making, production, creation
polemos	war, battle, fight
polis	city
politai	city dwellers
politeia	republic, constitution, fellow citizen
populus	a people, nation
populus Romanus	the Roman People
potestas	power
praxis	action

princeps	first in order, foremost
prostatês	guardian
provincia	sphere of duty
proxenos	public guest-friend, officially appointed patron or protector
psuchê	soul
regnum	kingship
res publica	the public thing, republic
scholê	leisure
severus	stern, serious, sober, grave, strict, austere, severe
socii	allies
soma dia somatos chorei	body passes through body
sophia	wisdom
sôphrosunê	temperateness, prudence, good sense
stasis	discord
subiungere	to join under a yoke
sumpatheia	sympathy
sumphronêsis	reconciliation
sumpoliteia	a federal union
sunkrasis	blending, compound
sunoikismos	concentration of dwelling houses, a living together
sunopsis	general view
sussitia	dining clubs, messes
technê	art
telos	end
terpsis	delight
thauma	wonder, marvel, astonishment
themis	family justice, that which is laid down not by statute but by custom
themistes	infallible decree, a kind of super-human wisdom, decree of gods or oracles
thes	wage laborer
thesmoi	sacred laws
thêtes	bottom income order, serfs
thiasos	guild, confraternity, company
tonos	tension

trittues	geographical voting areas, the number three
trivium	a place where three crossroads meet
ultimus finis	final end
urbs	city
utilitas	interest, usefulness, utility, use
virtus	greatness, moral rightness
xeinia	friendly gifts
xenêlasia	expulsion of foreigners
xenoi	strangers, guests, hosts, guest-friends
xunos	common, shared

INDEX

absolutism, 11, 196, 201, 207–208, 215–16
Adams, Samuel, 256–57
Adams, John, 260
Aeneus, 156, 213
aesthetics, 244, 246
agora, 18, 41, 49–50, 53
Alberti, Leon Battista, 163, 179
Alcibiades, 69–71
Aldus Manutius, 182
Alexander the Great, 81
Alexandria, 83
Althusius, Johannes, 195
American Revolution, 255
Amsterdam, 195
Anaximander, 46
ancient philosophy, 1
antinomian, 211, 224, 264–65
Antiochus of Ascalon, 106–107
architecture, 49, 84, 114–15, 166, 173–75, 181, 184–86, 198–201, 203, 225–26, 239–40, 286–88, 299–302
Arendt, Hannah, 155
aristocracy, 32, 34, 97, 118, 131, 155, 271
Aristotle, 78–79, 105, 140, 183–84, 195, 260
Arminius, Jacobus, 194
artisan, 31, 42, 79, 104, 174, 290
ascetic, 258–59, 267
assembly, 53, 59
associations, 81
Athens, 39–40, 55, 65–68
Atlantic, 255, 268
Augustan Age, 12, 238–46
Austen, Jane, 239

Baillie, Robert, 195
balance, 46, 49, 53, 59, 76, 157–58, 177, 226, 193–94
Barbaro, Daniele, 181
baroque, 196–205, 225–26
basileus, 18
beauty, 31, 49, 76, 130, 163, 237
Bernini, Gianlorenzo, 197, 202
books, 171
Brown, Arthur, 301
Brunelleschi, Filippo, 163, 177
Bruni, Leonardo, 155, 157–59
bureaucracy, 217–18, 230–32, 293
Burlington, Richard Boyle, third earl of, 240
Burnham, Daniel, 301
Byzantium, 119, 124, 126, 140, 182

Calvinism, 194–95, 256–59, 304
Campbell, Colen, 239
Carolingian Empire, 126
Catholic, 119
Catonian republicanism, 256, 258, 259
center, 66, 202
change, 206
checks and balances, 99, 242, 273
Chicago, 299
Christianity, 116–19, 127, 141, 142, 177, 305
Cicero, 100, 104, 106, 260, 270, 282–84
citizens, 33, 41, 42, 56, 59, 78, 103, 109, 246, 265–66, 282, 295–96
city, 19, 20, 21, 43, 45, 49, 76, 87–89, 93–94, 102, 115, 124–25, 127–30, 142–44, 155, 171, 207, 230, 268, 270, 282, 298

city squares, 203, 298
civic art, 67
civic religion, 43–44
civic tribes, 56–57
civilization, 58
clan, 16
classicism, 125, 130, 240
Cleisthenes, 55–60
clients, 103
colonization, 23, 28–29, 30
common sense, 242–44
Commonwealth, 221–34, 256
Commonwealthmen, 227–34, 256
commune, 130–37
companions, 20, 27
composition, 241
conflict, 50
constitution, 57, 95, 165, 167, 269–73
consuls, 97–98
contest, 21, 28, 34, 50–53, 83
continental republic, 261, 263
contingency, 222–23, 233, 236, 249
Coornhert, Dirck, 194
Corneille, Pierre, 196
cosmology, 46–48
cosmopolitan, 9, 85–86, 115–16, 125, 134
council, 40–41, 166
courts, 50
covenant, 208–13, 265
creation, 147–48, 150, 237, 243

Dafoe, Daniel, 248
Dante, 137, 139–47
de Quiros, Pedro Fernandez, 212–13
de Tocqueville, Alexis, 294–95
Declaration of Independence (U.S.), 277
Delian League, 67
demiourgoi, 21, 32
democracy, 68–70
denizen, 22–23, 297, 315
despotism, 228
dikê, 17, 19
dissatisfaction, 199–200
Draco, 56

Dürer, Albrecht, 197
dynamism, 69, 197–208

Edinburgh, 195
Egypt, 209
empire, 81–84, 1122–16
England, 193, 221–51
English Civil War, 222, 224
epic, 140
Epicureanism, 222, 289, 292
Eratosthenes, 83
eunomia, 72–73, 245
expansion, 45–46, 101–105, 116

federalism, 87–88, 135, 269, 272
feudalism, 118, 126, 170, 221
Ficino, Marsilio, 168–70
Florence, 128–29, 143, 144, 153–60, 164–68, 172–75
form, 19, 24, 66, 76, 149, 150, 197, 224, 242, 244, 245, 247
France, 196, 215, 298
freedom, 30, 31, 40, 96, 158, 292, 296
friendship, 81, 131, 289

garden, 287
geometrical, 48, 75, 78–81
Germanic tribes, 123
Ghibellines, 136–37
Giangaleazzo Visconti, 156
Gibbon, Edward, 112, 239
Gilded Age (U.S.), 299–301
Goethe, 173
goodness, 76
goods, 103–104
gothic, 177, 193, 228–29
Greece, 15–92, 102, 182–84, 209, 237, 238, 260, 270
Grotius, Hugo, 195
Guarini, Guarino, 199
Guelfs, 136–37, 144
guest, 26
guilds, 129

Hamilton, Alexander, 259
harmony, 51, 158

Harrington, James, 135
Hebraism, 210–13, 263–64, 266
Hellenistic Age, 81–89
hero, 25
hierarchy, 46–47, 53–54, 18, 209, 214
Hippodamos, 80
Hobbes, Thomas, 194–95, 227
Holbein, Hans, 197
Holland, 193
Homer, 25
House of Representatives (U.S.), 265, 272
household, 15, 27, 33, 35, 57, 103, 131
hubris, 60
humanism, 10, 105–108, 139, 153–60, 163, 171–72, 193–95, 238–42, 282, 285
Hume, David, 267
Hunt, Richard Morris, 301

imperialism, 101, 134–37, 238
industry, 251–52, 291
infinite space, 201–202
intellectual virtue, 77
interests, 275
Ionia, 45–51, 53, 80, 237, 302
Islam, 125

Janus, 94
Jefferson, 12, 277, 284–94
journey, 25–26, 33, 140–41, 304–305
justice, 16, 47, 51, 54, 73, 79–80, 98, 108, 110, 143, 184–88, 209, 214–15, 241

Kant, Immanuel, 303, 304
kings, 27, 46, 83–84, 94–95, 126, 135–36, 196, 215–21, 224–34, 238–39, 268
Kircher, Athanasius, 209
kosmopoiêsis, 9, 10, 12, 139–60, 148, 156, 237, 241–42

landholders, 40, 42, 79, 103–104, 117–ﾠ18, 228, 230, 259, 261, 263, 266, 268, 288
Lascaris, Giovanni, 171
law, 15–19, 48, 56, 99, 102, 110, 115, 214–15, 232, 245, 265, 283

Leibniz, G.W., 249
liberty, 95–96, 98, 158, 266, 268
libraries, 82–83
Lincoln, 296, 301
Lipsius, Justus, 194
Livy, 94
logos, 20, 69, 78, 81, 86, 152, 245
love, 71, 151

Machiavelli, 164–65
Marx, Karl, 295–96
McKim, Charles, 301
McMillan Commission, 301
measure, 39–54, 57, 79, 178–79
Medicis, 164–68, 172–74
mercenaries, 165
merchants, 33, 42, 78, 249, 267
metics, 22, 32,33
Michelozzo, 163, 166
mixing, 59, 87, 100
moderation, 60, 240
monad, 147–52
Montesquieu, 261
Monticello, 286–88
Mycenea, 15

Naples, 234
nationality, 101
natural law, 115, 260
nature, 28, 31, 52, 79, 234–36, 248, 264, 305
Neoplatonism, 139–40, 147–52
Neville, Henry, 227–29
New Jerusalem, 211–13
New York, 299, 301, 302
Newton, Isaac, 249
nomos, 56, 59, 60

Odysseus, 25, 248
oligarchy, 34, 75
oppositions, 51–54, 180, 185, 198, 237
order, 31, 49, 177, 234–38, 242, 246, 270, 304, 306–307
Orthodoxy, 119
Otis, James, 260, 269

Padua, 182–83
Palladio, Andrea, 181, 184–86, 240
Panaetius of Rhodes, 105, 284
Paradise, 145–46
parliament, 222, 229–30
Parthenon, 67
patriarchal, 15, 19, 58, 101
patrimonial, 15, 48, 98, 108–109, 112, 125
Peisistratos, 43
people (Florence), 133
people (Rome), 96–100
people (U.S.), 271–72
peregrination, 297–98, 304–307
Pericles, 66
Persia, 55
Philo of Larissa, 106–107
philosophy, 71, 75–78, 81, 274
Pico della Mirandola, Giovanni, 168, 170–72
Pietro da Cortona, 207
Pirenne, Henri, 123
Plato, 73–78, 105, 169, 174, 260
Plotinus, 116, 147–52
podestà, 132, 134
polis, 41, 44, 45
Pomponazzi, Pietro, 183
power, 45, 50, 52, 69, 94, 96, 100, 133, 173, 201, 208, 222, 229, 250–51, 273
producer, 246, 291
proportionality, 78–81, 170, 175–76, 185, 188
Protestantism, 211, 212, 223–24, 256–59, 262, 266, 281–82
Psellos, Michael, 140
public, 22, 82
public borrowing, 230
public things, 111, 114, 283
Pythagoras, 53, 58, 147, 150, 169, 260

radials, 203–204
Raphael, 180
rationalization, 233–34, 244, 248, 264
reason, 86, 148, 169, 243, 245, 247, 273–75, 306–307
Rembrandt, 197, 207

Remus, 94
Renaissance, 10, 163–86, 198–99
republic, 93–112, 154, 164–65, 193, 227, 258, 264, 268, 281, 294, 298, 316
rhetoric, 69
rhythm, 175, 302–304
Richelieu, Cardinal, 196
rights, 295–97, 304
romanticism, 247, 263
Rome, 10, 93–119, 153–54, 202, 205, 213, 227, 239, 265, 269
Romulus, 94–95
Rotterdam, 195, 234
Rubens, Peter Paul, 207
rule, 34, 74

Salutati, Coluccio, 155
San Francisco, 299, 302
Scipio Aemilianus, 105, 241, 270
Scotland, 195
sea, 24, 28–29, 123–24, 238–39, 250
Senate (Rome), 96–100, 113
Senate (U.S.), 265, 272
servitude, 30
Sforza, Francesco, 164
Shaftesbury, Anthony Ashley Cooper, third earl of, 11–12, 234–38, 270
Sicily, 135–36
skepticism, 108
slavery, 31, 42, 62–63, 117–18, 290–92, 296, 303
smallholder, 31, 102, 117, 228–29, 259, 288–89
Smith, Adam, 249, 251
social contract, 213–14
Socrates, 68, 75
Solon, 39–42, 56
soul, 72
sovereignty, 11, 214–15
Spanish America, 298–99
Sparta, 26, 32, 66–67, 227, 265, 266
speculation, 223
speech, 74, 78
speed, 204–205
Stamp Act, 255
standing army, 232–33, 293

Stewart, James, 267
stoicism, 84–87, 105–108, 115, 234–36, 260
stranger, 25, 28
sublime, 246–51
Supreme Court (U.S.), 273
symmetry, 49, 176–77, 179–80, 184–85
sympathy, 86–87
sympolity, 88

Tappan, David, 266
taste, 242
taxes, 117, 187–88, 255–56, 258, 268
territory, 260
themis, 16–17, 39
Tories, 226, 229, 239
trade, 23, 31, 33, 39, 124–25, 128–29, 130, 131, 133, 136, 195, 263, 266–67
truth, 106–107, 172
Turin, 205
Turner, Frederick Jackson, 276
tyranny, 43–44, 75, 155–56

union, 93, 111, 149, 150, 163, 276, 286

United States, 12, 255–307
University of Virginia, 277, 288

Velásquez, Diego, 197
Veneto, 181–82
Venice, 126, 128, 181–83, 193, 227
vice, 142–45
Vicenza, 181, 183
virtue, 52, 60, 72–73, 76, 84–86, 106, 109–10, 141, 151, 156, 159, 257, 274, 281, 283, 289
Vitruvius, 179, 184, 239
voluntary association, 293–97

Walpole, Sir Robert, 240
Walzer, Micahel, 210
war, 22, 27, 34, 46, 50–51, 101–102, 116–17
Washington, 301
Whigs, 226–27, 238
wilderness, 251, 262, 266, 287–88
Wölfflin, Heinrich, 179, 197
women, 57–58